FATHERS, MASCULINITY, AND AUTHORITARIANISM
IN LATIN AMERICAN CINEMA

Fathers, Masculinity, and Authoritarianism in Latin American Cinema

Irina Dzero

UNIVERSITY OF FLORIDA PRESS

Gainesville

Cover: *top*, Lieutenant General Jorge Rafael Videla swearing the oath as he becomes the president, 1976 (https://en.wikipedia.org/wiki/National_Reorganization_Process#/media/File:Jorge_Rafael_Videla_Oath.PNG); *bottom*, Promotional poster for *The Clan Puccio* (2015), directed by Pablo Trapero, reproduced with the director's permission.

Publication of this work made possible by a Sustaining the Humanities through the American Rescue Plan grant from the National Endowment for the Humanities.

An early version of chapter 4, "The Patrón: A Backslapping Predator with a Big Smile in Mexico," first appeared in *Periphērica: Journal of Social, Cultural, and Literary History*, vol. 2, no. 1, 2023, pp. 219–253.

This book will be made open access within three years of publication thanks to Path to Open, a program developed in partnership between JSTOR, the American Council of Learned Societies (ACLS), University of Michigan Press, and The University of North Carolina Press to bring about equitable access and impact for the entire scholarly community, including authors, researchers, libraries, and university presses around the world. Learn more at https://about.jstor.org/path-to-open/

Copyright 2025 by Irina Dzero
All rights reserved
Published in the United States of America

30 29 28 27 26 25   6 5 4 3 2 1

Content warning: This book contains stories and images of violence, sexual abuse, rape, racism, homophobia, hateful slurs, and other disturbing content that may be triggering for readers.

DOI: https://doi.org/10.5744/9781683405146

Library of Congress Cataloging-in-Publication Data
Names: Dzero, Irina, author.
Title: Fathers, masculinity, and authoritarianism in Latin American cinema / Irina Dzero.
Description: Gainesville : University of Florida Press, 2025. | Includes bibliographical references and index. | Summary: "Through an analysis of twenty-first-century films created in Latin America, this book makes the case that contemporary filmmakers are using the figure of the father as a metaphor for political leadership and that their work reflects a growing rejection of predatory and coercive authority in the region"—Provided by publisher.
Identifiers: LCCN 2024056872 (print) | LCCN 2024056873 (ebook) | ISBN 9781683405146 (hardback) | ISBN 9781683405290 (paperback) | ISBN 9781683405405 (ebook) | ISBN 9781683405481 (pdf)
Subjects: LCSH: Motion pictures—Latin America—History—21st century. | Masculinity in motion pictures. | Authoritarianism in motion pictures. | Motion pictures—Political aspects—Latin America. | BISAC: HISTORY / Latin America / General | PERFORMING ARTS / Film / History & Criticism
Classification: LCC PN1993.5.L3 D69 2025 (print) | LCC PN1993.5.L3 (ebook) | DDC 791.43098—dc23/eng/20250123
LC record available at https://lccn.loc.gov/2024056872
LC ebook record available at https://lccn.loc.gov/2024056873

| UF PRESS
UNIVERSITY
OF FLORIDA | University of Florida Press
2046 NE Waldo Road
Suite 2100
Gainesville, FL 32609
http://upress.ufl.edu

GPSR EU Authorized Representative: Mare Nostrum Group B.V., Mauritskade 21D, 1091 GC Amsterdam, The Netherlands, gpsr@mare-nostrum.co.uk

For Cate, Peter, and Maxim

CONTENTS

List of Figures   ix
Acknowledgments   xi

1. Introduction   1
2. The Reluctant Rapist and the Cult of Aggressive Masculinity in Peru   27
3. Arquímedes Puccio and Other Carceral Disciplinarians in Argentina   56
4. The Patrón: A Backslapping Predator with a Big Smile in Mexico   86
5. The Scold: Leadership as Emotional Abuse in Brazil   114
6. The Histrion and Fatherhood as a Stage: Bolívar in Colombia and Venezuela   145
7. The Profiteer: Political Freedom Becomes Consumer Freedom in Chile   172
8. Conclusion: The Clean-Shaven Father, Disfigured, Urinated Upon, Buried Alive, and Blown Up   201

Works Cited   227
Index   249

FIGURES

1.1. A military leader presides over a social gathering in *The Clan*   19
1.2. The father presides over his family in *The Clan*   19
1.3. The young woman offered to pacify the Dominican dictator Trujillo in *Feast of the Goat*   20
1.4. A family of kidnappers wearing masks of Perón, Evita, Videla in *History of a Clan*   21
1.5. The murderer at the dancing contest in *Tony Manero*   21
2.1. The bleeding Trujillo prepares to fire back in *Feast of the Goat*   31
2.2. The colonel's son dominates the slum in *Magallanes*   46
2.3. Magallanes is dwarfed by the Palace of Justice in *Magallanes*   47
2.4. Madeinusa smiling for the first time at the end of *Madeinusa*   50
3.1. The kidnapper brings a piece of cake to the hostage in *The History of a Clan*   62
3.2. The kidnapper rolls in place the door to the hidden prison in *The History of a Clan*   63
3.3. Puccio, wearing theatrical makeup, calls the hostage's wife in *The Clan*   69
3.4. Puccio sweeping the sidewalk in front of his house in *The Clan*   71
4.1. Officials line up to kiss the corrupt governor's hand in *The Perfect Dictatorship*   98
4.2. The police chief and the mayor kiss the drug lord's hand in *Hell*   100
4.3. Amaro kisses the bishop's hand in *The Crime of Father Amaro*   105
4.4. Andrés gives Catalina a slap on the behind to speed her up in *Tear This Heart Out*   111
5.1. The father hurries to kill his daughter with a tilling tool in *To the Left of the Father*   120
5.2. The father takes aim at his son as he walks away in *Behind the Sun*   123

5.3. The son dreading the electrical prod at the mental hospital in *Brainstorm*   127

5.4. The attractive and armed Captain Nascimento in *Elite Squad*   135

5.5. Jair Bolsonaro's signature finger-gun gesture   141

6.1. *The Liberator Simón Bolívar*, Tito Salas, 1930   147

6.2. *The Liberator*, Juan Dávila, 1996   148

6.3. *Fig. 202*, Juan Dávila, 2018   149

6.4. *El Colorado*, a carnival float in the streets of Pasto, Colombia in 2018   169

7.1. Gonzalo observing the empty soccer field of the razed slum in *Machuca*   178

7.2. René carries his son through the crowd celebrating the electoral defeat of Pinochet in *No*   188

7.3. The mime in "Free" soft drink ad and the pro-democracy campaign in *No*   190

8.1. The fascist leader points at and questions Pinocchio in *Pinocchio*   203

8.2. The fascist Captain Vidal seizes and shakes Ofelia in *Pan's Labyrinth*   204

8.3. The Stalinist father grabs his son by the arm in *Dance of Reality*   204

8.4. The father grabs his son by the neck in *Endless Poetry*   205

8.5. Captain Vidal stiches up the cut on his mouth in *Pan's Labyrinth*   211

8.6. Pinocchio makes fun of Mussolini in *Pinocchio*   212

8.7. The wife urinates on her husband in *Dance of Reality*   212

8.8. The son shaves his father's head and his Stalinist mustache in *Endless Poetry*   213

ACKNOWLEDGMENTS

I want to thank Mirna Trauger, Jim Fujitani, Vitelia Cisneros, Françoise Massardier-Kenney, and Héctor Fernández L'Hoeste for helpful comments and discussions, and Kent State University Research Council for awarding me the academic leave to work on this project. I am grateful to director Pablo Trapero and artists Juan Dávila and Carlos Ribert Insuasty for granting the permission to reproduce their work in this book.

1

Introduction

This book examines post-2000 films from Brazil, Argentina, Venezuela and Colombia, Mexico, Peru, and Chile in which the father is a metaphor of predatory leadership. To identify such a father as an urgent problem is a new trend in the cinema of the new millennium. I show this by examining the source stories these films retell. Many of these plays, novels, and memoirs were written in the 1970s, an era of oppressive dictatorships in Latin America. Unsurprisingly, in these stories the children perceive bad fathers as fate and languish under their dominion. But in the recent, post-2000 cinematic retellings of these stories, the children confront and even defeat their bad fathers. Unquestioning deference to authority diminished in the new millennium, and the films contribute to and shape this trend. These recent cinematic retellings of old stories compel viewers to look at their real-life rulers with a critical eye and hold them accountable.

I begin with the increased public scrutiny of authority figures that generated a wave of protests in Latin America in the 2010s. I then examine the different structures of domination contested in these demonstrations. I argue that the recent films I discuss explain these structures of domination with the figure of the father. The fathers we see in these films embody colonial, patriarchal, and racial domination. They are caudillos, caciques, and dictators who derive a deep pleasure from dominating others. If, as cognitive linguist George Lakoff posits, we understand political governance by means of the metaphor of the family, films about bad fathers contribute to the current contestation of authority on the deep level of metaphors and symbols, activating a visceral rejection of authoritarian and predatory leaders. Power beckons to people of different dispositions. The histrion enjoys basking in admiration of the crowds. The disciplinarian likes to set up secret spaces of obedience in which he can dominate his subjects fully. The profiteer likes to compromise on moral principles. The backslapping charmer forces on people a physical and affective rapport. The scold sets rules in order to berate people for breaking them. These dispositions help people rise to power but also make it impossible for them to leave it of their own accord. This is when they become predatory leaders. I turn to filmmakers and scholars who explain cinema's visceral impact, which produces affect and shapes beliefs. The filmmakers of the new century show us people who suffer but go out of their way to please the abuser. Watching these films exorcizes the abject instinct to comply.

Recent Protests and Contestation of Authority in Latin America

In the new millennium, corruption scandals are shared instantly on social media and government officials have become subject to intense scrutiny. More and more people engage emotionally with politics because they learn about it from someone they know personally ("How People Decide"). The 2021 Latinobarómetro report explains that the citizens are out in the streets protesting because they decided to leave Macondo, the town of mirages and cyclical time from Gabriel García Márquez's *One Hundred Years of Solitude*. This incendiary report opens with an allusion to the Communist Manifesto, "A specter is haunting Europe—the specter of communism" (un fantasma recorre Europa):

> A wave is sweeping Latin America (Una ola recorre Latinoamérica), in consequence of the egoism of its elites—the wave of the scarcity in which the majority of people live. This is because Latin Americans can no longer tolerate governments which protect the interests of the few, the concentration of wealth, the scarcity of justice, the weakness of civil and political guarantees, and the falling behind in building social guarantees. The abuse of power, privileges, and restrictions on pluralism are at the heart of the demand for equality before the law, respect, and dignity. (*Adios a Macondo* 1)

The report explains that from 2009 to 2020, the satisfaction with democracy in the region fell 20 percentage points (from 45% to 25%). More and more people are saying that the elites are ruling in the interest of the few rather than the majority (an increase of 19 percentage points). The elites are "called to the board" (llamadas al pizarrón; 38)—this metaphor shows particularly well how deference for authorities changed into exactingness. Citizens want "true" and "full" democracy, not its "degraded" version installed by the elites (43). Now "even the most illiterate of the region's citizens can see that they are treated badly, discriminated against, that they have rights and can demand them" because "they can see on the screen of their phones how citizens of other countries live and are treated" (6). The report calls to hold the ruling elites accountable in a peremptory, demanding tone.

Latin America has seen massive protests in the new millennium. Citizens learn the schemes for political and business elites to appropriate their money. The Odebrecht corruption scandal put many high-level politicians and even presidents in detention or jail. Odebrecht, the largest Latin American construction company based in Brazil, bribed politicians with campaign contributions and favors in exchange for state contracts. In Peru, all recent presidents were mired in the Odebrecht scandal and arrested. In 2019, ex-president Alan García shot himself when the police arrived to arrest him. Ex-president Alejandro Toledo, after denying accusations of corruption on Twitter, was arrested in the United States and extradited to Peru. Ex-presidents Ollanta Humala and Pedro Pablo Kuczynski were put in pretrial detention. In Ecuador, Vice President Jorge Glas was suspended and sentenced to six years in prison. Venezuela's former prosecutor alleges that Odebrecht paid $200 million to a Chavista politician and that Venezuela's president Maduro, implicated in the scandal, is blocking the investigation ("Odebrecht Case"). In Mexico, the recently arrested CEO of PEMEX alleged that Odebrecht funded the electoral campaign of former president Enrique Peña Nieto in 2012 in exchange for contracts. This is the first arrest of a government official implicating an ex-president in Mexico (Sheridan). In Brazil, the corruption investigation helped galvanize the revanchist revolt against the leftist Workers' Party governments and propelled to power ultra-conservative Jair Bolsonaro (Mello). Former president Luiz Inácio (Lula) da Silva was sentenced to seventeen years in prison. His successor Dilma Rousseff was impeached in 2016 on charges that remain unproven. The accusations of corruption can be weaponized to discredit and oust opponents.

Venezuela has been weakened by tremendous inflation, food shortages, and political instability. When Nicolás Maduro, Hugo Chávez's handpicked successor, declared he won reelection in 2019, massive protests broke out. The president of the National Assembly, Juan Guaidó, declared himself interim president in January 2020. Maduro's government opened a treason investigation against Guaidó. The US Department of State indicted Maduro on charges of drug trafficking and narcoterrorism in March 2020 and offered up to $15 million for information leading to his arrest or conviction ("Nicolás Maduro Moros—New Target").

In Colombia, a nationwide protest (El Paro Nacional) broke out in 2018. Despite the 2016 historic peace agreement that put an end to the decades-long war between the government and the radical left guerrillas, assassinations of social activists and ex-militants continued. Corruption is another driving force of the protests. In a 2018 anti-corruption referendum (Consulta Popular Anticorrupción), each question began, "Do you approve *of obligating*" ("aprueba usted *obligar*," my italics) elected officials to make public for the scrutiny of the citizens their assets, activities, contact with lobbyists, and other conflicts of interest. Instead of "consulting" with the citizens, these questions showed them the many ways in which officials can take advantage of their position of power. In hope of bringing Colombians together with this issue, conservative president Iván Duque supported the referendum and presented it to Congress, but it failed to collect enough votes to be mandatorily considered. Another related reason for the protests is the fact that Colombia is the second most unequal country in the region, according to the World Bank. As protesters put it, "We are the generation fed up with injustice and such deep inequality" ("The Pandemic Strikes" 24). Because of unemployment or underemployment, almost 40 percent of Colombians have no fixed income (Hernández).

In Chile, in 2019, a fare hike of thirty pesos (4 US cents) triggered massive protests. This was Chile, the most prosperous but also the most unequal nation in Latin America. During Pinochet's dictatorship (1974–1990), education, health, and services were privatized. The reason is today, as during the times of Pinochet, those who cannot afford to pay for top schools and hospitals feel left behind. Public school graduates scoring low on the university admission exam have little opportunity for social mobility. The graduates of elite schools, representing only 0.5 percent of all students, go on to fill 54 percent of leadership positions (Zimmerman). Because of the high cost of living and college tuition debt, Chileans today owe over 75 percent of their disposable income, which makes Chile one the most indebted nations in relation to GDP in Latin America (Cuevas). It is estimated that two-thirds of jobs are precarious. Over 50 percent of the workforce cannot accumulate enough savings to fund a minimally adequate pension (Sehnbruch, "How Pinochet's Economic Model Led to the Current Economic Crisis Engulfing Chile"). The massive and long-lasting protests, known as Estallido Social (Social Outburst), led to the vote in 2021 to form a constituent assembly and to rewrite the constitution inherited from Pinochet.

In Argentina, in 2019, people protested the policies of the right-wing president Mauricio Macri. Macri attempted to cut government spending to avoid defaulting on the country's tremendous external debt. He secured another emergency loan with the IMF in the amount of $56 billion and cut state subsidies on transportation, electricity, and water. Notwithstanding, inflation reached 44 percent; unemployment, poverty, and hunger rates increased; and the economy shrank 3.4 percent during his tenure (Gedan). On the wave of discontent, Cristina Kirchner, who opposes neoliberal policies and favors generous government spending and protectionism as well as price and capital controls, returned to power as vice president with her former chief of staff Alberto Fernández as president. The 200 percent increase in inflation helped right-wing populist Javier Milei win the presidency in 2023. Milei borrows his eccentric style and rhetoric from Donald Trump, Jair Bolsonaro, and Boris Johnson. Students and unions are now protesting cuts to the government spending and the proposed labor law reform (Alvarado).

In Mexico, protests address extraordinarily high levels of violence. A hundred people are murdered every day, and most perpetrators go unpunished. Corrupt security officials collaborate with criminals in exchange for bribes. Salvador Cienfuegos, who oversaw Mexico's army and air force from 2012 to 2018, was arrested in the United States on corruption and drug-trafficking charges. Identified as El Padrino ("The Godfather") of the powerful Sinaloa drug cartel, Cienfuegos diverted government military operations away from the cartel. Mexico asked to have Cienfuegos returned to the country to be investigated. Once back in Mexico, he was released and all charges against him were dropped (López). Another top security official, former Secretary of Public Security Genaro García Luna, who oversaw Mexico's federal police from 2006 to 2012 and was once considered a leader in the efforts to combat drug trafficking, is also currently under investigation for accepting bribes from the Sinaloa cartel to ensure secure transport for its drugs and to provide information about rivals and police probes ("Mexico Files U.S. Lawsuit"). Most Mexicans are well aware of the all-pervasive corruption: 34 percent of Mexicans who used public services in 2019 reported solicitation of bribes. Of 12,987 corruption investigations launched between 2013 and 2016, only 10 percent led to prosecutions, resulting in fifty-one convictions. The impunity of perpetrators is astonishing. According to Mexico's National Institute of Statistics and Geography, 93 percent of crimes are unreported or uninvestigated. Over 67 percent of Mexicans in 2018 believed that judges are corrupt (Martínez-Fernández 7). Less than half of Mexicans express support for democracy. Massive protest marches focus on especially outrageous cases, such as the still-unsolved disappearance of forty-three rural teachers' college students in Iguala in 2014, which was reportedly facilitated by municipal police. The years 2020 and 2021 saw mass demonstrations against femicide by women. Ten women are murdered daily in Mexico, and only one murder in ten is resolved (Barragán and Castañeda).

The wave of protests sweeping over Latin America is generated by the democratization of the region. It is no longer *comme il faut* to openly repress journalists, and it is not possible to suppress information when it gains traction on social media. Similarly, governments cannot control cultural production, especially cinema. In the days when filmmakers depended on the state for financing, a film like *The Perfect Dictatorship*, which shows how media companies promote corrupt politicians, could not be made (to be fair, the media company Televisa pulled out from sponsoring the film after learning what it was about). The films I examine here provoked vivid controversy and even death threats against the filmmakers (*Herod's Law* and *The Crime of Father Amaro*). They set the agenda for public discussion and for legislative initiatives (*Machuca* and *City of God*). They collected millions of mentions on Twitter and beat American blockbusters at the box office (*The History of a Clan* and *The Clan*). These post-2000 films contribute to anti-government protests because they activate the metaphors of the nation as a family and the father as a leader. The father *pater*nalistically controls his wife and children as subjects, extending his *patro*nage, or rather, his *patri*archal control over all people assigned to his sphere of influence, and treats whatever resources he can lay his hands on as his own *patri*mony. Patriarchy, patrimony, and patronage all come from *pater*, the Latin word for "father" (*páter* in Greek). These structures of domination will appear as predatory fathers in films, as I will show.

Patrones, Caudillos, Dictators, and Profiteers

The conquest of Latin America brought hundreds of years of servitude and serfdom upon the Indigenous people. The Spanish conquistadors settled territories with a population of about 32 million native inhabitants (compared to about 3 million in the US and Canada). Colonial Latin America became a caste society, with a small group of large landowners, officials, and clergy ruling over a vast Indigenous population (Reid 59). Andrés Reséndez in *The Other Slavery* explains how the Spanish monarchs were torn between declaring their new subjects free on the one hand, and on the other, using their forced labor to extract precious metals and produce valuable commodities. Slavery became an open secret. It existed surreptitiously, under various names and in different guises. Recipients of *encomiendas* and *repartimientos* were granted Indigenous workers in exchange for Christian instruction. One of the settlers wrote that enslaving Indigenous communities was the only way to obtain starting capital to get ahead in the New World: "In those days, we did not consider anyone a man until he had journeyed to the Indian rancherias, whether friends or enemies, and seized some children from their mothers to sell" (Reséndez 99). After Bartolomé de las Casas made public that colonists plundered, tortured, and even killed Indigenous peoples for fun, the Spanish monarchs prohibited slavery with the New Laws in 1539. The measure was met with hostility in the colonies: the envoy to Peru was murdered, and the envoy to Mexico, fearing for his life, convinced the monarchs to continue the encomiendas. Slavery became more insidious. Indigenous workers were given the status of "employees." They were to be paid a symbolic wage of one golden peso a year and were to work no more than six months a year for their *patrón* (master) for a maximum of three years. In practice, these limits were only declarative. Officials entrusted with ensuring compliance with these regulations were in collusion with the slavers. Governors were themselves slavers (Reséndez 213).

After independence, criollo elites feared that the enslaved would rise against them, as they did during the slave revolt in Haiti, the Tupac Amaru II revolt of Indigenous workers in Peru, the Canudos revolt in Brazil, and other smaller-scale revolts. Therefore, although slavery was prohibited de jure, it continued under the name of debt peonage. Liberal governments enshrined private property as a key to national progress, confiscated the land belonging to Indigenous communities, and sold or awarded it to commercial growers and industrialists. Indigenous people were put to work for white male-led households so this national progress could be achieved, explains Elizabeth Dore. Growers and owners lured peasants to come work for them with large cash advances. Instead of being paid, new workers were told they owed money to the *patrón* (the master) for clothing, food, tools, and mistakes or losses, real or invented. The patrones were obligated to discipline workers to avoid "disturbances," by publicly flogging and locking them up. As patrones needed more and more workers, laws were created to define most of the population as vagrants. People without trade, profession, income, or property; those who engaged in their profession or trade infrequently; people whose income was not sufficient for subsistence; and even people who frequented "bars and pool halls" were obligated to work for a patrón (Dore 117). Soon, everyone except those with an income of five hundred pesos or more was obligated to "render public service" and contribute to the nation's progress. Potential and runaway workers were rounded up and held in jail (with expenses for their capture and arrest added to their debt) until patrones in need of workers came to take them to work (Dore 131). Peonage was a lifelong social condition. As one patrón explained to an American journalist who pretended he wanted to buy enslaved workers, "We don't keep much account of the debt, because it doesn't matter after you've got possession of the man" (Reséndez 240). Another patron, who declared his peon a fugitive although the peon had paid his debt, was frank in court: "I didn't want his cash, I wanted his labor!" (Dore 145). Children inherited the debt of their parents. Peonage was racial and social slavery, and many generations were socialized in the submission and obedience to the patrón. On rare occasions when peons sued their masters for grave offenses, their complaints were dismissed. Judges were supposed to "presume peons are guilty unless there is manifest evidence to the contrary" (Dore 116). One case is especially striking: a parish priest sexually abused and held captive a peon's wife and blinded the peon himself in one eye, but the court refused to hold the priest accountable because "it would encourage men of [the peon's] social standing to show disrespect for people in authority" (Dore 63). Dore argues that this coerced servitude was to some degree consensual because it was embedded in the traditional structure of patriarchy (2). Peons continued to work for patrones even when they had no material need to do so. One peasant whose family inherited a fertile plot of land continued to work as peon for thirty years longer in hopes of finding a good patrón to help out in case of need, but never found one (Dore 163). This is how patriarchy guaranteed consensual submission and minimized resistance of the exploited who came to consider this system necessary to their survival (Dore 132). Peons were socialized into the belief that without a master they would have no one to turn to for protection and help (*socorro, ayuda, protección*), whereas masters felt it was natural for the Indigenous workers assigned to their house to provide free work.

Forced labor based on wage advances, known as *habilitación* and *enganche*, continues to this day. The UN special rapporteur Elisa Canqui writes that Indigenous children, considered the cheapest and most obedient labor force, are recruited to work in the most dangerous work environments: logging camps, cane sugar plantations, mines, distilleries, and charcoal production. In Bolivia (tropical areas of Santa Cruz, the northern Amazon, and the Bolivian Chaco), in Paraguayan cattle farms, in the Brazilian Amazon region, and in the Amazon basin of Peru, this exploitation is understood not as a crime but as "a cordial relationship" between the patrones and the Indigenous communities (Canqui 5). The colonial practice of *criadazgo* persists in Paraguay: poor families give their young children to rich families to be fed and raised. The children call their patrones "mami" and "papi," work as servants, and are subjected to floggings (Canqui 22; Frayssinet). In Argentina, work exploitation and trafficking in rural zones increased 44 percent between 2016 and 2018, in some provinces reaching 85 percent. These laborers often have no access to drinking water, healthy work conditions, or appropriate housing (Premici). In Mexico, exploitative work conditions are common in *maquiladoras*, export-oriented manufacturing plants on the northern border. Managers keep costs low for foreign companies by keeping the unions out and bringing workers from the South, explaining: "These people come to work hard, to suffer. They are willing to work for very little" (Johnson). Maquiladora workers work for decades for wages that barely cover food, and they cannot afford to keep their children in school. Pro-company ghost unions sign contracts on behalf of the workers. These unions, formed during the long rule of the PRI party, helped represent Mexico as a nation as "a low-wage, owner-friendly destination" (Johnson). Labor activism and strikes are rare in Mexico because union leaders, often chosen by the company itself, cooperate with the management. Workers say, "the union has always had us by the throat. Everyone is scared they'll be fired. That's why they haven't gone on strike" ("We Won't Be Trampled On"). In Brazil, hundreds of people, the majority of them children, are rescued every year from slavery-like environments of debt bondage, degrading work conditions, long hours, and no days off. From 1995 to 2019, more than 53,000 people were rescued (Teixera). Hundreds of companies—coffee farms, clothing sweatshops, cattle ranches, timber companies, construction industries, charcoal production plants—are put on the government's "dirty list" each year.

Another contemporary insidious form of consensual submission to an authority figure that originated in debt peonage is political clientelism. People in poor neighborhoods seek out a patrón and provide him unconditional political support in exchange for limited access to goods and services. As "clients" of that patrón, they attend rallies, plaster posters, and vote for him. At the same time, the transactional nature of this exchange is obscured because patrones act through intermediaries who live in the neighborhood, operate the party office, and build networks of influence under the guise of friendship and kinship. These intermediaries, known as brokers, distribute milk, school uniforms, medicine, sewing machines, zinc sheets, part-time jobs, and more to clients as "favors." Clients believe that brokers "sacrifice themselves" to help them and come to view them as friends and relatives of sorts. Clientelism is so deeply entrenched that even when the patrón fails to provide, clients look for a new patrón rather than quitting the system. Clientelism is resilient and adapts to changing governments and political systems. It makes real political democratic competition impossible (see Auyero and Benzecry on Argentina, Tosoni on Mexico, Lazar on Bolivia). In communities controlled by drug lords, these criminal authorities are the patrones: they solve people's everyday problems, permit candidates to campaign, and tell local community leaders which petitions to prepare (see Gay on Brazil, Tuckman on Mexico). Clientelism as a social practice of feigned friendship and kinship (*compadrazgo*) makes people think that politics is about hoping for favors rather than formulating demands. It engages the logic of reciprocity: once you accept a favor, you feel you must return it.

The patrones' expectation of being obeyed without having to deliver the help and favors expected from them stems from the long history of slavery and servitude and from the colonial arrangement of the power structures. Officials in the colonies were far removed from the metropole, where the laws and regulations were made, so they acted as they saw fit without fear of repercussions for not implementing these laws. Hence the famous maxim: "I obey but I do not comply" (obedezco pero no cumplo) (Reid 59). During the independence campaign, another kind of unchecked authoritarian leader emerged to fill the power vacuum—the caudillo (Lynch 437). Like the patrones, caudillos call themselves fathers and saviors and establish a visceral, personal connection with people (Weber 242). Caudillos are populists: they strive to mobilize masses of people in paternalistic and controlled ways. Juan Perón, Hugo Chávez, and Fidel Castro have been described as modern caudillos (Horowitz). Charismatic caudillos are averse to checks and balances enshrined in the post-Independence liberal constitutions and eliminate them overtly or inconspicuously. The fact that former presidents and "dark horse" candidates often win elections reveals "the new face of Latin America's old caudillismo," where loyalty to a person matters more than political institutions and political debate (Corrales 33). The cult of personality surrounding dictators and presidents in Latin America helps them concentrate power in their hands with the approval of the people (Rivas Molina). Finally, caciques need to be mentioned among leaders who tap into patriarchal authority and rule by coercion and consent. The cacique is essentially a collaborator, a "junior partner" of the colonial authorities and later the criollo elites, an Indigenous leader who exploits the members of his own community. He made his community members work beyond their labor draft dues and collaborated with the municipality or growers to help privatize the community lands (Dore 83).

The cruelty of dictatorial regimes that spread throughout the Latin American continent in the second half of the twentieth century shows the continuity of this form of domination with the ones it superseded. Like patrones, caudillos, and caciques, dictators also perceive citizens to be their property and dispose of them as they see fit. Alfredo Stroessner ruled Paraguay for thirty-five years (1954–1989), killing over four thousand people. In Argentina, over 30,000 people were killed during the relatively short rule of the military junta led by Jorge Rafael Videla (1976–1983). In Brazil, the military junta relied more on torture than killing (1964–1985). In Chile, Augusto Pinochet employed both torture and secret killings (1974–1990). Hugo Banzer, who ruled Bolivia as a dictator from 1971 to 1978 and employed a former Nazi to teach torture, was later elected as civilian president (1997–2001). These dictatorial governments revived the colonial narrative of protecting the nation entrusted to them. Like patrones of old, who were required by law to discipline their peons to avoid disturbances, dictators suspended the political rights of the subjects they perceived as dissenters and disciplined them as they saw fit. They justified the kidnappings and killings as a sacred mission to save Western, Christian civilization (Finchelstein 5). When the juntas stepped down, their members congratulated themselves on completing their mission with valor and granted themselves amnesty. The first democratic presidents protected these amnesties fearing military rebellions. The perpetrators denied feeling any remorse. Pinochet declared, for example, that his conscience is "very much at peace. I have no burden on my conscience. I feel uneasy about other things . . . I can worry about my grandson, my wife, my children, but regarding what you're asking, my conscience is clear" (Correa and Subercaseaux 114). Videla said the same: "Mind you, I don't repent of anything, I sleep very well at night" (Reato), as did the rest of the junta.

After 2000, truth commissions were formed under the pressure of victims' families and international human rights organizations. Personal narratives of survivors, as well as testimonies about torture and rape, provoked indignation and demands to bring the perpetrators to justice. First efforts in truth-finding kept the perpetrators' identities secret. Known perpetrators were protected by amnesty laws. Truth commissions had limited powers and mostly offered economic and symbolic reparations to some surviving victims. In 2001 and 2005, the Inter-American Court of Human Rights reached the decision that the amnesty laws were unconstitutional (Binder 1209). But in Brazil, the amnesty law the dictatorship passed in 1979 continues to prevent the investigation, identification, and trial of perpetrators. In Argentina, amnesty laws prevented investigation and truth-telling until 2000, when many cases were reopened. In Chile, truth-telling was for a long time divorced from judicial consequences for perpetrators, in the hopes of encouraging the perpetrators to share information about the disappeared (Collins and Hau 128). Although in Peru amnesty laws did not exist, the perpetrators' de facto impunity has been even more effective in preventing truth-telling. The predatory leadership model retains its hold on people. Many feel nostalgic about Fujimori, Pinochet, and other strongmen and vote for their ideological successors (Balasco 1178).

The last structure of domination embodied by the figure of the father in recent films is the neoliberal socioeconomic restructuring. Milton Friedman, an economist at the University of Chicago and an effective promoter of this model, saw the opportunity to test it in Chile when Augusto Pinochet took over. He trained Chilean economists who developed the reforms and personally advised the dictator. In the 1980s, neoliberalism conquered Argentina under Jorge Rafael Videla and later under Carlos Menem, Bolivia under Victor Paz Estenssoro, and Venezuela under Andrés Carlos Pérez. In the 1990s, it spread to Peru under Alberto Fujimori, Colombia under César Gaviria, Brazil under Fernando Collor de Mello, and Mexico under Carlos Salinas. With the exception of Videla, all these leaders were democratically elected. "The invisible hand of the market" was presented as a cure for government inefficiency, inflation, and unemployment (Klein 203). These ills were blamed on the import substitution development model of the first half of twentieth century, when countries invested in developing infrastructure and producing goods domestically. This model was successful, and governments began borrowing aggressively to capitalize on this strategy. However, in 1981 the world economy entered a recession and interest rates soared. As a result, Latin American countries found themselves burdened by immense debt. In Argentina, the national debt ballooned from $7.9 billion to $45 billion, and in Brazil from $3 billion to $103 billion, for example. A lot of this money was spent on the military, and much of it was moved offshore—Pinochet alone had 125 secret bank accounts (Klein 196). Governments turned to the international lending institutions, the International Monetary Fund and the World Bank, which provided loans on the condition that the governments cut social spending, offer state companies and services for privatization, and open domestic markets to imports. As a result of these reforms, many government employees lost their jobs. Companies and factories unable to compete with cheap imports closed, so these jobs were lost as well. Many employees of privatized companies also lost their jobs because new owners cut labor costs to maximize profits. Outsourcing and subcontracting made jobs precarious. Workers on these contracts complete the same tasks as permanent workers but work longer hours, receive inferior pay and benefits, and have no right to form unions. These two-tier contracts help the management sow jealousy among employees to deflect their anger from the management and prevent them from formulating common demands (Hughes; Manky). At the same time, low earnings make people take on debts to supplement their insufficient income and to service previous debts (Pérez-Roa). Chile, Mexico, Argentina, Panama, Costa Rica, and Colombia lead the region in the indebtedness of their households.

Aníbal Quijano argued that colonial America created a blueprint for the international division of labor. People who live in Latin America and, more generally, the Global South must work incessantly but remain poor. Historically, in colonial Latin America, only white Iberians had access to the administrative and military positions of any importance and were paid wages. In contrast, Indigenous and Black people were forced to provide free labor for the white settlers and Spain and, after independence, for the patrones in the name of the public good and national progress. The local elites in Latin America have always aligned themselves with Western elites rather than with Blacks, Indians, or mestizos. For centuries, people from the "inferior races," first as enslaved subjects and then serfs, were seen as "undeserving of wages," says Quijano (538). Today this model has spread to the entire world market, as the nations of the Global South, whose governments embraced neoliberal reforms, are coerced to work for multinational corporations for wages on which they cannot survive. This blueprint, which Quijano calls "coloniality of power," is naturalized, invisible, and pervasive (535). Policymakers blame the failure of neoliberal reforms to bring the promised prosperity not only on corruption and lack of dedication to the reforms but also on the peoples' laziness (Klein 235), another manifestation of Quijano's "coloniality of power." Even the economists of the IMF have become critical of neoliberalism. In "Neoliberalism—Oversold?" they argue that these reforms do not cure ailing economies. Instead, opening financial markets makes economies more likely to crash. Reducing public spending undercuts growth because it decreases the quality and quantity of employment, generates inequality, and hurts demand (Ostry, Loungani, and Furceri 40). In other words, the model that Friedman advertised as a pragmatic, efficient, and inevitable "road to freedom" led to the erosion of democracy, social goods, and rights. It was never voted upon but imposed from above, by dictatorial and democratic governments (Klein 450). The system remains in place with the unadvertised and sometimes reluctant consent of the political elite (Hay), and of the voters, whose political freedom is converted into the freedom to consume (P. Silva).

Harnessing Affect and Transgressive Realism in Film

Contemporary Latin American filmmakers operate in the global neoliberal system. They attract financing from global corporations interested in the return on the investment. In fact, films criticizing the neoliberal political system (that is to say, these same corporations that finance them) draw attention, are picked up for a wide distribution, and sell well. As Sofia A. Clennen puts it, "only two out of the ten top-rated, Latin America-connected, international films at the US box office do not have a fairly clear political message" (6). American and Spanish media corporations partner with their regional counterparts and invest billions of dollars in producing Spanish-language content. For example, Netflix produced a show entitled *The Head of Joaquín Murieta* in collaboration with the Mexican arm of Dynamo, the Colombian company that worked with Netflix on *Narcos*. Billion-dollar investments in "glocal" content energizes production: a Mexican producer says, "People are fighting for vans, equipment, no actor is free, everybody has 20 offers on the table. In general, it's the best time and the worst time if you're able to produce" (Kay). National governments provide some financing but also act in an entrepreneurial manner, to make a profit. The successful 2013 film *Instructions Not*

Included (*No se aceptan devoluciones*) was written, directed, and performed by Mexicans; produced by the US–Mexican film production company Pantelion Films; distributed by US-based, Canadian-founded Lionsgate; and screened by Chinese-owned AMC theaters (Clennen 1, 26). Today, Latin American filmmakers not only draw on big budgets but can also harness the Hollywood aesthetic and familiar genres to reach wide audiences and offer a meaningful critique of neoliberalism (Clennen, Tierney). Joanna Page argues that recent intimist films reverse the neoliberal drive to privatize the public sphere and subsume politics into economics. Focusing on the lives that appear to have become useless and futile, "cinema lends them transcendence," taking up the function of the state that it has forsaken (Page, *Crisis and Capitalism* 194). Similarly, Juan Poblete argues that films can send viewers back to the time that the dominant ideology of neoliberalism wants to obliterate, "a time when accessible public education, proper political representation, and equality for all were seen not only as worth fighting for but as feasible political goals" ("Memory of the National" 104). In the films, people who fully adhere to the neoliberal ideal of competition and individual success are murderous psychopaths (as in *Tony Manero*, *The Clan*, and *Angel*).

The palpable political agenda of contemporary Latin American films originates in the New Latin American Cinema (NLAC) movement of the 1960s and 1970s. Filmmakers from Brazil, Cuba, Argentina, Bolivia, Chile, and other parts of Latin America rejected Hollywood and its aesthetics as distraction. For them, cinema was a "populist and militant political project of national liberation that seemed achievable and oftentimes even inevitable (as in the 1960s), a project of denouncing and undermining authoritarianism" (Schroeder Rodríguez 237). Cinema was a form of public culture that had political impact, raised consciousness, and inspired revolution. They rejected emotion and used the techniques of Italian and French neorealism to foster critical thinking. These choices alienated the wide audiences they hoped to reach (Clennen 26). In the 1970s and 1980s, NLAC filmmakers shifted from militancy to embracing conventional genres, as in the Oscar-winning social melodrama *The Official Story*. They also employed neobaroque style of parallel, alternative worlds, "rich color palettes, claustrophobic mise-en-scènes, and characters who play roles in narrowly defined vertical social relations ... to denounce or parody patriarchal patterns of thought and behavior" (Schroeder Rodriguez 242). The NLAC films showed that socioeconomic realities and values are constructed and can be changed, undoing the rigid messaging of the 1970s dictatorships.

After the transition to democracy in the 1990s, which was also the time of calls for "reconciliation" and forgetting by democratically elected leaders who amnestied key perpetrators, cinema became more introspective and, some critics argue, responded to this call for consensus (King 265). National cinemas started rebuilding their cinematic production in the 1990s, as evidenced by the *retomada* in Brazil and the *nuevo cine argentino*, but it is after 2000 that production expanded and diversified (Cunha and Silva 4). Contemporary filmmakers continue to use innovative style. They focus on surfaces and create gaps in the narrative, omitting crucial scenes or marking insignificant scenes as important. They reveal characters and motivations not through dialogue but through gestures and positioning in space (Page, *Crisis and Capitalism* 41–45). The use of documentary aesthetics and even documentary footage, another common technique in contemporary Latin American films, may be used to create a critical distance from the characters and what they represent (Andermann 168; Oubiña 37; Bentes 115), or on the contrary, to take viewers into "the realm of intersubjectivity, of pure affect" (Page, "Beyond Reflexivity" 85). Some critics interpret this intimist, eclectic filmmaking relying on traditional story formats as "melorealism," exploiting "audiences' willingness and desire to be swept up in emotionally charged narratives in realistic settings" to make marketable "glocal commodities" (Schroeder Rodríguez 250). In contrast, Laura Podalsky influentially argued that filmmakers embrace emotion and affect to reframe political issues in a way that feels "authentic, true, and profound." Thus, even as engaging emotions became an important marketing strategy in the neoliberal era, filmmakers can harness affect, "embodied intensity," "strong feelings as yet unclaimed by meaning" to deliver an impactful political message (Podalsky, *The Politics of Affect* 32, 33).

Filmmakers explain that their goal is to capture raw reality, real people, real locations, and real emotions. Walter Salles incorporates spontaneous events that happen during filming, so "viewers wonder whether they are watching fiction or documentary." He mixes actors with non-actors and looks for "visceral quality of acting, everything coming from within," "total giving." He met his lead for *Central Station* when a shoeshine boy approached him to ask for money for a sandwich (the director was wearing sneakers and he could not clean his shoes). When the director asked him to do a screen test, the boy initially refused, saying, "I can't, because I've never been to the movies before" (interview with Demetrios 61, 91, 69). Claudia Llosa met her lead for *Madeinusa* (Magaly Soller, now a famous actress and singer) in a girl who sold street food in her rural village and did not know much about films (interview with Demetrios 383). "I can't do anything with an actor. I hate actors! They are poison! 'Oh, I need a close-up not from this side, but from this side. I can't say this line . . .'" says Alejandro Jodorowsky (interview with Ebiri). "I had former drug-dealers coaching actors and non-actors who would play drug dealers; former regular cops coaching actors who would play regular cops; and former BOPE cops coaching actors who would play BOPE cops," says José Padilha (interview with Demetrios 181). Fernando Meireilles worked with illiterate favela boys to whom he suggested scenes to improvise, then he suggested their lines to the scriptwriter, and then he suggested them back to the boys. All the while, the boys "did not know I was testing for the scenes" (interview with Demetrios 150). One of the actors in Jodorowsky's film was a heavy drinker, so Jodorowsky made him drink three bottles of tequila before shooting the scene of his suicide, musing philosophically, "If he dies . . . he dies" (Cobb 274). He heard an old drunk street woman singing, recorded her, and included the recording as a soundtrack for the suicide scene. "There are real sentiments, because all those people I found were not actors. Every person I showed had the problem I show in the picture. Real people I used, real tiger! I'm not a Hollywood company making fake everything" (interview with Wilkins). Sebastián Silva filmed the story of his family nanny-maid in his actual family house. He used his family's actual clothes, bed covers and sheets, and even his nanny-maid's photo album with photos retouched to the likeness of the actress who played her. During filming, the director found himself overwhelmed and gasping for breath, thinking, "'Whoa, I'm at home. And I'm filming my family!' It was stressful, and there were points with the stress that I would go to a bathroom, lock myself in and pant in front of the mirror, like, 'Fuck, what's going on, what's going on?'" (S. Silva). The emotions, confusion, and danger feel real and palpable in these films. The transgressive rawness makes viewers lower their defenses and experience the story viscerally.

Lúcia Nagib interprets this commitment to "the event of truth," to "producing reality" rather than mimicking it as an ethical stance. For these filmmakers, "the world is not a mere construct or discourse, but made of people, animals, plants and objects that physically exist, thrive, suffer and die. They feel part of, and responsible for, this material world, and want to change it for the better" (Nagib 15). Even though films today are more personal and introspective, more revelatory than revolutionary or didactic, "to reveal—to turn a mirror on a society, within the auditorium—can be a political act, highlighting social problems and prompting debate" (Demetrios 14). David H. Fleming reflects on taboo images and topics in these unsettling films and argues that they "engineer" "a cut, or a crack, in what [viewers] thought they already knew" (17). Matheou Demetrios compares watching these films "to eavesdropping on someone in a way that a documentary can't even approach" (260). I have argued that the physical and emotional nakedness of the people on the screen lures us in, teases out secrets and traumas, gives a new perspective on them and allows to rescript behaviors, especially in the face of abusive authority ("Under the Skin Cinema" 39).

The Nation as a Family Metaphor

The transgressive realism producing affect activates the deep metaphor I discuss in this book, of the nation as a family and the father as a political leader. When we watch these films, we understand they are not about one isolated father abusing one isolated family. The predatory father inflicts transgressive moral and physical damage on his subjects—that is to say, his wife, children, and subordinates. I compare these films to the literary sources that inspired them to prove my point that in the new retellings the children rebel, while the fathers surrender, and sometimes even repent. My analysis is primarily narrative to show that filmmakers shape a visceral rejection of predatory leaders. Stories, literary and cinematic, explain issues and show what is possible (Meretoja 4). Stories plunge us into a state of suspension known as narrative transportation: they make us forget who we are and where we are. Over time, people forget that the information and opinions they acquired came from a fictional source (Green and Brock 329). In fact, fictional stories can have more impact than nonfiction because people approach nonfiction with a critical eye and do not experience transportation (Plantinga 58). This is why stories can change opinions and inspire collective action (Mayer 66). As filmmaker Alejandro González Iñárritu puts it, "once the story goes into your brains, it's in your DNA. That's why I have a theory that the universe is not made of atoms, it's made of stories. Once the story gets into your bones and your body, it's there" ("Iñárritu on Film Metaphysics").

Cognitive linguist George Lakoff influentially argued that we use conceptual metaphors to understand complex issues. One such automatic, unconscious metaphor is Nation as a Family: the government represents the parent, and the citizens represent the children. People who believe that parents should set strict rules and punish the children who break them will support the authoritarian Strict Father metaphoric model. Conversely, people who believe that children become responsible and self-reliant because they are cared for and respected by their parents identify with the Nurturant Parent model of running the state and demand safety nets and democratic accountability for authority figures (Lakoff 15). The films I examine reframe the Strict Father leadership model as repulsive and lethal for the family and the nation.

Freud's mythical father of the primal horde, who exiled his sons and took all women for himself, is another Strict Father archetype. United, the sons killed and ate the father. After that, taken by remorse, they reinstituted the father as the sacred deity of the tribe, embodied by a totemic animal. But they also felt the need to reenact the killing of that primal Father in a periodic ritual, in which all members of the tribe must come together to devour the sacred animal (*Totem and Taboo* 166). The dead father becomes a symbolic function, the figure of the prohibition of incest in the Oedipus complex (*Totem and Taboo* 153). In the story of Freud's patient known as the Rat Man, the father comes to signify a general prohibition on sexual desire. At the age of three, the patient was beaten by the father for what Freud believes was masturbation. Lacking insults in his vocabulary, the boy shouted at the father, "You lamp!" "You towel!" "You plate!" Since then, he became a "coward," "terrified of blows" ("Notes" 316). He avoided marrying and was unable to have a healthy sexual life. He repressed the memory of the traumatic punishment and said that he loved his father more than anyone else in the world, but often caught himself wishing death or terrible torture upon him. Freud explained this paternal figure as a function of prohibition and command. Jacques Lacan conceptualized this prohibitive regulatory order as "The Name of the Father." In French, the "Name of the Father" sounds the same as the "No of the Father," so Lacan associated the paternal figure with laws, prohibition, and guilt. It entangles people in language and symbols and marks them with "hieroglyphics of hysteria, blazons of phobia, labyrinths of the Zwangsneurose [obsessional neurosis], charms of impotence, enigmas of inhibition, oracles of anxiety . . . , seals of self-punishment, disguises of perversion" (52). For Slavoj Žižek, the Name (and the No) of the Father signifies "perverse fantasies about what the person who is the bearer of this No 'really wants.'" The No of the Father is not a clear law, such as "You shall not kill" but "the truncated injunction 'You shall not!'—do what? . . . you yourself should know or guess what you should not do, so that you are always and a priori put in an impossible position of always and a priori being under suspicion of violating some (unknown) prohibition" (lxvi).

The scenes from the film stills examined below are examples of the audiovisual metaphors for the oppression and abuse predatory fathers unleash. The first two stills show the familiar situation of a family dinner. In many films, the family dinner looks like a hostage situation, which is indeed the case of the children in these films and of the society as a whole under a dictatorship. In figure 1.1, a scene from the 2015 Argentine film *The Clan*, a military leader presides over an official gathering of his associates and toasts to "duty," "honor," and "the homeland," with everyone in attendance raising their glass in unison. Figure 1.2 shows a different scene from the same film, in which one of these associates, a kidnapper and murderer, now presides over his family

Figure 1.1. A military leader presides over a social gathering in *The Clan* (2015).

Figure 1.2. The father presides over his family in *The Clan* (2015).

at dinner. Similarly oppressive family dinners appear in the Brazilian films *To the Left of the Father* (*Lavoura arcaica*, 2001) and *Behind the Sun* (*Abril despedaçado*, 2001). In the latter film, the father administers a smashing blow to his youngest child. In each of these scenes, we can plainly see the oppressive and claustrophobic atmosphere in these families and the violence the father yearns to unleash.

These scenes undo the received idea that the father always knows best and leads for the good of his dependents. There are many bodies in pools of blood in these films, but the female bodies are particularly impactful. The victims are often defenseless, trusting girls, such as the one dying from a clandestine abortion gone wrong in *The Crime of Father Amaro* (*El crimen del padre Amaro*, Mexico, 2002), or one raped by an impotent dictator in *The Feast of the Goat* (*La fiesta del Chivo*, Peru, 2005); see figure 1.3. We also see the father locking people in the family bathroom in *The Clan* (*El clan*, Argentina, 2015),

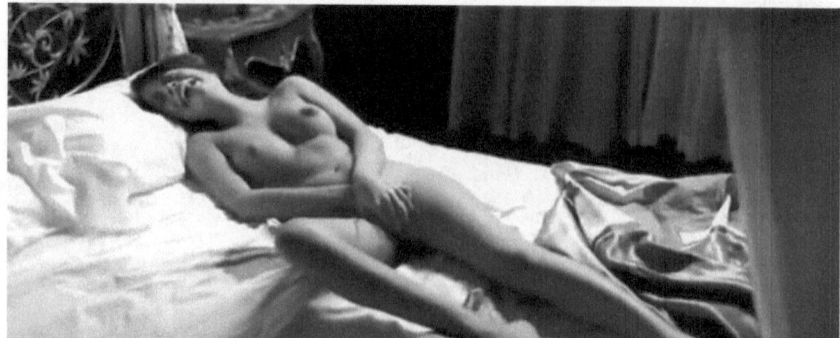

Figure 1.3. The young woman offered to pacify the Dominican dictator Trujillo in *Feast of the Goat* (2005).

or in a mental hospital, where they are subjected to electroshock, as were the hostages of the dictatorships in the 2000 Brazilian film *Brainstorm* (*Bicho de sete cabeças*).

Filmmakers use heavy theatrical makeup, masks, and stage costumes to show that these fathers only masquerade as benevolent protectors. In the 2015 Argentine film *The Clan*, a kidnapper and torturer tricks his son into helping him with kidnappings, saying, "Give me your vote of confidence, son" (dame tu voto de confianza), as if he were a political candidate running for a position. The actor wears a bright white foundation, eyeliner, and lipstick. Figure 1.4 shows a scene from *History of a Clan* (*La historia de un clan*, Argentina, 2015), in which the kidnapper, his wife, and son wear masks of Argentina's former president Juan Perón, his wife Evita, and the military junta leader Videla. Similarly, figure 1.5 depicts a scene from the 2008 Chilean film *Tony Manero* in which a cold-blooded assassin and criminal dreams of winning the Tony Manero look-alike contest.

There is a reason that the films I examine in this book are recent, post-2000 adaptations of stories written during the dictatorship times or earlier. The cinematic retellings transform these old stories entirely. It is not about removing a storyline or a character to make the story fit in a shorter time frame. It is about transforming the protagonists into the opposites of their literary counterparts and sending them on an entirely different trajectory—one of rebellion rather than resignation. The result is that the original story's moral message is changed. The filmmakers could not do it differently. Now they know with certainty that the dictatorship "saviors" actually engaged in kidnappings, torture, and clandestine murders, and that the money they bor-

Figure 1.4. A family of kidnappers wearing masks of Perón, Evita, and Videla in *History of a Clan* (2015).

Figure 1.5. The murderer at the dancing contest in *Tony Manero* (2008).

rowed promising spiritual rebirth and economic recovery was spent on the military or moved offshore. The filmmakers also lived through hopes of true democratization after the fall of these dictatorships, which for many people remained just that—hopes. In the films, the fathers are brought to justice by their emboldened children. Such retellings show that both filmmakers and audiences want to see predatory leaders fall.

An Outline of the Book

Each chapter identifies a different face of predatory leadership: the reluctant rapist, the carceral disciplinarian, the backslapping charmer, the histrion, the scold, and the profiteer. The concluding chapter focuses on films in which the composite figure of the predatory father is blown up, stabbed, urinated upon, and extirpated from existence, down to his name.

Chapter 2, "The Reluctant Rapist and the Cult of Aggressive Masculinity in Peru," features demented and sadistic fathers who abuse fourteen-year-old children. This violence—physical and verbal—against their most defenseless subjects is entirely unnecessary. The leader performs it as a job, a chore, almost reluctantly. This performative violence is a version of the ritual child sacrifice with which the pre-Columbian Inca empire inspired awe in the subjects. Figure 1.3 above, a still from *The Feast of the Goat* (*La fiesta del Chivo*), shows its ritualistic and sacrificial character. For Dominican dictator Rafael Leonidas Trujillo, rape of young women was a ritual by which he demonstrated to himself and his subjects that he can do his job as their leader. Now that Trujillo is old and ill, the ritual of raping became a chore. Mario Vargas Llosa, who wrote the novel that inspired the film, identifies primarily with the raped girl because as a child he was beaten and verbally abused. In the 2015 Peruvian film *Magallanes*, a colonel sexually enslaves a fourteen-year-old girl, to protect her, in a way, and to cope with fear. This mystery thriller recounts the routine capture and rape of Indigenous girls during the conflict between the Peruvian state and the terrorist organization Sendero Luminoso (Shining Path) in the 1980s. In the film, unlike the story that inspired it, the colonel's son is kidnapped and raped as well. In the 2005 film *Madeinusa*, the mayor of an Indigenous village picks his fourteen-year-old daughter as the winner of the beauty pageant, the Miss Virgin of a macabre parade, hoping to deflower her in the evening. In these films, rape is shown as a ritual of predatory leadership, which the leader completes because he must, out of a sense of obligation. It causes an emotional shock in the viewer and inspires disgust for aggressive masculinity.

Chapter 3, "Arquímedes Puccio and Other Carceral Disciplinarians in Argentina," looks at the men at the helm of the Argentine dictatorship of 1976–1983, who inspired confidence through their orderly and proper appearance and their passion for rules and routine. These qualities seem to many a guarantee that things in the country would go as they should. Little do people suspect that the man with carceral dispositions will go beyond conventional methods of enforcing his vision of order by creating places of clandestine detention. In just seven years the junta succeeded in detaining and killing over

30,000 people. In recent years, the man who personifies these carceral disciplinarians became the focus of several books and films. Arquímedes Puccio, who kidnapped people during the Dirty War in Argentina and killed them after collecting ransom, was a very proper-looking patriarch and a cleanliness aficionado who went to Mass with his family every Sunday. He made his family "help out" with clandestine detention, hiding hostages in the family house in a prestigious neighborhood. Places of clandestine detention make it possible for carceral disciplinarians to feel they can dominate people completely: the hostages were held in over six hundred secret detention centers often right in the middle of the city, so people walked right past them. In addition, the victimizers, both in Puccio's family and in the prisons, enjoyed chatting with their inmates, brought them cakes from home, and played cards with them to take a break. The films about Puccio reflect the scary nature of carceral disciplinarians—the homey normality and orderliness with which they go about their gruesome tasks. I look at films *The Clan* (*El clan*) and *The History of a Clan* (*La historia de un clan*), the true crime book *The Clan Puccio*, and the speeches of the dictatorship perpetrators Jorge Rafael Videla, Emilio Massera, Alfredo Astiz, Antonio Bussi, Miguel Etchecolatz, and Adolfo Scilingo. Just like Puccio, these leaders boast about their service to the Fatherland. Ridiculous and scary examples of the banality of evil, they refuse to repent of their crimes and draw from them the feeling of being special.

Chapter 4, "The *Patrón*: A Backslapping Predator with a Big Smile in Mexico," focuses on leadership as pretend kinship and friendship known as patronage in Mexico. The *patrón* and the people under his patronage form a close informal relationship, based not on rules or laws but on mutual expectation of favors. The patrón distributes goods and services to clients in return for their unconditional political loyalty. The patrones portrayed in the films are so charismatic and personable that no one can resist their charm even when they demand increasingly immoral favors. In *Tear This Heart Out* (*Arráncame la vida*, 2008), a middle-aged general marries a fourteen-year-old girl. He becomes governor, then senator, and his wife shares with him the prestige, wealth, and influence. In *The Crime of Father Amaro* (*El crimen del padre Amaro*, 2002) the seductive patrón is the bishop who trains a young seminary graduate to solicit money from the drug lords, to intimidate journalists, and to excommunicate priests who refuse to participate in these corrupt practices. In return, the bishop promises his disciple quick ascension through the ranks, and eventually, the bishopric. *The Perfect Dictatorship* (*La dictadura perfecta*, 2014) is about a charmingly unprincipled governor known as El Padrino, the godfather of the criminals and drug cartels operating in his state, and a young creative director of a TV channel, hired to propel him to presidency. These stories are metaphors of clientelism as *modus vivendi*, unthinking consensual compliance with corrupt power figures in exchange for favors. The young protagonists begin with small concessions to their enchanting *patrones* and, before they know it, they become engines of corruption themselves. In most of these films, the *patrón*'s subordinates kiss his hand, like peons of old.

Chapter 5, "The Scold: Leadership as Emotional Abuse in Brazil," identifies Kafka's father as the inspiration for many recent film adaptations. The writer's father scolded him to such a degree when he was a child that he believed himself to be physically and intellectually repulsive. He never married and died young. He believed he was the father's prisoner and compared his childhood to "a preparation for a hanging." The father laid strict rules for the family to follow but never followed them himself, using these rules only as a pretext to attack and abuse. Kafka poured his grievances into a letter to his father, which the father returned unopened. In the novels that inspired the films I examine, written in the 1970s, the fathers would rather kill or lock up their sons in a mental asylum than have them disobey. These stories are inspired by Kafka's short stories "Judgement" and "Home-Coming," as well as his letter to the father, so, predictably, the sons wither away. Amazingly, in the recent film adaptations of these novels these sons stand up to their fathers, as in *Brainstorm* (*Bicho de sete cabeças*, 2001) and *Behind the Sun* (*Abril despedaçado*, 2001). Kafka's famous tale "Metamorphosis" in which a dutiful son turns into a giant insect and worries most about making his father angry inspired the famous films *City of God* (*Cidade de Deus*, 2002) and *City of Men* (*Cidade dos Homens*, 2007).

Chapter 6, "The Histrion and Fatherhood as a Stage: Bolívar in Colombia and Venezuela," is about the leader who enjoys the histrionic dimension of power—to be admired and applauded by the crowds. For the leader, it becomes unthinkable to ever part with the position of power because the limelight becomes the meaning of his life. In his desire that the applause continue indefinitely, the histrionic leader begins leveling the political field just as a celebrity actor striving to overshadow his rivals onstage would. In the new century, the hallowed Founding Father Simón Bolívar came to be seen as more passionate for the limelight than for his patriotic cause. Chilean artist Juan Dávila, for example, portrayed him in his familiar image on horseback but not wearing pants and, in another painting, as a reclining Marilyn Monroe flashing a dazzling celebrity smile. We see this histrionic Bolívar in Colombian film *Bolívar I Am* (*Bolívar soy yo*, 2002) and the novel *The Feast of the Innocent* (*Carroza de Bolívar*, 2012) by Evelio Rosero. Rosero's novel inspired a carnival float paraded during the 2019 carnival in Pasto, the Colombian city that the Liberator destroyed. In this monumental work, Bolívar is the Devil himself, driving a chariot of death. He wears a mask and no pants, as in Dávila's painting. These criticisms counterbalance the appropriation and deification of Bolívar by Hugo Chávez, as can be seen in Venezuelan films, especially in *The Liberator* (*El Libertador*, 2013), and the Colombian series portraying Chávez as a histrion, *El Comandante* (2017).

Chapter 7, "The Profiteer: Political Freedom Becomes Consumer Freedom in Chile," focuses on the contestation of the neoliberal restructuring imposed by Pinochet. The belief that privatization of services and industries is more effective resulted in precarization of labor, with most current jobs lacking security and access to pensions and benefits. Labor precarization actually picked up speed when democratic governments took over. This is particularly striking in the mining sector, Chile's most lucrative industry, where three out of four jobs are precarious. The 1904 classic *Subterra* by Baldomero Lillo accurately describes the labor management: cutting costs on safety, not paying workers, and pitting them against each other. In the 2003 film adaptation, the workers are shown to work with the owner toward the economic and social progress of the country. *Machuca* (2004) shows how the privatization of education pits rich and poor children against each other and hurts them both, ending in arrest and disappearance for the poor child and lonely lifelong conformity for the rich boy. In *No* (2012), we see how entertainment and the freedom to consume substitute for political freedom. All three films introduce a new character—a father who likes the idea of democracy but does nothing because he profiteers from the neoliberal restructuring.

The concluding chapter, "The Clean-Shaven Father, Disfigured, Urinated upon, Buried Alive and Blown Up," discusses films by Guillermo del Toro and Alejandro Jodorowsky, in which the composite figure of the predatory father is extirpated completely, both physically and symbolically: *Pan's Labyrinth* (*Laberinto del fauno*, 2006), *Pinocchio* (2023), *Dance of Reality* (*Danza de la realidad*, 2011), and *Endless Poetry* (*Poesía sin fin*, 2016). The predatory father is urinated upon, blown up, buried alive, stabbed, disfigured, and stripped of his name. All the four films I examine have the same visual: a clean-shaven man with slicked-back hair, impeccable uniform and boots, grabs hold of a small child and looks at it with intense hatred. For some reason, the child in these films cannot understand simple commands. Obeying commands must come naturally to people, and especially to children, who depend on adults for their survival. The clean-shaven man in the films precipitates the rigid structure of the fascist crowd by giving people simple commands. The child's inability to follow simple commands threatens to implode the crowd from within. The clean-shaven man ends up with a gun pointed at the child because outside of the crowd his life has no meaning. The rebellion of the children against the authority of the predatory father reaches its apogee in these films. The man's pulchritudinous physique becomes smeared in abject body fluids and disfigured. Lacan's notion of the Name of the Father, which means the symbolic order of prohibitions, helps understand why the predatory father in these films is stripped of his name. These films rescript instinctual acquiescent behaviors in the face of authority and invite us to stop living in constant expectation of command.

2

The Reluctant Rapist and the Cult of Aggressive Masculinity in Peru

The rape of minors by an authority figure in a paradoxically festive atmosphere is a persistent focus of many Peruvian narratives. The rape of the most defenseless subjects is so outrageous and unnecessary that it must have a performative function. The festive context in which it occurs confirms that such rape is a public spectacle of domination. In this chapter, I will construe rape as a metaphor for the relationship between the authoritarian ruler and his subjects in numerous Peruvian films, novels, and plays. In the novel *The Feast of the Goat*, published in 2000 and adapted for the screen in 2005, Mario Vargas Llosa depicted the rape of a fourteen-year-old girl as a ritual sacrifice through which a dictator claims a godlike status, and the novel has had such a profound resonance that it continues to inspire new cinematic and theatrical adaptations. Another victim depicted by Vargas Llosa in his autobiography and the 1963 novel *The Time of the Hero*, both fictional and autobiographical, is a fourteen-year-old boy routinely beaten by his father. The boy's indoctrination into aggressive masculinity continues at a military academy, with rape-simulating rituals and punishments. Alonso Cueto's novel *The Blue Hour*, published in 2005 and twice adapted for the screen, and Alberto León's 2014 play *The Captive* are both about a fourteen-year-old girl captured to be raped by soldiers. Similarly, a fourteen-year-old girl breaks out of her condition of ritual rape by her father, the village mayor, in the 2006 film *Madeinusa* directed by Claudia Llosa. The imagery and symbolism of sacrificial festivals that always accompany rape in these works show that the perpetrators experience this simulation of child sacrifice as a nation- and community-building act, a means to experience transcendence. One tends to associate rape with an uncontrollable compulsion, but these rapists are unusually tired and reluctant. What used to be a perverse inner impulse has become a part of the job description of the predatory leader, no longer pleasurable and even downright stressful and challenging. The cinematic retellings of the original stories usually punish these rapists more harshly. We see them quiver in blood or vomit, sacrificed in their turn. Jelke Boesten, a researcher of violence against women in Peru, argues that predatory leadership in the public and private spheres is symbolically encouraged by the state because it systematically fails to punish rapists. Even after the fall of dictator Alberto Fujimori, iron-fist rhetoric continues to remain popular in Peru as we can see in the electoral success of Keiko Fujimori, currently investigated for corruption; Daniel Urresti, currently investigated for human rights abuses; and Ollanta Humala's brother, Antauro, a radical nationalist. The worshiped reluctant rapist in these Peruvian narratives is a metaphor for predatory leadership and its powerful hold. These narratives of rape inspire a disgust for aggressive masculinity.

Rape as a Sacrifice Ritual and Leadership Principle

Mario Vargas Llosa, Nobel Prize laureate for literature and one of Latin America's most famous writers, is known for his fascination with transgression. His influence is clear in all the writers and filmmakers discussed here. Alonso Cueto writes and lectures on Vargas Llosa, arguing that he helped shape (moldear) and understand Peru ("El aniversario"). Luis Llosa, who adapted Vargas Llosa's novel for the screen, is the famous author's cousin, and Claudia Llosa, who directed *Madeinusa*, is his niece. Salvador del Solar, who directed *Magallanes*, played the title character in the adaptation of Vargas Llosa's novel *Pantaleón Pantoja and the Special Service* (which also features human sacrifice). Santiago Roncagliolo, author of *Red April* (*Abril rojo*), another novel about sacrificial murders committed during a festival, described Vargas Llosa and contemporary Peruvian writers as a grandfather and grandchildren (Roncagliolo).

Human sacrifice in the ancient Inca empire made a profound impression on Vargas Llosa and returns obsessively in his writing. In *Captain Pantoja and the Special Service* (*Pantaleón y las visitadoras*, 1973), set in the northern Amazon city of Iquitos, a sect of religious fanatics crucifies people. They smear their faces with blood and even drink it to purify themselves of sin (131). Note the transgressive description of the child sacrifice. The old matron narrating denies taking part in it, although she may have. The child "had his little eyes closed, his little head fallen over his heart, like a miniature Christ. . . . He looked like a baby monkey from a distance, but that white body drew my attention. I approached, went up to the foot of the cross and then I realized. Oh, God, . . . when I'm on my deathbed I'll still see that poor little angel" (109, the Spanish diminutives *ojitos, cabecita, cuerpecito* make the reader shudder). In his later novel *Death in the Andes* (*Lituma en los Andes*, 1993), the inhabitants of an Andean town sacrifice and eat three people in a festive atmosphere to reenact the ancient yearly custom and "buy happiness and prosperity" for the year to come (276). Note the transgressive insistence on repulsive details when Vargas Llosa describes ancient human sacrifice in Peru: "the religious passion of the Chancas and Huancas for human viscera, the delicate surgery in which they removed their victims' livers and brains and kidneys and ate them in their ceremonies, washing it all down with good corn chicha" (158).

In 1983, Vargas Llosa chaired the committee investigating the massacre of ten journalists in the Andean village of Uchuraccay, during the conflict between the radical left organization Shining Path and the Peruvian government. The inhabitants mistook the journalists for terrorists. Vargas Llosa was much criticized for saying that the *comuneros* killed the journalists to obey ancient traditions rather than the orders of the paramilitary to kill all foreigners (as the Truth and Reconciliation Commission established in 2003). Indeed, the writer was strongly impacted by the magico-religious aspect of the killing. The victims were buried face down, as "devils" and foreigners. They suffered most wounds in their mouths and eyes because "the sacrificed victim must be deprived of eyes so it cannot recognize its torturers, and of the tongue, so it cannot speak and denounce them, and its ankles must be broken so it cannot come back to disturb those who killed it" (Vargas Llosa, Informe 24).

Vargas Llosa draws his knowledge about human sacrifice rituals from Sigmund Freud and Georges Bataille, writers he often mentions. In *Totem and Taboo* (1913), Freud defined taboo as a prohibition of something sacred—something at once holy, unclean, or dangerous. Killing a totem animal is taboo. However, it is an obligation to participate in the killing of that animal in a yearly ritual, when that animal is sacrificed—torn apart alive and eaten by all members of the community (Freud 224). Freud argues that the sacrificed totemic animal represents not only the deity but also the father of the primal horde. That father banished his sons to keep all women to himself. The sons rebelled, returned, killed, and ate the father (234). After that, they deified the father and established a patriarchal society, to punish themselves for this transgression and to divide authority among themselves. The community members perform ritual sacrifices to reenact the sacrifice of the primal father and to experience communion with him and with each other (255). The sacrificial killing of a sacred being is an ancient ritual to make members participate in and witness each other commit a terrible transgression together. In this way, sacrifice is constitutive of the community. Its yearly repetition ensures that its members stay together and increases their chances of survival.

French philosopher Georges Bataille was so fascinated by sacrifice that he founded a secret society called Acéphale (A Headless Man), whose members planned to have a human sacrifice but were unable to find an executioner (Hegarty 7). Bataille believed that sacrifice, a wasteful, unnecessary, excessive spending of lives, was used by humans to experience a communion with something bigger than themselves, something eternal and uncontrollable, the "sovereign world of the gods and myths" (Bataille 210). For Bataille, the sexual act is a reenactment of human sacrifice (18), as is the transgression of taboos. Literature is a way to explore and vicariously experience these hidden impulses of wasteful violence, as Bataille notes in *Literature and Evil*. Bataille's essay made a profound impression on Vargas Llosa. He wrote that literature knows and contains the inner sadist hidden in human beings, "muzzled and tied by the conventions of the community . . . panting at the boys with golden locks, brandishing a dagger, one hand of his flies" (Vargas Llosa, "Bataille or the Redemption of the Evil" 126). In his 2018 essay "New Inquisitions," Vargas Llosa said, again citing Bataille, that if literature is not allowed to speak about violence and misogyny, it will die, and then violence, left without a way out, will find its way back to real life (dejaría sin vía de escape aquellos fondos malditos que llevamos dentro y estos encontrarían entonces otras formas de reintegrarse a la vida; *Nuevas Inquisiciones*).

It is to explore this profundity of evil that Vargas Llosa wrote *The Feast of the Goat* (*La fiesta del Chivo*, 2000). The novel is about the Dominican dictator Rafael Leonidas Trujillo. Rape in this novel is a ritual sacrifice through which the dictator awes his subjects so they worship him. A histrionic sadist, Trujillo ruled for three decades (1930–1961) until he was assassinated. He was nicknamed The Goat (El Chivo) for his morbid pursuit of women, especially the wives of his close associates, to demonstrate his alpha male status. In his old age, suffering from incontinence and incipient impotence, this ritual raping became an unpleasant duty, a chore. In 2005, the writer's cousin Luis Llosa, known for several Peruvian TV series and later several Hollywood blockbusters, such as *The Specialist* and *Anaconda*, adapted it for the screen. The adaptation features an international cast and is in English. In the film, Urania (Isabella Rossellini), a successful New York lawyer, returns to Santo Domingo for the first time in thirty years. She treats her father, an invalid afflicted with Alzheimer's, with resentment and, as the story unfolds, we learn that he offered her to Trujillo when she was only fourteen. He was an educated man and Trujillo's close associate. He doted on Urania, his only daughter, and guarded her against the attentions of predators like Trujillo's handsome son Ramfis, another known rapist. But one day he woke up to find himself declared a traitor, removed from his post of senate president, and his bank accounts frozen. There was no reason for this demotion: he was randomly picked by Trujillo, who regularly victimized close associates to keep all of them worried

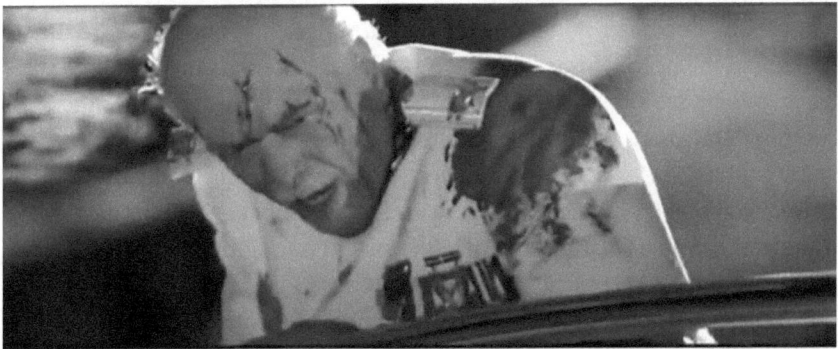

Figure 2.1. The bleeding Trujillo prepares to fire back in *Feast of the Goat* (2005).

and afraid. In a desperate attempt to win back Trujillo's good graces, Urania's father sent her to Trujillo's special house for romantic encounters. He told her she had been invited to a special party, a *fiesta*. This event explains the novel's title, *La fiesta del Chivo*. This festive setting and festive expectations paradoxically prefigure the rape that actually takes place, as in other stories, literary and cinematic, that I examine here. Urania was excited to go and help her father make peace with the Chief, although she did wonder what she would do at the mysterious party alone. Trujillo failed to achieve an erection to rape her, so he raped her with his fingers. After the rape, Urania never returned home to her father and escaped to the United States with the help of her school principal.

Throughout the film, Urania tells her story to her aunt and niece, with the invalid father present, looking tortured. The film focuses on the punishment of the cruel rapist and dictator. He was assassinated by a group of conspirators. The assassination scene is the climax of the film. The badly wounded Trujillo (Thomas Milian) gets out of the car and faces his assassins, calling out to them "Traitors!" He roars and raises his gun. The conspirators, one by one, unhurriedly fire at the dictator, and he collapses with a look of hatred on his face. Trujillo's hold over the country, which lasted thirty-one years, is at an end. The Benefactor, the Father of the New Fatherland, or simply Papá Trujillo, as children were obligated to refer to him, is dead. The director, Luis Llosa, wants to show that the predatory ruler can and should be defeated (figure 2.1).

The same ending and focus are found in the last five episodes of the 2014 telenovela *El Chivo*, produced by RTI Colombia and Univisión. Trujillo (Julio Bracho) also gets out of the car, trying to fight back, and is riddled with bullets just as dramatically. His wife looks on with scorn, and one of the conspirators tells him that no death could redeem what he did to his country before shooting him in the head. This is followed by archival footage showing Dominicans tearing down his statues, painting over Trujillista slogans, holding signs welcoming democracy and liberty, and casting their votes.

In contrast, in Vargas Llosa's novel, Trujillo's death changes nothing. His power is absorbed by his most unassuming accomplice. Trujillo dies in the middle of the novel, with no drama: the conspirators simply find him already dead in the back seat of his car. This is because the novel has a very different objective. Instead of celebrating the end of the dictator, the novel shows his rebirth in Joaquín Balaguer, the bookish intellectual who turns out to be as obsessed with power as was his deceased boss Trujillo. In the first part of the novel, Balaguer is a servile poet composing essays on the Benefactor's divine mission and serving as his puppet president. In the second part of the novel, Balaguer slowly absorbs all of Trujillo's power by playing the Trujillistas and the Americans against each other. Trujillo's chief of the secret police Johnny Abbes says in disbelief, "You are as dirty as I am. Nobody will swallow the Machiavellian ploy of you leading the transition to democracy," to which Balaguer replies calmly, "It is possible I might fail. But I must try" (usted está tan manchado como yo. Nadie se tragará el jueguito maquiavélico de que usted va a encabezar la transición hacia la democracia; Es posible que fracase . . . Pero, debo intentarlo; *Feast* 358). Balaguer admires the masterful machination that he has set in motion in order to "convince the world that with him as president the Republic is becoming a democracy" (convencer al mundo de que, con él en la Presidencia, la República estaba volviéndose una democracia; *Feast* 475). Vargas Llosa describes both Balaguer and Trujillo as inhuman: Trujillo's diabolical mark is the obsession with cleanliness and sex, while Balaguer's is abstinence from sex and absence of any interest in eating, drinking, or money. Their true passion is to have a whole country under their thumb and to see people dance as they pull the strings.

The novel was published in 2000, when Balaguer was running for the presidency for the eighth time. By then he was ninety-one years old and completely blind. Although he lost that election, Balaguer had served as president for twenty-four years (1960–1962, 1966–1978, and 1986–1996), almost as long as the sadistic dictator Trujillo. The mottoes of Balaguer's political campaigns were "No need to change what's good" (Lo bueno no se cambia 1974–1978), "Balaguer again and again" (Y vuelve y vuelve Balaguer 1986–1990), "Another four years and then we'll talk" (Cuatro años más y después hablamos 1990–1994), "Balaguer just keeps on going" (Y sigue y sigue Balaguer 1994–1998), and the very frank "whatever Balaguer says" (Lo que diga Balaguer

1994–1998). In 1997, Balaguer was forced to step down amid accusations of electoral fraud and having ordered the disappearance of his vehement critic Narciso González, journalist and academic. Regardless, the Dominican congressmen proclaimed him "the Father of democracy," "the Great Precursor of Dominican Democracy, Economic Development, and Political Stability and Governance" (Liberato 15). After he died in 2002, Balaguer's name was given to a highway, a metro stop, a plaza, and an airport. The Fundación Balaguer dedicated exhibitions to him and published books about him. Cultivating "anti-democratic interactions and paternalistic relations between the political leadership, the citizenry, and political elites," Balaguer showed "how a politician should act to be able to win" (Liberato 27, 24).

In this novel, Vargas Llosa found a powerful metaphor of predatory leadership—rape of a girl as a performative ritual sacrifice, facilitated by her father. This is why the novel continues to inspire new screen and stage adaptations. Colombian theater and film director Jorge Alí Triana, who adapted it for the stage in 2003 together with his twenty-two-year-old daughter Verónica Triana, decided that Trujillo and Urania's father should be played by the same actor (Armada). The novel was adapted for the stage more recently in 2019 by Natalio Grueso in Spain with over three hundred performances. The rape scene in the novel is so excessive and graphic that it provokes a spiritual shudder (or as Freud puts it, "holy dread," 20). Critics, including myself, have shied away from citing it directly and refer to it with euphemisms, as does the film adaptation, but it must be considered closely to recognize the wastefully excessive, transgressive aspect of human sacrifice. When she arrives at the promised fiesta, Urania soon understands what awaits her. She is paralyzed with disgust and fear when the smelly old Trujillo dances with her, forces his tongue into her mouth, and tries to seduce her. But when he cannot get an erection, he blames it on her; he orders her to stop playing dead and to perform fellatio on him—but nothing works (*Feast* 396). The description of this scene is extremely graphic, and Urania's aunt begs her to stop talking, but she continues, relentlessly. Trujillo fears she will go home and "laugh at [him] with [her] father," so he rapes her with his fingers, "digging, forcing them into her. She felt pierced, stabbed with a knife; a lightning bolt ran from her head down to her feet. She cried out feeling as if she were dying" (escarbaban y entraban en ella a la fuerza. Se sintió rajada, acuchillada; un relámpago corrió de su cerebro a los pies. Gimió, sintiendo que se moría, *Feast* 397). These lines evoke the stabbing and death of the sacrificial victim, but Trujillo is not satisfied. He is angry and vindictive: "Go on and screech, you little bitch, see if you learn your lesson" (Chilla, perrita, a ver si aprendes; *Feast* 397).

To force a scared girl into performing degrading actions, rape her, and then scold her with obscenities is absolutely unnecessary and excessive. Trujillo's anger shows that he is tired of performing what he understands to be his leadership ritual, to prove to himself and his subjects that he can continue being the leader. The sacrifice from which Trujillo draws, or thinks he draws, his supernatural powers, fails and he breaks into tears, taking it to mean that he can no longer govern his ungrateful subjects: "There is no justice in this world. Why was this happening to him now, after he had fought so hard for this ungrateful country, for these people without honor" (no hay justicia en este mundo. Por qué le ocurría esto después de luchar tanto, por este país ingrato, por esta gente sin honor; *Feast* 397). He later regrets that he did not kill Urania, as she could make his impotence known. He consoles himself that he will prove himself with a new girl in the evening (he is murdered on his way to that engagement). He prays to God, begging for help in raping her: "Dear God, do this for me. Tonight I need to fuck Yolanda Esterel right. So I can know I'm not dead. Not an old man. And can go on doing your work for you, moving this damn country of assholes forward . . . Don't be a miser, don't be stingy" (Dios mío, hazme esa gracia. Necesito tirarme como es debido, esta noche, a Yolanda Esterel. Para saber que no estoy muerto. Que no estoy viejo. Que puedo seguir reemplazándote en la tarea de sacar adelante este endemoniado país de pendejos; *Feast* 339). This transgressive prayer shows that for Trujillo rape is a sacred ritual he must continue to perform as the country's leader and that he is tired of it all. This reluctant rapist shows that predatory leaders must often *make* themselves go on abusing, even when they have lost any and all pleasure they may have derived from it in their younger years. If their "embrace with power" (as Ángel Rama calls it) did not asphyxiate other thoughts and emotions, they would have quit long ago.

We will recognize the graphic enormity of Urania's rape scene in Vargas Llosa's autobiographical descriptions of how he was abused by his father, and later at the military academy where his father sent him to learn what he terms *la hombría* (manliness) but is actually predatory masculinity, as I will show shortly. This must be why Vargas Llosa called Urania "the character with whom I identify so much," "the character who moved me profoundly. She is an entirely fictional character, but I feel she is more real than many historic characters in the novel. Her case greatly moved me while I was writing. I came to identify myself with Urania on a sentimental level, which did not happen with other characters." While researching for the novel, Vargas Llosa learned that offering girls to Trujillo by their fathers was so common that not all could be accepted. He felt "enormous anxiety and anguish" ("Eso no debe repetirse jamás" 52). These offerings demonstrated "the almost religious affection" they had for Trujillo as "an incarnate divinity," said Vargas Llosa (Navarro). Millions truly worshiped Trujillo. As Vargas Llosa reflects in the novel, they "do not merely fear him but love him, as children eventually love authoritarian fathers, convincing themselves that the whippings and beatings are for their own good" (*Feast* 63). Urania's father finally agrees to give her to Trujillo because he too thinks that Trujillo deserves this supreme sacrifice, as one of these supernatural "forces of Nature, instruments of God, makers of nations." He and his likes serve Trujillo not to gain power and money, as "vile people" think, but "out of love (*cariño*), compassion, piety (*piedad*, incorrectly translated as *pity*)" (*Feast* 314). The word "piety" tells us that Trujillo's closest associates also perceived his rape of girls as a duty and ritual and worshiped him for it. Trujillo extracted a "masochist vocation from the bottom of their souls" and they "needed to be spat on, mistreated and debased to be fulfilled," perspicaciously said Vargas Llosa in the novel (les sacó del fondo del alma una vocación masoquista, de seres que necesitaban ser escupidos, maltratados, que sintiéndose abyectos se realizaban; *Feast* 64). The sadistic brand of predatory leadership engenders masochistic disintegration of ethical anchors in the subjects who are made to watch and admire the atrocities committed by the leader.

Teenage boys in Vargas Llosa's works are subjected to rape-imitating rituals to indoctrinate them in the leadership principles they will later practice as future leaders of their families and their country. Vargas Llosa's first novel *The Time of the Hero* (*La ciudad y los perros*, 1963) features two boys who grew up with abusive fathers. One of the boys, Ricardo, is from a lower social class and discovers he has a father at the age of eight, when his mother brings Ricardo to Lima to live with his father. The father is distant and hostile. One night Ricardo hears him hit his mother. The boy tries to stop him, and the father beats him unconscious. The terrified child begs the mother to go back to their hometown, but she defends the father and tells the child he himself is to blame because he does not try to win the father over (conquistarlo). He must apologize for interfering, and they will live together happily, "like all families" (como en todas las familias; *Time* 120). Concluding that the mother is the father's accomplice, Ricardo submits himself entirely to the father, acquiescing when the latter scolds the mother for stupidity, incompetence, and even "whoring" (puterío; *Time* 214). The second boy, Alberto, comes from a privileged family. He is also reunited with his father at the age of eight. This father is a cold, indifferent womanizer who is cruel to both his mother and the boy.

Alberto and Ricardo meet at the military school, sent there by the fathers who worry they might grow into "fags" (*maricas*). The school teaches them the rituals of symbolic rape. One must aggress others to position oneself as a dominant male. Those who cannot aggress are labeled maricas. The initiation ritual at the military school described in Vargas Llosa's novel imitates group rape. Ricardo is urinated and spat upon and made to bark and bite other recruits like a dog. After that, they undress him and make him pretend to swim on the track. After that, he "imitated movie stars, polished many pairs of boots, cleaned a floor tile with his tongue, screwed a pillow, and drank piss" (imitó a artistas de cine, lustró varios pares de botines, barrió una loseta con la lengua, fornicó con una almohada, bebió orines; *Time* 54).

School sanctions for small infractions also imitate rape. In the "right angle" (ángulo recto) punishment, a cadet bends down before a soccer-loving sergeant who administers him a tremendous kick in the behind: "He put everything into it. Also, he kicked him with the toe of his boot. The cadet screamed as he fell forward, staggered on all fours for a couple of yards, and then collapsed." What the sergeant and the victim do next is astounding: the sergeant "glanced anxiously" at his superior, who "smiled at him." The kicked cadet also smiled: "Even Núñez, who had got up and was rubbing his buttocks with both hands, had a smile on his face" (Núñez, que se ha incorporado y se frota el trasero con las dos manos, también sonríe; *Time* 43). In these scenes, rape-imitating punishments elicit anxiety but also a display of pleasure, even from the victim. The cadets compete in manliness (hombría) by participating in ejaculation contests during group masturbation sessions and by making jokes about raping dogs and classmates. There is a scene in which they steal a hen, rape it, and roast it.

Alberto, who loves to read and write, manages to simulate adherence to the rituals of symbolic rape. He composes love letters and pornographic stories, which he sells to his classmates for cigarettes. He is nicknamed El Poeta (The Poet). In contrast, Ricardo, who has lived in mortal fear of his father, is unable to even simulate aggression. He is everyone's victim and is nicknamed Esclavo (Slave). Alberto and Ricardo would be friends if friendship were not viewed as weakness and "faggotry," *mariconería* (classmates immediately start calling Ricardo Alberto's wife). Ricardo, doomed all along at his home and at school, is killed by his most aggressive tormentor. Ricardo's father is distraught, but he defiantly tells Alberto that if he was "a bit strict" with his son, it was "for his own good" (por su bien). He continues to call his grieving wife stupid for blaming him for their son's death at the sadistic school. Alberto discloses to the school officials that Ricardo did not die in an accident but was killed by his classmate, but the officials, fearing a scandal, threaten Alberto with expulsion for his pornographic stories. Alberto fears the wrath of his father and withdraws his accusations. He graduates from the school and returns to his rich neighborhood of Miraflores. Dejected, he stops writing and decides that his father is a good example to follow, after all.

In *The Time of the Hero*, the schooling in symbolic rape perpetuates the model of predatory leadership. A "real man" starts a family with the objective of humiliating and dominating his wife and children, not to love them or care for them. In the public sphere, a "real man" obtains a position of authority not in order to care for his subjects but to dominate them. The 1980 adaptation of the novel by Francisco Lombardi makes it even clearer: the general who directs the school tells the students, "The country needs leaders in all spheres of human activity. And leadership is fought for and conquered. Our mission is to provide you with the personality capable of conquering that leadership!" It is all the more puzzling that the adaptation leaves out the fathers entirely. It fails to bring home the novel's epiphany that the fathers' abuse at home initiates the boys into the predatory leadership principle that is reinforced by the abuse at school, which the boys will teach to their children when they become men.

In Vargas Llosa's memoir *Fish in the Water* (*Pez en el agua*, 1991), we learn that the sadistic father from *The Time of the Hero* was modeled on the writer's own. Vargas Llosa's father abandoned his mother when he learned that she was pregnant. Vargas Llosa was growing up happily at his grandparents' house, surrounded by friendly uncles, aunts, and cousins. When he was ten, his mother met his father again at a party and ran away with him to Lima, bringing along Vargas Llosa. Very soon, Vargas Llosa hears his mother being beaten by his father, and he is savagely beaten in turn when he tries to intervene. His father begins to insult and beat them routinely. The writer recounts in masochistic detail how he humiliated himself asking for mercy, which enraged his father even more. Again, I draw your attention to the transgressive excess of the scene, which recalls Urania's rape from *The Feast of the Goat* and explains why the writer identified with her:

> When he beat me, I went off the deep end, and many times terror made me humiliate myself before him and beg his forgiveness with my hands clasped. But even that didn't calm him down. And he went on hitting me, screaming, and threatening to put me in the army as a private as soon as I was old enough to be a recruit so that I'd be set on the right path. When the whole scene was over and done with and he could lock me in my room, it was not the blows that kept me up all night, crying in silence, but the rage and disgust with myself for having been so afraid of him and having humiliated myself before him in that way.

> Cuando me pegaba, yo perdía totalmente los papeles, y el terror me hacía muchas veces humillarme ante él y pedirle perdón con las manos juntas. Pero ni eso lo calmaba. Y seguía golpeando, vociferando y amenazándome con meterme al Ejército de soldado raso apenas tuviera la edad reglamentaria, para que me pusieran en vereda. Cuando aquello terminaba, y podía encerrarme en mi cuarto, no eran los golpes, sino la rabia y el asco conmigo mismo por haberle tenido tanto miedo y haberme humillado ante él de esa manera, lo que me mantenía desvelado, llorando en silencio. (*Fish* 30)

For the young Vargas Llosa, the scolding that accompanies the beating is as scary, if not scarier, than the beating, just as in the rape scene in the *Feast of the Goat*. Vargas Llosa's father sequesters the mother at home, never allowing her to visit her family or friends. The boy is not allowed to go anywhere except school, leading him to engage in covert acts of rebellion. He starts praying and attending Mass to antagonize his father, who calls piety stupid. On one occasion, his father catches him on his way to Mass, breaking his order to stay at home. A terrible and humiliating beating ensues, accompanied by dirty words (*palabrotas*) that scare the child more than the punches:

> Without a word, he gave me such a hard slap on the face that it threw me to the ground; he hit me again and then shoved me into the car, where he began to say those terrible, dirty words that made me suffer as much as his blows. And, once we got back home, as he forced me to beg him for forgiveness, he went on beating me, as he warned me that he was going to straighten me out, to make a little man of me, because he wouldn't allow his son to be a sissy.

> Sin decir palabra, me pegó una cachetada que me derribó al suelo, me volvió a pegar y luego me metió al auto a empellones, donde empezó a decir esas terribles palabrotas que me hacían sufrir tanto como sus golpes. Y, en la casa, mientras me hacía pedirle perdón, me siguió pegando, a la vez que me advertía que me iba a enderezar, a hacer de mí un hombrecito, pues él no permitiría que su hijo fuera maricueca. (*Fish* 29)

As in *Time of the Hero*, the mother tortures the child in her own way by defending the father: "He wasn't so bad. He had his virtues. He didn't drink, didn't smoke, never had affairs, was so proper and so hardworking, weren't these great merits?" (No era tan malo. Tenía sus virtudes. No bebía una copa de alcohol, no fumaba, jamás echaba una cana al aire, era tan formal y tan trabajador. ¿No eran éstos, acaso, grandes méritos?). She tells him to make efforts "to win my father's affection, because he noted my hostility and resented it" (ganarme el cariño de mi papá, pues él me notaba hostil y eso lo resentía; *Fish* 30). Finally, after a particularly violent beating, Vargas Llosa's mother decides to take her son and leave the father. They escape and stay with their relatives. The father cuts them out of some photos, pierces them with pins in others, and throws their things in the street. But after a few days, the mother comes back. She makes several other attempts to leave, but she always returns. Vargas Llosa describes his mother's passion for this cruel man as "masochistic and tortured" and "excessive and transgressive": like a religious fanatic, she "wouldn't hesitate to pay the price of going to hell to prevail" (masoquista y torturado, excesivo y transgresor, pagar el precio del infierno para prevalecer; *Fish* 30).

Vargas Llosa's mother's devotion to her abusive husband must have informed the writer's portrayal of Trujillo's associates, who love him all the more when he tramples on them. The military academy to which the father sends him is another "sadomasochistic feast (fiesta)" (*Fish* 53). The excessive, sexualized, and transgressive description of the hazing fiesta evokes images of gang rape and sacrifice:

> We had to kick each other in the backside as we doubled over alternately, the one who kicked more slowly than the other was in turn kicked, hard, by the hazers. Afterward, they made us open our trousers fly and take out our penis and masturbate: the one who came first would be let go and the other would stay behind to make our torturers' beds. But, however hard we tried, fear kept us from getting an erection, and finally, bored by our incompetence, they took us to the soccer field. They asked me what sport I went in for: "Swimming, sir" "Swim on your back from one end of the field to the other then, *perro*."

> Doblados en dos, alternadamente teníamos que patearnos en el trasero; el que pateaba más despacio era pateado por los bautizadores, con furia. Después, nos hicieron abrir la braqueta y sacarnos el sexo para masturbarnos: el que terminaba primero se iría y el otro se quedaría a tender las camas de los verdugos. Pero, por más que tratábamos, el miedo nos impedía la erección, y, al final, aburridos de nuestra incompetencia, nos llevaron al campo de futbol. A mí me preguntaron qué deporte practicaba: 'Natación, mi cadete.' 'Nádese de espaldas toda la cancha de atletismo, entonces, perro.' (*Fish* 53)

The transgressive violence of the hazing ritual marks the young men with a compulsion to repeat it with other people ever after, as victims or as perpetrators.

Since the time the writer was first beaten by his father, he felt entirely powerless and under his father's total dominion. An obedient child, he never contradicted his father and was extremely polite. When his father tried to act friendlier later in life, the writer found himself unable to reciprocate. The father would see his son's portraits on the cover of magazines and, although flattered, he would always wonder why. But when his father read the depiction of himself in Vargas Llosa's 1977 novel *Aunt Julia and the Scriptwriter*, he sent Vargas Llosa a letter, commending him for understanding that he had been strict with him for his own good "because he always loved him" (había sido severo conmigo . . . por mi bien "pues siempre me había querido"; *Fish* 174). The writer left the letter unanswered. Enraged, his father sent another letter, this time accusatory and threatening. This letter too went unanswered. They never spoke again, and Vargas Llosa did not see his father again until his death.

The "terrible, burning rancor" of childhood dissolved somewhat with time, but the writer confesses that "even today, all at once the memory of some scene, of some image, of the years when [the father] had complete authority over me gives me a sudden hollow feeling in the pit of my stomach" (hasta ahora, a veces, de pronto, el recuerdo de alguna escena, de alguna imagen, de los años que estuve bajo su autoridad me causan un súbito vacío en el estómago; *Fish* 174). He became a writer to spite his father, who called writing *mariconería*, an occupation for "fags," "incompatible with pants and testicles" (incompatible con los pantalones y los huevos; *Fish* 37). Writing helped him make sense of the violence he had experienced as symbolic rape. In novel after novel, he describes this violence as a blueprint of predatory leadership passed on from generation to generation.

In 1990, Vargas Llosa ran for the presidency of Peru with the center-right Frente Democrático coalition. His decision to become the leader of the country appears to be another rebellion against predatory leadership, this time in the public arena. The story of the father and the election run in parallel in the memoir (Dzero, "*La fiesta del Chivo*, Novel and Film"). Vargas Llosa lost to a black horse candidate, agricultural engineer Alberto Fujimori. A diminutive man of Japanese heritage, Fujimori presented himself as a man of the people and attacked Vargas Llosa's neoliberal proposals. Soon after his victory, Fujimori implemented the same free-market reforms for which he criticized Vargas Llosa. More importantly, Fujimori's authoritarian inclinations became apparent to all. Two years after his election, he dissolved Congress and the judiciary. He attacked these institutions as "the old and rotten order of politicians, judges, and corrupt authorities who thwart real democracy" (los políticos, jueces y autoridades corruptas que impiden la verdadera democracia; Fujimori 4). The media, the military, the poor, and the middle class applauded the coup. Vargas Llosa bitterly commented that one cannot defeat strongmen and caudillos. People love them and believe they are "swift and efficacious" (*Fish* 272).

The undying hold of Vargas Llosa's father over him and Fujimori's triumph over him, as described in his memoir *Fish in the Water*, helps us understand why authoritarianism cannot be defeated in *The Feast of the Goat*, unlike in its film adaptations. In the novel, Trujillo is reborn in the inoffensive-looking intellectual Balaguer, who is just as power-hungry and authoritarian. Balaguer is a transparent allegory for Fujimori. They are both described with the same diminutive words: little face, little eyes, little hands (carita, ojitos, manitas). Balaguer is a "minute figurine" with thick, "nearsighted-man's glasses" (mínima figurilla, anteojos de miope; *Feast* 183). Fujimori is "a little man, tense and stuck-up" (un hombre menudo y algo rígido; *Fish* 244). They both have a machine-like, rehearsed quality. During the debate, for which the writer painstakingly prepared, Fujimori read his talking points and replies from little index cards without looking up, and the writer felt like a chess player facing a computer or robot (robots o computadoras; *Fish* 264). Balaguer is compared to "a radio actor or a professor of phonetics" (actor de radio o profesor de fonética; *Feast* 230). They are impenetrable. When Vargas Llosa offered to concede defeat after the results of the first round, Fujimori looked at him "for quite some time as though he didn't believe [him], or as though there were some hidden trap" (alguna trampa; *Fish* 244). Vargas Llosa thanked Fujimori in Japanese to make him laugh and establish a connection, but Fujimori held out his hand, emotionless, "without so much as a smile" (*Fish* 245). When Vargas Llosa met with Balaguer, he felt similarly unable to decipher the man. After talking to him for three hours, he left "perplexed," "with the absolute same ignorance about his personality as before meeting him." To his very direct question of how a man of Balaguer's erudition and education could have served the murderous Trujillo, Balaguer gave "a long explanation that had a very persuasive shape of something that didn't mean anything," and when the writer tried to recall that explanation, "it was simply smoke" (era simplemente humo; "Eso no debe repetirse jamás" 50). What makes Fujimori and Balaguer as enigmatic as Trujillo for the writer is their desire to exercise dominion over others as an end in itself.

And we can also understand why Luis Llosa adapted *Feast of the Goat* for the screen five years later in a more optimistic way. While Vargas Llosa was writing *Feast of the Goat*, Fujimori changed Peru's constitution to serve a third term and was unlikely to ever voluntarily leave office. Unexpectedly, the year of the novel's publication, 2000, became the year of Fujimori's downfall. Recordings of his chief of secret police Vladimiro Montesinos bribing politicians were broadcast on TV. Fujimori fled to Japan and was tried in absentia for murder, kidnapping, and crimes against humanity. Japan refused to extradite him, but he decided to return to Peru to run for president again in 2005. After he landed in Chile, he was detained and put under house arrest. Fujimori then announced his intention to run in Japan's Upper House elections in 2007. He was extradited to Peru and, after four trials, was found guilty of human rights abuses, bribery, and accumulating millions of dollars through graft. Fujimori was sentenced to twenty-five years in prison. He was the first democratically elected head of state to be convicted of grave human rights violations in his own country (Burt). By 2005, when the film adaptation was released, Alejandro Toledo had been serving as president of Peru for five years, professing his allegiance to democracy and social justice (accusations of corruption against him would not surface until later). The changed situation in Peru explains why the film adaptation celebrates the end of the dictator and the start of a new, different life. In contrast to the novel on which it is based, the film teaches a new intolerance for predatory leadership and an imperative to terminate it quickly and definitively.

Rape as a Bond-Forming Sacrifice

In the works of Vargas Llosa, rape is a duty and a chore of the predatory leader. His subjects worship him and bring him their daughters for this simulation of human sacrifice. Now I turn to stories in which rape is perceived by the perpetrators as a bond-forming and elevating sacrifice in situations of war. Writing about the Holocaust, Dominick LaCapra states that the enormity of this mass murder was, for the perpetrators, the source of redemption and transcendence. They performed these "sacrificial" killings with a "carnivalesque, 'sublime' elation" (269). The stories I will examine take place during the conflict between the Peruvian army and the terrorist group Shining Path (Sendero Luminoso) in the 1980s in the Andean highlands. Shining Path aimed to overthrow the Peruvian government and establish a Marxist-Leninist communist state based on Maoist principles, advocating for radical agrarian reform and the dismantling of existing political and social structures. They used guerrilla warfare, including violent attacks on government forces, infrastructure, and civilian targets, to destabilize the state and incite widespread unrest. The group recruited from Indigenous villages and violently repressed those who refused to join. The armed forces of the state used the same tactics. Suspected Shining Path recruits were tortured and killed in front of their families, or often alongside them. Raids in villages frequently turned into mass massacres. The Truth and Reconciliation Commission concluded that between 1980 and 2000, over 69,000 people died, of whom 79 percent were rural Indigenous Peruvians. Indigenous girls were captured and brought to the army barracks where they were promised freedom in exchange for submitting to gang rape. Afterward, they were shot.

The repercussions of the conflict are at the center of Alonso Cueto's popular 2005 novel *The Blue Hour* (*La hora azul*). Again, a fourteen-year-old girl is captured and raped, as a metaphor for the violence unleashed on the most vulnerable people. Cueto's original story exists in two versions and was adapted for the screen twice. The main character of the novel is a fourteen-year-old girl named Miriam, whose exceptional beauty draws the notice of a military commander. She is captured by army soldiers along with other girls and brought to the barracks. The practice was to rape and kill them. The commander rescues Miriam from gang rape and death to keep her for himself in sexual slavery. He acts as if he loves her, but she knows he will never let her go alive. After a year in captivity, she gets her guards drunk, changes into their clothes, and escapes, only to find that her family has been killed. Following the commander's death, his estranged son Adrián, a successful lawyer, sets out to find the mysterious girl. He travels to her home province in Ayacucho and listens to the stories of terrible suffering inflicted on these communities by Shining Path and the government forces. The *comuneros* tell him they had to witness the agony and death of their children, spouses, and parents. He finds Miriam, who now works as a hairdresser in a poor neighborhood of Lima and is raising a son who refuses to speak. Miriam feels no hatred toward Adrián's father, who seemed to have found in "loving" her a relief from the terrors of war. Miriam and Adrián become lovers and experience a symbiotic, mystical bond, which Miriam cuts short by killing herself. Adrián leaves his wife and children for a while, living with Miriam's phantasmatic presence. She "opened the doors of the palace of indifference" (palacio de indiferencia; 279) in which he used to live. Soon, however, he returns to his family and takes care of Miriam's son, his half brother. This "ethical awakening is short-lived" but "sincere" (Dickson 69). Like Adrián, readers finally learn the extent of the violence inflicted on the Indigenous rural people, of which, like Adrián, they had been unaware.

In 2011, Evelyne Pégot-Ogier adapted *The Blue Hour* for the screen with the same title (with Giovanni Ciccia as Adrián and Jackelyne Vásquez as Miriam). The director followed the novel closely though omitting the description of torture inflicted on Indigenous villagers and the sexual relationship between Adrián and Miriam, leaving only a kiss. Her goal was to show a "reconciliation of the father and the son, and of the two worlds, Adrian's and Miriam's" (interview with Ramos). The film was not enthusiastically received. Critics found the performances uninspiring and the script boring, failing to explain motives and actions (Zavala). After difficulties finding a distributor, Pégot-Ogier's film reached audiences at the same time as another screen adaptation of Cueto's story, *Magallanes*.

Magallanes (2015) enjoyed success with audiences. It incorporates some elements of *The Blue Hour* and is based on its shorter version, *The Passenger* (*La pasajera*). This story is a confrontation rather than reconciliation between the victim and the perpetrators, unlike in the previous film adaptation and the novel. The victim does not kill herself, and she frustrates the perpetrator's attempt to find forgiveness and redemption. The repentant perpetrator of the short story, Arturo Ochoa, brought the girl, Delia, to the barracks, and the commander told him to organize her rape by the soldiers. When he refused, the commander threatened to imprison him as a terrorist. Instead of killing Delia after the rape, as he was ordered, Arturo let her go. Now, twenty years later, Arturo is making ends meet driving a taxi in Lima, while the commander has developed Alzheimer's. Arturo remembers the commander's words, "I am leaving on a trip. Very far away. Where no one will find me" (Voy a irme de viaje. Muy lejos. Donde nadie me encuentre; 60). Arturo envies this loss of memory: "You escaped. I cannot forget. You are lucky to be like this. You escaped" (Usted escapó. Yo no olvido. Usted felizmente que está así como está. Usted escapó; 52). Arturo believes that what he did to the girl twenty years ago is the reason his wife and child died in a car accident as soon as he returned home from service. Guilt consumes him, as well as feelings of "hate, scorn, and vengeance" directed at the commander (el odio, el desprecio y la venganza; 47). One day, Delia steps into his taxi. Arturo recognizes her and attempts to redeem himself. He wants to give her the money that the commander had embezzled from the military pension fund and hid in his room, before he developed Alzheimer's and forgot about it. Arturo takes the money under the commander's serene gaze and brings it to Delia. But when Arturo tries to talk to her, Delia cannot bear to look at him. Although he took no part in the rape, or perhaps because of this, his "was the only face she remembered from that day. The face of that man. Not the faces of the soldiers who stood in line and who raped her, laughing and insulting her" (era la única cara que recordaba de ese día. La de ese hombre. No la de los soldados que habían hecho cola y que la habían violado, riéndose e insultándola; 35). At the sight of him, she begins to scream and shake uncontrollably. She throws the money into the air for passersby to catch. Seeing that he cannot make her forgive him, Arturo grows desperate and furious. He points his gun first at her head and then at his own. Delia then approaches him and moves the gun away, and this gesture comforts him enough to desist. He implores the policemen who arrive at the scene to put him in jail, but they refuse. Prisons are full, and Delia does not want to press charges. Arturo then goes to the commander's house, shoots him dead, and escapes. The unrepentant amnesiac perpetrator is brought to justice, but he does not even know what for.

Director Salvador del Solar chose to use thriller and melodrama elements in his adaptation of Cueto's story for the screen. He magnified the dimension of rape and, while the commander is not hurt in the film, his son is raped, too. What is more, it is revealed that the repentant officer, named Magallanes here (played by Damián Alcázar), had also forced sex on the girl, named Celina, in return for helping her escape. Later, the officer repents, suffering because he believes he loved Celina then and still loves her now. As in *The Blue Hour*, the girl was held by the commander for himself. She was known among the soldiers as "the colonel's girl" and "Ñusta," for her likeness to the fifteenth-century Inca princess who married a Spanish nobleman. "Ñusta" also denotes a virgin girl who presides at Indigenous celebrations of Pachamama, Mother Earth. Magallanes (his name refers to Ferdinand Magellan, the famous Portuguese explorer and navigator) keeps thinking about the girl and drawing her. To make Celina forgive him, Magallanes hatches a plan to extort money from the colonel's family. He conspires with a fellow former soldier, Milton, who misses the times in the mountains, the raping, and the killing. They kidnap the commander's son, a snobbish young lawyer, and demand a ransom. While Magallanes is away, Milton rapes the commander's son, saying, "I'll show you what I did with the *terrucas*." (*Terruca* is a derogative term for "terrorist," applied to females. We will later see a Peruvian elected official, accused of raping an Indigenous woman during the conflict with Shining Path, calling the victim *terruca* and denying her accusations.) When the usually meek Magallanes learns that Milton also raped Celina, he pounces on him, whimpering, "She was just a girl, asshole! Just a girl . . ."—knowing that he did the same to her. The zealous policemen, eager to please the commander's powerful family, discover that Magallanes is behind the extortion scheme. Magallanes begs to be arrested but no one is interested. Despite having been raped, the commander's son refuses to press charges to avoid bringing his father's crimes to light. Magallanes confesses to the inspector that he too raped Celina. The inspector replies, "No one here will prosecute you for that, Magallanes," and tells him to leave. In figure 2.2, the commander's son, released by Magallanes shortly before, is walking slowly, wincing from pain, through the shantytown near Lima

Figure 2.2. The colonel's son dominates the town in *Magallanes* (2015).

where he was detained. His face, shirt, and pants are smeared with blood, and he looks transfixed. In figure 2.3, Magallanes walks slowly alongside the Palace of Justice, as a metaphor of his penitent pilgrimage through life. These stills seem like mirror images but are exact opposites. The shantytown got back at the privileged man, but even when humiliated and punished he dominates the shantytown in the shot. In contrast, Magallanes is dwarfed by the imposing Palace of Justice. Metaphorically, this shot means that the abuse narrated in the story is systemic and institutionally sanctioned. The film adaptation highlights the lack of political will to bring perpetrators to justice, even when they themselves beg to be imprisoned, because justice would expose the important people who gave orders. The abuse is "systematic and symptomatic of a state and a country that never really respected the dignity and equality of the overwhelming majority of its citizens," said the director (Del Solar).

A similar story is told in the play *The Captive* (*La cautiva*, 2014) directed by Luis Alberto León. In this play, fourteen-year-old María Josefa is shot dead in a raid and is then raped by military men in the atmosphere of a religious festival. At the beginning of the play, the body of María Josefa is brought to the morgue together with the bodies of her parents, who were teachers and Shining Path militants. The pathologist tells his horrified assistant Mauro that after they clean her up, the captain will offer her to the soldiers as "a reward, revenge, and celebration" (recompensa, desquite, festejo). When Mauro realizes he can talk with the dead girl and see her move, he attempts to hide the upcoming rape from her. He disguises the situation as a quinceañera party—a

Figure 2.3. Magallanes is dwarfed by the Palace of Justice in *Magallanes* (2015).

celebration of a girl's fifteenth birthday and her transition from childhood to adulthood, typically involving a mass followed by a party. He dresses her in a white dress, and the girl tells him: "Let the guests come in, we will celebrate (*festejar*), I'll be the main meal of the feast (*fiesta*)." What is more, Mauro also reinvents the girl as her town's saint, whose birthday is celebrated in a festive procession. The decorations now include red and white paper chains and confetti. The bodies of two men, a Shining Path militant and a soldier, brought in with the girl, emerge from the refrigerator where the pathologist arranged them in an embrace. They dance a delirious dance and rape the girl. The drunken captain enters to rape her next, and Mauro disguises him as an Andean mythical deity, a jaguar with falcon wings. Mauro kills the captain. In retribution, the soldiers storm the room and kill Mauro. As in Cueto's story, the character who empathizes with the sacrificial victim is not only unable to prevent her victimization and rape but is actually making the rape worse, turning it into a soul-shattering spectacle. As for the perpetrators, they perceive the sacrifice of the girl as a bonding ritual that "brings the group together, as does mortal danger" (León).

The play was received with enthusiasm by audiences but provoked the anger of conservative politicians. It was investigated for making an apology for terrorism, even though the portrayal of the victim's parents, Shining Path militants, is clearly negative. The father was abusive, too, and tried to beat these ideas into María Josefa (enseñar a puñetazos) because in her heart she did not believe in their "triumph of the people" (León). The play is critical of Shining Path, so it must have been its excessive and transgressive performance of rape that angered politicians, some of whom were later accused of rape and murder during the war with Sendero. The play was performed and investigated during the presidency of Ollanta Humala, who is currently himself under investigation for ordering mass killings at the military base Madre Mía in the 1980s. Former soldiers testified that Humala, then known as "Captain Carlos," ordered them to bury eighteen people alive and burn one of them alive. Captain Carlos also allegedly gave women, among them a fourteen-year-old girl, to soldiers as gifts (regalos; "Las pruebas"). In 2017, the remains of seventeen buried victims were discovered. In addition, recorded telephone conversations of people close to Humala who attempted to bribe witnesses into retracting their testimonies were made public. The Madre Mía case was reopened the same year, but Humala has not yet been called to testify on these accusations (Quispe; Cabral). Humala's Interior Minister, Daniel Urresti, who called for the play to be investigated, criticized it as "macabre . . . obscene and immoral" (escabrosa; "Urresti: 'Fiscalía decidirá'"). Is it surprising that Urresti was also stationed in Ayacucho, the heart of the conflict with Shining Path in the 1980s, and is accused of murdering journalist Hugo Bustíos and raping an Indigenous woman who witnessed the murder to intimidate her? The woman, Ysabel Rodríguez Chipana, testified that Urresti raped her twice with her children present and threatened to turn her family into "dust and ashes" if she talked. Urresti laughed in her face while she testified in court, calling her a *terruca*. Urresti was cleared of all charges in 2018, but the Supreme Court annulled this ruling. In February 2021, Urresti's lawyer publicly resigned after evidence of attempts to bribe witnesses surfaced (Quiroz). Urresti was tried again and sentenced to twelve years in prison (Collyns). If these authority figures implicated in human rights abuses tried to sanction the play that dramatizes these abuses as an apology for terrorism, it must have stuck a nerve with them.

Overcoming Rape

Unlike all stories examined above, in *Madeinusa* and *The Milk of Sorrow* (*La teta asustada*), the female protagonists overcome rape as their inheritance and destiny. They rebel against their perpetual societal role as the sacrificial victim. Both films are written and directed by Claudia Llosa, who is the niece of Mario Vargas Llosa, and who belongs to a younger generation of artists. *Madeinusa* (2006) is set in an isolated fictional village called Manayaycuna, which means in Quechua "a place that no one can enter." It is Holy Week and, in this village, there is a tradition that for three days the inhabitants can do what they want without sinning because Jesus is dead and cannot see them. The mayor of the village, Don Cayo (Juan Ubaldo Huamán), is impatient for the festivities, planning to finally deflower his daughter, fourteen-year-old Madeinusa (Magaly Solier in her first role, which made her famous. She later starred in *The Milk of Sorrow* and *Magallanes*, among others). Madeinusa wants to be chosen as the Virgin in the village's beauty pageant, which would allow her to preside over the festivities and be carried around on a throne during the procession. A geologist from Lima named Salvador (Carlos J. de la Torre) finds himself stuck in the village. Madeinusa wants to escape to Lima, like her mother. She comes to believe she can use this stranger to escape. She sings a song to him in Quechua with a prophetic line: "I will steal your heart." Salvador is oblivious to the ominous name and appearance of the village and to Madeinusa's intentions. He finds the village and its dwellers repugnant and tells her that the "Made in USA" she saw on his T-shirt is not her name and is not a name at all. But Madeinusa has her own opinion: "It's my name. I like it." Madeinusa pursues him and offers him her virginity in an attempt to secure her escape from the village with him and to upset her father's plans. When her aunt sees blood on Madeinusa's legs, she scolds her for disappointing her father who waited such a long time, and washes her, while Madeinusa smiles triumphantly. Salvador, whose name translates as "savior," agrees to take Madeinusa to Lima after witnessing her father rape her (which he observes through a window, disgusted, but without intervening on her behalf). Madeinusa's older sister Chale, also abused by the father, is rancorous and mean to Madeinusa, and eagerly complies with their father's order to sew her sister's panties to her dress to prevent her from having sex with other men. On the eve of her planned escape to Lima, Madeinusa discovers that her father has destroyed the few treasures she inherited from her mother: a pair of earrings and two tattered magazine pages. She feeds him soup laced with rat poison. The failed savior Salvador also gets his due. He enters the house and looks on, stupefied, at Madeinusa and her agonizing father. When her sister Chale comes in and finds their father dead, vomit trickling from the corners of his mouth, Chale and Madeinusa start chanting that the gringo (Salvador) killed him, loud enough for neighbors to hear. We never see Salvador again. Madeinusa is shown leaving the village in the morning, alone, in the truck that Salvador had arranged to pick him up. We see her smiling for the first time as she listens to the chatter of the driver and tells him, "My name is Madeinusa" (figure 2.4).

Claudia Llosa, who wrote and directed *Madeinusa*, is a white woman and belongs to the Peruvian upper class. She studied filmmaking in Spain and now resides in Barcelona. She was criticized for representing Indigenous Pe-

Figure 2.4. Madeinusa smiling for the first time at the end of *Madeinusa* (2005).

ruvians as incestuous drunkards and the "abject Other" (Págan-Teitelbaum), reaffirming a view that justified genocide during the civil war with Sendero Luminoso (Zevallos-Aguilar), and creating an exotic Other for the enjoyment of international audiences (Shaw). However, as Dolores Tierney notes, her films are "self-consciously constructed to show awareness of the dominant classes' colonialist gaze and its problematic tropes, and by doing so, offer a counter perspective" (24). Actress Magaly Solier, who played Madeinusa, defended the film, saying that incest and abuse were common in the Indigenous community in which she grew up (Palaversich). Note that Madeinusa differs from other characters in the situation of rape discussed in this chapter. Madeinusa is not a victim but an agent of her liberation. She offers herself to Salvador but then gets rid of him as well as her father, "both men who had sex with her" (Palaversich). These men represent "patriarchal and (neo- and post-) colonial power." If Madeinusa appears ungrateful or unfeeling, it is because she "derails the religious and patriarchal scripts that regulate the behavior of women" (Palaversich). "She's like a princess, a warrior," said Llosa, "She doesn't understand fear, or passive emotions" (Smith). She "abolishes the law of the father" in a radical way, killing him in order to put an end to his dominion over her (Llosa, interview with Buntix).

In Claudia Llosa's following film, the 2009 Oscar-nominated *The Milk of Sorrow* (*La teta asustada*), the young Fausta (also played by Magaly Solier) also overcomes her condition of rape. The film begins with her mother singing to her in Quechua, recounting that when she was pregnant with Fausta she was raped by soldiers and forced to eat her dead husband's penis. Growing up with these tragic songs made Fausta painfully shy and almost mute from uncontrollable fear of people. To avoid her mother's fate, she places a potato in her vagina, which inflames her uterus, causes her to bleed, and makes her faint. Fausta forces herself to go out and work as a servant because she needs money to bring her mother's body to her native village to bury her there. Like her mother, Fausta constantly composes and sings songs in Quechua to cope with her constant anxiety. Her mistress, a composer, presents one of these songs as her own composition and performs it to a standing ovation. On their way back to the house, the happy Fausta remarks to the mistress that the audience must have liked the song, only to be ordered out of the car on the spot. But by the end of the film, Fausta liberates herself from the potato and her original condition as a symbolic rape victim and musters the courage to collect from her mistress's house the promised payment for her songs, a pearl for a song.

Madeinusa and Fausta are the first rural Indigenous female protagonists in Peruvian cinema (Atanacio). The dead father, covered in vomit, just as the blood-smeared Trujillo in figure 2.1, impresses on the viewer that sadistic authority figures can and should be deposed. In *Madeinusa*, the leader-rapist and the father coalesce into one character. The girls take control of their lives and overcome the legacy of rape that hovered over them as the only possible destiny.

The Impunity of Rapists and Appeal of Aggressive Rhetoric

Rape of minors by an authority figure is so pervasive in Peruvian narratives because it has been, and remains, part of everyday life and often remains unpunished. Jelke Boesten, who has studied violence against women in Peru from the civil war with Sendero Luminoso until the present, argues that the state itself set these patterns of behavior in the past and continues to do so now by leaving them unpunished. In 2012, Boesten wrote that in Latin America, Peru ranks highest for reported sexual violence against women, with an average of 6,881 victims each year. The actual levels of sexual violence are much higher. In 2009 alone, the Institute of Forensic Medicine conducted 34,153 forensic examinations of sexual assault victims in Peru. Few reported cases are processed judicially, and less than 10 percent of processed cases lead to convictions. The reported rate of domestic violence is growing, perhaps because the victims are more informed and encouraged to report it. In 2009,

95,749 cases of domestic violence were reported (Boesten, "The State and Violence" 362). By 2019, the number had nearly doubled, totaling 181,885 reports (Ministerio de la Mujer y Poblaciones Vulnerables).

The astonishing levels of violence against women in Peru may appear surprising because, under Fujimori, the country was the first in the region to adopt policies to protect women. Boesten explains that Fujimori introduced these policies in order to woo the progressive sector at home and abroad. These policies received inadequate funding, however, and the police and emergency center employees did not receive appropriate training. As a result, the policies were largely ineffective. Women who sought help were often reprimanded and sent home to their abusive husbands. Moreover, in 1997, a policy was introduced obligating women to go through a reconciliation process with their abuser, despite evidence of serious physical harm or long-lasting abuse. This policy received widespread approval from the conservative sector, which favored the preservation of the family unit at all costs. Non-Indigenous advocates of Indigenous human rights supported reconciliation as a more culturally appropriate strategy than divorce. The Peruvian state and the World Bank, the Interamerican Bank for Development, and the United States Agency for International Development (USAID) also favored this legislation because it removed domestic violence cases from the legal system, which they hoped would improve its functioning. While this law was repealed in 2001, in most instances, cases of violence against women remain within family law and are considered misdemeanors. When cases do go to criminal court, jail terms are usually annulled by a suspended sentence, and the victims are again exposed to the wrath of their aggressors (Boesten, "The State and Violence" 371). In 2016, two abusers receiving light sentences provoked angry demonstrations. One of them, captured on hotel security cameras naked and dragging his girlfriend by her hair through the reception area, received a suspended sentence. The other case received notoriety from widely circulated photos of the abused woman, with a disfigured face and stitches around her eyes. The boyfriend who beat her was released from prison after four years in pretrial detention. In both cases, the judges ruled that the injuries were minor and the victims' lives were not in danger. Boesten concludes that the primary goal of the state remains the preservation of the male-headed, patriarchal family structure in which men legitimately dominate women, and women are expected to tolerate a certain level of violence (Boesten, "Anger at Violence").

These sexual crimes are part of larger patterns of violence set by the patriarchal state. In Boesten's view, these patterns are directly connected to the widespread rape of Indigenous women by the military during the conflict with Sendero Luminoso and the fact that no perpetrator was punished.

The majority of rapes during that conflict, 83 percent, are attributed to the armed forces. Raping reproduced a system of privileges defining who could rape whom. Victims with whiter skin and education were reserved for the higher-ranked abusers. Indigenous girls, who often had no registration cards, were the easiest victims. The Truth and Reconciliation Commission identified 538 cases of rape, but only sixteen were investigated and presented for public prosecution. (Boesten, "The State and Violence" 367). The impunity of abusers reflects institutional sexism in the times of war and peace, as Boesten puts it. The state's lack of response and repeated attempts to exonerate the abusers with amnesty laws perpetuate the model of aggressive masculinity both in the private and public spheres.

Political scientist Lauren Balasco believes that the real reason Peruvian citizens feel unsafe is precisely the state's failure to hold those who are responsible accountable for their human rights violations. Just as they have failed to hold perpetrators of sexual crimes accountable, these politicians have ignored corruption and calls for reform within their own governments. Balasco also describes the lack of political will to reform the corrupt institutions of Fujimori's authoritarian regime. When Alejandro Toledo became president, he attempted, but failed, to reform the police. Torture has remained a widespread practice, including by military personnel, prison guards, and municipal security patrols. The judiciary system also failed to ensure the rule of law. The Toledo and subsequent administrations largely ignored an anti-corruption report drafted by the interim government of Valentín Paniagua, who succeeded Fujimori. Only a small fraction of the 1,400 judges, legislators, and state officials charged with corruption under Fujimori were convicted. The National Criminal Court, created in 2004 to hear cases of human rights violations, dismissed twenty-three cases, acquitted sixty-five military and police agents, and convicted only fifteen people. Reparations to victims were conflated with programs of assistance to the poor. This gesture deprived the victims of recognition and symbolic redress (Malca). Polls show that Peruvians do not trust the judicial branch or the police to investigate and punish criminals. They feel that legal means of ensuring security are failing, blame insecurity on democratization, and favor tough-talking politicians who declare themselves ready to use illegal means to get things done (Balasco 1188).

Many Peruvian politicians have been averse to investigating abuses and convicting the perpetrators, which would risk unearthing more evidence against authority figures and projects weakness. They prefer to attract voters through belligerence and shows of force. Fujimori's daughter Keiko named the party Fuerza Popular (Force of the People), with the rally chant "Vamos, con Keiko / ¡Vamos a la fuerza!" Until 2016, Keiko criticized the Truth and

Reconciliation Commission and was so popular that she nearly won the 2016 election. Despite being investigated on Odebrecht-related corruption charges, she ran for president again in 2021, promising to rule with a "firm hand" because "what is needed is a strong democracy that will make itself respected" ("Mano dura"). Daniel Urresti, convicted in 2024 for the murder of journalist Hugo Bustíos, had won the most votes during the 2020 congressional elections and ran for president in April 2021. Another popular tough-talking political leader is Antauro Humala, the brother of the ex-president. A xenophobic and homophobic hardliner representing the ultra-conservative left, Antauro Humala spent nineteen years in prison for an attempted coup against Toledo. Humala's party, the UPP (Unión para Perú), won votes in the poorest Andean zones (Noriega) that suffered the most during the conflict with Sendero Luminoso. In 2024, Antauro Humala founded a political party using his own name as an acronym (Alianza Nacional de Trabajadores, Agricultores, Universitarios, Reservistas y Obreros, Antauro), but it was dissolved for promoting antidemocratic activities (Carrasco Freitas). Aggressive rhetoric continues to exercise appeal on the symbolic level.

Conclusion

In the films and stories examined here, the rape of minors has many meanings. First and foremost, rape is a powerful metaphor of predatory leadership. It is a frank expression of what the leader plans to do to his subjects, if not physically, then morally. At the same time, we notice that, although some of these rapists are willing and moved by lust, many more are actually reluctant to inflict rape. This surprising reluctance means that rape is not an end but a means to something much broader and greater in scope. For some, rape has an educational value—the leader is trying to teach his subjects and to form his successors, who will perpetuate the system he created. We have observed the schooling in symbolic rape rituals in Mario Vargas Llosa's autobiographical and novelistic portrayals of his abusive father and the abusive school. These rituals are meant to ensure that boys will become dominating men and predatory leaders, of families and communities (*The Time of the Hero* and *Fish in the Water*). Other rapists view the act of rape as an obligatory ritual through which they bond in situations of war. We have observed these rapists in *The Blue Hour* and *The Captive*. A particularly reluctant rapist is the dictator in Vargas Llosa's *The Feast of the Goat*, who is so old that it is difficult or impossible for him to continue raping. It has become a stressful and even dreaded chore. In all of these instances, for the perpetrators, the rape of minors is not an end in itself. The act of violence against someone so vulnerable has the performative function of a child sacrifice ritual. This enormous transgression is a means to achieve transcendence, to rise beyond the rules and morals of ordinary mortals. These transgressive stories pierce like knives and elicit spiritual shudder in readers and viewers. The vicarious but lasting wounds that these stories inflict on our ethical imagination make us viscerally repudiate predatory leaders.

3

Arquímedes Puccio and Other Carceral Disciplinarians in Argentina

This chapter discusses the carceral variety of authoritarian fathers of the family and the nation. These fathers exude professionalism, self-discipline, and upper-middle-class respectability. The caveat is that these disciplinarians take their idea of order so seriously they will even build clandestine prisons to enforce it. I focus on the story of Arquímedes Puccio, who was arrested in 1985, together with his family. The people from his upper-middle-class neighborhood of Buenos Aires could not believe that this respectable patriarch, who went to Mass every week with his wife and five children, kidnapped his rich acquaintances, held them in his family house, and had them killed after collecting ransom. To "help" him, actively or passively, was his family's duty. This disciplinarian father enforced obedience in his family and in the private places of captivity that he set up for his hostages. When he was arrested, with a live hostage found in his basement, he denied the charges and pretended he was a victim of political persecution. After his release in 2011, he posed as a defender of justice and human rights. Nearly thirty years after his arrest, 2015 saw a resurgence of interest in Puccio's story. This veritable Pucciomania included *The Clan*, a feature film directed by Pablo Trapero; the miniseries *The History of a Clan*, directed by Luis Ortega; and *The Clan Puccio*, the true-crime book by journalist José Palacios, who interviewed Puccio after he was released on parole. *The Clan* was a box-office sensation—53 percent of Argentine movie-goers chose to see it on its opening weekend (Battle 2015). It won a Goya award and was selected as Argentina's submission for the Academy Award. The first episode of the miniseries *The History of a Clan* was the second most-watched television program, gathering nineteen million mentions on Twitter (now X) as it aired. Puccio's enigma continues to excite interest—in 2019, Gustavo Menéndez published his novel *The Day They Kidnapped Puccio*, and in 2021 Puccio was featured in an issue of La Mente Criminal book series titled *Arquímedes Puccio, The Sinister Clan Leader*. In 2022, Telemundo produced another miniseries, *The Secret of the Greco Family*, available on Netflix.

In this chapter, I show that films about Puccio's overt and secret disciplinarian practices provide insight into the last Argentine dictatorship (1976–1983). The name the regime chose for itself, the National Reorganization Process, reflects its disciplinarian drive. Like Puccio, the junta leaders inspired confidence with their proper deportment, for which they were known as "the Gentlemen of the Coup." Like Puccio, the leaders and commanders discoursed in public about order and the fatherland. However, in secret they launched the Dirty War, a campaign of state terrorism involving torture, extrajudicial murder, and systematic forced disappearances. They oversaw the incarceration and murder of over 30,000 people, the majority of whom were civilians (journalists, lawyers, students, and trade union members), for which purpose they set up over six hundred clandestine camps. Like Puccio, they argued they never killed anyone personally. Instead, they told their subordinates that these secret disciplinarian practices were their sacred patriotic duty. For these carceral disciplinarians, the truly perfect citizen can be fashioned only in clandestine places of detention. They are convinced that their public subjects (whether family or civil society) will only behave when they know they can at any moment join the incarcerated subjects, kept chained at arm's length in the bathroom at Puccio's house, or right in the middle of the city, in police stations, public buildings, and even schools that were transformed into torture centers during the dictatorship. Like Puccio, the dictatorship disciplinarians posed as saviors of the fatherland and innocent victims of political persecution. Like Puccio, they refused to acknowledge the mass secret killings. Also like Puccio, they drew from these unavowed crimes an incomprehensible certitude of moral rectitude, redemption, and renewal.

I begin this chapter by examining Puccio's domineering charm in films and books. I then identify the disciplinarians' rituals—assigning places and tasks, cleaning (preceded by dirtying), secrecy, and messianism, as they are practiced in Puccio's and the dictatorship's clandestine prisons. I will then focus on the banality of evil and the magnificence of evil, the two ways in which theorists explain the unrepentant behavior of the perpetrators of mass atrocities. I will conclude the chapter by examining several notoriously self-righteous dictatorship disciplinarians—junta leader Jorge Videla; Navy Admiral Emilio Massera; commanders Alfredo Astiz, Miguel Etchecolatz, Antonio Bussi; and Adolfo Scilingo, the whistleblower who later denied everything, like the rest of them.

Puccio in Films

Pablo Trapero, who directed the feature film *The Clan* (*El clan*, 2015), said he made the film for his son because his own father passed on to him the message of fear. When he was thirteen and showed interest in joining the school council, his father told him to stay out of student government because the dictatorship did not spare even school-age children (interview with Leigh). Moreover, Trapero was intrigued that Puccio's neighbors refused to believe that the Puccios were guilty, both because they were so proper and looked so much like them. The neighbors felt that "people from their social class did not readily engage in this kind of crime," as opposed to, say, financial schemes. "The upper middle class is often idealized, and for them it is normal to make decisions on the fate of other people," said Trapero (interview with Hopewell), and we understand that his Puccio is a metaphor for the Gentlemen of the Coup.

At the beginning of the film, we see a military commander at the head of a long table, proposing a toast to the fatherland. All present, including Puccio, cheer and drink. Then we are transported to Puccio's house, where now he sits at the head of the table, and his family members all bow their heads to him in silent prayer (see figures 1.1 and 1.2 in chapter 1). This is another hint that Puccio's family will be used as a micromodel of the society under the last Argentine military dictatorship. On the outside, Puccio is a perfectly respectable man. Little do his neighbors suspect that the middle-class safety and security that Puccio projects will be the end of their own security and life. In vain do they take anti-kidnapping courses in the United States. Puccio lets himself into their car by simply waving for them to stop with a friendly smile. One can say it is a masquerade, but for Puccio it is not. He is a disciplinarian, and his whole reason for being is to subject others. He is convinced that he can and should have people under his control, and this is why he creates his private places of obeisance where he can make his delusions come true.

Trapero created Puccio as a proper and pious *pater familias*. Puccio sweeps the sidewalk in front of his house several times a day, for which he is known in the neighborhood as "the crazy sweeper" (el loco de la escoba). He goes to Mass every week. He patiently sits with his daughter through her math homework and strikes up friendly conversations with his future victims. Guillermo Francella, who plays Puccio in the film, is known for his comedic roles, and he masterfully switches between Puccio's charming persona and his other face with dead eyes. One riveting sequence (also in the trailer) shows a routine evening at Puccio's house. Puccio massages his wife's shoulders as she makes dinner. She says she's lucky to have a husband with a magic touch and puts chicken and rice on a plate that he holds out, quipping good-humoredly, "this man must be starving" (se nos va a morir de hambre este hombre). Puccio carries the plate through the living room, tells one son to take his feet off the side table and go help his mother, says to the other son "it's rice and chicken for dinner," opens the door to another child's room to tell her it is dinnertime, and then pushes open another door to a bathroom where a blindfolded man seated in the bathtub breaks into sobs. Puccio sits down and, with a voice of a tired teacher, dictates a letter to the hostage's family which the hostage writes, weeping disconsolately. Puccio is patient and routinary with his hostages. It is clear he has been doing it for a long time. The bathroom is a historical fact but also a metaphor. Family members do not ask Puccio what he does in the bathroom, as they do not in any other family. The mother treats the capture and torture of people as her husband's work. When she learns that her son Alejandro wants to stop "helping out" the father, she lovingly rebukes him: "He has no one else to trust. If you don't help him, it's hard for him" (No tiene en quién confiar. Si vos no lo ayudás, es difícil para él).

For Puccio, kidnapping is a routine activity he learned as a member of the Peronist death squad, the Triple A—Argentine Anticommunist Alliance—operated by an arm of the police and the army, tasked with suppressing left-wing activism during the rule of Perón's second wife, Isabel, which preceded the coup. Puccio's acquaintances from these times occupy high positions in the dictatorship. He socializes with a commodore and a general, who pleasantly inquire about his wife and kids. Puccio is retired but continues to kidnap on his own even after the fall of the dictatorship. He stares with a blank expression at Alfonsín, the democratically elected president, perorating about human rights on TV. To find out what this is about, he heads over to the commodore's office, presenting an appropriate ID and moving about the building with the ease of a regular. The commodore's aide does not let him in, however, because "things are complicated right now" (las cosas están bastante espesas) and tells him to watch out for himself (guárdese). When Puccio repeats in disbelief, "Me, watch out for myself?" (¿Que yo me guarde?), it becomes obvious he has never had to watch out for himself before. We see how routine Puccio's work was during the Dirty War, how omnipotent the repressors felt, and how perfectly ordinary and respectable they looked. This is why the director said, "I am more afraid of this kind of person than I am of the bastard who attacks you openly" (Trapero).

Puccio's family members are his "public" hostages, and his oldest son, Alejandro, is coming of age. Alejandro (played by Peter Lanzani) is a strong, handsome young man and a celebrated rugby player. Puccio lies to his son, telling him that some people threaten the family and extort from him a large sum of money in order to get Alejandro to help kidnap the first hostage, Alejandro's friend. Alejandro "helps out," expecting his friend to be released after they receive the ransom. He is shaken when his friend is killed, but to his father's face he says only thank you, receiving from him wads of banknotes and a paternal word of caution: "Be careful, this is a lot of money" (ojo, es mucha plata). Generally, Alejandro follows his father's orders because he grew up with unquestioning obedience to him. After they are arrested, Alejandro seems relieved, visibly hoping his father will take on all the responsibility and rot in jail, releasing him from his grip. This is not part of Puccio's plans. Instead of confessing, he wants Alejandro to hit him in the face so that he can pose as a political prisoner. Alejandro's incredulous refusal, "No way!" (ni loco) shows how badly he wants his father to say that it was all his fault and that he, Alejandro, was forced to participate. Then Puccio deftly provokes him, telling him that he is a fake star and champion, that he owes everything to him. "You did it for money, Alejandro! For the money you took from my hands! Now you must act like a man" (Lo hiciste por plata, ¡Alejandro! ¡Por plata que recibiste de mi mano! ¡Ahora tenés que actuar como un hombre!). Furious, Alejandro hits him, just as Puccio wanted. The following day, Alejandro tears himself away from the guards and jumps from the fifth floor of the courthouse, in the first of his four unsuccessful suicide attempts.

The miniseries *The History of a Clan* (*La historia de un clan* 2015) was written and directed by the son of Ramón (Palito) Ortega, a singer and entertainer who went so far as to make propagandistic films for the dictatorship. One of them, *Dos locos en el aire* (1976), was filmed on an air base with a clandestine torture center (García). His son, Luis Ortega, often expressed his fascination with criminals and later directed *Angel* (2018), a film about the blond, adolescent Argentine serial killer Carlos Robledo Puch, who operated during the dictatorship and went unnoticed by the police because he did not look like "a subversive." In *The History of a Clan*, Puccio (played by actor Alejandro Awada) is a more obvious sociopath than in Trapero's film. The mother (Cecilia Roth) behaves as if she is unaware of what her husband is doing. When Puccio and his associate, retired colonel Franco, are in the bathroom where the hostage is held, the mother brings the colonel his usual glass of milk and appears not to register the presence of the hostage. When the younger children ask her what is going on, she looks genuinely puzzled. She cleans the bathroom after the hostage is taken to be killed, mumbling about "your father's experiments." She denies this other reality with such intense conviction that she succumbs to Alzheimer's at the end of the film, as did the dictator's accomplice in Mario Vargas Llosa's *Feast of the Goat* and the perpetrator in Alonso Cueto's *La pasajera*, discussed in chapter 2.

Silent acquiescence figures prominently in the titles of books on the topic of memory of the Argentine dictatorship. Journalist Gabriela Cerruti titled her memoir about growing up during the dictatorship *The Heirs of Silence* (*Herederos del silencio*), portraying a society in denial, gripped by the paranoid fear that something would happen to them or their family. Sebastián Carassai in his book *Argentine Silent Majority: Middle Classes, Politics, Violence, and Memory in the Seventies* shows how people relied on circumlocution, ambiguity, and the impersonal *se* construction when recalling how police kidnapped people in the streets in broad daylight. The fear to ending up in one of the clandestine camps and disappear paralyzed thinking and action.

In this film, the father, Puccio, and his son, Daniel, truly enjoy their prisoners' company. The testimonies of those who survived the Argentine death camps come alive in this film. One such survivor said that a guard "would sit on the floor of your tube and play chess, chat. And not about politics or information or people in the camp, but other things—what was going on in the world, soccer, whatever. Like someone who'd visit you at home. He'd talk about his kids, he talked a lot about his little girl. He worried if she shouldn't get good grades. He was preoccupied if a plant at home was dying" (Feitlowitz 85). This guard "felt more at home with the prisoners than with his fellows, his colleagues," and even brought his little daughter to meet his favorite prisoners once. "It was insane. The torturers and victims were all living together. Torturers were in constant contact with those they tortured," and "when they wanted a break, they came to play *truco* [a card game] with the prisoners" (Feitlowitz 84). Another survivor recalled that his torturer behaved as if they were friends: "He told me personal stuff. He got divorced and then married again, he brought me soccer magazines, at Christmas he brought me sweet bread made by his sister-in-law" (Verbitsky 58). Another former prisoner said the guards brought a TV so they could enjoy the World Cup together. The prisoners were still shackled and cuffed, but their blindfolds were lifted. They all shouted "Go-o-o-a-a-a-1-1-1-1!" each time their team scored, as is customary in Argentina (Feitlowitz 94). In the film, Puccio's son Daniel also brings a TV into the bathroom where the hostage his age is held to watch the World Cup together and enjoys hanging out with him. Daniel wistfully confides to Alejandro that the hostage has become his best friend, that he has told him things he never told anyone before, and that he will miss him. Puccio too confides to his last hostage that he is glad to have her here in the basement because it is difficult for him to relate to other people. The victim tentatively proposes that they could still relate if she were free, but he points out that it would not be the same (no sería lo mismo), to which she nods in agreement (Verónica Llinás's unforgettable performance helps grasp the hostage's dis-

Figure 3.1. The kidnapper brings a piece of cake to the hostage in *The History of a Clan* (2015).

consolate closeness with the torturer). Puccio's associate, the retired colonel Franco, brings a piece of cake from Puccio's birthday to another hostage in the basement and sits with him awhile in gruesome silence, holding a balloon and staring expressionless at the terrified man (figure 3.1). This is a reference to the nightmarish clown Pennywise who keeps his victims underground in Stephen King's *It*, Pablo Gullino reminds us (5).

The place of obeisance in this film resembles a theater. An area of the basement is set apart, like a stage, by the "curtain" of sliding metal fence gate. There is another "curtain": a large piece of furniture on wheels that the hosts roll into place to hide their private theater from the uninitiated (figure 3.2). Puccio consecrates it beforehand by bringing a priest to read a prayer and sprinkle it with holy water. Puccio whispers to the first hostage to occupy it, "life is not a dream, it is a theater" (la vida no es un sueño, es un teatro, an allusion to Calderón de la Barca's play). This powerful visual metaphor also brings to mind that in clandestine camps the torture chamber was known as "quirófano," or operating theater. "The only furniture in the operating theater was a metal table on which the torturers strapped us down," recalls a survivor. "This was a very sinister place, the walls were so covered with blood and stains that you could barely make out that it had once been painted yellow. The smell of burned flesh, blood, sweat and excrement, especially since there was no ventilation, made the air heavy, suffocating. The torturers took turns and kept a written copy of their 'work.'" In one camp there was a rhyming sign in the

Figure 3.2. The kidnapper rolls in place the door to the hidden prison in *The History of a Clan* (2015).

operating theater that said, "If You Know the Answer, Sing; If Not, Just Take the Sting" (Si lo sabe, cante, si no, aguante; Feitlowitz 65). The torturers spiced up their routine work with humor and performativity. In addition, having a hostage provided a constant opportunity to indulge in voyeurism, as Alejandro in Ortega's miniseries often does.

Alejandro is portrayed by Chino Darín, who has experience playing villains so sympathetic and charming they hardly look like villains. In this film, Alejandro understands that he is a hostage, too. He says to his brother that they are all their father's hostages—just that those who live above ground eat a little better than those kept in the basement (comemos un poco mejor). To learn that his father keeps other people as literal hostages convinces him there is no escape and that he must do what his father says. Fascinated by the profundity of his moral fall, he daydreams of making love to his mother and killing his father, like Oedipus. He goes down to the basement, as if descending into Hell, and furtively spies on the hostages, his face expressing empathetic horror at their fear and suffering. Puccio, the father, frames his activities as sacred rituals. He invents a blood oath for the members of the gang, which includes two more men besides himself and his sons. He also insists on giving his hostages a "Christian" death. When Puccio pressures his subordinate to kill a hostage, the man fires into the trunk rapidly without looking at the victim. Puccio upbraids him for not doing it right. But the hostage is unharmed and sobbing from fear. They take him out, remove the blindfold, and tell him to walk across the field to where his family is waiting for him. As he walks away, with a transfixed and happy gaze, they all fire at him. Their faces are solemn, too: they have given him a "Christian" death in that he died hopeful. The director said that criminals know and appreciate that they are different from other people. "Crime gives you an identity. You can be a petty thief, but you feel you are someone" (el crimen te da una identidad. Aunque seas un raterito, sos algo; Ortega). Crime, torture, and murder can be made into sacred rituals and sources of superior power, knowledge, and identity, as we will see with messianic dictatorship disciplinarians in the final section of this chapter.

Love Your Neighbor, Your Fatherland, and Your Broom: The Real Puccio

In 2011, Puccio called journalist Rodolfo Palacios, who was writing a book about famous Argentine criminals, and boasted they were nothing compared to him. Palacios traveled to General Pico, the city in La Pampa Province where Puccio was released on parole after twenty-three years in prison, and spent time with him. Although Palacios shared his materials with Luis Ortega, the real Puccio who emerged in these conversations is probably even scarier than his fictional portrayals. Although this banal and dirty man is now eighty-two, he has lost none of his desire to dominate others. He goes around taunting passersby: "Señora, do you know who I am? Young man, do you know who I am? Butcher, have you seen me before? Friend, did you ever see a picture of me in the newspapers?" (Señora, ¿sabe quién soy? Pibito, ¿sabe quién soy? Carnicero, ¿me tiene visto de algún lado? Amigo, ¿nunca vio una foto mía en los diarios?; 6). He enjoys their reaction when he tells them his name: "They just fall on their asses. And I shit my pants laughing. I shit myself laughing in their faces" (Y muchos se caen de culo. Se caen de culo. Y yo me cago de risa. Me les cago de risa en la cara; 6). He enjoys being feared, and the purpose of his taunts is to intimidate and establish dominance: "Don't worry, señora, I won't kidnap you, because you don't have a cent anyway" (igual quédese tranquila que no la voy a secuestrar porque no tiene un peso). "I like asking people whether they are afraid of me," he tells the journalist. He is at his scariest when he speaks of young people because he is dying to give them advice (aconsejar; 6). He laments that "they have no moral compass or profession" and "go about their lives confused" (no tienen norte ni profesión, 21; andan confundidos; 6). Obsessed with sex, Puccio boasts of having been with over two hundred women and continues preying on them. He scolds girls who show their "hole" (muestran el ojete) to a male and get pregnant irresponsibly and then tells of a fifteen-year-old who comes to ask him to help with a utility bill and whose makeup he interprets as a sign that she wants to have sex with him. He talks about his desire to kill—he has a list of thirty "enemies," including judges, investigators, and others. But "God does not allow killing," Puccio says piously, so he just hopes to outlive them and has already crossed out half of the names on his list. He congratulates himself that he has no money to buy a television, scolds a TV anchor who must be having lots of sex with her boyfriend, and says that if he called her on her show he would have sent her a bullet by phone (le mandaría un tiro por teléfono; 21). All this is said with a hearty laugh, as if it were a joke. "To laugh is the most important thing you can do," "you don't have to be bitter about things," Puccio keeps saying threateningly (lo más importante es reírse, no hay que ser amargado; 94).

Puccio loves to talk of power and leadership. In his earlier days, he worked as a diplomat and got to shake hands with Perón; Tito, the dictator of Yugoslavia; and Franco, the dictator of Spain (his diplomatic career ended when he was arrested for smuggling a suitcase with weapons). He also admires Hitler—a "great man who made Germany a powerful country" (77). He lies that he was a guerrilla leader: "in my armed struggle organization, I gave orders . . . I enjoyed prestige there. I was respected" (dentro de la organización armada daba órdenes, ahí yo tenía prestigio. Me respetaban; 122). Prison was another opportunity for leadership, and he even warned the guards, "When I take the reins, I'll dress you all in pink" (cuando yo agarre la manija, voy vestir a todos de rosa; 122). He boasts that he was feared and respected in prison and addressed as "don" (master, mister): "don Arquímedes." He declares that he is very well respected in his church and will soon become a pastor (Soy muy considerado en la iglesia. Algún día seré pastor; 21). He also plans on becoming a political leader to guide Argentine youth: "Soon I will dedicate myself to politics . . . I want to become a candidate for something or other. I want to appeal to the young people" (en breve me dedicaré a la política, quiero ser candidato a algo. Hacer un llamamiento a los jóvenes; 31, 46, 115, 94). At the same time, he exhibits a profound hatred for these young people because they do not know who he is and are not afraid of him. While in prison, he earned a law degree, and he was upset that at the graduation ceremony the young graduates had no idea who he was. "Even now, an old man, I can blow them out of the water, I'll fuck them straight up. With my limp dick. I could teach those insolent brats many things. They need a bit more time in the oven or a slap in the face. You know? If they listened to me and learned from my experience, things would go a bit better, they would love their fatherland, their ideals, their neighbor, again. You know?" (aun así, viejito y todo, me los fumo bajo el agua, me los cojo de parado. A pija muerta. Podría enseñarles muchas cosas a esos mocosos insolentes. Les falta un golpe de horno o una cachetada. ¿Estamos? Si me escucharan y aprendieran de mi experiencia, las cosas irían un poco mejor, recuperarían el amor por la Patria, por los ideales, por el prójimo. ¿Estamos?; 7). Puccio's idea of leadership is dominating people sexually, physically, and psychologically.

This domination, real in the past and now entirely imaginary, secretly inspires Puccio and keeps him avid for life. "I am a special being. I work miracles," he says (Soy un ser especial; Hago milagros; 94). "All doors are open to me. I am a lawyer and an accountant, not some bum, got it, dude? I don't consider myself defeated. In the past, I ate caviar, now I drink crappy whisky. Neat. Real men drink it neat" (A mí me reciben en todos lados. Abogado y contador, no cualquiera, che, ¿estamos? No me considero vencido. En una época comía caviar, ahora tomo whisky berreta. Y sin hielo. Los machos lo toman solo; 8). His favorite topic is his virility and strength. In prison, he became an evangelical and uses it as another reason to feel born again. He cites Apostle Paul (2 Cor 5:17): "Therefore, if anyone is in Christ, he is a new creation; the old has passed away, behold, the new has come" (Así, pues, el que está unido a Cristo es una nueva persona; las cosas viejas se terminaron y todas son nuevas). He asks the journalist to check out his biceps and boasts, "Do I look deflated like an old hag's tit? No, I'm strong" (¿Acaso me ven caído como teta de vieja? Estoy fuerte; 7). Puccio cites Almafuerte's poem about falling and getting up and says it was written about him: "I fell down and got back up a thousand times. And I'll keep doing it" (Me he levantado miles de veces. Y lo seguiré haciendo; 31). He uses his secrets as bait. He lured Palacios with promises of grand revelations: "You don't know what you are missing. Those other guys [famous Argentine criminals] are nothing. When you get to know me, you'll fall on your ass. You'll learn from me. I'm very generous and share my wisdom" (Te falto yo. Esos no existen. Cuando me conozcas, te vas a caer de culo. Vas a aprender conmigo. Soy muy generoso y comparto mi sabiduría; 76). Needless to say, he does not reveal anything, just like the dictatorship repressors I discuss below. "It's all baloney," "my family was normal," he says (es todo verso, mi familia era normal; 11). The closest one can get to the topic with him is an ominous pronouncement of the kind, "They can say what they want, imagine, make things up, judge me, but only I know the truth of this story. And I'll take it to my grave" (pueden decir lo que quieran, imaginar, inventar, juzgar, pero solo yo sé la verdad de esta historia. Y me la voy a llevar a la tumba; 11). He draws strength from his secret and assumes the stance of an offended victim. He says he visited the Nazi camps and saw the gas chambers, the mass graves, the soap, and felt terrified and "just so sad to even think that people accuse me of keeping prisoners in my house. Who could think of such a thing! That I would hold people hostage in a bathtub or in my basement? I used my house to live in it, not for anything else. Why would I do that! My family lived there!" (De solo pensar que me acusan de tener prisioneros en casa, me da mucha tristeza. ¿A quién se le ocurre que puedo tener gente secuestrada en la bañera o en el sótano? A mi casa la usaba para vivir, no para otra cosa. ¡Cómo voy a hacer eso! Ahí vivía mi familia; 31). "I don't feel remorse for anything," "I never killed anyone. Never," Puccio says again and again, and we will see that the disciplinarians of the last Argentine dictatorship say the same thing (No me arrepiento de nada. Nunca maté a nadie, jamás; 122). They are not interested in killing because it reduces the contingent available for disciplining, and do it only out of necessity.

Puccio's family is a micromodel of the Argentine society under the dictatorship. Some of the family became active torturers, while other family members acquiesced in silence, too scared to ask questions. The judge said the whole family must have been aware of the hostages, but they all denied knowing anything. Puccio's wife, Epifanía, a math teacher, was released for lack of proof. Silvia, the oldest daughter who taught drawing at an art school, denied all knowledge. Adriana, who was thirteen, was not even questioned. The younger son, Guillermo, escaped to Australia well before the arrests. Only Puccio's oldest sons, Alejandro and Daniel, were positively incriminated by the two other gang members. Daniel was released, pending trial, and fled the country. He left an apology letter for the last victim, who survived. He said he was profoundly sorry for what she had suffered, that he did not know what he was doing at the time. He said he would give her the letter personally, but he understood that she would "possibly" not want to see him (Palacios 72). Alejandro, who was sentenced to life in prison, said that his father was a terrible narcissist who used to lock him up in a bathroom (was it the same one in which he later held his hostages?). "If he did not care about me, his son, how could he care about the suffering of others?," Alejandro asked (Palacios 66). "He was terribly authoritarian. You had to do everything exactly as he wanted," complained Alejandro. "My only crime was to be the oldest son in a family where the father's authority made me believe that he was unquestionable, sublime, never wrong. This authority was imposed on me from my childhood onward" (Palacios 66). Alejandro said that prison at least afforded him the relief of finally being out of his father's reach. These excuses and his four suicide attempts constitute a sort of a confession. At the same time, Alejandro always maintained he was innocent, arguing that he was a successful man, the star player of the Argentine rugby team and an owner of a business (a luxury sporting goods store that served as a front for the kidnapping business). "Why would I do something like that?" (por qué iba a hacer algo semejante; Palacios 65), Alejandro asked—ironically, the same words his father often used. While in prison, Alejandro studied psychology and married his neighbor, who wrote letters to him. He was released in 2007 after twenty-two years in prison and died a few months later. No one came to his funeral, just as no one attended his father's.

Arquímedes Puccio himself enjoyed every kidnapping profoundly. He loved to call the young wife of one of the hostages and chat with her, complimenting her on the blouse she was wearing and telling her not to cry because it would be a shame for such a pretty lady to look ugly (Palacios 43). Conversing with desperate relatives evidently gave him pleasure and a feeling of absolute power. His final hostage, whom he lacked time to kill, revealed that Puccio also loved to joke with his victims. Once he asked her if she wanted chicken and rice for dinner and brought her a plate with a chicken bone picked clean and one grain of rice. When she broke down crying, he scolded her for ingratitude—did he not bring her chicken and rice as promised? (Palacios 63) After his release from prison, no one in his family wanted to see him or talk to him. The journalist shudders to hear Puccio complaining of feeling lonely: "I am a gregarious person. I don't like being alone. I like to be with people, chat with them, tell stories" (Tengo un espíritu gregario. No me gusta estar solo. Me gusta estar reunido con gente, charlar, hacer favores, contar anécdotas; 94). To have no one at one's disposal, either in public or in secret, must be extremely difficult for a disciplinarian.

In interviews, Puccio's disciplinarian identity shows through his supposedly friendly persona in sudden violent verbal outbursts. The films use makeup and masks. Guillermo Francella, who plays Puccio in Trapero's film, wears eyeliner and lipstick in the scene shown in figure 3.3, where he is on the phone with the victim's wife. His usually half-closed, dead eyes are wide open and full of excitement. In many scenes he also wears the bright white foundation used by stage actors. In Ortega's film, Puccio and his family wear elaborate rubber masks (see figure 1.4 in chapter 1). Puccio and his wife are Perón and Evita—Puccio admired Perón (as well as Hitler, Franco, Mussolini, and Tito). Puccio's son Alejandro wears the mask of the dictator Videla, and his son Daniel the mask of the soccer coach that led Argentina to win the 1978 World Cup, thereby strengthening the junta's prestige. These masks of the country's leaders worn by a family of assassins and accomplices (this scene is also the film's poster) are a powerful metaphor. Viewers are invited to consider that Puccio is not a random psychopath but the real face of the "gentlemen" of the dictatorship. They share the noble, patriarchal deportment and "the goody-goody aura, a certain air of false innocence to make you think

Figure 3.3. Puccio, wearing theatrical makeup, calls the hostage's wife in *The Clan* (2015).

they'd done nothing wrong" (aura santurrona, cierto aire de falsa inocencia: pareciera que no hubiesen hecho nada), write biographers of Videla, the leader of the junta (Seoane and Muleiro 71).

Puccio's ridiculous patriotic and pedagogical pathos helps to explain the unrepentant disciplinarians of the last Argentine dictatorship. Like them, Puccio used his family and family home to torture people and considered himself an exemplary Christian and family man. Like Puccio, the unrepentant disciplinarians of the Argentine junta are torn between the desire to speak of what they did and the desire to hide it. Like Puccio, they brag about their self-sacrificial love for the homeland, call themselves innocent victims, and decry the violation of their human rights. The temptation is great to say that these lofty words contradict the actual practice of torture and killing, and to understand this contradiction as hypocrisy and falsehood, as Marguerite Feitlowitz suggested in her book *The Lexicon of Terror*. But Puccio and the perpetrators themselves see no contradiction between their words and practice. For them, the grand words of family, fatherland, and duty do not mask but rather arise from causing enormous suffering for disciplinarian purposes.

The Disciplinarian's Rituals: Ordering, Dirtying and Cleaning, Secrecy, and Messianism

Disciplinarians are known for their love of order. The dictatorship aired TV ads calling upon the public to recall the "disorder, terrorism, and stagnation" of the past and compare it to the orderly present. Disciplinarians long to show everyone their place and modalities of life in the system they designed. The ads of the "Argentines, to victory" campaign each featured a person thinking out loud, "My country needs me. What can I do?" The man in voiceover firmly assigned them their tasks: the worker was told to work, the teacher to teach children the achievements of the regime, the student to study. The ads ended with the line "everyone doing their own work, protecting what belongs to us all" (cada uno en lo suyo, defendiendo lo nuestro, "Propaganda en la dictadura argentina").

Civil society had to be compartmentalized so the people would know better than to meddle in the leader's business. In the clandestine carceral world, the hostages are assigned to places with no such hassles. We see this assignment of people to space in the films. Puccio's first hostage sits in a bathtub, chained to the wall; the second sits, bound, in a wooden wardrobe in his home office. The last hostage spends almost a month in a tiny, windowless cement cell in the basement, chained to the wall. These dirty places of captivity transform people into unclean animals, making the act of discipline appear almost necessary and legitimate. The hostage who survived said her captors scolded her for stinking up the place at the same time that they removed the paint bucket she was given as a toilet. Puccio's nickname was "the crazy sweeper" (el loco de la escoba) because he obsessively swept the sidewalk in front of his house and liked to say, "We must keep San Isidro clean" (Hay que mantener San Isidro limpio; Palacios, 85). In Trapero's film, Puccio is shown rhythmically sweeping the sidewalk in front of his store, covered with prison-like shutters (figure 3.4). In Ortega's film, he is sweeping in front of the boarding house where he lives after serving his sentence. Puccio is emotionless and aloof throughout the film, and this emotionless disengagement enables him to kidnap and torture, as psychologist Albert Bandura shows. But the action of rhythmic sweeping absorbs Puccio fully.

When the real Puccio was released from prison, he continued his cleanliness rituals. He scolded his landlord, who complained that he swept and cleaned: "He must be the only person in the world who complains that someone cleans" (se queja porque barro y limpio. El único tipo en el mundo que se queja porque alguien limpia; Palacios). Cleaning also means killing. To get his accomplices to kill a hostage, Puccio would say, "You have to clean him—

Figure 3.4. Puccio sweeping the sidewalk in front of his house in *The Clan* (2015).

think about your family" (Tenés que limpiarlo, pensá en tu familia; Palacios 26). For Puccio, cleaning is a metaphor for controlling and dominating. He sent a journalist a photo of himself with a broom with the following inscription: "Best wishes to my new friend Rodolfo, in the hope that this enthusiastic friendship will be the beginning of a promising future on the path to truth and the respect of rights, of law, freedom, the Constitution, and the human rights for which I fought so much" (Con el mayor afecto al reciente amigo Rodolfo, en el deseo de que esta entusiasta amistad sea el inicio de un prometedor futuro en camino a la verdad y al respeto y vigencia del derecho, la ley, la libertad, la Constitución y los derechos humanos por los que tanto he luchado; Palacios 127). We can see that the real Puccio is even feistier than his fictional counterparts. With a broom in his hands, Puccio feels and talks as if he were important again.

The disciplinarians of the dictatorship were also cleanliness aficionados. A TV ad of the time depicted Argentina "as a fat cow attacked by a virus or germs" (Finchelstein 126; "Propaganda en la dictadura argentina"). Admiral Emilio Massera called the navy officers "the clean of heart" and fit to "clean a sick country" (limpios de corazón, limpiar un país enfermo; Massera 127, 22). "They [the detainees] were all cleaned up," said another perpetrator about the disappeared (los limpiaron a todos; Astiz). Military chaplains comforted repentant officers with the parable of the weeds (Matthew 13:24), saying that someone needed to "pluck out the weeds" (eliminar la maleza) so the wheat could grow (Scilingo 69). The officers who inquired about the disappeared were themselves "cleaned up" (Scilingo 89). The clandestine death camps were the places of dirtying that preceded the "cleaning." The rituals of the camps—torture, rape, and spray-painting prisoners with swastikas—transformed them into dirty life forms that needed to be purged (Finchelstein 120; Feitlowitz 179; Franco 13). One perpetrator described the infamous camp at the Escuela Mecánica de la Armada (ESMA): "There were detainees of all ages. Some were clean, others stank. A few of them were fat, others thin and shaking. You could hear someone cry. Some prayed. No one talked. The air was impossible to breathe, humid. You could feel the terror of those who were there, while they shifted their shackles trying to keep them away from the wounds on their smashed ankles" (Scilingo 49). Survivors recall feeling the "alienation provoked by one's own tortured body," from the "festering sores" and the blindfolds that turned them into "a little animal with an animal's fear of death" (Feitlowitz 76). The inmates themselves fought to remember that they were human because the rituals of torture repeatedly reduced them to dirty physical substances: "The physical evidence goes against you, you're so weak, so sick and so tormented, you think, if you *can* think: I *am* my shit; I *am* these stinking wounds; I *am* this festering sore. That is what you have to fight. And it's goddamn difficult; because whenever they feel like it, they replenish the physical evidence that goes against you" (Feitlowitz 76, original italics). The victims are made to feel filthy and abjectly dependent on their torturers.

The morbid appeal of kidnapping stories is that they represent everyone's worst fear. Modern audiences explore this fear vicariously through film. Yet people like Puccio were emboldened and enabled by the military dictatorship and, at the time, these fears could become everyone's reality. Ostensibly, dictatorial leaders detained people for a purpose, a reason. Puccio kidnapped for ransom whereas the dictatorship kidnapped to heal and correct the sick subjects—subversives, atheists, Communists. At the same time, as Hannah Arendt reminds us in *Eichmann in Jerusalem* (1963), torture camps in totalitarian Nazi Germany and the Soviet Union were anti-utilitarian and anti-pragmatic: they hindered both industrial development and war operations. Their purpose was different: they existed to transform individuals into "bundles of reactions" that "can be exchanged at random for any other" (438). More importantly, the camps existed so everyone in the society under control could be randomly selected and transferred to this place of the living dead where dignity and psyche were destroyed (447). "The society of the dying established in the camps is the only form of society in which it is possible to dominate man entirely," writes Arendt (456). Rodolfo Walsh, an Argentine writer who was killed during arrest, said in his open letter to the Junta that the purpose of the camps is not to extract information but to mash up "the human substance until it breaks, as it loses the dignity already lost by the executioner, the executioner's dignity, which you yourselves already lost" (Walsh). Clandestine places of detention destroyed the very idea of resistance in the mind of those who remained free. The disciplinarian uses them to control people through deep irrational fear.

Secrecy is another ritual of the disciplinarian because he knows he can dominate people only in hidden places where no one can interfere. At the same time, secrecy infuses torture and murder with a sacred, messianic meaning. Puccio made the members of his gang swear a blood oath that they would never reveal what they did. He lured journalist Rodolfo Palacios to come visit him by promising to reveal his secrets, but he never told him any. In the same way, the Junta leaders denied that disappeared people were killed. When he was on trial in 1984 and 1998, the dictator Videla denied that these people had been murdered. Later he acknowledged that they were killed and that he knew about it, but refused to reveal details: "You want us to reveal where the remains are? But what can we point to? The sea, the River Plate?" (Seoane and Muleiro 181). Federal police officer Julio "El Turco Julián" Simón, who was accused of torturing prisoners; Miguel Etchecolatz, the head of several torture centers; and admiral Emilio Massera all made a point of insinuating they had records and archives (Feitlowitz 248; Scilingo 272) that they never revealed to authorities. Videla's biographers wrote in 2016 that the motives of the dictatorship-era killers remain shrouded in "mystery," "obstinate mutism," and "silence" (misterio, mutismo tenaz, silencio; Seoane and Muleiro 3). In describing Videla—"he wants to talk, and he wants to keep quiet" (quiere hablar y quiere callar; 3)—his biographers accurately describe all these perpetrators, as well as Puccio. Albano Harguindeguy, the interior minister of the Junta, angrily replied to an American journalist who would not stop asking him what happened to his disappeared Argentine colleagues, "I am not Jesus, I can't tell them, Lazarus, rise and walk!" ("Albano Harguindeguy"). In preserving the secret, he could not abstain from making obscene insinuations. When three mothers searching for information about their disappeared daughters came to see Harguindeguy in 1977, he said to them first, "Señoras, we are family men" (nosotros somos padres de familia). Then he showed them a notebook and said, "See, in this agenda I keep the names of my friends. Your daughters left the country, and do you know where they are? In Mexico, working as prostitutes" (Ven, esta agenda la tengo llena de nombres de amigos míos. Sus hijas se fueron del país y ¿saben dónde están? En México ejerciendo la prostitución; "El día en que las Madres encararon a Harguindeguy"). Even in 2011, Harguindeguy made the same obscene insinuations while denying families information on the disappeared: "It is very difficult to determine who disappeared, who emigrated, and who is a prostitute who left for work; or maybe it's a husband who got divorced and left, or a girl who disappeared after she quarreled with her daddy because he wanted her to go to bed at 9 p.m.

on Saturdays and Sundays" (Es muy difícil determinar quién es desaparecido, quién es el emigrado y quién es la prostituta que se fue a trabajar; el marido que se divorcia y se va, la nena que está en desacuerdo con el papá que quiere que se duerma a las 21 del sábado y domingo y desaparece; Reato).

As keepers of secrets, disciplinarians remained the masters of their victims' destinies even beyond death, by means of obscene insults. In 1984, when a Jewish family published an announcement in newspapers seeking information about their disappeared son, they received the following message: "Jew, son of a Bitch: I am the one who killed the SHITHEAD OF YOUR SON and the Whore of your DAUGHTER-IN-LAW. THAT MAKES 2 ZIONIST JEWS LESS IN THE WORLD. If you only knew where we BURIED them! You would die, you motherfucking Jew" (Judío, hijo de Puta: Yo soy uno de los que mató al MIERDA DE TU HIJO y la Puta de tu NUERA. SON 2 JUDÍOS SIONISTAS MENOS EN EL MUNDO. ¡Si vos supieras dónde los ENTERRAMOS! Te morirías, Judío puto). Those who wrote the letter avoid face-to-face confrontation and taunt the family with real or purported secret knowledge. The secret can never be revealed so that the family can never overcome their loss (Finchelstein 169). The secret allows the perpetrators to exercise domination beyond their victims' death and, now, over their families. This secret knowledge injects the perpetrators with a feeling of omnipotence and gives them identity. "What binds these men together is a firm and sincere belief in human omnipotence," a solid conviction "that everything that exists is merely a temporary obstacle," Arendt wrote about the Nazis (378). The camps were a place where they could realize the principle of "everything is possible" to the fullest (395). "We thought we were omnipotent" (Nos creímos omnipotentes), Harguindeguy mused after he was arrested (Reato). Jorge "Tigre" Acosta, in charge of the ESMA death camp where five thousand people were killed, told prisoners he spoke to "Jesucito" to decide who would live and who would die ("Según el 'Tigre' Acosta"). Having fellow human beings at their mercy is rewarding, exhilarating, and empowering for the torturers.

Why do these disciplinarians refuse to feel guilty for their crimes? There are two explanations that may be complementary. The first, known as "the banality of evil," was coined by Hannah Arendt during the 1961 trial of Adolph Eichmann, the Nazi official who very efficiently organized the murder of six million Jews in the Nazi death camps. Eichmann actually escaped to Argentina and lived there under an assumed name before being captured by Israeli agents and tried in Jerusalem in 1963. At the trial, Eichmann argued that he never so much as hurt, not to mention killed, another human being and had no personal hatred for Jews. He simply did his job the best he could, and no one among his acquaintances and superiors or even the Jewish leaders who collaborated with him ever told him that what he was doing was wrong. This is why Arendt defined his behavior as "thoughtlessness" and more famously, as "the banality of evil"—if ordinary well-intentioned people are convinced that something is their duty, many of them will go above and beyond to "wreak more havoc than all the evil instincts taken together" (Arendt 288).

Arendt's "banality of evil" inspired several famous experiments. Solomon Asch found that when shown a picture of a short line and a long line, 75 percent of people would agree that a visibly shorter line was longer if the rest of the group said it was so (Brannigan 6). In Stanley Milgram's experiment at Yale medical school, people were instructed by an actor in a lab coat to deliver ever-increasing electric shocks to a "learner" (another actor) when "the learner" gave incorrect answers. The participants could not see "the learner" but could hear the person scream and beg them to stop. Notwithstanding, 65 percent used all thirty switches, ranging from 15 volts (Slight Shock) to 375 volts (Danger: Severe Shock) to 450 volts (marked XXX). All participants continued to 300 volts. When people feel they must conform, wrote Milgram, "*loyalty, duty, discipline* . . . refer not to the 'goodness' of the person per se but to the adequacy with which a subordinate fulfills his socially defined role" (146, emphasis added). That is to say, the participants' desire to obey the authority in the lab coat overshadowed all other concerns. Philip Zimbardo's Stanford prison experiment was stopped after one week instead of two because his graduate student (who later became his wife) told him it was immoral. She was the only person to do so. One-third of the students who were randomly assigned the role of "guards" grew sadistic. All "prisoners," also chosen at random, became depressive (Zimbardo 170). Being forced into the identity of the guard made people enjoy the submission and suffering of the prisoners "entrusted" to them. More recent studies indicate that situations of subordination, such as military training, cause cognitive degradation (Doris and Murphy), moral disengagement (Bendera), and distorted normativity (Pauer-Studer and Velleman). The "banality of evil" means that under certain conditions people of any social class, gender, age, and education can become agents of mass atrocities.

The miniseries *The History of a Clan* discussed earlier exemplifies the banality of evil. When the police raid the house and liberate the last hostage, she walks out of her basement prison to discover that it is the first floor of an ordinary family house. She meets the fearful and resentful gaze of the arrested mother, daughters, and Alejandro. She "visits" the house, studies with fascination the usual upper-class décor, complete with many family pictures crowding the walls and the piano, and bursts into laughter. After imagining her torturers as alien monsters, she is shocked to see that they look so absolutely ordinary.

The second explanation of unrepentant mass murderers and torturers can be described as "the magnificence of evil." Criminologist Augustine Brannigan, who coined this phrase, suggests that perpetrators commit atrocities not only to conform but also because they enjoy it. In *The History of a Clan*, Alejandro tells his sobbing mother who comes to visit him in prison, "I kind of liked what we did. Didn't you?" (un poco me gustaba lo que hacíamos. ¿A vos no?). Arendt herself noted that at times the dispassionate bureaucratic Eichmann seemed to take pride in the magnitude of the suffering he had inflicted on others. For example, he boasted to a fellow Nazi that he would jump into his grave laughing, knowing he had on his conscience the death of millions of enemies of the Reich. The Nazi ideology infused his petty and boring life with meaning and solemnity (Arendt 136). Eichmann knew what he was doing, and it made him feel important.

Similarly, American theorist of the Holocaust Dominick LaCapra explained the elation experienced by the perpetrators by the enormity of the transgression. Participating in mass torture and murder is felt as "a sort of secular sacred, related to something that goes beyond ordinary experience, and is almost, if not altogether, transcendent." The perpetrators experienced "a fascination with unheard-of transgression," an "extremely cruel, at times gleeful, pleasure in the suffering of others; and scenes that are almost like those out of a carnival—scenes of bloody massacre, where people are elated at what is happening, and in ways that may be incomprehensible to them, themselves" (LaCapra). In this framework, mass murders come to be seen as a mission for which only select, special, morally superior individuals are fit and as a means of spiritual regeneration, says Italian historian of fascism Emilio Gentile (22). Perpetrators find redemption and regeneration in the enormity of the suffering they cause, says historian of Argentine fascism Federico Finchelstein. These theorists often cite Heinrich Himmler's words to SS officers after they killed thousands of Jews in Poland; he told the officers that they were different from ordinary people who only talk about doing something like this and never dare to actually do it. He called them *anständig*—decent and morally beautiful (Finchelstein 141). Violence on a massive scale comes to be experienced as a sacred ritual, so the perpetrators feel special and superior to others.

Indeed, the disciplinarians of the Argentine dictatorship also viewed themselves as a messianic group, "a group of men so special, so rare in their human quality, so eminent in their courage," as Massera described them (un conjunto de hombres tan especiales, tan raros en su calidad humana, tan eminentes en su coraje; Massera 126). The officers carrying out kidnappings, torture, and murder were hailed as saviors, redeemers, martyrs, and heroes (Videla 28, 15, 22). Like the Nazis, they tricked the victims into helping in their own extermination. The victims were told they would be transported to rehabilitation facilities in the north. They were told to dance to merry music to celebrate their liberation. Afterward, they were injected with a sedative, which they were told was "a vaccine." They walked by themselves into an airplane, and, once in the air, to the door in the bottom of the airplane out of which they were pushed into the sea to their death. The perpetrators and the military chaplains explained that the victims' deaths were Christian because they died happy, expecting to be freed. Puccio also believed that it was important to give "Christian" death to hostages. In *The History of a Clan*, he tells the hostage to walk and meet his family, and when the hostage begins walking, with tears of hope in his eyes, Puccio shoots him dead. The officers tasked with throwing prisoners off airplanes perceived the death flights as a sacred ritual of communion and a supreme act for the sake of the Fatherland (comunión, un acto supremo por la patria; Verbitsky 47). Videla said the military men agreed to keep the murders secret because ordinary Argentines would have been unable to bear it (no se hubiera bancado; Seoane and Muleiro 231). Only messianic men were strong enough to do what they perceived to be their duty, and to do it right, with appropriate solemnity.

Convicting these self-righteous perpetrators and enforcing their incarceration has been a long struggle in Argentina. While incarcerated, they made emotional and dignified declarations, presenting themselves as victims of their old political enemies who now dominate the institutions they worked so hard to save. At first, they found refuge in impunity laws, and then pardons, commuted sentences, and house arrests. The first democratically elected president of Argentina, Raúl Alfonsín, feared that the military would rebel again, so only the leaders of the Junta were tried; four of them received life sentences in 1985. To appease the military, in 1986 Alfonsín passed the Full Stop Law (Ley de Punto Final). Its objective was to minimize the number of lawsuits filed against the repressors by setting a limit of sixty days, after which no new complaints would be accepted. This measure backfired, and the courts were flooded with hundreds of complaints, again provoking military unrest. Alfonsín then passed the Due Obedience Law (Ley de Obediencia Debida) in 1987, acquitting lower-rank officers on the grounds that they were following orders. The next president, Carlos Menem, set free the imprisoned Junta leaders in 1990 and encouraged the nation to move on. Open cases against the repressors were either closed or stalled (Balardini 65).

The twenty-first century was a turning point. International and domestic human rights organizations made the repressors' impunity a major social agenda. Néstor and Cristina Kirchner promoted the trials, proclaimed the date of the coup (March 24) National Remembrance Day, and established museums and memorials at the sites of the detention centers. The Armed Forces made efforts to distance themselves from the convicted repressors. Future army officers were permitted to study at public universities where human rights were part of the curriculum. Old cases were reopened and organized into mega cases with hundreds of repressors and thousands of witnesses. The number of convictions in human rights abuses cases in Argentina is the highest in Latin America, but appeals and delays make it difficult to enforce them. Several repressors provoked a scandal by running for public office while their conviction was being appealed (Balardini 66). Also, there have been new attempts to replace incarceration of notorious repressors with home arrest, although these efforts have been abandoned in the face of massive protest demonstrations ("Provocación ante el aniversario del golpe"). What is not changing is the dictatorship disciplinarians' unrepentant and proud stance, which, like Puccio's, would be ridiculous if it were not so scary.

The Proud Dictatorship Disciplinarians

Torturer Alfredo Astiz perceived kidnapping, detention, and torture as affectionate work. Known as the "Blond Angel of Death" for his celebrity-actor looks and blond hair, Astiz infiltrated the Madres de la Plaza de Mayo (the organization of the mothers of the disappeared), pretending to be looking for a disappeared brother. He gained their trust and helped capture two members and two French nuns, who were thrown from a plane into the sea (the perpetrators jokingly called them "the flying nuns"). Astiz remembered this time as "routine, everyday work," and, more disturbingly, expressed affection for the prisoners: "we even felt affection for each other. Because gradually you come to like the people you live with for many days. . . . I took a liking to some of the Montoneros" (hasta nos teníamos afecto. Porque uno le va tomando afecto a la gente con la que tiene que convivir muchos días. Yo a algunos Montoneros . . . les llegué a tomar afecto). But he refused to give details: "We won't talk about these things anymore. There is no need to know them. Those who want to know them are psychos (morbosos)" (Astiz, interview with Cerruti). The interview caused a public outcry. Astiz was discharged from the military, although then-president Menem and high military commanders tried to protect him, but he remained free until 2005. At his trial in 2008, he said, "I will never say I am sorry for having defended my fatherland" ("El gobierno incluyó"). At his 2011 trial, Astiz cast the perpetrators as victims. He complained that the witnesses defamed innocent officers—now old men who could make no sense of the false allegations and were illegitimately deprived of freedom, while their families suffered from "stress, suffering, and psychological disorders," and their children were "deprived of paternal affection" with "total impunity" (Astiz, "Palabras finales"). When convenient for him, Astiz recognized human rights, but only his own.

Admiral Emilio Massera, the mastermind of the disappearances, also shrugged at the accusations. He said at his first trial, "I feel responsible, but I don't feel guilty, simply because I'm not guilty" (me siento responsable pero no me siento culpable, sencillamente porque no soy culpable; Galarza). This sentence appears almost verbatim in the 1990 play *Paso de dos* by Eduardo Pavlovsky, in which a man tortures and strangles his female victim. He says, "I can only say that I'm absolutely responsible for everything and I repent for absolutely nothing because my actions are the only thing in which I can find any meaning" (Sólo puedo decir que soy absolutamente responsable de todo, de absolutamente nada me arrepiento, porque mis actos son lo único donde puedo encontrar algún sentido; Pavlovsky 11). As of this writing, this play is still performed regularly to a full house, with many in the audience weeping during the performances. Lover of grand words and former student of philology, Massera said that time would show he was a great man: "my children and my grandchildren will say with pride the last name that I left them" (mis hijos y mis nietos pronunciarán con orgullo el apellido que les he dejado; Galarza). In 1995, pardoned by Menem, Massera said, "I live at peace and happy," "I made my penance before Jesus" (Vivo tranquilo y feliz, hice un acto de contrición ante Jesucito). He saw himself as a bookish intellectual who disliked violence: "I never gave the order to kill anyone, I never tortured anyone. I never saw an electrical prod, and I don't know how to use this device. I don't even go around armed—I don't like weapons" (Nunca di la orden de matar a nadie, nunca torturé. Jamás vi una picana, ni sé cómo se maneja ese aparato. Ni siquiera ando armado: no me gustan las armas; Scilingo 272). And yet it was Massera who lectured to the navy officers that mass killing of prisoners was their sacred and ineluctable duty (these speeches were compiled and published as a book). He was investigated for kidnapping and suppression of the identity of minors (some of the disappeared were high school students), as well as for having ordered torture, execution, confinement in illegal detention centers, and the drowning of prisoners. However, in 2005 Massera was diagnosed with dementia, and all cases against him were closed. Recall that Puccio's wife succumbed to dementia in Ortega's *History of a Clan*. The continual effort to suppress these memories in order to deny them publicly caused them to genuinely lose their memories.

The dictator Jorge Rafael Videla, a lanky, self-effacing, and ascetic man is perhaps the most recognizable face of the dictatorship. Borges and other intellectuals had lunch with him shortly after the coup in 1976 and praised him as "a real gentleman" (todo un caballero). Borges later changed his position to criticize the Junta (Anguita and Cecchini). Videla was a very peculiar leader—he had "no commanding talent" and was a barely tolerable orator. At the military academy, he was the student "who stood out the least" and always avoided taking sides, said his former classmates (Seoane and Muleiro). His superiors described him as not very intelligent but an excellent executor. His main goal was to receive "un sobresaliente" (the highest mark), narrate his biographers Seoane and Muleiro (129). His acquaintances described him as so attached to rules that "if he saw his child cross the street on a red light, he would make him cross the street again" (Seoane and Muleiro 131). He believed in absolute obedience to norms emanating from institutions or some higher authority. His "fantasy was to transform the entire country into a military barrack" (105). "Political ideologies bothered him, altered his routine of getting ready for the 9 of July parade, when his soldiers, all impeccable, all looking alike, march in formation with a 15-inch step, eyes right, with him at the head, of course" (Seoane and Muleiro 129). When put under house arrest, he would not step onto his balcony in fear he would be breaking the rules. When first incarcerated, he had the key to the door through which he could escape, but since he was forbidden to use the key, he never did. He would always finish his walk ahead of time, to make sure to comply with prison rules. Videla "was molded by the army as an empty subjectivity, ready to be completed and endowed with meaning, within the confines of the classroom of the Military School and the barbed wire separating the barracks from civil society" (Seoane and Muleiro 71). He spoke of the disappeared as if they were abstract entities, not people. At a press conference in 1979, he said that "the disappeared cannot have a special treatment, he or she is a disappeared person, has no entity, is neither dead nor alive, is disappeared. This is why we can do nothing about it" (mientras esté desaparecido no puede tener un tratamiento especial: es un desaparecido, no tiene entidad, no está ni muerto ni vivo, está desaparecido. Frente a eso no podemos hacer nada; "Jorge Videla, el dictador que nunca cuestionó su accionar"). In 2011, he still felt good about what they called between themselves "the Final Disposition/Disposal" (Disposición Final; compare to the Nazis' "Final Solution"): "It was the best solution we found . . . it created an ambiguous sensation in people: they weren't there, it was unknown what happened to them" (era la mejor solución que encontramos, creaba una sensación ambigua en la gente: no estaban, no se sabía qué había pasado con ellos; Reato). When he was incarcerated, he assumed the stance of a sacrificed victim, "a scapegoat" society chose to redeem its collective guilt. He claimed to be rendering one more service for his country. "Note that I repent of nothing, I sleep very well every night," insisted Videla (Ojo, no estoy arrepentido de nada, duermo muy tranquilo todas las noches; Reato). His biographers concluded that he feels, like Eichmann, "neither pity nor sorrow. He feels the nothing of the banality of evil, the nothing of the bureaucracy of death" (Seoane and Muleiro 222). Indeed, of all the perpetrators discussed here, Videla is the most like Eichmann: shy and diffident, at his best when obeying orders.

Antonio Domingo Bussi, a military commander responsible for over a thousand disappearances in over thirty clandestine centers in Tucumán, was a weepy variety of the unrepentant disciplinarian. He declared at his trial in 2008, his voice hoarse and fighting back tears, that "the figure of the disappeared person is a psychological ploy created by guerrilla fighters to hide their combat losses" (la figura del desaparecido es arbitrio psicológico creado por los guerrilleros para encubrir sus muertes en combate) despite family members in the audience holding photos of the disappeared in his face. One former subordinate testified that Bussi tortured two detainees and beat them to death with a hose; another testified that Bussi personally conducted executions and fired first to act as an example to the soldiers (Ginzberg). After the dictatorship, Bussi won the position of governor of Tucumán, and then it came to light that he had a secret bank account in Switzerland. When asked about it, Bussi broke down in tears, saying he forgot to declare it. Soon, seven more foreign accounts were found, but Bussi was again elected, this time to the Lower House of Congress in 1999. The Congress deemed him morally unfit for the post because of his participation in the dictatorship's repression and embezzlement. In 2003, Bussi won elections again, this time as mayor of San Miguel de Tucumán, but he was arrested before he could assume the post. At his trial, he again broke down in tears. Pronounced guilty of the murder of senator Guillermo Vargas Aignasse, Bussi said, "I've never seen him or had any relationship with him in my entire life" (No lo vi ni lo traté en toda mi vida). About the camp detainees, he said, weeping, "We were not trying to torment them and much less physically eliminate them" (No se buscaba mortificarlos ni muchos menos su eliminación física). He concluded, sobbing, "I am a victim of those we defeated on the battlefield and at the ballot box" (Soy víctima de una venganza de los derrotados en las armas y las urnas; "Bussi, el militar de hierro que terminó a las lágrimas").

Miguel Etchecolatz supervised twenty-one illegal detention centers in the capital and personally conducted torture ("Condenaron a Miguel Etchecolatz"). He led the operation known as the Night of the Pencils, in which ten high school students were kidnapped and tortured. Six of them were never seen again (the 1986 film *La noche de los lápices* was based on the testimony of one surviving hostage). Etchecolatz intimated that he knew what became of them but refused to reveal the information. While protected by the impunity laws, he published a book, *The Other Campaign of Never Again*, in which he spoke of his "honesty, sensibility, self-denial, and self-sacrifice" (honestidad, sensibilidad, renunciamiento y sacrificio); lamented the current "loss of faith" (pérdida de la fe); and declared, "I never had or thought or was inconvenienced by any feelings of guilt . . . For having killed? I was the executor of the law made by men. I was the Keeper of divine precepts. For these two reasons, I would do it again" (nunca tuve ni pensé, ni me acomplejó culpa alguna . . . ¿Por haber matado? Fui ejecutor de la ley hecha por hombres. Fui Guardador de preceptos divinos. Por ambos fundamentos, volvería a hacerlo; Etchecolatz 15, 124). His daughter changed her last name and joined the march to protest the court's decision to grant her father house arrest in 2017 (that decision was revoked). She said that when her mother tried to leave him, her father threatened to kill her and her children. When he left home for work, she and her brother would pray that "he would never come back, that he would please die" (para que nunca jamás volviera. Que por favor se muera; Mannarino). His religiosity gave him another justification for abuses: "he would cross himself and kiss his holy cards. He considered himself beneath God but above other mortals. My brother J.M. and I used to say that when he prayed, he ate the saints" (se persignaba dándoles besos a las estampitas. Él se consideraba por debajo de Dios pero por encima de los mortales. Con mi hermano J.M. decíamos que cuando rezaba se estaba comiendo los santos; Mannarino). The years of trials and imprisonment did not change Etchecolatz. During his 2014 trial, he was photographed smiling and holding a little note saying "kidnap Julio López"—a cruel joke because López, a key witness in his 2006 trial, had indeed disappeared during the trial. As his life imprisonment sentence was read to him in 2018, Etchecolatz smiled and kissed the rosary ("Condenaron a Miguel Etchecolatz"). The same year, Etchecolatz asked to be restored to the rank of the Buenos Aires policeman. The leader of the Abuelas de la Plaza de Mayo commented, "he probably feels proud of what he did." His request was denied ("Estela de Carlotto"). This torturer, like the others, not only never repented but took comfort and pride in what he did.

Navy captain Adolfo Scilingo was the only perpetrator who repented, at least for some time. Tormented by guilt, Scilingo approached a journalist and revealed that he threw thirty drugged prisoners into the sea from an airplane. He came forward because his superiors, Massera and Videla, did not answer his letters, in which he urged them to acknowledge the death flights and reveal the names of the eliminated enemies. He said that the commanders' denials made officers like him, who obeyed what they thought were legitimate orders, feel like criminals. "Why do they not answer my letters? Do you think they will write back?" Scilingo obsessively asked the journalist (Verbitsky 22 and 26). Scilingo said that after the flights he alienated himself from his family and sought refuge in alcohol and pills. His interlocutor, journalist Horacio Verbitsky, who only by accident escaped the fate of Scilingo's victims, used words that provoked Scilingo's anger: "gang," "kidnappings," "torture," and "murder of victims," and each time Scilingo defensively corrected him: "the Navy," "detention," "interrogation," and "elimination of the enemy." Scilingo revealed that all officers took part in the weekly death flights on rotation, but they never spoke about it among themselves. They perceived it as a sacred ritual and considered colleagues who quit traitors (Verbitsky 17). It is this secret framework of heroic service that Scilingo wants his superiors to make public because without it he would be a common murderer. Instead, they deny everything, and that means he was involved in something shameful and criminal rather than heroic: "They are hiding the truth. Why are they hiding the truth? People hide the truth when they do something they shouldn't be doing" (se oculta la verdad. ¿Por qué se oculta? Se oculta cuando se está haciendo algo que no corresponde; Verbitsky 40).

"What am I supposed to do with my thirty dead men?" (¿Qué hago con mis treinta muertos?) Scilingo lamented at every public appearance (Verbitsky). Protected by the Due Obedience Law, he resolved to speak about the death flights publicly and force his superiors to take this burden of guilt off his shoulders. Scilingo did not back down, even after he was kidnapped in a police vehicle and the kidnappers carved the initials of the journalists he had spoken to on his cheeks and forehead. Scilingo flew to Spain to testify for judge Baltazar Garzón, who was investigating the disappearance of Spanish nationals in Argentina during the dictatorship. The judge ordered his arrest, and Scilingo said he expected it. He repeated his previous statements, saying he was prepared to accept "the sentence that I deserve" (la [condena] que corresponde; Herrera). During the years spent in pretrial detention, he changed his mind. At his trial in 2006, he retracted all his previous statements and said that his lawyers and the judge conspired to have him publicize "a total fantasy, fabricated to sensitize the public opinion and help judge Garzón" (la fantasía más grande del mundo fabricada para sensibilizar a la opinión pública y ayudar al juez Garzón; Sáiz-Pardo). He was sentenced to 1,084 years in prison to serve the legal maximum of thirty years. A model prisoner, he is entitled to thirty days of conditional liberty a year but is denied further leniency because he now refuses to repent or even acknowledge what he did. The prison psychologist noted that Scilingo speaks of his actions with coldness and detachment. For example, he said he picked 28 for the number of his victims because he got married on the 28th, and that the flights didn't take place weekly as he had said before: "there were just one or two" (hubo uno o dos solamente; Kalizsky). He cynically dares to prove what he himself so many times confessed: "Go ahead, tell me the name of even one of my supposed victims. Read the entire sentence and you'll see that there isn't a single name in it and there'll never be. And the juridical doctrine says that a case like this must be archived because there are no proofs that would lead to a sentence" (A ver: dígame el nombre de alguna de mis supuestas víctimas. Lea toda la sentencia y verá que no hay un solo nombre y nunca lo habrá. Y la doctrina jurídica dice que si en una causa como ésta no existen identidades de las víctimas debe ser archivada porque no hay elementos probatorios que permitan condenar; Kalizsky). Scilingo proclaims himself an innocent victim and hopes that "the time will come when people acknowledge his honor" (a que en algún momento se llegue a reconocer su honorabilidad; Altozano). In the end, Scilingo reclaimed the identity of unrepentant disciplinarian.

Conclusion

In many ways, the disciplinarians' argument that they killed no one personally (so why, they insisted, were they being tried and sentenced?) is actually a confession. Killing the hostage they had previously disciplined and reduced to a simple bundle of reactions puts an end to all the fun. They killed out of necessity, to make space for new people, because disciplining is a never-ending process and the space for disciplining is sadly limited. To replace and dispense with old hostages is a purely administrative matter, although the disciplinarians often develop affection for the prisoners and may miss them. The card games, the TV to watch a sports game together, the soccer magazines, the cake slices the disciplinarians bring from home to their prisoners and other tokens of affection are little thank-you gifts for letting them experience absolute domination. Unlike histrionic leaders who enjoy seducing crowds and basking in their admiration, the diffident, uncharismatic disciplinarians know that no one will willingly shower them with applause. They cringe when they need to speak in front of unknown crowds and prefer the captive audience of those they have plucked at random from the mass of their public subjects, whose freedom they can end at any moment. Repentance is absurd and unthinkable for the disciplinarians. Their declared goal is order, tradition, and religion, and, in this respect, they go above and beyond to establish and enforce rules for their prisoners. They think of themselves as professionals, even heroes, working for the greater good of their fatherland and family. Films and books about Puccio, a convicted kidnapper and torturer perorating pell-mell on patriotism, ideals, his fight for human rights, sexual prowess, and his admiration for Hitler, show how ridiculous but dangerous he and the likes of him are, how hungry they are for manipulation and control. The last Argentine dictatorship gave Puccio the opportunity not only to operate his own clandestine prison—for profit—but also to realize his urge to discipline others completely and to think of himself as a leader and a special being. I have discussed Puccio as a metaphor of the infamous dictatorship disciplinarians who also refuse to feel guilty or divulge what happened to their victims. They are dying of old age, but their dignified denials combined with pretensions of greatness continue to disturb. These disciplinarians came to consider themselves a messianic group, and the mass murders they ideated as supreme acts of service to their fatherland. We should be on our guard with such seemingly dependable men if we do not want to experience firsthand the carceral component of their leadership.

4

The Patrón

The Backslapping Predator with a Big Smile in Mexico

This chapter is about the charming, backslapping leader who establishes a pretend friendship with people in order to make them commit dishonest acts for him as a small personal favor. The leader operates by forcing a personal, intimate rapport on his subjects and gets offended if someone mentions that what he does or asks others to do is against the rules. This inappropriate closeness he forces on people is a bad omen for them. He makes light of his subjects' personal boundaries, just as he makes light of laws and regulations, and if his subordinates happen to displease him, he will not think twice about hurting or even killing them. The relationship he establishes with his subjects replicates the relationship of the benevolent patrón with his peons from the times of debt servitude. The peons have the obligation to work for the patrón for free to pay off their supposed debt and hope for his protection in times of need. In the contemporary political framework, this practice is known as clientelism. Clients (the modern version of peons) trade their political agency for access to goods and services. Loyalty to the patrón is beyond morality and rules. This widely accepted and largely unconscious social practice produces an inherently anti-democratic political system. Clients assume they must curry favor with officials rather than formulating political demands, and officials assume that their position of power is an opportunity for rent-seeking rather than public service.

Films use memorable images to depict these patrón–client relationships. We see clients kissing the patrón's hand to seal their subordination, just as gang members kiss the hand of the mafia boss, except here one owner of the hand is a bishop and the other a governor (*The Crime of Padre Amaro* and *The Perfect Dictatorship*). In the quadrilogy of comedies directed by Luis Estrada, the same actors take turns playing the role of a patrón in one film and a client in the other. This tells us that all individuals, no matter how honest, will eventually find themselves sucked into the system and become clients or *patrones*. Films also show the relationship between patrones of like standing known as *compadrazgo*. In the film, these *compadres* (literally, co-*fathers*) gather in intimate settings to discuss how to launder bribes from drug traffickers and criminals, expropriate lands and businesses, eliminate adversaries, and parody their own campaign lines to general roaring laughter. Once people pawn themselves to the corrupt patrón, clients lose all moral anchors. The films denounce these corrupt informal relationships disguised as friendship and kinship as the main obstacle to democratization. They expose the eagerness to subordinate oneself to a corrupt patrón as perpetuation of predatory leadership. In *Tear This Heart Out*, the adaptation of a novel written during the long rule of the Partido Revolucionario Institucional (Institutional Revolutionary Party, abbreviated as the PRI), filmmakers reinvent the novel's complicit and lethargic heroine as the agent of change. She puts an end to her predatory ruler, the husband, and her subordination, setting an example for the audience.

In this chapter I will first outline the origins and workings of patronage and clientelism. Next, I will focus on Luis Estrada's cinematic crusade against the corrupt patrones and their all-too-eager-to-oblige clients. The chapter's last section will show that filmmakers changed their literary sources written well before the 2000 defeat of the PRI, *The Crime of Padre Amaro* and *Tear This Heart Out*, to expose clientelism as the political structure of domination that must be recognized and rejected. I will conclude with the visceral and lasting cognitive impact these films have on viewers, who describe them as "stuck in my mind," "too real," and "shocking."

Clientelism in Mexico

Although the PRI, the hegemonic party that ruled Mexico, was defeated in elections in 2000, corruption has continued to thrive in Mexico. The defeat of the PRI was celebrated as the long-awaited transition to democracy, auguring the freedom of the press, accountable power structures, and popular participation and monitoring of power. Two decades later, Mexico is the fifteenth largest economy in the world, but 44 percent of Mexicans, or nearly half the population, live below the poverty line ("Ranks of Mexican Poor"). Democratization and frequent anti-corruption campaigns did not decrease corruption. On the contrary, the disintegration of old networks of domination and neoliberal reforms coupled with the privatization of state companies and services created opportunities for rent-seeking officials. Mexico leads Latin America in the solicitation of bribes. Corruption costs equal 10 percent of Mexico's GDP. The large informal sector employs 60 percent of workers and two-thirds of firms do not pay taxes. Companies obtain contracts through bribery and provide overpriced and inferior services (Martínez-Fernández 9). The PRI or not, democracy or not, to the cordial backslapping bosses, parties and governance frameworks are mere formalities that they can make light of or use to their benefit after they have secured the loyalty of the right people.

These coerced exchanges are actually to a large degree consensual. The study of corruption in Mexico by political scientists John Bailey and Pablo Parás shows that almost everyone admits to participating in corrupt exchanges, actively or passively. When asked who initiates corruption, "a third of the respondents said that it is the public official; an equal number said it is the individual; another third said it is both" (67). When asked to rate themselves as "Corrupt" or "Clean," only 27 percent rated themselves as "very clean." Questionable actions are perceived as "somewhat smart" or "very smart": 42 percent think it is smart not to pay the bus fare, 40 percent will not say anything when given more change than owed, and 33 percent approve of inventing a false excuse (Bailey and Parás 73). There is a widespread fatalism about corruption, as many perceive it as embedded in the system or culture. 44 percent believe that bribes are necessary, 55 percent believe that most people are corrupt, and 60 percent believe that honest people will become corrupt if they gain access to a public office (Bailey and Parás 74).

We see that people not only acquiesce when they are invited to participate in a questionable exchange, but often are eager to participate and even to initiate them. The informal beliefs, rules, and transactions that facilitate and naturalize corrupt practices take root in the social practice called clientelism. Clientelism is an analytical category to understand informal relationships of power. It describes the exchange of goods, favors, and services between socially unequal people or groups (Schröter and Tosoni). These exchanges seem voluntary but are actually obligatory because they engage the logic of reciprocity, the take and give (*toma y daca*). Accepting a favor from someone obligates us to reciprocate with a favor in return. Some people give, while others receive, and those who are takers today will be givers tomorrow (Tosoni 50). These exchanges are not rationalized as transactions because they are spaced over time and the parties never discuss them in terms of price (Tosoni 51). This is why scholars describe clientelism as a habitus, a term proposed by sociologist Pierre Bourdieu that means "a way of making sense of the world, learned in and through daily interactions" (Ayuero and Benzecry 190). People look for an authority figure to whom to subordinate themselves socially and politically in exchange for access to credit; services; crops; land titles; jobs for the municipality, the party office, or a state company; and basic survival supplies, such as "food, medicine, clothes, shoes, coffins, school materials, appliances, bricks, zinc sheets, cash," and even "marihuana and other illegal drugs" (Zarazaga 33).

The transactional nature of clientelism is also obscured by the fact that the patrón acts by means of his intermediaries (also called brokers), people who live in the neighborhood and whom the clients know personally. This is why the clients perceive these intermediaries as friends and selfless helpers. "It is not the state that is perceived as the distributing agency; it is [the brokers, their neighbors] Matilde or Juancito. And as they are the ones who distribute the goods, they are seen as not having any obligation at all to do it; they do it because they really want to, because they care, because they 'sacrifice themselves for people'" (Auyero 314). Consequently, people are socialized to believe that they cannot demand anything from state officials or choose candidates who may do a better job. When the patrón fails to deliver, clients look for another patrón instead of quitting the system altogether. Clientelistic networks exist as "schemas of appreciation, perception, and action in the mental structures" of the people socialized into these exchanges. To be loyal to the patrón is a prerational modus vivendi (Auyero 32). When people are socialized in this system, subordination, both social and political, feels perfectly natural. Moreover, personal probity makes no difference in this system. The distinction between what is corrupt and what is not melts in the relationships of unequal power masked as kinship and friendship, and the language of loyalty and affection. People explain their loyalty to the patrón as "the given word," "not failing one's promise," "integrity," "nourishing and not abusing one's contacts" (Roniger 37), "gratitude and collaboration" (Auyero 308). The exchanges are experienced as a "moral obligation to friends, acquaintances, and relatives, the way to express mutual respect," and, as such, one cannot help but perceive them as moral (Schröter 150).

In the films, we see that the corrupt charmer actively seeks out gullible prey, but people socialized in this system are often only too eager to respond to his advances. People seek out a patrón as much as the patrón seeks them out, and often run to offer their services before being asked. Their ensuing political and social subordination is to a great degree consensual, which makes it difficult to pity them. Also, films show the social groups that historically find themselves in the position of social and political subordination: the rural Indigenous and urban poor. Slavery and serfdom to which Indigenous populations were subjected after the conquest are the root of clientelism (Warf and Stewart 137). When the abuse and killing of the enslaved Indigenous population by the Spanish settlers became public, the Spanish monarchs prohibited slavery. But since they needed the metals and resources that enslaved populations extracted, slavery continued to exist under different names and became more insidious. "Formal slavery was replaced by multiple forms of informal labor coercion and enslavement that were extremely difficult to track," explains historian Andrés Reséndez in *The Other Slavery* (320). To prevent the abuses of the *repartimientos*, the system of *encomiendas* was instituted, a forced labor system in which Indigenous individuals were "distributed" to the Spanish settlers. The enslavers were supposed to provide instruction in the Christian faith, pay their workers a symbolic salary, and put them to work only for a certain period of the year. Protections of Indigenous peoples were regularly legislated but not enforced because officials and governors were themselves slavers. In practice, abuse went unrestrained, and slavers appropriated the land of native peoples under their "patronage."

After independence in 1821, bondage to the master took the shape of debt peonage, a legally codified, lifelong serfdom. Peasants were offered cash advances and promised wages, but soon they were told that they owed the patrón for clothing, equipment, and mistakes, real or invented. Debt was a ploy to entrap entire families to work for the master for free: wives were locked up in textile workshops to "pay off" the husband's debt, children were signed up as peons by their fathers or signed themselves up to stay together as a family. When haciendas were sold or inherited, peons went with the haciendas. Peons could not be sold but their debt could, and they "went with it" to work for the new master. As Yucatán planters explained to an American journalist posing as a buyer, "We don't keep much account of the debt, because it doesn't matter after you've got possession of the man." Peons were sold together with their photographs and identification papers, because "if your man runs away, the papers are all the authorities require for you to get him back again," explained the planter (Reséndez 240). Debt was passed on to the children. As owners of businesses and haciendas required more and more workers, a new legislature was introduced to define everyone not in possession of a large income as vagrants and obligate them to work for a patrón. "Vagrants" were rounded up and kept in prison with the costs of capture and detention added to their debt until a patrón came and took them to work (Reséndez 264, Dore 117). Liberalism and nationalism, paradoxically, worsened the subjugation of Indigenous communities. With the enshrinement of private property, communal lands were expropriated and granted to entrepreneurial patrones, while the former owners of these lands were called to work for these patrones in the name of national progress (Dore 159). In "North American Slavery," Reséndez shows how actively the Mexican state legislated on issues of peonage, symbolically giving its blessing to the practice of serfdom. The state recommended ways to keep accounts with illiterate laborers, prohibited or encouraged flogging and locking up runaway laborers, allowed laborers to abandon masters who did not pay, or prohibited laborers from ever leaving their masters. Legal documents show how widespread this form of involuntary servitude was. One governor rejected the corporal punishment of peons because it would have affected one-third of his state's population (Reséndez 605). In the state of Yucatán, the lucrative industry of growing a plant for making binder twine resulted in the enslavement of three thousand Koreans, eight thousand Yaqui Indians, and 125,000 Mayas (606). Elizabeth Dore explains that the patrón symbolically represented the father of his peons. This patriarchal arrangement made the coerced social and political subjugation of large groups of Indigenous and mestizo communities to the senior male appear natural (Dore 131). Workers continued to offer their labor and obedience because they expected the patrón to reciprocate with help and protection. One peasant inherited land but continued to sign up as a peon for thirty years longer, hoping all the while to find a good patrón (Dore 112). Social and political subordination to a patrón was a public and personal duty for large groups of the population.

The 1910–1917 Mexican Revolution freed these peasants from their "masters" when the new constitution established rights for this social group the first time in the country's history, including the right to land and labor rights. However, the PRI replaced the landowner–peon relationship with the patrón–client relationship, positioning itself as the master patrón. To incorporate peasants and workers into these new domination networks, the PRI created professional associations for them, Confederación Nacional Campesina (CNC) and Confederación de Trabajadores Mexicanos (CTM). To survive, workers and peasants depended on subsidies, credit, and aid that these organizations provided on a personalized basis, merely to maintain them at a subsistence level (Seffer 204). The leaders of these organizations maintained their leadership positions and workers and peasants received aid because they accepted their place in the clientelist pyramid of subordination and loyalty. Social programs, such as PRONASOL (Programa Nacional de Solidaridad), instituted in 1989 under Carlos Salinas to contain the popular discontent, also operated as a clientelist pyramid. Seffer explains that the PRI's mass clientelism (or corporatism) has been a means to manage social conflict (208). The party claimed that it provided personal aid through these organizations to empower the peasants and the workers. In effect, it worked to fragment the subordinated classes to prevent class-based mobilization and the collective questioning of the regime (Seffer 210).

Clientelist, pyramidal organization of power based on personal loyalty to the patrón is the direct opposite of the impersonal, bureaucratic, and rational organization of power in a democratic society. Although some scholars hoped clientelism would disappear after the electoral defeat of the PRI in 2000 (Holzner 224), it continues to thrive in the atmosphere of competitive politics. Clientelist distribution of resources is "help," "social work," and "support," unless your opponent is doing it—then it is decried as vote-buying (Hagene 156). Despite many efforts to reorganize power structures and establish agencies that track corrupt exchanges, clientelism prevails. Officials continue to seek rents to finance clientelism because the parties they represent must have the resources to distribute in order to win elections (Singer 3). We can see this in the film *Herod's Law* when the new mayor finds the public funds' coffer empty and the regional party boss gives him a copy of the constitution and a gun to fill it. Clientelism fosters impunity for rent-seeking officials because punishing them would weaken the political group as a whole (impunity as a consequence of clientelism is the topic of all films). Politicians resist reforms that would increase transparency and accountability and strengthen the rule of the law (Singer 4). "In Mexico law enforcement and politics are not about public service. There is no culture among bureaucrats and politicians that they owe their loyalty to the public," writes political scientist Tony Payan (20), bringing to mind a scene from *The Crime of Padre Amaro* where a city mayor sternly says to his compadres: "I govern for my people, not for the Party!" "No shit," responds one of them, and all burst into laughter. Former president Enrique Peña Nieto is currently being investigated for corruption and bribery (Rama). In general, despite numerous allegations of corruption, no former Mexican president has been formally charged with corruption before. In the Mexican public administration, "informal practices such as corruption, fraud, bureaucratic patrimonialism, and clientelism have become part of the rules of the game, as meaningful, if not more so, than the many laws and regulations" (Sabet 27). The same informal rules govern the interaction of police with the citizens—police officers solicit bribes and leak information to the perpetrators (Sabet 27). According to the UN Special Rapporteur, 98 percent of crimes go unresolved (Martínez-Fernández 6) because Mexicans fear retaliation from criminals allied with the police. Corrupt security officials enter into clientelist relationships with drug cartels. Genaro García Luna, who oversaw the Mexican federal police from 2006 to 2012, was considered a key force in the fight against drug cartels, but in effect he diverted military operations from them in exchange for bribes. Another top security official, General Salvador Cienfuegos, who oversaw the Mexican army and air force from 2012 to 2018, was identified as The Godfather (El Padrino) of the Sinaloa cartel (Martínez-Fernández 9). He was arrested and charged in the United States. However, when Mexico asked to extradite and investigate him, he was cleared of charges after less than two months, with then-president Andrés Manuel López Obrador calling the US investigation "unprofessional" ("Mexico President Backs Dropping of Drug Case"). During the rule of López Obrador, who positioned himself as the crusader against "the mafia of power," 80 percent of state contracts in 2020 were awarded directly, without public bidding, and many went to his known associates. Relatives and associates of the former president were implicated in corruption scandals, but no one was sanctioned (Loret de Mola).

In the 2010s, Mexican writers, politicians, journalists, and artists were asked by journalists María Scherer and Nacho Lozano whether they agreed with the phrase "We all carry a little priísta inside." This phrase was coined by journalist Carlos Castillo Peraza, who said that the priísta system of informal rules and transactions built on trying to please the boss remains strong in Mexican society. In the interviews, respondents were also asked to describe what their inner priísta looks like. Writer Juan Villoro says, "We have this social amiability that derives not from the need to express ourselves with politeness but from the need to keep social relationships well-oiled [and] from searching for consensus, which we understand not as an agreement for the sake of a common cause but as mutually beneficial pacts between rival groups" (Tenemos una amabilidad social que deriva no de la necesidad de expresarnos con cortesía, sino de la necesidad de mantener relaciones sociales bien aceitadas, la búsqueda de un consenso, no entendido como llegar a acuerdos para una causa común, sino como pactos de beneficio mutuo entre grupos rivales; Scherer and Lozano 13). The reluctance to displease the boss becomes "obedience that leads to ever-increasing levels of courtship, servility, and corruption. The boss is never wrong, and you must please the boss at all costs," says politician Marcelo Ebrard, former head of government of Mexico City (obediencia que lleva a niveles de cortesanía, servilismo y corrupción cada vez mayores. El jefe nunca se equivoca y hay que agradar al jefe como sea; 18). "This is not even obedience, this is submission. This is where [the famous joke] comes from, 'What's the time?—It's whatever time you say, Mister President.' This is submission disguised as discipline," opines journalist Joaquín López-Dóriga (Tampoco es obediencia; es sumisión. De ahí el: "¿Qué hora es? La que usted diga, Señor Presidente." Es sumisión disfrazada de disciplina; 167).

The metaphors these politicians, writers, and artists use to describe informal corrupt political practices in Mexico evoke animalistic, instinctual predation and domination: food chain, chain of complicities, chain of corruption, the mafia, and the army. Roberto Gil Zuarth, president of the Mexican Senate since 2015, says, "It's like a food chain: You begin as a small fish, you grow, you rise in the ranks, you behave yourself, and maybe tomorrow something will come your way, but if you don't behave yourself, it's almost certain that tomorrow nothing will come your way" (Es como una suerte de cadena alimenticia, en la que hoy eres charalito, creces, asciendes, te disciplinas y quizá mañana te toque algo, pero si te indisciplinas, es casi seguro que no te toque mañana; 30). Writer Sabina Berman compares the corrupt political system with "the alcoholic, womanizing father who has other families, who is never home, and who is out painting the town red, so everyone at home is mad at him. Then he comes home and the mother says, 'Be nice to Daddy, he is the giver of everything,' so everyone welcomes him with a smile. This is our political system, and this is the relationship between the citizens and this corrupt father" (el padre mujeriego, borracho, que tiene otras familias, que se ausenta de la casa y se va de juerga y todo mundo en casa se queda muy enojado. Después regresa y entonces la mamá dice 'no vayan a ofender a su papá porque es el dador de todo,' y se le recibe sonriente. Ése es nuestro sistema político y ésa es la correspondencia entre los ciudadanos y ese padre corrupto; 186). There is a consensus that corrupt exchanges between the people in position of authority and the citizens became "a code of unwritten rules," "the priísta code of what you can and cannot say," "everyday cultural practice," and "the pragmatic political code to understand public service as the space of self-enrichment" (78, 104, 122, 144). These frank words, from journalists, artists, and powerful politicians alike, reflect an exasperation with clientelist submission.

Many of these politicians and artists quoted the pyramid metaphor with which Mexican poet and diplomat Octavio Paz described the way the patrones in the Mexican political system view those below them. The *tlatoani* (Aztec ruler) saw the world from the top platform of the truncated pyramid where he stood together with priests offering human sacrifices to ancient gods. The ruler and the priests incarnated the ancient gods, and they accepted the worship of the people massing below them as their due. The new colonial masters inherited the pyramidal structure of power that reflects the serene, eternal, "impersonal continuity of domination" of the tlatoani (continuidad impersonal de la dominación; 311). "The power belonged, without question, to the incarnations of ancient gods and priests whose place was on the top of the pyramid, and now it belongs, also without question, to the successors of the Aztec rulers: the Spanish viceroys and the Mexican presidents" (sus herederos y sucesores: Virreyes, Altezas Serenísimas y Señores Presidentes; 305). The pyramid metaphor appeared in Paz's 1969 essay "A Critique of the Pyramid" ("Crítica de la pirámide"). This is an apposite metaphor. The pyramid now rests on consensual clientelistic submission, with networks of personal loyalties concatenating from the bottom to the top.

Clientelism in Luis Estrada's films

The films I examine show how people are seduced into accepting these informal rules and power relationships. The stories have the narrative arc of a bildungsroman in which well-intentioned, ordinary people begin their pilgrimage to perdition, starting by small concessions to a corrupt patrón. They comply with the easy demands first, as apprentices. By the time they understand what they got themselves into, they already became accomplices. At this point, they either rebel or become corrupt patrones themselves.

Luis Estrada is known for biting satirical films that openly criticize the Mexican political and business elite. His films all feature the corrupt patrón as a wonderfully charismatic and cordial predator with a dazzling smile and clients that are all too eager to respond to his advances. *The Perfect Dictatorship* (*Dictadura perfecta*, 2014) was the highest-grossing Mexican film of the year and the third highest-grossing film of all time in Mexico. The title comes from Mario Vargas Llosa, who called Mexico "a perfect dictatorship" on air in 1990, causing a scandal. The writer made this comment spontaneously during an interview on Televisa, the TV company that prided itself on being the "soldier of the PRI." "So much is Mexico a dictatorship," Vargas Llosa said, "that all Latin American dictatorships since I can remember have tried to create something equivalent to the PRI" (Trevino-Rangel 30). In Vargas Llosa's description, unlike in the Soviet Union or Cuba, the Mexican dictatorship was perfect because it was "camouflaged." Although elections were held regularly, all institutions, unions, and organizations were co-opted by the PRI.

The Perfect Dictatorship demonstrates that political domination is now exercised by and through media companies, which can sell the audience on the politician who pays the most. The media are so powerful that they can fan the flames of any political scandal, extinguish it, or make up a fake scandal, depending on the wishes of the person paying for the coverage. In 2012 it was revealed that PRI presidential candidate Enrique Peña Nieto paid Televisa to manipulate news coverage in his favor (Tuckman, "Mexican Media Scandal"). In Estrada's film, a charming and corrupt governor hires a Televisa-like company to make him president of Mexico. At the beginning of the film, the company airs security camera footage in which the governor sniffs wads of banknotes with delight, having pulled them from a briefcase presented to him by a criminal with whom he is obviously on friendly terms. The audience is made to think that this is democracy at work, where the media ensure that all Mexicans, even the most powerful of them, are equal before the law. The host of the show, with a grave voice and an earnest expression, issues a warning to all the corrupt men in power: "No matter who you are and the party you belong to, we will tell the truth about you to our viewers" and announces an instant poll, "Do you think the governor should resign?" But all this is a simulacrum of democratic transparency and popular participation. People can vote all they want, but this scandal is just a trick to distract their attention from the president's recent blunder in the conversation with an American official that Mexicans will gladly take on jobs that "not even Black Americans want" (an actual remark made by Vicente Fox in 2005, when he was still president).

In the film, the political scandals have no political consequences because media companies have full control over the audience's attention, which they are able to manipulate as they see fit. The charming governor pays an exorbitant bribe to the media company executives and they create a fake news story to present him as a selfless hero. The calls to resign in front of his palace change into cheers and acclamations. The corrupt exchange between the governor and the media executives stresses the fact that democratic transparency in the context of the neoliberal devotion to "the market" simply gave bribery a new format and terminology. Bribery became as legitimate as purchasing a service. The media executive (played by Tony Dalton) begins the exchange with a show of sternness, citing the company's noble "sole commitment to the viewers and, above all, the truth" (único compromiso con el televidente y sobre todo, con la verdad). The governor flashes a dazzling smile and pleads, "Don't tell me there is no other way to do things!" (¡No me diga que no hay otra manera de hacer las cosas!), opening a briefcase stuffed with money. The executive sternly asks whether the money is offered as a bribe or as a donation to the channel's foundation. "Of course, this money is for the foundation!" (¡Claro que estos dineros son para la fundación!) exclaims the governor, relieved to learn this new procedure for offering a bribe. The executive then cites the channel's other commitment: "to ensure the highest dividends for our shareholders" (entregar las mejores cuentas a nuestros accionistas) and pitches to the governor "the Premium Package" of public image improvement for some twenty million dollars. The governor pays no heed to his consternated aides who say that he would need to mortgage the state to raise that money. It dawns on him that he can do better and buy the "package" that would make him president of Mexico. The executive tells him to not get excited, that for this he would really have to mortgage the state, but the governor exclaims, "My great state has money for that and more!" (¡mi gran estado da pa' eso y pa' más!). The deal is concluded. We see that the media executive's commitment to democratic transparency is just a ploy to establish a clientelist relationship with corrupt politicians for the benefit of both parties.

The executive's young apprentice Carlos (Osvaldo Benavides) is instrumental in perpetuating this system. He will do everything to please his patrones, the executive and the corrupt governor, to become a patrón like them. He hatches a plan to organize a kidnapping of two twin little girls from an upper-middle-class family and then have the governor rescue them. This plan is carried out by an army general, secretly contracted by the channel. The channel crew turns this news story into an emotional telenovela. The charismatic and charming Damián Alcázar, who plays the governor, relishes the depravity of his character. With the same bright big smile on his face, the governor bribes, murders, and delivers campaign lines such as "If you give me your trust and work together with me, in the not-too-distant future our Mexico can change!" (Si me dan su confianza y trabajamos juntos, ¡en el futuro no muy lejano nuestro México puede cambiar!). When an honest politician passes proof of the governor's corruption to Carlos, this eager client reports everything to his patrón, the corrupt governor, who subsequently has that politician shot, slandered on TV, and killed. At the film's conclusion, the corrupt governor is inaugurated as president of Mexico. At his side stands Carlos's ex-girlfriend, a telenovela star, whom he passed over to the lustful governor in another corrupt exchange (Peña Nieto married a telenovela star who helped him promote his presidential campaign in 2012. They divorced in 2019). The governor accepts the presidential sash from his predecessor (who looks very much like Peña Nieto). Even the kidnapped girls and their parents, who had suffered so the governor could become president, are co-opted as clients. The girls are offered parts in a telenovela and, as the film ends, they sing *Ode to Joy* on a TV show, completely out of tune, with the parents smiling with pride. The filmmakers overemphasize the new colorful eye-candy cinematography and the always moving camera used in news reporting, attention-capturing techniques that were first developed in the United States and later adopted throughout the world. The public is shown absorbing the glitzy images on the TV screen, mouth agape, clueless of the corrupt exchanges taking place behind that screen. The title's reference to the "perfect dictatorship" leads viewers to conclude that this fake democratic transparency is simply a fun new format for the patrón-client exchanges to continue business as usual. In figure 4.1 we see a police chief and local authorities massing around the corrupt governor to congratulate him, with his aide bending to kiss his hand. The other henchmen stand in line, as it were, to kiss his hand next. The composition of the shot illustrates their symbolic status as peons and the governor's status as patrón.

Estrada pioneered the topic of clientelism in the first film of his quadrilogy, *Herod's Law* (*La ley de Herodes* 1999). It was released just before the 2000

Figure 4.1. Officials line up to kiss the corrupt governor's hand in *The Perfect Dictatorship* (2014).

elections and caused such a scandal that it was said to have contributed to the defeat of the PRI. In the 2000 election, the candidate Vincente Fox from the Partido Acción Nacional won the presidency. The attempts of the PRI and the PAN to sabotage the film brought even more people to the theaters. The director said that the film foreshadowed "a shared feeling of enormous unease, of having had enough" of the priísta culture (una sensación colectiva de un enorme malestar, de un hartazgo; Scherer and Lozano, 107). It is 1949, and the hero (also played by Damián Alcázar), a good-natured janitor, finds out to his surprise that he has been appointed interim mayor of a rural community. He arrives there brimming with enthusiasm and ideas, only to discover that the box with the municipal funds is empty. His patrón, a regional party boss, explains that it is up to him to extract these funds from his constituents and provides him with the party badge, a gun, and a copy of the Constitution. The new mayor quickly becomes corrupt and cruel. He extorts money from the townsfolk and hides it in his copy of the Constitution, carving a hiding place in its pages, in a memorable image of how patrones treat the law. He goes around his village drunk, firing a pistol and shouting that he is the authority in the village. Shortly thereafter, the villagers rebel and try to lynch him, as they did his predecessor. The protagonist narrowly escapes and is promoted in the party hierarchy. In his speech at Congress, he energetically declares that the PRI must remain in power forever to defend the ideals of the Revolution.

Estrada made his following film, *A Marvelous World* (*Un mundo maravilloso*, 2006), six years after the 2000 defeat of the PRI. This film mocks the cynical neoliberal policymakers of Vicente Fox's government and marvels at the readiness of the people they impoverished to please them. In the film, the new head of the Department of the Economy cuts subsidies and public sector jobs and argues that to fight poverty one should simply wait until the poor starve and die. We see broad swaths of the population who lost their jobs and fell into utter poverty. One of them is a good-natured homeless man (again Damián Alcázar), who becomes the symbol of the opposition to neoliberalism, by accident and much to his surprise. One night, he climbs onto the rooftop of Mexico City's World Trade Center building to sneak into a hotel room to spend the night but is discovered by the police and the media. When the journalists pressure him to confirm that he was going to publicly commit suicide to protest the government's austerity measures, the hero answers with a sly smile, "If you say I was, then I was, but if you say I wasn't, then I wasn't" (Si usted dice que sí, pues sí; si usted dice que no, pues no). Government officials promise him money and a house, so he says that he climbed the building to show his support for the government. After that, the hero is thrown into jail. The cheaply built house given to him by the government officials collapses on itself. The film ends with an oneiric sequence: the hero and his other homeless friends are shown eating and enjoying themselves in the comfort and décor of a suburban home, in slow motion, with dreamy faces. We wonder if they somehow finally got lucky, but the camera rolls back and we see the bodies of the owners and their children in the garden, whom the heroes have killed. Sayak Valencia explains this unexpected and unrepentant cruelty in *Gore Capitalism*. Neoliberalism and globalization made many people redundant and, on top of that, convinced them that they should look for happiness in consuming more and more things. This is when people become what she calls "*endriago* subjects"—they entrepreneurially engage in crime and killing, to be not a victim but a success (26). What they seek cannot be obtained by working because there is no more honest well-paying work, so they have recourse to necroempowerment (crime and killing), just like the entrepreneurial clients in Estrada's films.

Another charismatic patrón and his good-natured client are featured in Estrada's 2010 film *Hell* (*El infierno*). Deported from the United States back to his town in northern Mexico, the hero (also played by Damián Alcázar) discovers that drugs have become his town's sole business. The city mayor, the chief of police, and top antinarcotics agents and officers run errands for the short-fused local drug lord (Ernesto Gómez Cruz). The hero begins working as a mechanic but joins the cartel when his friend tells him to, enjoying the easy money and pretty women. When he learns how deep corruption runs, he decides to report everything to a professional-looking agent who works for the new security agency created to oversee the existing corrupt ones. The

Figure 4.2. The police chief and the mayor kiss the drug lord's hand in *Hell* (2010).

agent obligingly thanks him and makes a call to the drug lord. At the end of the film, the protagonist brings a machine gun to the rally at which the drug lord publicizes his candidacy for the position of mayor, guns down the corrupt people on the stage, and is himself gunned down. The film explains that the war on drugs is not leading anywhere because the cartels enlist or coerce the loyalty of the public officials. The scene in figure 4.2 depicts the mayor promising that he and his compadre the police chief will do everything possible to make the drug lord happy, after which they take turns kissing his hand and rush out, with a telling gesture of adjusting their pants. Earlier, when the hero (Alcázar) was presented to the drug lord, he also kissed his hand. The officials call the drug boss "don José," but his workforce call him patrón or, if referring to him, his wife, and his son, patrones. In other words, in the film, the drug business is run like a patriarchal hacienda. All characters are bonded to the patrón's household, like the peons of old.

Luis Estrada marveled that he was the first Mexican filmmaker to tackle government corruption with the political satire genre. He sees filmmaking as an opportunity to explain to audiences how corruption works:

> It's a curious thing: *Herod's Law* was the first film in the history of Mexican cinema that spoke about the PRI and the corruption and impunity that surrounded its reign for seventy years. *Dictadura perfecta* is the first film in the history of Mexican cinema that satirizes the president. This sounds weird. Because in any real democracy—and we'll talk about whether this country is really a dictatorship or a democracy or what—this is something common, everyday. (interview with Partlow)

The director knows that cinema reaches wide audiences and explains complex issues with symbols. For him, filmmaking is not only an artistic pursuit but also a citizen's duty: "I'm not a political scientist, I'm not an analyst, I'm not a politician. I'm a film director, a screenwriter, who works with fiction, who works with satire. . . . I'm also a citizen. I'm also a person who has been worrying about this country and trying to understand it for many years. I'm passionate about history" (interview with Partlow). A reviewer of the film expressed the same idea: "To see a pompous intellectual attack a TV company on a university TV program is not the same as watching an actor portray the anchor of the most important Mexican evening news program who manipulates his sources" (Cueva). The director also understands his films as a duty of a father to a son, saying that he made *The Perfect Dictatorship* because he became a father (Pablo Trapero expressed the same idea when speaking of his film *The Clan*, discussed in chapter 3). For the director, it is a moral obligation to explain that corruption affects everyone because it "has become an integral part not only of our culture, but our idiosyncrasy, our way of comprehending reality" (interview with Scherer and Lozano, 107). We see that Estrada wants to expose the strong perceived need to seek out a patrón and go along with whatever he does.

Damián Alcázar, the actor featured in all Estrada's films discussed above, is a patrón in two films and a client in two other films. That is to say, he either kisses other people's hands or has his hand kissed. This interchangeability of roles means that the system will make everyone a patrón or a client, and no one can refuse to participate. There is a lot of physical contact between men in the patrón-client relationship, a lot of backslapping to charm them, hand-kissing to seal the domination arrangement, and, in some cases, there is rape (when the client is a woman) and even killing of the client. This intimate, bodily rapport forced by the handsy patrón on the client dispenses with rules and ceremonies and can easily change from pleasurable to lethal on the client's end, as is the case of most clients in Estrada's films. If they are not killed, they become like the patrones, ruthless and unprincipled. The physicality of the patrón-client relationship brings out its total inappropriateness.

Padres and Compadres in *The Crime of Padre Amaro*

The Crime of Padre Amaro (*El crimen del Padre Amaro*, 2002) was nominated for the Best Foreign Language Film Oscar. It was the biggest box office draw in Mexico ever, attracting over 800,000 viewers on the first weekend. Roman Catholic groups in Mexico called it "a work full of hate towards our Holy Church and priesthood" (una obra cargada de odio hacia nuestra Santa Iglesia and sacerdocio). The conservative PAN government also took it as an affront (Aznárez). The film retells a controversial 1885 Portuguese novel, transforming its corrupt hero into a sympathetic man to explain how clientelism works. The patrón in this film is a charismatic backslapping bishop, and the hand-kissing client is a recent seminary graduate. The handsy bishop is all smiles with his young client and if they walk together he always leads him by the elbow. It is really remarkable that this patron–client relationship is the central point of the film, considering that it did not even exist in the Portuguese novel that inspired it. So daringly did the film lay bare these intimate and corrupt relationships that it became an instant success with audiences and the object of fierce attacks by the parties who felt offended.

The client character, played by Gael García Bernal, is complex and sympathetic. He has the intention of doing good for the community entrusted to him, but just as eagerly follows the corrupt example of his patrones. When his reckless actions lead to a disaster, he sincerely weeps and mourns, but he will not confess that he is responsible. We see that he will soon get over his grief and continue his immoral and dishonest actions, even though they make him uncomfortable. Director Carlos Carrera explained that he wanted a likable Amaro and looked for an actor "who projected goodness" (que proyectara bondad). Accordingly, actor Gael García Bernal "set out looking for ways to love his character and to identify with him" (fue a buscar la forma de querer a su personaje para identificarse con él; Carrera's interview by Fernández). The novel's exceptionally violent and vile Amaro became not only ordinary but likable in the film. This is what the director's objective was: "I just wanted to portray the moral descent of a character, which is something that could happen to any of us" (Rodríguez 62). Together, the director and the actor created the same type we saw in Estrada's films: a man with good intentions but also a client's soul, all too eager to pawn himself to the charming backslapping patrón. Mexican critic Luis García Orso felt sympathy for Padre Amaro and thought that such characters "mirror us all in some aspect of our human itinerary. . . . They are men with hopes and temptations, who feel the joy of their ministry and sadness at their mistakes, who feel the pain of others, illness, solitude, sexual attraction, confusion, the blinding sway of power and ambition" (nos reflejan a todos algo de nuestro propio itinerario humano. . . . hombres con ilusiones y con tentaciones, con las alegrías de su ministerio y las tristezas de sus errores, que sienten el dolor de los otros, la enfermedad, la soledad, la atracción sexual, la confusión, la ceguera del poder y la ambición; Orso 101). In contrast, American critic Stanley Kauffmann found Father Amaro immoral and unforgivable: "And for all these aberrant actions, what does he suffer? Nothing. Hawthorne's Dimmesdale ends with exposure and death.

Padre Amaro just goes on being a priest, apparently in the belief that expiation lies in priestly service, as before" (24). In these clashing appraisals we see that the film gives clientelism a human, sympathetic face in its main character. The intention, however, is not to whitewash clientelism but to show that it leads to perdition, of the hero and the community that he leads.

The film is based on an 1875 novel of the same title by Portuguese writer Eça de Queirós. In this novel, Amaro is mean, violent, and corrupt from beginning to end. He joins other corrupt priests who masquerade as Portugal's spiritual leaders. After graduating from the seminary, Amaro arrives in Leiria, a town in central Portugal. Amaro realizes that as a priest, he is important and powerful. Rich widows generously reward the attention he gives to their perverse religious fantasies. Violent and lustful, often compared to a raging bull, Amaro finds priestly duties and abstinence morbid. Realizing that his mentor, Canon Dias, lives with his widowed landlady as husband and wife, Amaro quickly seduces the landlady's teenage daughter Amalia. When she gets pregnant and threatens to tell everyone to convince him to marry her and keep the baby, he beats her. He sends her away to give birth in secret and takes his newborn son to a sham foster mother who kills her charges. Amalia soon dies from grief. Amaro moves to the capital and jokes with Canon Dias that he now only has affairs with married women. Amaro and Dias lead the entire nation to moral and intellectual degradation. In the last pages, the two priests meet a politician who thanks them for keeping Portugal out of trouble, saying, "Look at this peace, this prosperity, this contentment! Other countries envy us while we have respectable clergymen like you," and both priests reply, "Without a doubt" (351). Portugal remained a monarchy until 1910—much longer than its neighbors, France and Spain. Eça de Queirós blames it on the alliance of the conservative ruling class and the priests.

In the screen adaptation, the story comes alive in modern-day Mexico to expose the corrupt *compadrazgo* between the priests, drug traffickers, and the town and party officials. The parish priest, Amaro's mentor, accepts money from a drug lord to build a world-class hospital. The bishop launders these "donations" and the mayor helps out as well. The bishop intimidates journalists who dare to unveil these corrupt exchanges and excommunicates the sole good priest who wants to help his community, which has been oppressed by drug traffickers. Ernesto Gómez Cruz (who played the patrón in Estrada's *Hell* discussed above) shines as the corrupt bishop, making his character's absolute lack of moral principles almost lovable by deploying his charismatic cordiality, just like Damián Alcázar in *The Perfect Dictatorship*. The bishop establishes a physical rapport with Amaro and then asks him to carry out immoral tasks for him as a personal favor. Under the influence of this corrupt patrón, the young seminary graduate soon finds himself breaking most of the commandments. It is symbolic that these commandments are chanted at the film's beginning. Amelia (Ana Claudia Talancón), whom Amaro is seducing, recites the commandments to her young Sunday school students during the catechism lesson in a playful way, and they chant them in chorus after her. Amaro and Amelia exchange an enamored look just before one of the kids inquires what the word "formicate" (fornicate) means. In this symbolic scene, Amaro does not know yet that he will take God's name in vain, bear false witness, commit adultery, and even kill.

Gael García Bernal plays Amaro with his trademark ambiguity (filmmaker Alejandro Iñárritu said that he has "the face of a good boy who could also be a son of a bitch" [una cara de niño bueno que podía ser un hijo de la chingada]). Amaro is likable and disarming in his selfish weakness. The opening scene shows that he means well and intends to help people as a good priest should. As he rides the bus to his new parish, he listens compassionately to an old man in the seat next to him who plans to open a business with his savings. When robbers hold up the bus, the old man loses his savings and Amaro gives him some of his money. Amaro also admires the film's only good priest, Natalio (Damián Alcázar) and loves Amelia. He frantically drives the bleeding girl to the hospital after the back-alley abortion and weeps disconsolately when she dies on the way. In the last scene, the transfixed and trembling Amaro, with tears streaming down his face, begins Amelia's funeral service with "Forgive me, Father, for I have sinned." The congregation intones Amaro's prayer. They have no idea that Amaro is confessing to having caused Amelia to die and asking for their forgiveness. Amaro appears frightened and profoundly repentant. But who, if not Amaro himself, had spread the rumors that Amelia's pregnancy was her former boyfriend's doing?

Unlike his literary counterpart, Amaro becomes corrupt under the influence of corrupt patrones. The director said, "In the novel he has a corrupt soul from the start. In the movie we wanted to show the moral fall of the character. Amaro arrives with good intentions," "turns into a survivor of power structures, and then does everything to keep his position of power" (Carrera, "El conflicto"). Indeed, Amaro cannot say no to his desires or to the enticements of a corrupt patrón. Each time he acquiesces in a corrupt practice, he knows it, and his face expresses an almost physical discomfort. He sees that his mentor Father Benito (Sancho Gracia) lives with a woman but, instead of confronting him, he begins an affair himself. Amaro knows that Father Benito attends parties given by the local drug lord and is building his dream community hospital with the drug money. But when this information appears in the local newspaper and the bishop asks Amaro to make them publish a

Figure 4.3. Amaro kisses the bishop's hand in *The Crime of Father Amaro* (2002).

retraction, Amaro cannot say no. Next the bishop entrusts Amaro with bringing the threat of excommunication to the good priest Natalio to dissuade him from supporting his parishioners as they fight off drug traffickers. The bishop also receives money from the traffickers so he protects them by portraying the resisting peasants as anti-government guerrillas. Amaro knows that this is not true and that Natalio is the only good priest he has ever met. He even makes a half-hearted attempt to defend Natalio before the bishop. But when the bishop hints that he picked him as his successor, Amaro forgets his objections. We see him kiss the bishop's hand as the bishop looks on, sealing their client–patrón contract (figure 4.3). Recall that Ernesto Gómez Cruz, who plays the bishop, also has his hand kissed in *Hell* (figure 4.2), as the fearful drug lord whom his employees and the city authorities call patrón. Actually, Amelia kisses Amaro's hand too at the beginning of their romance, bringing out the erotic inappropriateness of this ritual.

In the film, Amaro's mentor, Father Benito, is also earnest and sympathetic, unlike his Portuguese prototype, the cynical Canon Dias. He wants his parishioners to have a hospital and sees no ethical problem in accepting drug money for this noble objective. This plotline is based on facts. In 2005, when the Pope expressed concern over reports that the Mexican Church accepted money from drug traffickers, bishop Ramón Godínez Flores objected that Jesus did not ask Mary Magdalene where she got the money to purchase the expensive perfume with which she washed his feet. A noble purpose can transform money, said the cardinal: "You don't have to burn the money only because its origin is bad. You have to transform it instead. All money can be transformed, just as a corrupt person can become transformed" (Bañuelos). Also unlike his literary counterpart, Father Benito genuinely loves the woman he lives with, Amelia's mother. Amelia is his daughter in the film and he tries, unsuccessfully, to protect her from Amaro. At Amelia's funeral, Benito is the only person who knows that Amaro is the cause of his daughter's death. In a wheelchair from the heart attack caused by suppressed grief, he frantically turns and rolls out of the church unable to watch Amaro hold a service for her. Benito, like Amaro, started with good intentions, but in pawning himself to the corrupt patrón he accomplished the opposite of what he wanted to do. Compared to his callous novel counterpart, Canon Dias, who makes sexual advances toward Amelia after learning about her affair with Amaro, Benito is a good man who lost his way.

Scriptwriter Vicente Leñero, who also wrote the script for Estrada's *Herod's Law* discussed above, explained that everyone, including journalists, were clients of the government during the PRI rule. He recounted how newspaper owners and journalists had no choice but to be clients of the government because "the government was the owner of everything, even paper. You couldn't publish a newspaper if you couldn't get paper. This is why journalists agreed to little concessions, some of which were quite corrupt, for example, selling eight columns of your newspaper for a specified amount" (interview with Day 19). To get access to paper and resources, newspapers published pro-government content for a fee, "as if they were ads" (como si fueran anuncios). Business owners were also clients of the government, and if the government punished a newspaper by withdrawing its paid content, so did business advertisers (interview with Day 20). These "small acts of treasons, small transactions, ideological, mental, or personal ones, difficult to gauge or evaluate" were routine (Day 20). Leñero said that the Mexican Catholic Church was hostile to the film for exposing it as a clientelist pyramid: "What made the Church hierarchs and their acolytes so angry was that we denounced how corruption and power turns a loyal priest into a parish priest, a loyal parish priest into a bishop, a loyal bishop into a cardinal" (interview with Cherem 18). The scriptwriter intentionally made Amaro into a client, which was not at all the case in the novel on which the film is based.

The director, who likes to make films about "very ordinary and common" people (Carrera, interview by Fernández), and the scriptwriter, incensed by corrupt exchanges, changed the Portuguese source story to explain clientelism in Mexico as a pervasive, understandable, and even expected behavior. The film shows that submitting to corrupt patrones insidiously corrupts the individual and the community. As a viewer commented, the film is about "the ladder of sin" (*The Crime of Padre Amaro:* User Reviews). This is Father Benito's realization, as he watches Amaro, the younger version of himself, repeat his mistakes and worse. The despair in Benito's eyes indicates that Amaro's apprenticeship is complete. Amaro became a new unprincipled father for the congregation and, with him as leader, the congregation is in an even worse position than with Benito. Like the characters of Estrada's films, Amaro too is a "sujeto endriago:" he does not make mistakes in choosing the right patrón. Now he is kissing the bishop's hand, soon many other people will have to kiss his.

Wife as Client in *Tear This Heart Out*

This 2008 film features another charming backslapper: a corrupt governor of Puebla with ambitions to become president of Mexico. The story is set in the first decades of the twentieth century. The politician recruits a beautiful, young, inexperienced girl as his wife and client to appear at his side at rallies, write his campaign speeches, and not meddle in his corrupt dealings. Here the physical contact the patrón forces on his client–wife to establish rapport is sexual seduction and, at times, disciplinary rape, to show her who is the master when she makes attempts at insubordination. For her services, the wife receives expensive presents, such as a mansion in the capital, and the position of social visibility. It is interesting that the heroine of the 1985 novel of the same name that inspired the film accepts her submission as fate and becomes more and more complicit until she loses all will to resist him. The novel uses marriage and family to show how the clientelist system works. Corrupt men come together during intimate family dinners and wives, cognizant of their husbands' corrupt dealings, organize these meetings and keep out. They accept their subservient status and discuss "births, servants, and hairdos" (85). Generals, politicians, union leaders, and other powerful men eat separately from the women. They call each other *compadres* (this word appears 31 times) and *amigos* (58 times), which means they are either patrones and clients or patrones of equal standing. At these intimate dinners, they strike their deals and decide how to frame them by means of public policy. Men engage in so much physical touching that the wife marvels at them. She thinks they do it because they cannot express affection toward each other like female friends do: "the men began to embrace and clap one another on the back. Men are priceless. Since they can't kiss, or say sweet things, or rub one another's swelling bellies, they do all that hugging and thumping, accompanied by loud talk and guffaws. I can't imagine what they see in it" (122). But we know that this is the way to establish personal rapport to dispense with ceremonies and laws as meaningless formalities and to replace them with personal favors. It is to establish client–patrón relationships that they embrace, hug, and clap each other on the back.

The most ambitious of these men, Andrés Ascencio, is constantly touching, hugging, and slapping someone on the back. It is no coincidence that the first thing his future wife feels when she meets him is his arm on her shoulder. He establishes a physical rapport with her before even saying his first words to her: "Suddenly he put his hand on my shoulder and said, 'Isn't it true that they're all assholes?'" (pendejos; 1). Catalina is not even fifteen yet, but she immediately responds to his ambition and charisma. She too is ambitious and wants to be important and special. Andrés takes her to the sea to establish sexual contact with her, during which she feels nothing and tells him so. He could not care less: the physical rapport he initiates with people is one-way and predatory in nature; he aims to establish influence over them, not to be influenced by them. Soon he tells her to prepare for the wedding. She is surprised but complies. At the ceremony, she is surprised he does not let her sign her maiden name on the marriage certificate or allow her to order the juice she is used to having at meals during the wedding celebration. She appeals to her father to get the juice, and the waiter stands at attention waiting for a senior male to confirm or cancel the order made by a woman. When her father tells the waiter to bring the order, Andrés disciplines him: "remember that she isn't your little girl anymore and that at this table, I am in charge" (Acuérdese que ella ya no es su niña y que en esta mesa mando yo; 13). He seems to like that Catalina is feisty and has a mind of her own because he obtains more enjoyment from dominating someone who resists. Early on, dissatisfied with her first sexual encounter with her husband, she seeks information on how women achieve orgasm. She feels bored with other wives and would rather go talk to the men, even though she knows it is not "proper" (no era correcto; 85). Once she opposes her husband at dinner and he reminds her afterward that she is a woman and should know her place. Catalina is intelligent and curious, and Andrés likes making her do what he knows she objects to, with jokes and physical contact, including forcing sex on her.

The charismatic Andrés effortlessly charms everyone and is the center of attention at all parties and meetings. A skillful public speaker, he talks of serving the poor even as he confiscates their land and possessions through intermediaries. He talks about protecting workers, while personally killing striking workers to break strikes. He grows immensely rich and powerful; becomes governor, then senator; and plans to become president. Catalina aids his ascension. At first, she enjoys the freedom of wealth—horse riding, traveling, and owing properties by the sea and in the capital, servants, and attention. When she learns that her husband has other women and does not think twice about eliminating people who thwart his plans, she cannot bring herself to leave this life. When he brings home his children from another woman, she accepts them. When she learns her husband is behind mysterious assassinations, she remains with him. She is unable to leave behind her grand house and the privileges that come with it. Only once does she try to leave Andrés, but she cannot stand riding the bus with uncouth commoners and returns home (55). Eventually, Catalina accepts his behavior as appropriate for a man of his standing. She cannot bring herself to confront him, even when he orders the killing of the man she fell in love with, musician Carlos, her husband's childhood friend. Perhaps Andrés kills Carlos out of jealousy, although it is also likely that he wants to punish Carlos for challenging his status as a patrón. Carlos provided support to his political opponents and even, as his friend, had the guts to tell him to stop interfering in union elections.

Catalina's reactions to these attacks on her feelings and dignity are that of a client who cannot even think of defying or leaving the patrón. Instead of becoming angry at her husband, who she knows is behind Carlos's assassination, she lashes out at her dead lover: "Why did he have to get mixed up in politics? Why didn't he stick to conducting his orchestra, composing his strange music, talking with friends and poets, and fucking me? Why this idiotic rage for politics?" (¿Por qué se metía en política? ¿Por qué no se dedicaba a dirigir su orquesta, a componer música rara, a platicar con sus amigos poetas y a coger conmigo? ¿Por qué la fiebre idiota de la política?; 216). She has his tomb filled with the flowers her lover admired when they made love in the field the day before, although when she throws some in herself, she snaps, "Now you have your flowery grave, imbecile" (Ya tienes tu tumba de flores, imbécil; 229). When she learns Andrés has killed peasants to expropriate their communal lands, she demands an expensive horse. When he arranges "an accident" to get rid of his daughter's inconvenient boyfriend and marries her off to his *compadre*'s son, both the daughter and Catalina demand a Ferrari. Even after Carlos's murder, Catalina continues to sleep with Andrés. She writes campaign speeches for him, painting him as a champion of the common man, "at the service of each and every one of you," working "for tranquility and progress," and he praises her: "one would think you're a man" (pareces hombre; 273).

Like other clients of corrupt *patrones*, Catalina changes under Andrés's influence. She becomes lethargic, burdened by the guilt of complicity with a bad man in exchange for favors. She copies him. Andrés takes mistresses and Catalina takes lovers. He abandons the children, and so does she (this can hardly be interpreted as feminist resistance, like some critics suggest—Lavery

204; Bailey 140; Bodevin 166). He lies, and she lies too. She would have drifted through life like that until her death, but one day, a wife of a peasant her husband killed comes to see her and gives her a poisonous herb. Catalina is in no haste to use the poison and does not think about it. Only when Andrés fails to secure the presidency and feels that his luck has run out does she begin serving him the poisonous tea. As he gets weaker and weaker, she continues to tell Andrés that he will get better soon and lies with him until he dies. After his death, she continues talking to him in her head, scolding him for not leaving her alone even from the grave, because now she must deal with all the other wives.

Andrés is as irresistible as the other patrones I examine here. The writer said she wanted to show that Andrés, "as any cacique and dictator," is "charismatic, enchanting, funny, and full of life and even though he is arbitrary and devastating with people, people like and love him" (Mastretta, "Women" 37; "La escritura" 332). It is interesting that the person who wrote the script in the new century could not fathom how Catalina could stand living with such a corrupt and cruel man. The writer relates her conversation with the scriptwriter:

> The woman who was writing the script would come and tell me, "But I just don't get how this woman can continue living with this man who she thinks killed her lover. How can she keep living with him?" And I'd tell her, "Well, if you don't get that, you don't get this character. This character is not me." I wouldn't have been able to keep living there, but I'm not her. She had no choice but to live there and she knew that from the beginning of the book, because she does leave her house but comes back. She can't be away from it even for a day. She boards a bus, and she realizes that she can't, she asks herself, "What kind of life is this?" And she goes back. She has no energy to leave or to fight, and she knows it. (Mastretta, "La escritura" 332)

The scriptwriter's incapacity to understand such protracted, masochistic tolerance for corrupt authority means that it no longer seems plausible in the new century, and the film adaptation reflects that. The novel's achievement is to show that it is next to impossible for people socialized in patrón–client relationships to leave their patrón, no matter how corrupt, because they do not see themselves outside of this relationship. Mastretta said that the novel is about "the bad habits of doing politics from which continue to affect us" (los malos hábitos de hacer política que aún padecemos; "Entre la aventura"). Daniel Giménez Cacho, who played Andrés in the film adaptation, said that these corrupt practices shaped the Mexico of today: "The film shows how our

Figure 4.4. Andrés gives Catalina a slap on the behind to speed her up in *Tear This Heart Out* (2008).

system was born and forged, how the seeds of degradation in which we live today were planted.... We are children of fraud, hypocrisy, and impunity" (se ve el nacimiento de cómo se forja nuestro sistema y cómo se van sembrando las semillas de la degradación que vivimos actualmente.... somos hijos del fraude, de la simulación, de la impunidad; Caballero). Roberto Sneider, who directed the adaptation, highlights Catalina's complicity: "she loves the benefits provided by the power which she sustains" (ama los beneficios que le trae el poder que sustenta). The audience will find this behavior familiar, says the director: "We recognize ourselves in these characters and we learn how we are complicit in the fact that these kinds of relationships have endured until today, in love and in politics" (nos reconocemos en esos personajes y terminamos por descubrir de qué forma somos cómplices de que ese tipo de relaciones exista hasta nuestros días, tanto en el terreno amoroso como el político; Sneider). The filmmaker defines his objective to reveal clientelist political subordination disguised as friendship and kinship.

Catalina (Ana Claudia Talancón) in the film also loves her privilege and wealth at first. In the film Andrés enjoys bodily and morally seducing and domineering Catalina as much as in the book as is evidenced by the slap on the behind he administers to her in figure 4.4. The change between the book and film, however, is Catalina's willingness to endure this domination. Very soon, she becomes confrontational. She resists, disagrees, and takes action. She stands up to her husband. Catalina's stance in this adaptation is the opposite of the subservient posture of the hand-kissing clients in the films discussed above. In the film, she remains with her husband out of fear: he threatens to kill her if she leaves him, saying that there can be widowed presidents but not divorced ones (hay presidentes viudos pero no divorciados). In the scene where she boards the bus to leave Andrés, his bodyguard compels her to return. In contrast, in the novel Catalina is free to leave at any time. Also, we do not see her demanding horses, Ferraris, or other luxuries in exchange for her subordination in the film.

In addition, the cinematic Catalina is more moral. The scriptwriter resisted including even Catalina's first lover, a childhood friend she turns to for comfort after she sees Andrés with another woman, until the novelist insisted (Mastretta, "La escritura" 332). In the film, Catalina never takes another lover after Carlos, unlike in the book. After Carlos's death in the film, Catalina openly weeps over his body, unafraid of Andrés, whom she kicks out of her bedroom and does not sleep with again. This Catalina seeks out the poisonous herb herself to avenge Carlos. She poisons Andrés at the apogee of his might, as he prepares to assume the presidency, rescuing not only herself but also the entire nation from this corrupt man. The complicit and lethargic heroine of the 1985 novel becomes an agent of change in the 2008 film. Catalina puts an end to her handsy patrón and to her physical and moral subordination to him, setting an example for audiences. Sánchez Prado argues that this film is "uninteresting" and that it "erases Mastretta's subtle critique of the PRI regime" (111). The film has a different point to make. The heroine no longer wants to kiss the hated hand and rescripts the behavior of always acquiescing in the face of a corrupt authority.

Conclusion

The films examined in this chapter illuminate another face of predatory leadership: the patrón who smiles, hugs and slaps on the back, and then demands total submission. Forcing on people this physical rapport masked as friendship and kinship, the leader establishes domination. This domination is modeled on debt servitude, in which peons obeyed and worked for the patrón in exchange for "protection" that more often than not never materialized. Socialized into the contemporary version of this social practice, known as clientelism, people find it natural to have a patrón and surrender their political agency. It is the clients' eagerness to comply with a corrupt patrón and enlist in his service that all these films expose and show as wrong. As we watch the films, we feel a desire to tell these people, "Stop, don't do that!" as they prepare to comply with their patrón's next immoral request, even though they know that it is a wrong thing to do. The films instill a visceral repudiation not only of this cordial backslapping predator with a big smile but also of his unreasonably servile clients. We can see this repudiation in the viewers' reactions to these films on IMDb. Viewers of *The Perfect Dictatorship* found it difficult to laugh because it felt "too real," so much so that they felt "stuck" and "hurt." One viewer wrote, "I can't explain how I felt while watching the movie. Every single detail is so real that it hurts. I could simply replace the names of the characters with the names of real politicians. Our countries in South America are experiencing everything that is shown in the movie." Other viewers wrote that the film felt "too real," "too realistic," "a realistic window into Mexico." Another impressed viewer declared that "every Latino person MUST watch this movie, and it should be watched in colleges" (*The Perfect Dictatorship*: User Reviews). The film *Tear This Heart Out* also felt "so accurate" because "nothing has ever changed really," wrote a viewer. Attending the packed premiere in Puebla, where the events in the film take place, another viewer wrote, "Some nervous laughter could be heard from the members of the finest families of the region. You do guess what they thought of this portrait" (*Tear This Life Out*: User Reviews). The controversial *Crime of Padre Amaro* compelled more than a hundred viewers to express how they felt. They say the film shows "how Mexico really is," "just the way it is in the real Mexico," "so realistic that it scares." The film has a physical impact: it is "disturbing," "powerful," "hard to watch," "shocking," "stuck in my mind," "wow," "everyone was walking out of the theater with a 'wow' face," "makes you think, makes you experience, like good movies do." These reactions show that films are not just stories about a corrupt governor, a wife oppressed by her husband, or a priest who fell in love but also metaphors for a society built on misplaced loyalties. The viewers come to realize that clients seeking corrupt patrones are also to blame because they perpetuate the corrupt system. This is why the viewers find it difficult "to know who to root for," the predatory husband or his complicit wife in *Tear This Heart Out*, and cannot pity Amaro because going along with the bad patrón's requests "damages you until the day you lay to rest." "The so-called 'abused' are no better," says one viewer, "probably equally corrupt and greedy if they get the chance to be so" (*The Crime of Padre Amaro*: User Reviews). The films instill a rejection of both the patrones and the clients—that is to say, they compel us to reject the corrupt system as a whole.

5

The Scold

Leadership as Emotional Abuse in Brazil

In this chapter, I look at several recent Brazilian films about fathers who do not love their sons. These films and/or novels on which they are based are inspired by Franz Kafka's writings. As a child, Kafka was tyrannized, ridiculed, and scolded by his father to such a degree that even as an adult he could not overcome his feelings of shame and guilt. To avoid becoming like his father, he never married. He died at the age of forty. In *Brainstorm*, *To the Left of the Father*, and *Behind the Sun*, the father would rather have his son killed or committed to a mental institution than let him escape from his control. The stories that inspired the films were composed during Brazil's last military dictatorship (1964–1985). Amazingly, when they were adapted to the screen in the twenty-first century, the abused sons stood up to their fathers. Interestingly, Kafka's father called him an "Ungeziefer," a parasitic insect sometimes translated as "cockroach" (the Nazis later called the Jews this same word). Being called that made Kafka write the famous story *Metamorphosis*, in which a shy and obedient son turns into a giant insect, a repulsive, nonhuman being that anybody can kill at any time. This condition, theorized as "bare life" (Agamben) and "the living dead" (Mbembe) became the topic of several famous Brazilian films—*City of God*, its sequel *City of Men*, and *Elite Squad*. The heroes are residents of poor urban enclaves (favelas) and because they are perceived as "vagabundos" and "marginais" (delinquents), they can be killed with impunity at any time. In line with the general trend to demand social and political rights for "the sons," *City of God* and its sequel give their heroes a future and make the audience care for them, unlike the novel on which they are based. This is how films on the symbolic level shape a demand for a nonabusive political leadership. For the first decade and a half of the new century (2002–2016), Brazil's presidents responded to this demand. Lula da Silva and Dilma Rousseff talked about Brazil's poor as citizens whose rights have long been violated and practiced a leadership that does not threaten or ridicule. In contrast, with the film *Elite Squad* and Jair Bolsonaro's presidency, we witness a relapse. The film's policeman executes people as "bare life," seeing them as the "cockroaches" of Kafka's story. This policeman, an abusive character who is also, unsurprisingly, a bad father, should have inspired fear, but many in the audience took him for a hero, an incorruptible tough guy. Many Brazilians voted for Bolsonaro, who also promised that "criminals will die like cockroaches," taking him for such a man. But there are signs that Brazilians came to understand that threats, insults, and mockery hurt the whole nation, not only the groups that he attacked. Bolsonaro's failure to secure a second term show that more Brazilians came to recognize in him the abusive father, a man who screams about law and order only to break laws himself—a lawless man.

Kafka's *Letter to My Father*

When Kafka wrote his famous letter to his father in 1919, the emotional abuse of children had not yet been identified as an issue. Now it is known that emotional abuse is similar to physical abuse in shaping a child's personality for life. Repeated name-calling, mocking, threats, and gaslighting (criticizing to sow self-doubt and confusion in the child's mind) can have a profound and irreversible neurological impact. Victims of emotional abuse may develop post-traumatic stress disorder, depression, inability to trust, failure to thrive, personality disorders, low self-esteem, aggression, anxiety, and emotional unresponsiveness. Abuse negatively impacts feelings about enjoyment of living, prospects for future life, purpose in life, chances of having a happy marriage and expectations for being a good parent (Binggeli et al. 24, 30). Kafka struggled all his life with these consequences, but because victims internalize abuse, he blamed himself almost as much as his father even as he narrated the name-calling, threats, and humiliations to which he was subjected. Shame, guilt, and fear followed him into adulthood, and he was convinced that he was intellectually weak and physically repulsive (Fichter 367). Kafka wrote his famous letter to his father to explain, as the father demanded, why he was "cold, remote" and even "afraid" of him. The father wondered why he was eager to do anything for "strangers" while unwilling to "move a finger" for him, "not even get a theater ticket" (*Letter* 1). "I am the result of your education and my obedience," Kafka explained, and we see the internalized shame and guilt that burdens him (19). We learn that his father's "education talk consisted of abuse, threats, a mocking laugh and peculiar self-pity" (19). Charming with strangers, the father was always "disappointed and depressed at home by your children, particularly me," the writer specifies dejectedly (20). Kafka's father was always resentful and angry, and his children felt it physically: "abuse was scattered everywhere, so your words rang in my mind, and sometimes you were almost deafening" (19). This permanent aggression was unwarranted, and Kafka knows it: "You reproached me without cause" (27), but the guilt and fear continue to haunt him. The writer recalls that one night when he was little and went on whimpering for water, his father swooped him up and left him on the balcony in his nightshirt outside a closed door. Kafka was struck that his father did that to him "almost without reason." Since then, he was always worried the father could do that to him again at any time, and this fear remained with him forever (18). When he did not scold, the father mocked him with sarcastic questions: "Can't you do it properly?" "Have you already too much to do? And so, naturally, you have no time?" (19). He mocked the people his son took interest in and, later on, mocked his fiancées, so Kafka never married. Derision was backed with threats. One graphic threat, "I'll rip you apart like a fish," made a deep impression on the child: "that was dreadful to me, even though I knew that nothing bad would happen (yet as a young child I didn't know this), but your words served as a sign of your power, and you always seemed capable of doing something" (21). Family meals were an opportunity for the father to give everyone a piece of his mind: "You shouted left and right at the table and tried to grab someone—or pretended to—until mother came to rescue" (19). The father would tell one of the children, for example, "She has to sit ten meters from the table, the fat lump," or sit in angry silence, "like an embittered enemy" (23). The father also screamed at his store assistants and threw merchandise on the floor for them to pick up (35). There is nothing one could do to please the father because everything was simply "the occasion for the ever present storm within you to break loose" (23).

Even though he did not recall his father physically striking him, for Kafka it was almost worse because he lived fearing it. He compares his life to the preparation for a hanging that was postponed. Once the prisoner has seen "the noose before his face," he "is left to lament his existence for years" (24). Moments of calm and affection were so rare that Kafka breaks into tears when he remembers one, when he was in bed with a fever one day and his father silently waved at him as a sign of encouragement: "at such times one could lie down and cry for one's good fortune—as I am crying now as I write" (25). The experience of abuse became part of him and, although childhood was far behind him as he wrote the letter, he felt "stuck. I am not twenty years more experienced, just twenty years more wretched" (70).

Kafka's *The Home-Coming* in *To the Left of the Father* (*Lavoura arcaica*)

This sad letter sounds even sadder to know that the mother returned it to the writer unopened by the father. Even though the father demanded explanations of why his grown son was cold with him, deep inside he knew the reason only too well. He refused to acknowledge the secret reality of abuse by not opening the letter. He felt entitled only to gratitude and obedience, as Kafka explains in the letter: "You said that I must thank your work for my lack of need, for my life of peace, warmth and abundance" (30). Kafka paid dearly for this outward comfort, as the scolding father always denied him the right to speak or act on his own: "You denied me any word—'No word of contradiction!' And you threatened me with your raised hand" (19), "whenever I tried to decide anything, you restrained me" (59).

We see this controlling and exigent father in the 1975 novel *Ancient Tillage* by Raduan Nassar (*Lavoura arcaica*), adapted to the screen almost verbatim by Luiz Fernando Carvalho in 2000. The quotations from the novel cited below also appear in the film. The film was given the title *To the Left of His Father* in English, which is a line from the novel that explains where the son sits at the dinner table and signals that this is a wrong side. The director said that the novel is a political metaphor for the collision of the oppressors and the oppressed. He was fascinated by the "alchemy" of Nassar's baroque and metaphorical language (Campi and Pompermaier). The father's house is big and beautiful, but all family members must follow strict rules. At the dinner table, they bow their heads to listen to the father's sermons about "love, union, and our work alongside our father" and "the unique emotional and spiritual ties that bind us" (O amor, a união e o trabalho de todos nós junto ao pai, peculiaridades afetivas e espirituais que nos uniam; 24). Each family member must "participate in the work of the family, bring fruit into the home and help to replenish the common table" (participando do trabalho da família, trazendo frutos para casa, ajudando a prover a mesa comum; 25). The family is a "solid trunk, faithful hand, loving word and wise principles" (o mesmo tronco, a mão leal, a palavra de amor e a sabedoria dos nossos princípios; 25). But even one misstep can destroy this microcosm: "if only one member were to make a false move, the entire family would topple" (bastava que um de nós pisasse em falso para que toda a família caísse atrás; 25). Beyond the confines of the home rage chaos and hostility so the children should "never wander beyond our doorway, always answer our father when he spoke" (não nos afastando da nossa porta, respondendo ao pai quando ele perguntasse; 24). The happiness one could imagine beyond the father's realm is "no more than an illusion" (não passando de ilusão; 50). We will see almost identical statements in the speeches of the military dictator who ruled Brazil when Nassar was writing this novel.

One rebellious son (Selton Mello) flees the family home because he feels stifled and because there is a secret, incestuous passion between him and his sister (Simone Spoladore). He breaks the patriarchal taboo but, in a sense, as Ilja Braun notes, he literally follows his father's teachings that there is nothing worthwhile outside the family home and all pleasures are to be found within: "we have discovered a miracle, above all, we have become whole within the confines of our own home, confirming Father's words that happiness is only found in the bosom of the family" (descobrirmos acima de tudo que nos bastamos dentro dos limites da nossa própria casa, confirmando a palavra do pai de que a felicidade só pode ser encontrada no seio da família; 104). Thus, the fear of the father that his subjects should escape from his control brings a worse disaster on the family—incest.

The older brother brings the prodigal son back to the family home, as in the biblical parable, but the pain and strangeness of this return actually come from Kafka's take on the parable, the short story *The Home-Coming*. In this story, a young man returns to his family home, but everything feels so strange and hostile that he stops in front of the closed kitchen door, behind which he knows he will find his parents. He cannot bring himself to enter that kitchen, as if aliens or monsters were lying in wait for him there: "Who is going to receive me? Who is waiting behind the kitchen door? Smoke is rising from the chimney, coffee is being made for supper. Do you feel you belong, do you feel at home? I don't know, I feel most uncertain" (493). The grownup son stands at the door, listening in: "I hear nothing but a faint striking of the clock passing over from childhood days, but perhaps I only think I hear it. Whatever else is going on in the kitchen is the secret of those sitting there, a secret they are keeping from me. The longer one hesitates before the door, the more estranged one becomes." He cannot bring himself to enter because he, too, has a secret: "What would happen if someone were to open the door now and ask me a question? Would not I myself then behave like one who wants to keep his secret?" (493). This story reverses the prodigal son parable and captures the denied reality of the abusive family. These secrets on both sides are the repressed memories of scolding and shouting, and of humiliations, inflicted and suffered. It is too painful to reenter this secret reality and pretend that it is not there. The why of the abuse always remains an impenetrable secret for the child who has committed no sins or crimes and yet is punished by the very people who must love and protect him. Kafka's prodigal son never makes it home. He escapes in fear that "someone" (the monsters—his parents) would open the kitchen door and see him.

Like Kafka's nameless hero, André, the wayward son from Nassar's novel, is also struck by the eerie silence and emptiness of the house upon his return, even though all the windows are illuminated and everyone is home. André also stops at the kitchen door, where his parents are waiting for him, and also hears the family clock ticking: "rigorously marking the silence, our familiar wall clock was judiciously working through each second" (marcando o silêncio com rigor, estava ali o nosso antigo relógio de parede trabalhando criteriosamente cada instante; 216). Unlike Kafka's hero, André finally enters the kitchen, although he should not have because his secret is too heavy. André's father wants to know why he left, and he is outraged to hear his son say that this loving family environment is "hostile," that it feels like a prison. Just like Kafka's father, he will have none of that. André says:

> You can't expect a prisoner to serve happily in the jailer's house; by the same token, Father, it would be absurd to demand a loving embrace from someone whose arms we've amputated; the only thing that makes less sense is the wretchedness of the maimed person who, lacking hands, applauds his torturer with his feet.

> Não se pode esperar de um prisioneiro que sirva de boa vontade na casa do carcereiro; da mesma forma, pai, de quem amputamos os membros, seria absurdo exigir um abraço de afeto; maior despropósito que isso sô mesmo a vileza do aleijão que, na falta das mãos, recorre aos pés para aplaudir a seu algoz. (144)

Compare these resentful lines to Kafka's argument that he cannot bring himself to marry because his father turned marriage and family into a prison: "It is as if a prisoner wanted not only to escape from his prison (which perhaps could be done) but also to convert his prison into a holiday camp for himself" (Kafka, *Letter* 73). André's father commands him to speak clearly and humbly, "Answer me as a son should, above all, be humble in your manner, be clear as a man should" (me responda como deve responder um filho, seja sobretudo humilde na postura, seja claro como deve ser um homem; 148). But just like Kafka's father, he soon tells the son, "Be quiet!" and "I am telling you to hold your tongue! I will have no depraved wisdom contaminating the ways of this family!" (dobre a tua língua, eu já disse, nenhuma sabedoria devassa há de contaminar os modos da família!; 149). André surrenders and says, "I shouldn't have ever taken one step beyond our front door; from now on, I want to be like my brothers, I'm going to give myself over to the discipline necessary for my assigned tasks" (não devia ter me afastado um passo sequer da nossa porta; daqui pra frente, quero ser como meus irmãos, vou me entregar com disciplina às tarefas que me forem atribuídas; 150). André submits to his father because this is what he has always done.

As in the parable of the Prodigal Son, André's father gives a feast to celebrate the return of the prodigal son. At the feast, the overjoyed sister makes

Figure 5.1. The father hurries to kill his daughter with a tilling tool in *To the Left of the Father* (2001).

everyone uncomfortable with her sensuous dancing. The father grasps the outrageous secret, seizes a cutlass, and slashes the dancing daughter to death. The mother loses her mind and the children, young and old, see their world crumble and cry out, "Father! Where is our shelter? Where is our protection?" "Father! Where is the union of our family?" (onde a nossa segurança? onde a nossa proteção? Pai! Pai! onde a união da família?; 169). The father seems to suffer more than everyone else: "the patriarch himself, wounded at his very maxims, the patriarch now possessed by divine wrath (poor Father!), the guide himself, the tables, the law itself had gone up in flames" (era o próprio patriarca, ferido nos seus preceitos, que fora possuído de cólera divina [pobre pai!], era o guia, era a tábua solene, era a lei que se incendiava; 169). The tight control that helped him run his family with such ease destroyed it in the end. In figure 5.1, the father turns on his child with a lethal weapon, as we will see other fathers do.

Raduan Nassar wrote this novel during the military dictatorship, and it is the cruelest of these dictators who talked about familial unity the most. Emílio Garrastazu Médici (whose portrait occupied a prominent place in Bolsonaro's office while he was a congressman), in power from 1969 to 1974, was a former director of the secret police. He ideated and controlled several secret police organizations that conducted torture, rape, and castration; performed arbitrary arrests, imprisonment without trial, and executions; and dismembered and hid bodies (Vieira 76; Dassin). Médici's government was popular and it coincided with the period of economic growth known as the Brazilian miracle. This period ended with the shock of 1979, when escalating oil prices caused the system to unravel (Roett 63). Médici entitled his speeches *My Constant Concern, Our Family, A Big Family of My People, A Well-Deserved Trust*, and the like. He depicted the government as a loving *pater familias* who trusts and loves the people, and they trust him in return. He said the people must "incorporate themselves in the grand designs of the government which pursues the interests of the nation" (Garrastazu Médici 197, 13). Thanks to his firm guidance, Médici implied, Brazil is a "great and generous family, noble and understanding, vigorous and courageous" (84). The subjects must all contribute to the common cause, guided by the leader: "Each and every one, with inexhaustible devotion and efficacy, contributed to our social and economic progress: each individual in their area of expertise but all in obedience to the general course of action outlined by the Executive Power" (13). The leader and the subjects live in perfect harmony: "our success is the labor completed together, by the governing and the governed" (84). The leader warns that beyond the confines of the Brazilian family rages chaos: "In the middle of the tempestuous universe, the Brazilian family is calm and confident" (14). Elsewhere "economic growth often leads to political and social instability," but Brazil enjoys "the atmosphere of order, peace, harmony, and safety" (84). These lines were delivered while people were tortured and killed, and they must have inspired the character of the father in *Ancient Tillage*, in addition to Kafka's works. The book and the film show that taking away all freedom and agency from people, as authoritarian leaders and fathers do, cannot make them happy. Instead, complete containment and complete obedience will result in twisted obsessions and cause a total breakdown of the family unit and metaphorically, of the nation.

Kafka's *Judgment* in *Behind the Sun*

In *Behind the Sun* (*Abril despedaçado*, 2001), we see the son stand up to and walk away from his father, which is not at all the case in the renowned source novel by the Albanian writer Ismail Kadare, *Broken April*. Written in 1978, the novel allegorically represents the stifling atmosphere under the Stalinist dictator Enver Hoxha, who ruled Albania for forty-one years, from 1944 until his death in 1985. The novel is set in the 1940s in the Albanian High Plateau, where life is lived according to the Kanun, the ancient consuetudinary law code. All families are tied together by blood feuds. A blood offense must be avenged until all males of the feuding families are dead. To refuse to participate is to become a pariah to whom "nothing could be handed" "except with the left hand passed under one's thigh" (Kadare 42). In the novel, young Gjorg obeys his father and kills the man who killed his brother, knowing that he will soon have to die in turn. He has thirty days of truce to pay the death tax, after which he will be shot, as his father reminds him. The death tax must be paid in a deserted castle, where Gjorg must wait for an unknown number of days to be able to pay. A beautiful woman falls in love with Gjorg, but he is shot the day the truce is over.

This novel evokes Kafka's *Castle*, as well as *The Trial*, one of Kadare's favorite books, in which the main character, K., finds out that he is sentenced to death by invisible authorities. Another Kafka story, *Judgment*, must have given Kadare the idea of the name Gjorg for *Broken April*. In this short story, a young man Georg (in Albanian Gjorg) also dies to obey his father. The story begins with the young man musing on how to tell a friend that he got engaged. Then he goes to his elderly father's room, planning to move him to his own bigger and brighter room. In a flash, the decrepit old man springs to life and grows into an overpowering mad presence. He claims with absurd conviction that his son's friend is actually his friend and ridicules his fiancée. Finally, Georg's father thunders, "I sentence you to death by drowning!" In response, the son runs out of the house and jumps off a bridge, mumbling, "Dear parents, I have always loved you" (Kafka, *Judgment* 16). Kadare based his novel on the composite hero of Kafka's works—the obedient timid man hopelessly entangled in the workings of some implacable and inscrutable power.

Kadare's novel also described his life under the rule of the Albanian dictator Enver Hoxha. Hoxha thought of himself as a Francophile intellectual, but during his rule 100,000 people were imprisoned and five thousand killed. In *Broken April*, the father implacably enforces a senseless law and dooms his son to death. The son in this novel cannot rebel any more than the writer himself could rebel against Hoxha's regime. Incredibly, in the 2002 Brazilian film adaptation of this story (titled in English *Behind the Sun*), the son comes to realize that he is not bound by the father's laws and walks out on him. Director Walter Salles co-wrote the script and had previously directed the Oscar-nominated *Central Station*, in which the faith of the little boy Joshua in his father, a carpenter named Jesus, changes him from a drunkard and a womanizer into a father who cares. Similarly, in his reworking of Kadare's novel, Salles sets out to defeat the Kafkaesque father and free the son. The fact that the father cannot be changed is not the reason to brood over one's unhappy fate or die trying to please him. It is simply the reason to cut all ties with the father and move on—we can recall that "going no contact" with "toxic" family members has become a popular trend in recent years. Walter Salles often said that he disliked stories about the "inescapable, something that was not able

Figure 5.2. The father takes aim at his son as he walks away in *Behind the Sun* (2001).

to change" and preferred characters who "give themselves a second chance, undergo a second baptism, redefine their place in the world," "change the state of things, the pre-established order" (Salles, Interview). After 2000, such optimism became possible.

The adaptation transports Kadare's story to the Northern Brazil of 1910, where blood feud was also common. The young hero's family press sugar cane, work that was previously done by enslaved people. The father says that they have nothing but their honor and expects his two sons to obey him in everything. Life is repetitive and bleak. The two bulls that walk in a circle all day to turn the wheel of the cane press represent the two brothers who must do as the father tells them. The circular rut made by the bulls stands for the joyless life of the parents and the cycle of the blood feud which the sons will have to perpetuate. The older son obeys his father: he kills his brother's killer and prepares to be killed in turn. This is when the brothers meet a beautiful itinerant circus performer and realize there is a world beyond their father's. The little brother is fascinated by *The Little Mermaid* book she gives him, a tale about a mermaid who decides to become human. The older brother (Rodrigo Santoro) falls in love with the girl. The night when the avenger comes, the little brother puts on his brother's hat and leads the avenger away. The avenger cannot see well without his glasses and shoots the boy dead. The other son realizes that his brother sacrificed himself to set him free and walks out of the family home, his gaze fixed on the road leading away from his past life. He is hardly aware or does not care that the father, despite his grief over the dead younger son, grabbed a gun to kill him for refusing to perpetuate vengeance, and would have done it if the mother hadn't stopped him (figure 5.2). The son walks away from the family home, never to return, with a transfixed, luminous gaze into the future that lies ahead. Salles's mission as a storyteller is to instill hope, so in his take on Kadare's novel the son not only survives but leaves his father's house unafraid, looking forward to seeing the world.

Kafka's Letter to His Father in *Brainstorm*

The son in *Brainstorm* (*Bicho de sete cabeças*, 2001) is tricked by his father into entering a mental hospital where he will be detained because the father found marijuana in his pocket and thinks he is becoming a disobedient addict. Austregésilo Carrano Bueno wrote the source novel, autobiographical *The Song of the Damned* (*Canto dos malditos*) in 1976, during the dictatorship. In the novel, the son is captured and subjected to electroshock and other torturous treatments as lessons in obedience. The Brazilian dictatorship used electroshock to torture. As Carrano Bueno recounts his own story we see that he is still wondering how his own father could put him through such an ordeal. In the novel, he describes the general atmosphere of repression of the young people by the dictatorship, describing how the police capture long-haired hippies, torture them and disparage them with sensational headlines such as "Hairy Pothead Rapes a Minor!" (49). After the author was locked up in the mental hospital, no one bothered to conduct tests to confirm that he was indeed an addict, no matter how many times he begged them to. Instead, the personnel administered shocks to him, stuffed him with sedatives, and put him in solitary confinement as a matter of procedure. His only diagnosis is the father's words in his file that he is "nervous, disobedient and aggressive toward everybody" (inda muito nervoso, desobediente e agressivo com todos; 67). This is enough to keep him locked away and tortured. As a nurse puts it, "If you don't listen to anyone and do whatever crosses your mind, . . . you sure have some kind of a problem" (Se você não escuta ninguém, quer fazer o que lhe vem à cabeça . . . algum problema você tem!; 67). The youth prays that the doctor who administers electroshock does not come: "I felt like a wounded and cornered animal, trapped in that room. A seventeen-year-old boy, with pimples on his face, not even a trace of facial hair yet. Locked up, waiting for the shock! A place I had never dreamed of visiting. Locked up! Waiting for the shock. Going through nightmares that would make any grown man fearful" (Sentia-me um animal ferido e acuado, preso naquele quarto. Um garoto de dezessete anos, espinha na cara, barba nem pronunciada. Preso, esperando o choque! Um lugar que jamais sonhara conhecer. Preso! esperando o choque. Passando por pesadelos que fariam qualquer machão adulto ficar temeroso; 102). The son shudders to think that the father prefers to lock him up here just like that rather than talk with him: "It's a nightmare, my God, this isn't happening... It can't be real!... Dad... why did you do this to me?... You didn't have to bring me here. Why don't we talk, dad? Why don't we fucking talk?!" (é um pesadelo, meu Deus, isto não está acontecendo, não pode ser real... Não é real, meu Deus! Pai... por que você fez isso comigo?... Não precisava me trazer para cá. Por que não conversamos, pai? Por que não conversamos, porra?; 57). When they release him, he is a changed man, forever traumatized. Because he has a record of being interred in a mental hospital, he will be returned there repeatedly during his life.

This individual experience of one youth during the dictatorship metaphorically represents the experience of Brazilian society. During the dictatorship, interning undesirable people in mental hospitals was a frequent procedure. Private hospitals received government funding with almost no oversight. The number of private hospital beds increased from 14,000 to 98,000 because "the madness industry" was very lucrative (Miguel 256). Undesirable social elements were compared to pathogens that contaminate and disrupt the natural, organic order. The Colonial Hospital of Barbacena in Minas Gerais became the symbol of psychiatry as an instrument of control more than treatment. In 1973, a visitor compared it to a concentration camp. It was overcrowded, with one psychiatrist per four hundred patients, and short on clothing and food. An estimated 70 percent of patients did not receive a proper mental diagnosis, just like the author of *Song of the Damned*. Internment in mental hospitals continued until 2000, when the Mental Health Reform Law was adopted. The law replaced internment in psychiatric hospitals with community-based service networks that promote recovery, social inclusion, and human rights. *Song of the Damned* was the first testimony of the abuse in mental institutions in Brazil. In 2003, Lula da Silva thanked Carrano Bueno for his work on mental health reform (Catunda). Significantly, Bolsonaro pursued legislation to dismantle the Reform's achievements, reducing local mental health organizations, resuming the hospitalization strategy, and investing in psychiatric hospital beds. Bolsonaro criticized the Reform as "ideology" and proposed to replace it with "scientific methods" such as electroconvulsive therapy and hospitalization of children and adolescents. As the Brazilian dictatorship of which he is fan, Bolsonaro used medical language to pathologize his enemies—leftists, communists, and the LGBTQ community (Miguel 264)—to diminish his political opponents as abnormal.

The 2001 film adaptation of the novel *Brainstorm* (*Bicho de sete cabeças*) transposes the story to modern times. The film ends with the father repenting of wanting to discipline his son and weeping from shame and sorrow. Luiz Bolognesi, the film's scriptwriter, explained that he was inspired by Kafka's

Letter to My Father when writing the script for *Brainstorm*. And yet, just like Walter Salles in *Behind the Sun*, he rescripts the tragic story on which the film is based *and* Kafka's *Letter*. Bolognesi conceives the father and son relationship as "a toxic love and hate" and ends the film with a promise of catharsis and reconciliation (Bolognesi 13, 17). The film is framed as the young hero's letter to his father because when the family comes to visit him at the hospital the father refuses to believe his son and keeps saying that the doctor is the best psychiatric authority in Brazil and has published many books. The film excels in portraying the hospital and its torture practices as a malevolent, Kafkaesque universe that captures its young victim. Figure 5.3 shows the hero transfixed at the sight of the approaching electric prod. The tool is an allusion to the *picana*, an adapted cattle prod, used to interrogate detainees during the dictatorship. It is the head doctor who is the actual drug addict in the film. Permanently high, he looks over his domain with satisfaction and gives orders to capture more homeless people to retain government financing. The young hero (Rodrigo Santoro, who played the protagonist in *Behind the Sun*) writes to his father: "There's no way out, it's not fair. I hadn't done anything. Once you told me, 'I got this far in life, who knows where you'll get.' Here ... I got here. This is my place. You managed to make me smaller than you. Your world outside is too big for me" ("Não há saída, não é justo. Eu não tinha feito nada. Uma vez que você me disse, 'Cheguei tão longe na vida, quem sabe onde você vai chegar.' Aqui ... cheguei aqui. Aqui é o meu lugar. Você conseguiu me fazer menor do que você. Seu mundo lá fora é grande demais para mim"). And yet, while Kafka's father did not care to even open the letter, in the film the son *makes* him open and read it—as he hands it over to him, he stubs a burning cigarette into his hand. After reading the letter, the father weeps and brings his son home. Once again, we see the son in the film defeating the father and reclaiming his freedom, in contrast to the original story.

The film's title comes from the song "Bicho de sete cabeças" by Geraldo Azevedo and Elba Ramalho. This expression means "a very hard obstacle to fight or a complex thing to do," but translated literally, it means "a creature (animal or insect) with seven heads." The sudden transformation of the son into a "creature" (um bicho) to be shut away also calls to mind Kafka's *Metamorphosis*, featured prominently in the films about the urban poor to which I now turn.

Kafka's *Metamorphosis* in the films *City of God* and *City of Men*

Sørbøe and Cruikshank argue that residents of poor urban enclaves, such as the favelas of Brazil, have long been perceived and treated like *homo sacer*, a

The Scold: Leadership as Emotional Abuse in Brazil · 127

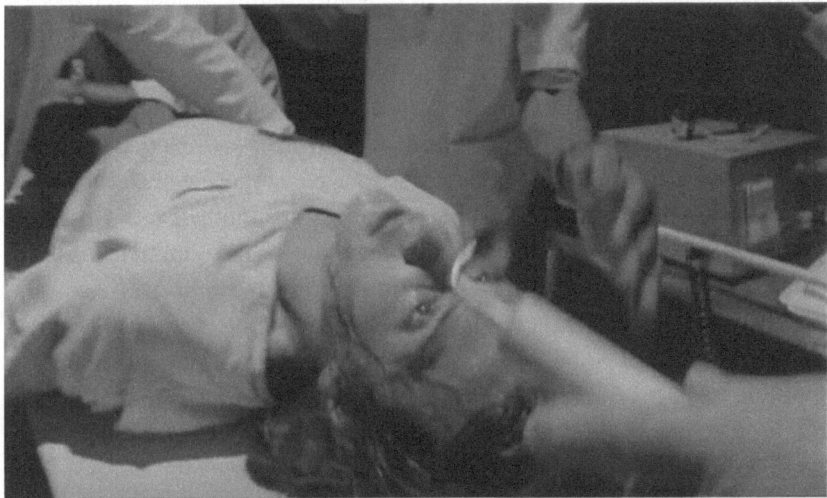

Figure 5.3. The son dreading the electrical prod at the mental hospital in *Brainstorm* (2000).

figure in Roman law denoting someone who was banned from society and had all of his rights as a citizen revoked. This is why he can be killed without the killer being regarded as a murderer and why he cannot be sacrificed in a religious ritual. Philosopher Giorgio Agamben, inspired by Michel Foucault's concept of biopolitics, founded this theory of state power on the concept of homo sacer. *Sacer* means not only "sacred" but also "*unclean,* cursed," and this is the condition of many people in today's societies who are "included in the juridical order solely in the form of [their] exclusion (that is, of [their] capacity to be killed)" (Agamben 2). They are "bare life" or bodies, *zoê* in Greek, as opposed to political beings (citizens), who are "qualified life," *bios*. The state decides who will be "bodies" and who will be "citizens," and this division is "the hidden foundation on which the entire political system rest[s]" (7). From Kafka, Agamben takes the idea that in totalitarian societies, the laws that divide people into "citizens" and "bare life" are entirely arbitrary. In Kafka's stories, and especially in *The Trial*, Agamben finds a perfect illustration of how people may find themselves suddenly deprived of their rights for no reason at all: "law is all the more pervasive for its total lack of content and a distracted knock on the door can mark the start of uncontrollable trials" (Agamben 35). The prisoners of the Nazi extermination camps were reduced to bare life by the word of the Fuehrer, which was "the perfect source of law" (Agamben 73).

The perfect illustration of suddenly finding oneself in the position of "bare life," a repulsive, nonhuman creature, is Kafka's *Metamorphosis*, the short story that underlies the rest of the films examined in this chapter. In the story, traveling salesman Gregor Samsa awakes one day to find that he has turned into a gigantic insect. Gregor is a timid and dutiful son and, although he dislikes his job, he is proud to provide for his parents and his younger sister, an aspiring violinist. After his astonishing transformation, Gregor must spend his days and nights in his room under the sofa. He cannot eat or sleep because he is worried that he will disgust his sister, scare his mother, and—his worst fear—anger his father. The one time he crawls out of his room to listen to his sister play violin, his father hisses at him and threatens him with his walking stick, so he rushes back to his room. Soon everyone in the family agrees that Gregor cannot go on living with them, and the following morning he is found dead in his room. The maid joyfully tells the family she took care of the mess (Gregor's dead body), to which they do not deign to respond, as if Gregor never existed. In many translations, the insect into which Gregor turns is a cockroach (the policeman in *Elite Squad* uses that word, as we will see shortly). But the word Kafka used in the original German is *Ungeziefer*, which means more generally any pest, vermin, or parasitic insect. *Ungeziefer* is what Kafka's father liked to call him when he was little (*Letter* 82) and what the Nazis called the Jews (Despiniadis 69). This word assigns the "bare life" status to the people so designated.

In his best-selling novel *City of God* (*Cidade de Deus*, 1997), writer Paulo Lins portrays the residents of the favela City of God as "bare life," persons whose lives do not matter. The novel was adapted to the screen in 2002 and is now among the most popular Brazilian films. The author lived in the favela himself and conducted interviews with the residents (*favelados*) for an anthropology project when he was a student at the university. His achievement was to show that the gangsters and drug traffickers who also live in the favela exploit the favelados (Castro Rocha). This is why all favelados are seen as de facto or potential "bandidos," "malandros" (crooks), "bichos-soltos" (loose animals), and "vagabundos," or their accomplices, for which reason policemen can kill them with impunity. The favelados are "segregated economically as poor, racially as Afro-Brazilian, and territorially in the favela" (Cruikshank 8). Simply by virtue of being born in a favela, its residents cannot aspire to a decent job, no matter how well they do in school. Love and friendship are obstacles to survival. Because of this permanent lack and danger, the community is torn apart by racism, misogyny, and homophobia. Everyone can be a victim of horrific violence at any time, at the hands of the police or each other. A Black man dismembers the white baby his wife gave birth to, a jealous husband buries his wife alive, a man kills his ex-girlfriend who began dating a cop, a gangster beats up his mother for telling him to tidy up his room, a queer is viciously attacked by people of all races, genders, and ages. Small children are beaten by their parents if they fail to bring home money, so they organize gangs to get some. The policeman explains to a passerby who asks him to spare a boy's life that "This thing ain't human—this here's an open sewer, a rabid dog!" (isso aqui não é gente, não, isso aqui é uma vala aberta, um cachorro raivoso; 97). Little children are shot by stray bullets fired by gangsters and policemen alike, and these bloody bodies are the only thing that makes them change hatred for sadness for a little while, reminding them that they are all "bare life."

The novel's author, Paulo Lins, also wrote a poem about a favelado who describes himself as "an ugly fetus in the belly of Brazil" and a *bicho*, animal or insect, "illuminated by the weak light of the streetlamp." "I can steal your daybreak," says the hero, which sounds like an ironic and absurd threat. He is registered by society as a "bicho," and like the hero of Kafka's *Metamorphosis*, he terrifies people when he tries to speak to them. When Gregor's supervisor comes to reprimand him for not coming to work on the day of his transformation, Gregor opens the door of his room and tries to convey that he will be back at his desk in no time. The supervisor backs away from him in horror and runs for his life. The narrator of Lins's poem also cannot make himself understood because people see him as "bare life" and either fear or ignore him. The poem's narrator says that his voice is "without an ear [to hear it], like a breath without phonemes / a voice dead in the throat. / My word-life is mute in the legal world / which makes me your criminal" (Voz sem ouvido, voz morta enterrada na garganta, E a palavra vida muda no mundo legal / me faz teu marginal; Lins quoted in Oliveira Rocha). The social outcast, *bicho* and *marginal* of this poem is precisely "bare life." He is alive but cannot be seen or heard. He lives in order to be excluded from the "legal world" of citizens with rights.

In 2002, *City of God*, a film adaptation of Lin's novel was released, followed by a sequel, *City of Men* in 2017. Critic João Cezar de Castro Rocha said that these films infantilize Lins's novel in that they offer "false promises" that the favelados can cross into the world of people with citizenship rights (Castro Rocha). But it is uncontestable that the adaptation gave its protagonists national and international visibility, by tapping into the bildungsroman genre and action and gangster film codes (Tierney 148). Director Fernando Meirelles and scriptwriter Bráulio Mantovani adapt Lins's novel into the story of one favela resident, Rocket (Buscapé in Portuguese, played by Alexandre Rodrigues), who becomes a photographer, which gives him a voice and a means to change the public perception of all the favelados. The film opens and closes with the famous shot of a chicken running for its life during a shootout between the police and the gangs. Like the chicken that is everyone's prey, Rocket is armed only with his camera and can only run, although "in the City of God, if you run away, they get you, and if you stay, they get you too," he tells us in the voiceover. Rocket is incapable of violence. He cannot bring himself to hold up a bus in order to get the money necessary to buy a camera because the bus driver lets him ride free and tells him to study and get out of the favela. One day, the cruel drug boss, Lil' Zé, tells him to take pictures of his gang. A journalist of the newspaper where Rocket works as a delivery boy accidentally sees these pictures and publishes them. Rocket thinks he will be killed, but Lil' Zé appreciates his newfound fame. Soon Rocket shoots even better pictures, of policemen releasing Lil' Zé in exchange for his cash stash. Next, Lil' Zé is killed by a group of teens who want to take over his business, and Rocket photographs his dead body. By the end of the film, Rocket says with pride that his name is "no longer Rocket—I am now Wilson Rodrigues, photographer" (Ninguém mais me chama de Buscapé, agora sou Wilson Rodrigues, fotógrafo). Despite his success, in the film Rocket chooses to stay in the favela, unlike his counterpart in the novel. The director explains: "You can't just go away and let the place burn. It would be wrong. All he wants is an opportunity in life: the country needs to give that opportunity. So we changed it. He still lives in the favela, but he has a decent job. He effectively says, 'I don't get much money, but I'm included. I'm part of society. I have a life of possibility.' And that's it" (Meirelles 142). The filmmakers transformed the character from "bare life" into a citizen with rights (and a camera, like themselves). Lula, when he was president, thanked the filmmakers and said that the film influenced his favela security policy (Meirelles 145). The film was nominated for an Oscar in four categories and is one of Brazil's most famous films.

In the sequel, *City of Men* (*Cidade dos Homens*), the favelados become even more relatable and exemplary. Director Paulo Morelli and scriptwriter Elena Soarez frame the solution to exclusion as a decision on the part of the excluded to become a caring and present father to his son. The film follows two friends, Laranginha (Darlan Cunha) and Acerola (Douglas Silva), minor characters from Lins's novel, but invents a new story for them, also with a bildungsroman arc. Both friends will soon turn eighteen. Laranginha wants to find his father, even though his grandmother tells him he is not worth looking for: "He never even showed up when you were born. He went to play soccer. Your father was a bum. He didn't work. He slept all day. What use is a father who doesn't care if his son is dead or alive?" (Seu pai era um vagabundo. Não trabalhava, dormia o dia todo. Pai que tem um filho e não quer saber se o filho está vivo... não quer saber se o filho está morto! De que serve um pai desse?). But Laranginha perseveres and finds his father, just released on parole after twenty years in prison. Laranginha's father wants nothing to do with his son at first, but later he shows signs of affection, cooking him a birthday meal and giving him a check for $200. But the boys also learn that he killed Acerola's father, even though they were friends, like the two boys. He was robbing a shop where Acerola's father worked as a guard and shot him in the back. This father cannot change: after his release from the penal system, he begins forging checks and soon returns to prison.

The lesson for the friends is to be good men even though their own fathers failed them. Acerola is himself a father already, and at the beginning an avoidant and neglectful one. He even wants to leave his girlfriend after she becomes pregnant. It is his friend Laranginha who rebukes him, asking if he wants his son to be like them, "always getting into trouble." It would have been different if they had both had fathers to take them to school and for walks, and to make sure they were okay. Acerola agrees to be a father to his son, but he is not good at it. For example, he forgets him at the beach with other teenage friends, and if it were not for one conscientious girl, the little boy would have surely drowned. The friends work together to be good fathers. They refuse to become soldiers in a gang and escape from the favela. Acerola comes to pick up his little son and tells him, "I love you. From now on, it's you and me. I'm going to bring you up, take care of you. Now it is just you and me, together" (Eu te amo. Daqui pra frente é só eu e tu, tá? Eu que vou te criar agora. Eu que vou cuidar de você. Agora é só nós dois). At the end of the film, the little boy walks between the two friends, holding their hands. They walk away from the favela that rises behind them and then turn to look at it as they cross the road. In the film, Acerola and Laranginha are very different from their counterparts in Lins's novel, two loafers who smoke pot and manage drug dens. The thought of quitting crime, not to mention becoming good fathers, never occurs to them.

Thus, both film adaptations of Lins's novel *City of God* produce a metamorphosis of Lins's Kafkaesque nonhuman creatures (bichos). Rocket, Laranginha, and Acerola are no longer "bare life" but rather people viewers will care about and recognize as fellow human beings. These films follow the trend I identified in *Brainstorm* and *Behind the Sun*: providing the sons with ways to overcome their condition of abusive neglect. To use George Lakoff's metaphoric models of the family and national leadership, the films shape a demand for a parent and leader who listens and helps—a Nurturant Parent, rather than a strict father who disciplines and punishes.

Kafka's *Metamorphosis* in the film *Elite Squad*

The 2008 Brazilian film *Elite Squad* (*Tropa de elite*) directed by José Padilha breaks the trend of emancipating the sons and seems to call for the Strict Father's return to the family and politics. In this film, we return to the "malandros," "vagabundos," "bandidos," "marginais," and "baratas" (cockroaches) of Kafka's *Metamorphosis*, but now we are invited to identify with a man who plays the part of the reliably cruel father rather than the scared son. The film is based on the 2006 book *Elite Squad* (*Elite da tropa*) written by ex-police officers André Batista and Rodrigo Pimentel together with anthropologist Luiz Eduardo Soares. The book makes it impossible to identify with the hero/narrator, the leader of a BOPE squad, a special police unit in Rio. The hero enjoys creating new torture methods, such as putting the "vagabundo" into a cistern of water and sticking electrical wires into it, which he names Miami Dolphins because the victim jumps so gracefully. He and other officers laugh during torture sessions because, well, "what else were we going to do?" (Mas a gente ria, ia fazer o quê?; Soares 29). He mutilates his victims and then is repulsed by their disfigured faces and bodies. The narrator relates how they shot a suspect in the head and his eyes popped out "like billiard balls," so he "got a bit nervous and asked to execute the criminal once and for all. He was already turning into a monstrosity" (Fiquei um pouco nervoso e pedi para executar o marginal de uma vez. Ele já estava mesmo virando monstro; 36). The "vagabundos" who start begging for their life turn into the monsters of Kafka's *Metamorphosis*, which he cites. Unlike in other stories, the hero is looking at them from the father's point of view, with repugnance:

> a kind of metamorphosis happens to the dying—so you'll know I'm not an idiot, I should mention that it reminds me of a Kafka story by that name, about a guy named Gregor Samsa who turns into a cockroach.... In the metamorphosis in which a scumbag becomes a monster—as we say in the BOPE—the son of a bitch seems to regress, becoming a child and starting to cry for his mother. It's goddamn hard to take.

> acontece uma espécie de metamorfose com o moribundo—para você ver que eu não sou nenhuma besta, devo lhe dizer que isso me lembra um conto do Kafka com este nome e que conta a história de um sujeito chamado Gregor Samsa, que vira barata.... Na metamorfose em que o vagabundo vira monstro—como a gente diz no BOPE—, o filho da puta parece que regride, volta a ser criança e começa a chamar pela mãe. (É de lascar 36)

Note that the insect into which Gregor Samsa turns is translated as "cockroach" (barata)—Bolsonaro is also fond of this word, as I will show shortly. The helplessness of the "vagabundo" makes the executioner more pitiless, reminding us of Gregor's father in Kafka's *Metamorphosis*. When his father chases him back into his room, Gregor would like to run faster to demonstrate that he is happy to comply but cannot move quickly enough on his numerous but weak feet because "even in his earlier life his lungs had not been very reliable" (*Metamorphosis* 146). Gregor could have escaped by scaling the walls and the ceiling, but he is too scared his father will think he is not complying. "And so Gregor did not leave the floor, for he feared that his father might take as a piece of peculiar wickedness any excursion of his over the walls or the ceiling" (146). The father "bombards" him with apples, and one of these apples hits him in the back, incapacitating him. In a scene from the *Elite Squad*, a boy is running away from the BOPE just like Gregor. The officers accidentally killed that boy's brother while trying to scare them into telling where they hid their guns. The terrified boy tells them where the guns are, but "it's too late now"—everybody understands that he must be killed too. The boy runs around the house from them like Gregor from his father: "He begged, shrieked, climbed onto the sink, slid down the sofa, jumped over the refrigerator, pushed over the TV" (implorava, guinchava, subia na pia, deslizava pelo sofá, saltava geladeira, empurrava a TV; 57), but the officers set off an "apocalypse" with their machine guns until nothing remains of the place but shards, plaster, bones and blood on the ceiling and the floor, and the paralyzed mother, who the whole time begged for her sons' lives, upstairs. The executioners reason that she can go on living because she did not see them (58). Policemen kill indiscriminately in favelas. They are the instruments of a new way of "managing multitudes," which Achille Mbembe called "necropolitics." To practice necropolitics is to deploy weapons "in the interest of maximum destruction of persons" and to create "death-worlds, new and unique forms of social existence in which vast populations are subjected to conditions of life conferring upon them the status of living dead" (Mbembe 40).

We are not surprised to learn that when the merciless BOPE officer was a child, he too was in Gregor's position with his own abusive father. "When he would scold me, my father used to interpret my silence as indifference and disrespect. The result was that my silence was usually followed by a smack in the head. A grenade inside my head" (Quando me chamava a atenção, meu pai costumava interpretar meu silêncio como sinal de indiferença e desrespeito. O resultado é que o silêncio geralmente era sucedido por um cascudo. Granada na cabeça; 51). Feeling like a grenade about to explode is a frequent metaphor in this novel. The father's abuse turns him into another angry and pitiless man. The narrator makes it plain that he is an antihero, a sadist, but in the film this book inspired he could be—and was, in far-right groups—taken for a hero, "a patron saint of outlaw justice" (Cabral).

The Black hero of the novel becomes white in the film. Played by Wagner Moura, he is very attractive and charismatic in his black uniform (figure 5.4). In the film Captain Nascimento is an expectant father, and the film's central question is whether he will be a good father to his son. He would like to be a good father, and he begins looking for his replacement so he can take a desk job and take care of his son. Unfortunately, this job changes him irrevocably. He says to his wife on the phone in the beginning of the film, "My love, I want to be with you too, but I have to work" (Meu amor, também queria estar com você, mas estou trabalhando). He listens to his unborn son's heartbeat on the phone while watching corrupt policemen sell guns to traffickers. When he finally holds his newborn son, he thinks about work (Laukkanen 177), about a lookout boy who he made identify the traffickers during an arrest, who killed him in retaliation. He comes to enjoy telling people what to do so much that he can no longer have a conversation with his wife: "Only one thing drove me crazier than making my own mistakes. It was Rosane telling me what to do. The worst part was, at times, even though I knew she was wrong, I obeyed" (Só tinha uma coisa que me deixava mais irado que erro em operação. Era Rosane dizendo para mim o que eu tinha de fazer. E o pior é que, às vezes mesmo sabendo que ela estava errada, eu obedecia). Soon he explodes at his wife, telling her who is in charge: "Don't you ever open your mouth to talk about my job again! I give the orders in this house! Not one word about my team inside this house! Am I clear? You got that? I give the fucking orders!" (Não abra mais a boca para falar do meu trabalho nessa casa. Quem manda aqui sou eu! E você não vai mais abrir a boca para falar do meu batalhão nesta casa! Você está entendendo? Você entendeu? Quem manda nessa porra sou eu!). When he comes back home to find a note in place of his wife and son, he nods to himself, like a man who accepted his tragic mission. The filmmakers portrayed him as a bad father, but also as a necessary evil. He hates corrupt cops and does not take bribes, although if he did, many people would not have died.

Unsurprisingly, the film shows that the training to join his elite corps is more about emotional abuse than building physical stamina. The recruits are attacked by the BOPE officers, who punch them, hit them with guns, and yell at them, "Go back to where you came from!" "Do you know why your number is 0–1? Because you'll be the first to give up. And I'm gonna make you do it! Ask me to quit! If you don't, you're fucked!" The recruits are not allowed to

Figure 5.4. The attractive and armed Captain Nascimento in *Elite Squad* (2007).

talk back or strike back, they must take the beating and the insults obediently or quit. When the "coaches" dump a pot of food on the ground, the recruits have only two minutes to eat it with their mouths like dogs. The "coaches" cheer when a recruit quits and erect a cross for each quitter at the end of training. The recruits who endure until the end are the champions in taking gratuitous abuse. Out of one hundred officers, only five or less make the cut to become the necessary evil. However, this seems to solve nothing. The hero is like a Sisyphus who must roll a huge rock up the hill eternally, and his rock becomes heavier and heavier every day with the weight of new dead bodies.

The film *Elite Squad* made such a profound impression that about twenty million people watched a leaked copy of it before it opened in theaters. Captain Nascimento must have inspired Brazilians to vote for Jair Bolsonaro as an incorruptible "tough guy," speculates José Padilha, the film's director. This is wrong, he says, because Bolsonaro is more like the militia man from *Elite Squad 2* (interview with Almeida Moreira). Militiamen are ex- or off-duty policemen who form illegal death squads and eliminate favela traffickers to set up their own extortion and protection rackets (Phillips). The film was meant to "grab you by the balls," make you sympathize "with the fucking torturer," feel "fucking guilty" and think about the issues more, said Padilha and cited the number of PhD dissertations based on his films (interview with Matheou 185). He says that the film's message is that "a society cannot sustain itself if its police believe in the idea that violence is something that you control with violence, which is of course a stupid idea" (interview with Matheou 174). Padilha takes pride in his film being not only commercially successful but also provoking intellectual discussions. However, many people cannot engage with characters critically. Therefore, if they really like Captain Nascimento's black uniform and that emblem with an impaled skull with guns, they will not identify police violence as a problem. Accordingly, Ivana Bentes has argued that violence against the poor in this film is a hallucinatory spectacle that holds the viewer hostage and lends credence to conservative discourse blaming everything on the favelados themselves (109).

Perhaps it is not surprising that Padilha was critical of Brazilian presidents who practiced the Nurturant Parent leadership style. He criticized Lula da Silva and lauded the tough-looking judge Sérgio Moro, who sentenced the former president to nine years in prison. He also supported the impeachment of Lula's successor Dilma Rousseff. In the 2018–2019 Netflix show *The Mechanism* (*O Mecanismo*), which he directed, Padilha idealized Moro as articulate and selfless, while the real Moro struggles with Portuguese grammar and makes strikingly basic mistakes when speaking in public (Ribke 55). In contrast, he portrayed Lula and Dilma as inept, unable to pronounce simple sentences while practicing campaign speeches, and more preoccupied with how their hair looked than what they said. Recently, however, Padilha called himself "an idiot" because it was revealed that Moro exchanged messages with the prosecutor to influence the investigation of Lula and because he became Bolsonaro's Minister of Justice and Public Security. Padilha said he would vote for Lula "without blinking an eye" to remove Bolsonaro from the presidency (Nery).

The Return of the Abusive Father to Brazilian Politics with Jair Bolsonaro

Bolsonaro rose to power on the crest of the revanchist revolt against the inclusive rhetoric and redistributive policies of Lula and Dilma, candidates from the left-wing Workers' Party (Partido dos Trabalhadores, PT). Both Lula and Dilma spoke of the state as a caring parent who must compensate poorest citizens for decades of neglect. Their programs lifted millions of people out of poverty. Bolsa Família, Lula's main social assistance program, provided cash transfers to twenty-five million people on the condition that their children went to school and were vaccinated. Fifty percent of placements at public universities and technical institutions were reserved for Black, Brown, and Indigenous people, public school graduates, and low-income students. By the end of Lula's second term, poverty rates had fallen by 50 percent. Thirty-seven million Brazilians joined the emergent lower middle class. Minimum wage rose by 75 percent from 2002 to 2013 (Costa 73). In favelas, the PT governments implemented two important programs. PAC-favela, a subprogram of the Accelerated Growth Program, funded large-scale projects in construction, energy, transport, and logistics. The second program, UPP (the State Police "Pacification" program) was designed to improve the security of favela residents by combining police occupation of favelas with social and educational programs such as social services, job training, and cultural activities (Sørbøe 105).

Scholars note that the PT governments failed to include these reforms as citizenship rights in the constitution or reform the tax system to change the entrenched socioeconomic inequality. The PAC and UPP programs also drew criticism (Sørbøe 110; Costa 73). At the same time, on a symbolic level these leaders had an immense impact. Brazilians saw an uneducated iron worker and a woman become president. These presidents drew attention to the "bare life" status of the poor (Sørbøe 111). Lula said, for example, that inclusive and participatory democracy means that "this Palace needs to learn to welcome blacks, Indians, women. And this Palace needs to learn to welcome those who never get to even come close to the Palace, not to mention go inside it." Lula repeated over and over that the Brazilian government failed to provide rights and opportunities and is in "decades and decades of social debt to the Brazilian people" (Silva). In his view, the government is responsible for the poverty of its citizens and must adopt policies to lift them out of poverty and violence:

> Poverty is not God's work, but the work of those who governed this country, and if youths turn to crime, it is because the government failed them ... When we see on TV a young man being arrested, this young man is a victim of policies—social, educational, and economic—that we never had in this country. For this reason, it is the state who is to blame that this young man became a criminal. ("Lula defende")

Lula, a man, even portrayed himself as a mother rather than a father: "Don't make a mistake: even though I am the president of everyone, I will keep doing what a mother does: I'll first take care of the most indigent, the most fragile, those who need the Brazilian state the most" (Silva). Dilma Rousseff, who succeeded Lula, also presented the state as a caring mother. In all her speeches she expressed her pride in being the first woman president, and asserted herself as a mother, a daughter, and a grandmother: "But a woman is not only courage. Affection, as well. It is with this immense affection that I will care for my people" (Rousseff). We recognize Lakoff's Nurturant Parent model of political leadership, in which the leader wins the respect and trust of the citizens by encouragement and help rather than punishment.

The revanchist revolt against the PT government led to a smear campaign against Dilma and Lula. Dilma was accused of corruption and budget peddling on charges that remain unproven and was removed from the presidency in 2016 (Sørbøe 122). Lula was accused of money laundering and accepting bribes from the construction company Odebrecht in exchange for government contracts. He was arrested and sentenced to nine and a half years in prison, but the charges were annulled by the Supreme Court. The smear campaign against the left weakened the public trust in the institutions of democratic governance and political parties and helped Jair Bolsonaro win the presidency in 2018 (Mello).

Bolsonaro holds an ultra-conservative, hierarchical view of society, which his supporters consider moral and fair (V. Castro). Lakoff terms this political leadership model Strict Father morality (as opposed to Nurturant Parent morality practiced by the PT leaders). In this model, the moral order is a hierarchy with God at the top (Bolsonaro's campaign motto is "Brazil Above Everything, God Above All"). Lakoff describes this worldview as a pyramid: "God has dominance and moral authority over human beings. Human beings have dominance and moral authority over nature (animals, plants, and natural objects). Adults have dominance and moral authority over children. Men have dominance and moral authority over women" (Lakoff 105). Whites have dominance and moral authority over nonwhites (Lakoff 82), and the rich have dominance and moral authority over the poor. If one is poor, this means they are lazy, lack talent, or have some other moral weakness. In Bolsonaro's worldview, and his concept of social justice, "explanations in terms of social forces and class make no sense" (Lakoff 203). Disciplining and excluding are legitimate means to enforce this order, which is perceived as natural and moral. Non-heterosexuals, feminists, and leftists threaten this "natural" order of things (Lakoff 82) and should be censured.

Bolsonaro's supporters embrace the Strict Father morality. They are attracted by his theatrical virility because they think that only a strong government can fix Brazil's problems (V. Castro). They view Bolsonaro in messianic terms, as a savior at a time when Brazil is torn between good and evil, shadows and sunshine. They take Bolsonaro's insults directed at his political adversaries as honest talk. Bolsonaro's supporters confess to knowing little about his actual economic and social proposals. They feel he is right to attack the left because they believe that leftist policies took away their privileges, which they believe are earned through hard work and dedication. If Afro-Brazilians suffer from disadvantages, they must overcome them themselves and not be granted quotas at universities (although the interviewees could not name any of their acquaintances who did not gain admission because of the quotas). Similarly, the interviewees say that recipients of the Bolsa Família did nothing to deserve help, even when they themselves or their acquaintances also benefited from it (V. Castro).

But Bolsonaro is not a typical conservative. What his supporters love him for most is his leadership style of public insult and offense. They call him "legend" and "myth." Theodor Adorno described this enjoyment of humiliation, doing it and watching an authority figure do it, as one of the traits of authoritarian personality. Such style confirms for many people the "power and 'toughness'" of the man who uses it. Such leader and the people who follow him display a "preoccupation with the dominance-submission, strong-weak, leader-follower dimension; identification with power figures;" "exaggerated assertion of strength and toughness" (Adorno et al. 228). Bolsonaro is a self-confessed admirer of Hitler and openly supports eugenics (Leal). We recognize his fascistic leanings by his comparing criminals to cockroaches, like the torturer cop in *Elite Squad*. Bolsonaro said that criminals "are going to die in the street like cockroaches, and this is how it should be," and promised impunity for policemen (Os caras vão morrer na rua igual barata, pô, e tem que ser assim; Brennan). He joked with his Black supporter with an Afro, "Are you breeding cockroaches in that hair?" (The supporter took it to mean that he and the president enjoy a special kind of intimacy; Travae). Asked by Black singer Preta Gil how he would react if one of his children fell in love with a Black woman, Bolsonaro replied, "I don't run this risk. My children were very well educated and didn't live in an environment like, unfortunately, yours" (Travae). He called the Indigenous people whose land cannot be used for commercial purposes "parasites" who live in "zoos" (V. Castro). He said that *quilombolas*, Afro-Brazilian residents of settlements established by runaway slaves, "weren't even fit for breeding" (V. Castro). He attacked the quotas for Black and Brown students in higher education, arguing that he had "never enslaved" anyone and hence neither he nor Brazil as a whole had a debt to repay to Brazil's majority Black population that was enslaved for three hundred years. He said he would not enter into a plane flown by a "quota pilot," nor allow himself to be operated on by a "quota doctor" (Lum). In 2022, a Black man with a disability, Genivaldo de Jesús, was pulled over for riding a motorbike without a helmet (as Bolsonaro often does). Policemen stuffed him inside their vehicle and threw in a teargas bomb, and he died in this improvised gas chamber. Bolsonaro called the victim a "suspeito" (suspect), "bandido," and "marginal" (Pereira).

Bolsonaro also made similarly gratuitous and sadistic comments about women, non-heterosexuals, and leftists. These verbal comments always evoke physical abuse—hitting, torture, killing, and rape. For example, he dedicated his vote to impeach Dilma to the memory of Colonel Brilhante Ustra, the only person in Brazil to be convicted of torture during the military dictatorship, who headed the unit where Dilma was allegedly tortured (Mello). When Michelle Bachelet, former president of Chile, criticized rising police violence in Brazil, Bolsonaro responded that she "is defending the human rights of vagabonds" (vagabundos) and implied that it was for a good cause that her father was tortured and died in prison during the military dictatorship: "If Pinochet had not defeated the left in 73—among them your father—Chile would be a Cuba today" (Phillips). Bolsonaro attacked a fellow congresswoman, Maria do Rosário, and said that she is "not worth raping, she is very ugly." Similarly, he said that women should be paid less because they get pregnant. He said he is proud of his four sons and that he fathered his daughter "in a moment of weakness" (V. Castro). He recommended giving a good thrashing to a son who shows signs of being gay (Lum) and said he would rather learn that his son died in a car crash than that he is a homosexual (V. Castro). He vowed to send socialists and other "Reds" "to the edge of the beach. It will be a cleaning never seen in the history of Brazil." This is another awful threat, because the "edge of the beach" refers to a Navy base at Restinga da Marambaia, in Rio de Janeiro State, where the Brazilian military dictatorship tortured and killed dissidents (Rocha et al. 136). He said that the mistake of the Brazilian military dictatorship was "not to kill off the Commies," and that Pinochet's mistake was "not killing enough people" (Leal). He called human rights activists criminals: "the only advocates of human rights in Brazil are bandits, rapists, hoodlums (marginais), kidnappers, and crooks" (V. Castro).

The Lover of Law and Order Is a Lawless Man

Bolsonaro, like his supporters, believes that violence against people he considers immoral is right. He is famous for his finger-gun gesture (figure 5.5). This gesture, frivolous and performative, a kind of a prank, matches perfectly with the fathers in the stills from the films examined above, who grab a weapon and rush to attack. This gesture is deeply symbolic and models the mistrust and belligerence with which the citizens are supposed to treat each

Figure 5.5. Jair Bolsonaro's signature finger-gun gesture, 2019 (cropped). Photo by Marcos Corrêa/PR. https://creativecommons.org/licenses/by/4.0/deed.en

other. Bolsonaro admired Brazil's last military dictatorship and reinstated the commemorations of the coup day, March 31. As congressman, he hung portraits of the dictatorship leaders in his office. As president, he tripled the number of military personnel in civilian posts in the federal government to nearly 1,100. His vice president is a former general (Nikas). Before the 2022 presidential election, he was trailing Lula in the polls, so he began undermining the public trust in the election results and declared that "a new class of thieves has emerged who want to steal our freedom. If necessary, we will go to war" (Nikas). This "law and order" man was threatening a coup. In the first round, he finished with 43 percent to Lula's 48 percent and attempted to criminalize polling firms for predicting "false" results. He lost the election to Lula and went silent for a few days, while his supporters blocked highways in a bid to overturn the election. When he reemerged in public, he neither acknowledged his defeat nor mentioned Lula at all. Instead, he said he understood his supporters' "indignation and the feeling of injustice over the electoral process." Only his chief of staff said they would begin the transition process (Spigariol and Nikas).

Like all authoritarians, Bolsonaro believes that only *he* is fit to rule, only what *he* says is right. This is just how Kafka described his father: "In your armchair you ruled the world. Your opinion was right, all other opinions were mad, extreme, freakish—not normal.... And you could condemn the Czechs, and condemn the Germans, and condemn the Jews—all of them in each and every respect—until the only man left undamned was yourself. Just you alone remained" (*Letter* 9). Kafka's father issued strict rules for everyone, but never bothered to follow them himself. The authoritarian creates rules only to have a pretext to abuse and control his terrorized subjects and to have the pleasure of breaking these rules in front of them. "Almost every meal was for me a festival of malice and spite," writes Kafka:

> Bones could not be held in the hand and picked clean, except by you. Vinegar could not be slurped, except by you. It was vital how the bread was cut, but you could cut it with a knife dripping in sauce. One had to be careful not to let crumbs fall to the floor, but when we had finished most lay under you. One could not be distracted at the table; you cut your nails, sharpened pencils and cleaned your ears with toothpicks. But please, father, understand me correctly: these were completely insignificant details, yet they oppressed me, because you, a great man of authority, could lay down rules for me, and ignore them. And through this I saw that the world was divided into three parts: in the first lived the slave, me, under laws invented solely for my life but to which, without understanding why, I could never fully adjust; and in the second part lived you, infinitely far from me, busy ruling, giving commands and being angry when they weren't followed; and in the third lived everybody else, happy and free from commands and obedience. (*Letter* 13)

Such a family gathering, with the father screaming and breaking his own rules, is an appropriate metaphor for Bolsonaro's recent meeting with his ministers, the recording of which shocked the public. With at least forty insults, threats, and curses, Bolsonaro scolded governors, senators, the Supreme Court, and the ministers themselves, who looked away, ashamed and confused (Galarraga Cortázar). At the meeting, Bolsonaro, who rose to power as an anti-corruption crusader, was furious that he could not replace the chief of police to shield himself and his sons from criminal investigations (Londoño et al.) The authoritarian lays down laws for others but considers himself above them because he is right—not intellectually but organically, as Kafka so well explained: "And you became for me that puzzle which belongs to all tyrants: the law lay in your person and not in your wisdom" (*Letter* 9). The louder the father and the politician screams about rules and discipline, the more obvious it should be that he himself is a lawless man.

Conclusion

German philosopher Walter Benjamin said that "the fathers in Kafka's strange families batten on their sons, lying on top of them like giant parasites" (Despiniadis 31). Kafka's stories are parables of the father who slowly poisons his son with continuous emotional abuse. The father's taunts, mockery, and threats become part of the son's identity. Kafka wrote a letter to his father to explain why he does not seek him out or show affection like the father expects. Returning the letter unopened, Kafka's father refused to acknowledge the reality of emotional abuse, and so its slow poison continued to spread. Kafka's struggle with his father took place in his imagination and his stories. He lost that battle and died when he was only forty, before his father. But the intensity of this struggle—Kafka believed that books must be like "an ax for the frozen sea within us" (Thiher)—was a revelation for anti-authoritarian thinkers. Elias Canetti, author of *Crowds and Power*, wrote of Kafka: "Since he fears power in any form, since the real aim of his life is to withdraw from it, in in whatever form it may appear, he detects, identifies it, names it, and creates figures of it in every instance where others would accept it as being nothing of the ordinary" (87. Canetti's book will be my focus in the concluding chapter). For many philosophers, including Walter Benjamin, Michel Foucault, Theodor Adorno, Hannah Arendt, and Giorgio Agamben, Kafka's father helped theorize abusive political authority. The films discussed in this chapter are inspired by Kafka's letter to his father and his short stories. However, if Kafka and his heroes seek to withdraw from the father and his inscrutable power, in these films, the sons in the films stand up to him. The son leaves his house even as the father prepares to shoot him in the back (*Behind the Sun*). He sticks a burning cigarette into his hand and forces him to open the letter recounting his abuse, watching him weep (*Brainstorm*). The son shuns his violent and neglectful father and clings to his own little son as if he were the sole meaning and goal of his life (*City of Men*).

The sons in these twenty-first-century Brazilian films escape the father's doomed universe because Brazilian leaders at the beginning of the century purposefully adopted the inclusive discourse of a caring parent. They depicted the poor working class as citizens whose rights have long been violated and implemented affirmative action and redistributive policies. With Bolsonaro and his gun-like gestures and words, we witness the return of the abusive leader who mocks and threatens the left, the poor working class, women, Afro-Brazilians, Indigenous Brazilians, and members of the LGBTQ community. Bolsonaro also calls people he dislikes cockroaches (*baratas*), just like the violent policeman in *Elite Squad* who likens his victims to the insect from Kafka's *Metamorphosis*. It is important that films in which the son stands up to the abusive father are made. People who watch them become vicarious bystanders of abuse, and through these films, they may be more likely to recognize abuse when it becomes their political reality. It has been shown that bystanders of continual abuse experience almost as much stress as the victim. Witnessing abuse makes bystanders feel afraid, sad, powerless, guilty, and ashamed (Janson et al.). When we watch films, we experience these emotions indirectly and learn what the victims feel and why abusing others is wrong. These films instill in people a visceral repudiation of leaders who taunt and threaten. They teach audiences to see through such leaders' talk of order and discipline the familiar cruel coldness of a bad father and a lawless man.

6

The Histrion and Fatherhood as a Stage

Bolívar in Colombia and Venezuela

Films about the predatory father of a family or a nation often depict the man as an actor, suggesting he is not what he appears to be. The father is only pretending to be a good leader while pursuing a sinister hidden agenda. In chapter 3, we saw the Argentine kidnapper and murderer Puccio assume a cordial persona to gain the trust of his victims. In the films, Puccio wears heavy theatrical makeup and even an actual mask to show that this persona is merely a facade. In the Chilean film *Tony Manero*, discussed in the introduction, another killer practices dance moves with deadly determination to win a dancing contest and cares deeply about his snow-white performance suit. In the Peruvian novel and film *The Feast of the Goat*, discussed in chapter 2, the Dominican dictator Trujillo rapes performatively, to inspire awe. In this chapter, I discuss a leader to whom power beckons as a locus of attention and acclaim, as the stage beckons to an actor. The leader ignites his followers with a performance of messianic inspiration, offering them a leading role in the destiny of the fatherland. The followers partake in the leader's power and satisfy their thirst for obedience, as philosopher and cultural theorist Theodor Adorno explains. In turn, the leader draws energy from the collective enthusiasm of his followers. Power as a performance venue with guaranteed constant acclaim becomes an end in itself for the leader, an addiction. To leave the spotlight becomes unthinkable, so the leader demands absolute loyalty from his people and interprets dissent as treason. If he feels the admiration for him fade, the leader doubles down on seduction and charisma and failing that, on repressions, like an actor would if a rival attempted to steal the show. This histrionic facet of predatory leadership can best be grasped in recent artistic portrayals of Simón Bolívar, the revered hero of the Spanish American wars of independence, precisely because, until recently, men consecrated by history and tradition as the Founding Fathers were safe from such attacks.

Bolívar's comrades in arms portrayed him in two different ways: as a selfless visionary and as a selfish performer. The former president of Venezuela Hugo

Chávez and the Colombian radical left movements championed the first, heroic Bolívar and claimed that, like him, they were fighting to liberate Latin America from the control of the imperialist West and the local oligarchies. I examine three Venezuelan films that glorify Bolívar and indirectly, Chávez— *The Liberator*, *The Diary of Bucaramanga*, and *The Man of Difficulties*. The second, unflattering portrayal of Bolívar as a self-serving manipulator was endorsed by Karl Marx himself, to the embarrassment of Marxists (Aríco 55). Consequently, in Colombia, Bolívar is often portrayed as an actor and addict of the limelight—with irony in Jorge Alí Triana's film *Bolívar I Am*, with derision in Gabriel García Márquez's novel *The General in His Labyrinth*, and with indignation in Evelio Rosero's novel *The Feast of the Innocent*. Colombia recently released two historical telenovelas recounting the life of Bolívar and Chávez. In *Bolívar: una lucha admirable*, The Liberator is depicted as a selfless hero, but both Venezuelan actors who played him criticized this glorification. In *El comandante*, Chávez is portrayed as a consummate actor who uses Bolívar to conquer the spotlight (Andrés Parra, who played Chávez, said he had to play a better actor than himself). The attack on the hallowed figure of the Liberator is an act of symbolic *lèse-majesté*. Artists portray Bolívar with his pants down (Dávila and Insuasty), or suffering from malodorous flatulence (García Márquez) and even pedophilia (Rosero). That the Liberator became a straw man for attacks on predatory leadership is a warning to leaders and citizens. What if the messianic man is simply an actor, an addict of the limelight?

Bolívar Without Pants in Pop Art Style

We can easily grasp the recent transformation of Bolívar from visionary into histrionic leader in the paintings shown below. In *The Liberator*, painted by Venezuelan artist Tito Salas in 1930, Bolívar projects dignity and benevolence (figure 6.1). Juan Dávila, a Chilean artist based in Australia, parodied this canonical painting in his 1994 work *Liberator Simón Bolívar*. His version shows Bolívar as a half-caste with a woman's breasts peeking out of the uniform. He has no pants, and his exposed penis is barely covered by the saddle. He holds up his hand in a "Fuck-you" gesture. The painting provoked a scandal, and the Chilean government had to issue a formal apology to Venezuela, Colombia, and Ecuador. Dávila had since painted several other Bolívars. Some newer versions portray him as a young lumpen in a military uniform and a modern military boonie hat (often worn by guerrillas), with his pants down to his knees. The lumpen flashes a grin with a missing tooth as he takes aim at someone with a gun (figure 6.2) or making a different "Fuck-you" gesture. Note

Figure 6.1. *The Liberator Simón Bolívar*, by Tito Salas, 1930. Oil on canvas. Licensed under CC BY 4.0.

that the cloud around Bolívar's head in the original painting becomes a halo in Dávila's desacralizing versions. These paintings deride the man, Bolívar, but also people's need to idolize someone to give their lives meaning and purpose.

In another work, Dávila recreated Bolívar in a dystopian black-and-white

Figure 6.2. *The Liberator*, by Juan Dávila, 1996. ©Juan Dávila, courtesy of the artist and Kalli Rolfe Contemporary Art.

landscape, with a robot-head creature with a machine-gun hand whizzing along on a horse. Dávila also painted a Bolívar with the face of a glamorous female celebrity, reclining on his arm with feminine grace. His general's uniform dissolves to the epaulets and the embroidered collar (figure 6.3). Take note because in the last representation of The Liberator I will discuss, as a figure on a carnival float, Bolívar will also be missing pants and retain only the epaulets and collar from his uniform (figure 6.4). Dávila's painting shown below is stylized as a postcard of the Andes. The background landscape shows a large, generic American budget hotel at the foot of a picturesque, snow-

Figure 6.3. *Fig. 202*, by Juan Dávila, 2018. Acrylic on photographic paper. ©Juan Dávila, courtesy of the artist and Kalli Rolfe Contemporary Art.

covered mountain. Meanwhile, the locals are still without running water and scoop it from a stream in the background. Bolívar's face immediately brings to mind the photo of Marilyn Monroe's face, with a halo of blond curls and a seductive smile, which became even more famous after Andy Warhol made multiple clones of it in pop art style. Bolívar's pose comes from another famous shot of Monroe, made to be printed on postcards.

In this work, the painter portrays Bolívar as an actor who basks in the admiration of the crowds, a cult figure, just as Warhol transformed Monroe's face into an emblem of unthinking mass worship of charismatic celebrities in 1967. Dávila said he aims for "a language of disobedience," to undermine "the lineal language of history and the military" (Dávila).

Dávila follows in the footsteps of Colombian artist Beatriz Gonzalez who first applied ironic pop art style to Bolívar. In 1976, Gonzalez depicted the majestic equestrian portrait of Bolívar mentioned above (figure 6.1) with synthetic enamel on a very small rubber flag. In 1974, González made *Mutis por el foro*, a pop art version of another dignified depiction of Bolívar, the 1930 *Death of the Liberator* by Pedro Alcántara Quijano Moreno. In the original painting, the deceased Bolívar lies in his bed, covered with the flag of Gran Colombia and surrounded by a large group of officers in resplendent uniforms. In the pop art version, the prostrate Liberator is literally lying on the bed—he is painted on a metal bed bought at a flea market—and his entourage has been removed (Reyes 155). Like Dávila, González believes that "art says things that history cannot tell" (González). These pop art depictions of Bolívar deflate the worship of political leaders because constant acclaim habituates the leader to see himself as an irreplaceable savior and redeemer, *vox dei* and *vox populi* (the voice of God and the voice of the people; P. Castro 15).

Bolívar, the Reluctant Dictator

Bolívar's professed reluctance to assume and hold the position of supreme authority is almost a cliché. And yet, he served as president of the Second and Third Republic of Venezuela (1813–1814 and 1817–1819), the dictator of Peru (1824–1827), and the president of Bolivia, which was named in his honor (1825). Also, for eleven years, he ruled over Gran Colombia, which constituted today's Venezuela, Colombia, Ecuador, and Panama, as well as parts of northern Peru and northwestern Brazil. He served as president of this vast territory from 1819 until 1930, when he resigned and died a few months later.

Bolívar's famous Angostura Address (1819) reveals that he feared democratic elections. At first, he laments that his position of supreme authority is a "fearful and dangerous" burden on his "slender resources." Following Rousseau, Bolívar warns that one man in power is a recipe for disaster: "nothing is more perilous than to permit one citizen to retain power for an extended period. The people become accustomed to obeying him, and he forms the habit of commanding them; herein lie the origins of usurpation and tyranny" (Bolívar 183). However, Bolívar goes on to argue that one should not rely solely on elections because people are too ignorant to know who should rule over them: "one should not leave everything to chance in the elections, because people fool themselves too easily" (201). Therefore, the people should not be allowed to choose their rulers or have a say on how well they rule. Senators should not be elected. They should be "a new race of men," serve lifetime appointment and pass them on to their sons, and "if the people of Venezuela do not applaud the elevation of their benefactors, they do not deserve to be free and will never be free" (196). The same should be true for the president. He should have "an even greater authority" than the British monarch, serve until his death, and choose his successor (192). Bolívar sees the president as the Sun King and the Unmoved Mover (God) in one: "The President of the Republic comes to be in our Constitution, as the Sun that, firm in the center, gives life to the Universe. This supreme authority must be perpetual" (Bolívar 240). This poetic image of the lifetime president appears in the constitution Bolívar wrote in 1826 for the newly created Bolivia, named in his honor. Bolívar attempted to impose this constitution on Gran Colombia as well, but it was rejected by the Congress. In other words, Bolívar says he does not wish to establish aristocracy but this is exactly what he does; he warns against concentrating power in one man and then warns that not doing so would result in anarchy.

These consistent ambiguities reveal Bolívar's authoritarian bent. He pretended to assume power reluctantly, presented himself as an agent of history, and bequeathed this strategy to caudillos who dominated the region for the next century (Andrade and Lugo-Ocando 75). Bolívar exemplifies political Caesarism, a system in which the ruler represents his subjects in his person and expects from them only perpetual acclamation. The messianic leader denigrates elections and debate as formal, unauthentic democracy. What would be the point of consulting with the people if the providential man *is* the people, as Chávez, Bolívar's admirer, would say in the twenty-first century?

Bolívar Admired and Vilified by his Contemporaries

The messianic and heroic Bolívar emerged in the memoir of his faithful chief aide general Daniel Florence O'Leary. "Bolívar had a personality admirably suited to the dangerous undertaking of freeing his country. Young, active, brave, and unselfish, he devoted all his life and thoughts to this end," wrote O'Leary with admiration (55). Every time he assumed authority as the supreme chief, president, or dictator, Bolívar "utterly detested" it and only accepted it "to save the country from anarchy" and because he "had to agree to the fervent wishes of the people" (145). He sacrificed himself to the interests of his nation. In addition, he detested "liars and gossips" and was "so loyal and gentlemanly that he would not allow others to be discussed unfavorably in his presence" (140). Bolívar liked praise, but "flattery angered him" (140). He was a genius commander and defeated "experienced adversaries commanding troops very superior in numbers" (73). He was a great public administrator, "almost miserly with public funds" and "prodigal with what was his own" (140). Champion of liberty, "he had great regard for the sublime mission of the press" (142). He called himself "a soldier" and "a simple citizen" (362) and gave away all gifts presented to him. The insinuations that he harbored the desire to be the emperor of the territories he liberated were lies to damage his reputation, according to O'Leary.

Another Bolívar aide, Henry Louis Ducoudray Holstein, painted an entirely different Bolívar—a consummate performer who wore a mask and squashed free speech and rivals without mercy. "He prefers circuitous roads and dissimulation to frankness" (2:222), "he is very dissembling, and very dexterous in finding out various secret means to intrigue, and to gain his aim by numerous windings and doublings—he openly professed to be a warm patriot, a disinterested soldier, who wished for the welfare of his country, but was always anxious to save his reputation and zealous to preserve his authority" (1:224). In one instance, Bolívar mocked and disparaged one of his generals, but the moment that general walked into the room, Bolívar "met him at the door and embraced him warmly, as a dear friend," and conversed with him for hours (2:236). When Bolívar believed people could be useful to him, he was charming with them, but he removed his mask as soon as they served their purpose:

> He spares nothing to gain those he thinks will be of present use to him. He is officious in rendering them little services; he flatters them, makes them brilliant promises; finds whatever they suggest very useful and important, and is ready to follow their advice. A third person suggests something to him, or he meets with some unexpected success. Instantly he resumes his true character, and becomes vain, haughty, cross and violent; forgets all services, and all obligations, speaks with contempt of those he had just courted, and if they are powerless, abandons or sacrifices them. (2:236)

For Holstein, Bolívar was an autocrat, unwilling to share his power with anyone, in the times of war or peace. He governed incompetently and tyrannically, suspending freedoms and rights: "the security of persons and property depended on [his] will and decree," "the liberty of the press was a mere name" (1:219). As a result, he "destroyed the welfare of Colombia and that of Peru" (2:270). Being a man of "limited talents," Bolívar could not suffer men of "character, experience, and knowledge" for fear of being "found out" in this unflattering comparison (2:3). "His favorite occupations were being in the company of his numerous mistresses, and lying in his hammock surrounded by his flatterers," who amused him by criticizing the people he disliked (1:156). Incompetent loyalists thrived: "Those who flatter and please him best, get the best offices, without the least regard to their qualifications" (2:263). Profligate with public funds, he wasted money on his favorites and on festivities because he knew well that "so long as he reigns, he shall not want money" (2:266). As a skillful performer, he carefully staged his public appearances, telling "his friends and creatures" "what he intends to do and how they are to act" (2:264). Bolívar arranged his entry to Caracas in a triumphal car, in the manner of Roman emperors, except his car was drawn by "twelve fine young ladies, very elegantly dressed in white, adorned with the national colors, and all selected from the first families in Caracas. They drew him, in about half an hour, from the entrance of the city to his residence; he, standing on the car, bare-headed, and in full uniform, with a small wand of command in his hand" (1:151).

Holstein and another Bolívar's aide whose memoirs are another important source about Bolívar, General Louis Peru de Lacroix, note that The Liberator admired Napoleon Bonaparte, and copied both his appearance and rhetoric. Holstein wrote that Bolívar imitated Napoleon in his proclamations and by sporting a simple uniform amid the splendor of his suite: "[Bolívar] is ambitious, absolute, and jealous of his command, like [Napoleon]. On public occasions he is simply dressed, while all around him is splendid, like Napoleon, and he moves quickly from place to place like him. With respect to military and administrative talents, there is no resemblance between them" (Holstein 2:238). Peru de Lacroix recounted how Bolívar enviously praised Napoleon's smart way of visually distinguishing himself: "What numerous and brilliant General Staff Napoleon had, and what simplicity in his dress! All who surrounded him were covered in gold and rich embroideries, and he only had his epaulets, a hat without distinctions and a plain jacket" (Lacroix 82). Like Napoleon, Bolívar hungers for the admiration of the multitudes, and he feels satisfaction in having become, like Napoleon, "a center of attention, or if you like, the curiosity of almost the entire continent, and you can also say of the whole world" (82). While Bolívar professed a hatred for Napoleon for crowning himself monarch and destroying the Republic, he also styled himself after Napoleon, as a "simple soldier" and "citizen" who sacrificed everything for the country. In his Angostura Address, Bolívar borrowed the idea that "nothing is so dangerous for the people as a weak executive" from Napoleon's 1806 speech to the congress: "weakness in the executive is the greatest of all misfortunes to the people" (Bonaparte, "To the Legislative Body"). Even Bolívar's famous 1830 self-sacrificial farewell, "If my death can heal and fortify the union, I go to my tomb in peace" (Bolívar 281), is very much like Napoleon's 1815 farewell, "I offer myself as sacrifice to the hatred of the enemies of France" (Bonaparte, "Proclamation"). We will see that writers and filmmakers deride Bolívar's love of grandiloquence and pomp.

Ironically, Karl Marx, the founder of modern communism and anti-imperialism, chose Holstein's histrionic Bolívar. In the *New American Cyclopaedia* entry on Bolívar, Marx describes him as a petty criollo aristocrat who "pretended," "plotted," "conspired," "contrived," and "dissimulated" as a champion of liberty in order to make "the whole of South America into one federative republic, with himself as its dictator." A cowardly man and a worthless commander, Bolívar wasted lives and protracted the war. He schemed and plotted to return to power until his very last breath: "He effected his retreat from Bogota in a very slow manner, and contrived, under a variety of pretexts, to prolong his sojourn at San Pedro, until the end of 1830, when he suddenly died" (Marx, "Bolívar y Ponte"; this sentence sums up the García Márquez's novel about Bolívar, discussed below). Marx was even harsher on Bolívar in a letter to Engels. He called him a "most cowardly, meanest, and most wretched louse" (feigsten, gemeinsten, elendesten Lump, Marx, Letter), and compared him to Faustin Soulouque, who was elected president of Haiti and soon proclaimed himself Emperor.

The Heroic Bolívar in Recent Venezuelan Films

Still, this scathing criticism was brushed off as a misunderstanding or eurocentrism on the part of Marx (Arico 55), and in the twentieth century Bolívar became a powerful symbol for South American left-wing intellectuals. The famous "Song for Bolívar" by Chilean poet Pablo Neruda ("Canto a Bolívar," 1950) erected Bolívar as the creator and redeemer of Latin America. The poem begins as the Lord's Prayer but is directed to the Liberator: "Our Father who art on the earth, in the water, in the air," "all bears thy name, Father, in our land." Sugarcane, tin, the bird, the volcano, the potato, saltpeter, rivers, planes, bell towers, and "our daily bread"—they all bear Bolívar's name. In a somewhat macabre way, the body of the dead Liberator sprouts to the surface. From "the seed of thy dead heart," "from thy little brave captain's corpse," suddenly "thy fingers spread out in the snow." Multitudes of hands, all red, from all over the world, reach out to clasp Bolívar's hand sprouting from the ground. The dead Liberator's sword and banner call out to the living to gather into armies under his name. This Bolívar is God the Father ("our Father who art in heaven") and God the Redeemer, who died and rose from the dead in order to save the oppressed. Later in life, Neruda witnessed Chinese peasants prostrating themselves in front of Mao's portraits and became aware of Stalin's death camps. Neruda became disillusioned with "Maostalinism, a repetition of the cult of a socialist deity" (Neruda, *Confieso* 331). We are left to wonder whether he might have taken back the Bolívar he deified as another possibly dangerous messianic man.

Neruda's godlike Bolívar remains with us, as we can see in the posters of three recent films from Venezuela I will now discuss. Bolívar looms as god the creator over the mass of people in posters of *The Liberator* and *The Diary of Bucaramanga* and offers himself as a sacrifice to his cause, as Christ the redeemer in the poster of *The Man of Difficulties* (Bolívar, challenged to a duel by a fellow patriot, refuses to shoot). Bolívar, who in real life was a man of small stature with a high voice, comes through in these films as both the charismatic demigod and the tender martyr. This is because Venezuelan leader Hugo Chávez founded his regime on the cult of Bolívar and himself.

The 2013 Venezuelan film *The Diary of Bucaramanga* (*Diario de Bucaramanga*), directed by Carlos Fung, is based on the diary of Bolívar's aid Peru de Lacroix. In this film, Bolívar tries to pass his decisions democratically but fails to gather support and proclaims himself dictator. In 1828, Bolívar called the congress of Ocaña. He waited with his generals in the nearby city of Bucaramanga, to make sure the Congress passed his new centralist constitution, with a lifetime presidency (for himself) and a hereditary Senate. Bolívar (Simón Pestana) entertains his inner circle with pleasant anecdotes of his love and military conquests, but he rages when he finds out that the congressmen have rejected his constitution and are trying to push a federalist constitution. Bolívar takes power into his hands and assumes dictatorial powers, only for the sake of "unity" and "peace," and his lover Manuelita Sáenz praises this decision. She saves Bolívar from an assassination attempt plotted by his disgruntled enemies, Padilla and Santander. The film makes the memoir's author, Peru de Lacroix, into a character in the film (played by Patrick Delmas). Expected by his father-in-law to spy on Bolívar, Peru de Lacroix becomes Bolívar's sincere admirer, saying, "I never betrayed you, your cause is my cause, I believe in your vision, I believe in one great nation" (Jamás le traicioné, su causa también es la mía, creo en su visión, creo en una gran nación). In the film, Bolívar assumes the dictatorship reluctantly, only to complete his historic mission to create and save the united Latin America. The film's director, Carlos Fung, expressed his admiration for "the eternal president" Chávez and "his dreams, his struggle, his commitment" to reviving Bolívar's project ("Estrenan in Zulia").

Another messianic Bolívar appears in the 2012 Venezuelan film *The Man of Difficulties* (*El hombre de las dificultades*), directed by Luis Lamata. When the film opens, Bolívar is in exile in Jamaica, after losing a battle to the royalist forces in 1815 (the rancorous Holstein wrote that he escaped there after deserting his army). During this exile, Bolívar petitions the president of Haiti, Alexandre Pétion, for military support in order to relaunch the liberation campaign. His antagonist is the agent of the Spanish empire, El Polaco (Jorge Reyes). Bolívar's other antagonists are his fellow patriots, but he is magnanimous: challenged to a duel by one of them, General Montilla, he fires into the air. (In a much better-known dark episode of his biography, Bolívar actually ordered the execution of a fellow patriot, General Piar, fearing that he would challenge his authority.) The filmmakers explain that their Bolívar is a tribute to Chávez. Roque Valero, who played Bolívar in the film said, "Commander Chávez was the first to take Simón Bolívar off the pedestal and transform him into a living human being. We continue his work by means of a script. We have a real Bolívar, who suffers, weeps, faces difficulties and must overcome them" (Valero 2014). Ironically, the Bolívar of this film is uncharismatic and unsubstantial and is more convincing as an adventurer and womanizer.

Bolívar is even more like Chávez in the 2013 Venezuelan film *The Liberator*, where he confronts Western bankers who want to subjugate the country he liberated. In this film, Bolívar (played by Edgar Ramírez) constantly speaks to the masses of ragged people, who follow him as if enchanted. The scene when Bolívar crosses into Venezuela in 1813, to mark the beginning of the pivotal "Campaña Admirable," sets him apart from the Colombian general Francisco de Paula Santander, the future president of Colombia. Santander refuses to cross into Venezuela because his orders are to stay in Colombia, and he is "the man of the laws" (which is Santander's nickname, hombre de las leyes). In contrast, Bolívar follows a calling. His democracy is authentic, not rule-based, like Santander's: he always asks directly whether the soldiers want to follow him, and they always do. Like other political Caesars, he consults with the people only to hear a yes.

In this film, Bolívar has enemies he will be unable to defeat—the perfidious foreign bankers who invested in his campaign in order to wrestle this vast market from Spain. British banker Martin Torkington (Danny Huston), who has "a nose for money, like a pig with truffles," offers to fund the campaign and says with disarming frankness: "It is not often that an entire continent comes into play." Soon, Torkington comes to visit Bolívar in Venezuela, and they talk on an idyllic beach. Bolívar asks the banker what he wants in return for his help. Torkington casts a greedy look around him, inhales aggressively, and replies, "I should like to buy a house here but with Spaniards in power it would be impossible." He says forebodingly, "We have plans for the continent." Bolívar rejoins, "We make our own plans," but later, he turns to him again for assistance. Torkington provides Bolívar with the money needed to continue his campaign, saying, "Here is my investment in the future of the continent. Money is freedom!" He returns to collect his due when Bolívar is the president of the vast Gran Colombia, asking to let the British open and operate Gran Colombia's first bank. Bolívar is indignant: "Do you think the Congress will allow it?" Torkington cunningly rejoins, "We did not ask the Congress. We asked you." The British just want to help the new republic build its "basic infrastructure," argues the banker, but Bolívar knows what they want: "What you're asking is to control our financial system. That is not infrastructure, it is invasion, an affront to the freedom we won." "Simón!" pleads the capitalist like an offended old friend. "President," Bolívar corrects him, "Respect this office and the people." The banker retires with a foreboding, "Long live The Liberator!" Immediately after that, the film cuts to the final scene: Bolívar's assassination by unnamed killers. The film supports Chávez's claims that Bolívar did not die from tuberculosis but rather was killed by his enemies. Claiming that Bolívar was killed, Chávez implied that he too is under threat. This narrative of danger was meant to compel Venezuelans to unite around him and protect him and their country. It also reflects Chávez's criticism of the International Monetary Fund and the World Bank, which make their loans conditional on cutting government spending and opening domestic markets to private and foreign investors and casts these measures as essential to democracy.

All three Venezuelan films glorify Bolívar through Chávez and Chávez through Bolívar. When he assumed the presidency in 1999, Chávez, too, said he would serve only one term, but after each successive term he extended that horizon: until 2012, then 2021, then 2030, then 2050 . . . (Carroll 272). But he died in 2013 after a battle with cancer. He led a coup in 1992 and failed, but his first appearance on TV following the failed coup made him instant celebrity, a hero, and later, president. After winning the presidency in 1998, Chávez changed the constitution, increasing the presidential term to six years and introducing two consecutive terms (at that time, even his allies from the pro-government party Podemos accused him of seeking lifelong power). In 2007, Chávez attempted to amend the constitution again, extending the presidential term to seven years and allowing the president to run for reelection indefinitely. When this proposal failed in the referendum, Chávez still pushed the lifetime presidency by passing an amendment to abolish the two-term limit for all public offices, including the presidency, in 2009 (Cannon 64). As

Raúl Baduel, his old comrade-in-arms and his Defense Secretary said, "Power changed Chávez." Everyday president's work "was small potatoes for him. He preferred to be elsewhere saving humanity . . . It became obvious that the only thing he cared for was being president for life. The mask kept slipping" (Carroll 149). Baduel was imprisoned in 2009, placed under house arrest six years later, and returned to prison in 2017, where he died in 2021.

Chávez transformed Bolívar into a cult figure, the great Father of the new socialist fatherland. He would leave an empty seat for Bolívar at meetings and prayed to him. In a macabre spectacle reminiscent of Neruda's poem, Chávez had Bolívar's remains exhumed in 2010 to prove that he was poisoned by his enemies who wanted to destroy Gran Colombia. Although forensic experts could not confirm this theory, Chávez held on to it. In addition, Chávez presented to the public a new portrait of Bolívar supposedly based on his remains, in which the Liberator resembles Chávez himself (Wallis). Chávez conflated himself with Bolívar and Jesus and used religious symbols to cast himself as a messianic man. Chávez led his admirers to think that through him they acquired an identity and voice, because he represented them all. His catchphrase was "I am not Chávez. I am the people" (Chávez no soy yo. Yo soy el pueblo; Block 242). Because he was "the people," Chávez understood dissent as treason and repeated, "I demand absolute loyalty to my leadership, because I am not me, I am the people, *carajo*" (Block 242). In his last TV appearance in 2013, Chávez announced that his cancer had returned while the camera continuously cut from his face to the large portrait of Bolívar above him, the bust of Bolívar at his side, Bolívar's sword, and the large cross in his hand. Chávez kept saying that, should he die, Venezuelans must elect his handpicked successor Nicolás Maduro and unite around him (Maduro was Chávez's driver in the early stages of his career). He also kept kissing the cross, saying that faith in Jesus had saved him. He repeated that he was the people, that Chávez knew the heart of the people and the people knew the heart of Chávez. He congratulated his followers that they had created their fatherland (patria), and restored it to Bolívar, the Father (padre). The enemies are only waiting to destroy it, "so our answer should be unity, unity, and, again, unity. As Bolívar used to say, 'Let's unite, or anarchy will devour us.' Unity, unity, unity," Chávez kept repeating like an incantation ("Hugo Chávez").

Venezuelan political analyst Carlos Rey argued that for both Chávez and Bolívar, unity meant unconditional loyalty to them and their "vision." If the leader is the people, true and participative democracy means obeying the leader's directives. Political debates and parties thwart the harmony between the leader and the followers and hinder authentic democracy. When the leader manages to trick or scare the people into thinking that only he knows how to build "the new Kingdom of God on Earth," "there will be no limits on the extent of his power or the sacrifices he will demand from the people" (Rey 181). Chávez borrowed from the playbook of democratic Caesarism, says political scientist Colette Capriles. He told the people they were the subject of politics but also that he incarnated them entirely in his person. The people, the supposedly protagonistic "pueblo elector," were reduced to perpetually acclaiming whatever Caesar says and does.

Why are people so eager to gather around a providential autocrat when they are the first to suffer from his deluded decisions? Theodor Adorno showed that people with authoritarian personalities tend to conform to conventional norms and exhibit a submissive attitude toward authority while being hostile toward out-group (*The Authoritarian Personality*). In addition, they get caught up in the logic of performance, as Adorno showed in "Freudian Theory and the Pattern of Fascist Propaganda." Participating in a rally can stir the emotions of the people in attendance "to a pitch that they seldom or never attain under other conditions" (123). Losing their individuality and becoming part of the crowd, the primeval horde, they experience elation. The leader assumes the role of the horde's omnipotent father. He makes them believe that the entire world is against them, and they admire the leader because he promises to protect them. At the same time, the leader plays the part of "the great little man"—a man just like his followers, only better. Thus, the followers partake in the leader's greatness, and at the same time satisfy their "passion for authority" and "thirst for obedience" (126). In turn, the leader draws his power from the collective strength of his admirers (126). Paradoxically, the exaggerated theatricality of this collective performance strengthens the symbiotic bond between the leader and the followers. In fact, the followers do not have to really "believe in the leader. They do not really identify themselves with him but act this identification, perform their own enthusiasm, and thus participate in their leader's performance" (127). Knowing that the leader is "a ham actor," and aware of the "fictitiousness" and "phoniness" of his performance, the followers applaud him all the more zealously (127). Both the leader and the crowd follow the logic of the performance, of the make-believe, and they give each other energy and identity.

Chávez's histrionic personality drew the attention of journalists, political analysts, writers, and filmmakers. When Chávez won the presidency in 1999, Colombian writer Gabriel García Márquez met him and wondered whether he was a savior or an illusionist (García Márquez, "El enigma de Chávez"). Stage, performance, and spectacle are common metaphors in books about Chávez's "socialism of the 21st century" and his "Bolivarian Revolution." In his book *Comandante: Hugo Chávez's Venezuela*, journalist Rory Carrol wrote that Chávez "bestrode society like a colossus, commanding attention, everywhere his voice, his face, his name. It did not matter whether you despised or adored him—you looked. Covering Venezuela was like wandering through a vast, boisterous audience that simultaneously booed and cheered the titan who turned the presidential palace, Miraflores, into a stage" (16). The grand performance ended in a fiasco: "Venezuela atrophied. Nothing worked, but there was money and spectacle. An empty revolution, then. No paradise, no hell, just limbo, a bleak, misty in-between where ambition and delusion played out its ancient story" (292). Rafael Uzcategui in *Venezuela: Revolution as a Spectacle* also compares Chávez's Venezuela to an "epic production." Chávez claimed that he made the dispossessed the agents of change, but during his presidency the private sector experienced more growth than social economy. Incompetent and corrupt loyalists were appointed to lead the economy and the nationalized companies. When global oil prices tumbled in 2014, the country's economy collapsed. What Chávez called "popular power" turned out to be the familiar domination by the elite. Uzcategui described Chavismo as a "media spectacle," "a pseudo-world," which exists only in "the long speeches, the never-ending display of urban housing projects, agricultural co-ops, and plants managed by their workers—all of which disappear when the actors march off the television screen." To create his leadership persona, Chávez tapped into the cult of the male military hero and macho values. He wore a military uniform and used belligerent vocabulary: "the enemy within," "socialism or death," electoral "battle," and others (Uzcategui). Chávez was a media Caesar, says Colette Capriles. The weekly show *Hello, Mr. President* (Aló Presidente) with Chávez speaking, singing, and talking with random people and associates for hours on end, was not direct democracy, as he claimed, but the spectacle of it (Capriles 58).

Accordingly, the 2017 Colombian series *El Comandante* portrayed Chávez as an actor. It was created by writer and columnist Moisés Naím, former Venezuela's Minister of Trade and Industry and former editor-in-chief of *Foreign Policy* magazine. The series shows Chávez say one thing and do another—without premeditation, almost instinctively. For example, he tells the mother of a girl he is courting that she would finish school at the locality in which he is stationed, and that he had already spoken with the principal. He is inventing all of it on the spot, and later he tells the girl that one should always tell people what they want to hear. The girl looks worried, and soon she learns that Chávez has affairs with other women. But even these affairs seem to be merely the collateral of his need to seduce everyone personally. It is impossible to know what Chávez really thinks and what his "Revolution" means, other than him being in the spotlight as its leader indefinitely. When his close associate tells him that things are worse than before they came to power, Chávez explodes with anger and tells him to leave. His first encounter with the press is shown in slow motion, as a life-turning event. He speaks into the camera in the wake of the coup that failed because he got distracted or afraid and when his leadership was most needed, he was talking with a bust of Bolívar instead (episode 14). When he sees cameras pointed at him, this confused and insecure man transforms into a perfectly focused vector of energy. He becomes a celebrity after that first public interview, and crowds gather to demand his release from prison. When he is released, people gather to cheer him. They place portraits of him in their homes and light up candles in front of them as if he were a saint. This Colombian show makes it clear that what they want is to believe a man, idolize a man, and for some reason, Chávez is the man who can give them that and they are grateful to him for it. They demand nothing else of him and do not care if their life does not improve. Similarly, all Chávez wants and is able to offer is being this idol, this receptacle in which people can place their adoration. His last communion with the admiring crowds is also shown in slow motion. In this scene, Chávez campaigns for presidency in 2012, already exhausted by his battle with cancer. Although he now moves with difficulty and is in constant pain, he is so energized by the prospect of speaking to a large audience that he runs up the steps leading to the stage, rejecting an unflattering raincoat his aides try to put on him. He walks around on the stage talking with excitement, happily oblivious to the pouring rain, like his fans. After his performance, he tumbles down the steps into the arms of his friends, in slow motion, and passes out (episode 102). These shots are highly symbolic, showing how exercising power and being the center of attention can become ends in themselves. Cultural critic Ángel Rama in his book about Latin American dictators brilliantly summed up the obsession with power: "this voracious and crushing passion . . . leaves no place in the soul for anything else, dries out all spiritual life and is punished by a complete loneliness," "until nothing survives this embrace of power which in the end becomes empty of any appeals that it once offered" (Rama 52). Throughout the show, Chávez is called an "actor," "clown," "liar" (actor, buffón, mentiroso) by his antagonists. The fillers Chávez constantly uses such as "yo . . . de verdad . . ." (I . . . the truth is . . .), "fíjate" (look), "compañero," "compadre," "amigo," repeated *ad infinitum*, become his essence, rather than discursive strategies used to establish rapport. Although he has nothing to say, he has a pathological desire to speak, seduce, and be admired. The Colombian actor who played Chávez, Andrés Parra, said that the main challenge of the role was "to play an actor who is better than yourself" (Parra). Incidentally, and to Nicolas Maduro's great anger, before playing Chávez, Parra also played the drug lord Pablo Escobar in the telenovela *Patrón del mal* (the title literally translates as "the master of evil"). Note that Parra opined that Escobar is "a joke" compared to Chávez!

This is why when the new Colombian show about Bolívar was announced, Maduro condemned it beforehand, expecting some dirty trick of the likes of *El Comandante*, but after he watched it, he wished it had a thousand episodes instead of sixty ("Maduro se retracta"). As we can see from the title, *Bolívar, una lucha* (battle) *admirable*, this 2019 Colombian production runs contrary to the general trend in Colombia to portray Bolívar critically. In the poster of the show, Bolívar looks like Christ the Pantocrator, similar to the godlike Bolívar in the posters of the three Venezuelan films discussed above. Produced by the Colombian company Caracol and distributed internationally by Netflix, the show commemorated the bicentennial of the Independence and aimed to portray the birth of independent Latin America in a dignified and grandiose manner. The most expensive Colombian TV production to date (Finol), it was well received in Latin America but alienated international audiences unaccustomed to the telenovela format and its sentimentalism. While the producers and the creator said they wanted to portray Bolívar as a human being, the result was a Bolívar who speaks and acts like a hero (Quintero). His lover, Manuela Saenz, is the only character to occasionally question his decisions: "But dictator, Simón! Dictator! They will claim it was what you wanted all along! They will call you a tyrant!" (episode 56). Bolívar passionately explains that he must save the united Gran Colombia, and this explanation is enough to reassure Manuelita. Interestingly, both Venezuelan actors who portrayed Bolívar in the film said that everyone grew tired of the image of Bolívar as redeemer and savior during the two decades of Chavismo. Actor Luis Gerónimo Abreu, who played the adult Bolívar in the Colombian series, said that Bolívar's determination bordered on madness. He also opined that Bolívar would have been insulted by Chávez's "Bolivarian Revolution" and would have removed his name from it (Abreu). The actor who played the young Bolívar, José Ramón Barreto, said that Venezuela has had about enough of the cult of boots and needed not one Liberator, but thirty million Liberators, meaning all Venezuelans (Barreto). Both Venezuelan actors expressed frustration with the charismatic male hero they played in the show.

Bolívar the Histrion in Colombia

More generally, however, in Colombian films and novels (and several recent popular history books, see the conclusion for some scathing titles), Bolívar has come under increased criticism in recent decades. Chávez's belligerent attacks on the conservative president of Colombia Álvaro Uribe is one reason for this critical attitude. The second reason is that in Colombia, Bolívar was also appropriated by radical left movements as an Indigenous symbol of anti-imperialism in the post-Marxist world (Chernick 68). Unsurprisingly, Chávez often expressed his support for the FARC, claiming that they have a "Bolivarian project," which is "respected here in Venezuela." The guerrillas received refuge and some military aid from Venezuela, although its officials denied it (Acosta). These movements sought to overthrow the Colombian government and establish a socialist state, using terrorism, kidnapping, and other violent tactics. The government responded with similar violence and the country plunged into a five-decade bloody conflict. The umbrella group of these guerrilla movements, active from 1987 to the early 1990s, called itself Simón Bolívar Guerrilla Coordinating Board. The guerrillas stole and paraded Bolívar's battle swords. The 19th of April Movement (M-19) stole Bolívar's sword from a museum in 1974. "Bolívar, your sword returns to the battle," the guerrillas declared, to achieve a second independence, "this time total and definitive" (M-19). They restituted the sword in 1991 and transitioned to a political party. Another radical left movement that stole Bolívar's sword was the FARC (Revolutionary Armed Forces of Colombia, Fuerzas Armadas Revolucionarias de Colombia), an organization with a more troublesome record and history that cuts across classes in terms of victims, which relied on kidnapping, extortion, and drug trafficking to finance their operations. They presented the stolen sword to the left-wing Continental Bolivarian Movement founded in 2009 in Caracas. In 2010, a FARC commander was filmed with another sword, saying, "the Great Hero has come back, . . . his sword will shine in the first line of combat, fighting, opening the paths of hope, of definitive independence, of the victory of the Liberator's political and social project" (*Rebelión*). The FARC disarmed and transitioned to a political party in 2017.

There is so much resentment and so many people died or were displaced during the conflict that Colombians voted against the peace deal with the FARC in 2016, rejecting amnesty and community service for the guerrillas as inadequate reparation for the violence they had unleashed. This is why in Colombia, Bolívar receives some of the animosity people feel for radical left guerrillas and Chavismo. Historians and artists have wondered why these pseudo-democratic and de facto authoritarian movements claim Bolívar as their symbol and mentor. Colombian writers and filmmakers use irony and scornful pity to reflect and model the demand for non-authoritarian, non-messianic, and non-histrionic political leadership. Accordingly, on the poster of the film *Bolívar I Am*, we see a sulking Bolívar with a pigeon sitting on his head. The cover of the novel *The General in His Labyrinth* features Bolívar's *empty* hammock. On the cover of the novel *The Feast of the Innocent*, Bolívar is either the monstrous creature from Bosch's *The Garden of Earthly Delights*, who devours people alive and excretes them for further tortures (2012 edition) or the Devil himself (2019 edition).

The Bolívar that Gabriel García Márquez created in his 1989 novel *The General in His Labyrinth* (*General en su laberinto*) is obviously an actor who is able to hide his enormous ambition under the mask of humility only with an equally enormous self-discipline. This constant repression causes violent mood swings: for example, Bolívar insults and curses his young loyal aide after losing a game of cards to him (these details are borrowed from the memoir of Peru de Lacroix). Bolívar is traveling up the Magdalena River, on his last voyage from Bogota to Santa Marta, where he will die before his intended departure for Europe. All the while, he compares the pitiful welcome he receives from the townspeople on his way with his triumphal entry into Caracas in a chariot pulled by six young girls (an anecdote borrowed from Holstein and Marx). García Márquez quietly mocks Bolívar's need to seduce people, "the terrible power of his charm," "capable of parting oceans and moving mountains" (capaz de apartar océanos y derribar montañas con su terrible poder de seducción; 217). No one believes his "repeated renunciations from power" anymore, and his line "My first day of peace will be my last day in power" becomes a popular song. The city walls are scribbled with "He won't leave and he won't die" (ni se va, ni se muere; 13). And still Bolívar is surprised that no one voted for him in the last presidential election. "Not a single vote for me?" he asks incredulously. "Not a single one," responds the narrative voice somewhat sadistically (¿Ni un solo voto por mí? Ni un solo; 29). Finally, he leaves Bogota, and his path is strewn with symbols of death, disease, and ruin—a rabid dog, stoned and hanged from a tree near a schoolhouse (187); another "filthy, emaciated dog, suffering from mange and a paralyzed paw" (113) whom he adopts and names Bolívar; and funerals (121). Ravaged by tuberculosis, he shrinks to such smallness and lightness that when he falls on the stairs he cannot roll down the steps, and when he comes out to the ship deck his aides worry that a gust of wind will carry him off. He suffers from malodorous flatulence and diarrhea. And yet, as soon as he learns that a faction wants him back as president, he springs back to life and spends days and nights planning his return. Again, we are in the presence of the histrion. Throughout the novel, he is shown to be doing one thing but thinking another. Not even his friends believe him. A bishop comes to confess him when he is on the verge of dying but storms out of the room without saying a word "in a state of consternation," refusing to officiate at the funeral or even to attend it (267). García Márquez was criticized for such a disconcerting portrayal of the Liberator, as a man for whom being needed, important, and powerful became an addiction, a narcotic. The writer was accused of stripping "Latin Americans of one of the few heroes we have" (Rohter). García Márquez serenely riposted that he felt very close to Bolívar, came to "love him a lot and have a lot of compassion for him" (García Márquez, Interview). Derisive pity is perhaps one of the most powerful means to pulverize the cult of a man. In one scene, Bolívar makes love to a very hairy girl and then "lovingly" shaves her from head to foot, including eyebrows. The girl, "her soul in shreds," asks him if he really loves her, and he answers "with the same ritual phrase he had strewn without pity in so many hearts throughout his life: 'More than anyone else in this world'" (213). In this jocular scene, García Márquez paints Bolívar as a clownish narcissist.

The 2003 Colombian film *Bolívar I Am* (*Bolívar soy yo*) shows how addictive it is to find oneself even for a short time in the role of a messiah and how eagerly people gather around messiahs. An actor playing Bolívar in a telenovela becomes convinced that he really *is* The Liberator and vows to make his dream come true. José Alí Triana, who wrote and directed the film, witnessed such a metamorphosis take place in the actor who played Bolívar on the set of the telenovela he directed two decades before. The star of that telenovela, Pepe Montoya, came to be treated by everyone as if he really were Bolívar, and Triana noticed that even off the set the actor also began dressing like Bolívar and speaking with grandiloquent words and gestures. On one occasion, local peasants who were told that Bolívar would come to visit them arrived at the set with vegetables, chickens, suckling pigs, and brandy for The Liberator and asked him to help with roads, the school, water supply, and the FARC and paramilitary violence. The actor, Pepe Montoya, answered he would be happy to help with "all these stupid things (pendejadas) you are asking me to do," but first he has to win all his battles, "in Bomboná, Pinchincha, Junín, and later, Ayacucho" (Martínez). Pepe Montoya would also come to political gatherings and beauty pageant panels as Bolívar (Silió).

Triana recreated this eerie transformation of the actor into a charismatic character in *Bolívar I Am*. The actor who plays Bolívar in a telenovela (Robinson Díaz) comes to believe he really is Bolívar, and everyone immediately plays along. Even his mother talks to the actor as if he were Bolívar. The president of Colombia (Jairo Camargo) brings him along to the summit of the Bolivarian presidents in Santa Marta. "Bolívar," who is actually an actor, says to the president: "You do your theater, I will take care of politics" (usted se ocupa del teatro, yo de política). At the summit, "Bolívar" says he rose from the grave to bring back Gran Colombia. "My name was used for the worst," says "Bolívar" gravely as he turns to face the president of Peru: "for mediocre schools, useless hospitals, constitutions which no one follows"; "to justify a coup," he continues, turning to the president of Venezuela; and "the barbarity of the armed struggle," concludes Bolívar turning to the president of Colombia (mi nombre ha sido utilizado para el peor: para los colegios mediocres, hospitales que no sirven, constituciones que no se aplican, para justificar el golpe de estado, y la barbarie de la lucha armada). The actor takes the president of Colombia hostage and tells the other presidents to meet him in Bogota. He sails down the Magdalena River to Bogota, reversing the moribund Liberator's last voyage. Immense crowds gather to salute him as he sails by. Suddenly, guerrillas storm the boat, but only to present the actor with Bolívar's sword and pledge to fight at his side to make his dream come true. "This has nothing to do with my dreams," "Bolívar" objects acrimoniously (Eso no tiene nada que ver con mis sueños). As they all arrive in Bogota for the supposed recreation of Gran Colombia, the security forces shower them with bullets. Amid blood, smoke, and shell casings, the expiring "Bolívar" says "Cut!" with a happy smile. Triana, who also wrote the script for the film, said he made "a tragic tropical farce," "a parable about our history and of what is happening today" (Triana). He added, "Everyone has their own vision of Bolívar," said Triana, "and my Bolívar is a utopian delirious dreamer" (Silió).

Another recent Colombian film about the utopian dream ending in violence with a possible reference to Bolívar is *Monos* (2019), directed and cowritten by Alejandro Landes. A group of teens, kidnapped as children by the guerrillas, "train" and guard a kidnapped American researcher, first in the isolated mountains, then in the jungle. As their dwarflike commander lines them up and lectures to them on patriotism, we see the stripes on his sweatpants: red, yellow, and green, the colors of the flag of Bolivia, the country named in honor of Bolívar who wrote its quasi-monarchical Constitution. The teen soldiers' isolation from the world and their subordination to a nebulous idea leads them to kill the commander, punish and hunt each other down for betraying "the cause," kill civilians, and kidnap their children to raise them as soldiers.

A similarly chilling story about young people united by the cult of Bolívar who end up killing civilians and each other is told in the 2012 novel *The Feast of the Innocent* (*La carroza de Bolívar*) by Evelio Rosero. In this portrayal, Bolívar does not even care to put a good mask on. A group of students in Pasto in the 1960s organize into a kind of guerrilla cell and call themselves a theater group for cover. Here, theater is, again, a symbol of deluded individuals seeking attention. The novel draws on the history of Pasto, an Andean city in southern Colombia. The city staunchly opposed Bolívar's forces because many of its inhabitants were Indigenous people and Afro-Colombians who saw an opportunity to negotiate their entitlements and obligations with the

Spanish crown. They viewed Bolívar as a tyrant and an invader (Echeverri 224). When Pasto's elites signed the capitulation with Bolívar, the popular classes continued to fight against him. Bolívar decided that they needed to be "crushed to their core" and, on December 24, 1822, which became known as Black Christmas, Pasto was taken and pillaged for three days. Soldiers killed more than four hundred civilians (roughly one-fourth of the city's inhabitants), including women, the elderly, and children. Property was confiscated, and the surviving men were conscripted into the army and marched to Peru. On the way, many died and some were tied in pairs and thrown alive into the Guáitara River to save ammunition, which the victimizers called "marriage" (Echeverri 207).

Pasto is known for its yearly carnival at which fanciful floats (*carrozas*) are paraded through the streets. Rosero's novel *La carroza de Bolívar* (for the English translation, its title was changed to *The Feast of the Innocent*) tells of one such float. Justo Pastor, a local gynecologist and history aficionado, has local artisans build a float to depict Bolívar's crimes. He plans to use this float to reveal Bolívar's true face to the large crowds that come to Pasto for the carnival. He is also writing a biography of "the so-called Liberator" (el mal llamado Libertador), depicting him as a cruel and violent man. Justo Pastor and his friend, Arcaín Chivo, professor of history, draw their information about Bolívar from Marx and José Rafael Sañudo, the Pasto-born historian who published in 1925 *Studies on the Life of Bolívar* (*Estudios sobre la vida de Bolívar*), which earned him the name of "an ungrateful son of his fatherland" from the Colombian Academy of History (Rodríguez-Bravo 54). Sañudo portrayed Bolívar as motivated exclusively by "the delirium of greatness" (Sañudo 161). He quoted Bolívar's sayings which make obvious his extreme narcissism and pride, such as "my name is a talisman, I know the roads of victory, and peoples live under my laws," and "Here there is no other authority but mine; I am like the sun among my lieutenants, if they shine, it is I who lend them my light" (Sañudo 275). Sañudo argued that Bolívar "unleashed a storm on Colombia whose darkness did not dissipate even a century later," and became "a paragon for those devoured by ambition" (Sañudo 271). The novel's protagonist, Justo Pastor, repeats Sañudo's conclusions: "Bolívar provided a disastrous model that would turn itself over time into Colombia's political culture. What did Bolívar teach the whole host of politicians who would succeed him throughout Colombia's History? Firstly, to think only of themselves: of power. Next, to think only of themselves, of power, and, then, power again, and so on, and so on to infinity" (Bolívar dio el desastroso ejemplo que se convertiría con el tiempo en cultura política colombiana. ¿Cuánto enseñó Bolívar a toda la caterva de políticos que en la historia de Colombia le sucedieron? Primero a pensar sólo en sí mismos: el poder. Después a pensar sólo en sí mismos: el poder, y luego otra vez el poder y así sucesivamente hasta el infinito; 96). Again, the Bolívar of this novel is an actor playing the role of a savior—he "schemed, deceived, dissembled" (intrigaba, enredaba, disimulaba; 100). The novel's author, Evelio Rosero, repeated these ideas in his interview almost verbatim (Rosero).

On a symbolic level, the novel portrays Bolívar as a child molester. The protagonist records two family legends about how Bolívar made two underage girls perish at the hands of their family members. Bolívar sighted his first victim at a dinner party organized by her father for the victors, to protect his daughters from being raped by Bolívar's soldiers after they took Pasto. Bolívar chose the youngest daughter, thirteen years old and holding a doll, abducted her, and returned her pregnant. The family locked her up for life with her newborn daughter until they both died of old age. The other victim was a beautiful and mentally handicapped fifteen-year-old. Her grandmother managed to save her from the three-day Pasto massacre, but the girl was noticed and claimed by Bolívar. The grandmother promised to prepare her properly. When The Liberator arrived to pick her up, she handed her over to him, washed and perfumed, and dead, as he realized after galloping away. The preyed-upon, dead young girl is a powerful metaphor of predatory leadership, as discussed in chapter 2 on Peru, and it is shocking to see it applied to Bolívar.

The student militants who venerate Bolívar in the novel and believe they are fighting for social justice set out to punish the doctor for his attacks on Bolívar and destroy the float which he designed to depict Bolívar's devastation of Pasto. They declare their history professor "the enemy of the people" for reading Marx and Sañudo to them, drag him into the street and make him crawl like a snake. The students also decide to execute another "enemy of the people" and pick an unsuspecting off-duty police officer on his way to buy milk. Only one member, the inoffensive poet, has the courage to carry out the execution. The rest of the group, ashamed of their own cowardice, turn against him after that. The poet is the only one of the group who realizes that their rebellion is pointless. Instead of spying on the doctor, as he was assigned to do, the poet tells him he will be killed as "the enemy of the people" if he is not careful. At the end of the novel, this one repentant student is sentenced to die as a traitor by the rest of the "rebels." The doctor will likely suffer the same fate, but the carnival float is saved from destruction and hidden until more propitious times.

It is extraordinary that the carnival float from *The Feast of the Innocent* really did materialize in the streets of Pasto during the 2018 carnival (figure

Figure 6.4. *El Colorado*, a carnival float created by Carlos Ríbert Insuasty in the streets of Pasto, Colombia, in 2018. GVI Live. *YouTube*, 18 Mar. 2018, www.youtube.com/watch?v=jUYnCrN6IFY.

6.4). The float, named *El Colorado* after a street in which the Pasto massacre turned particularly gruesome, took three years to make, claims its designer Carlos Ribert Insuasty ("Reportaje"). The float is swarming with 140 colorful figures and dozens of live participants in its balconies, dressed in military uniforms who throw confetti at the crowds and work the float's moving parts. A raging Bolívar charges forward on a furious, red-eyed horse, his punishing arm flung forward. Leading him on is an enormous and flirty skull of Death, which grins and makes eyes at the crowds. The skull carries Sucre (Bolívar's general who commanded the massacre), brandishing his sword and surrounded by excited little devils, plump and mischievous like cherubs. Enormous infernal dogs violently pull the float over the bodies of dead and dying people pierced by knives and brandishing knives. Just as in Dávila's paintings, Bolívar is missing pants. His general's uniform is only a costume, a disguise. It is reduced to only the embroidered collar, epaulets, and cuffs, exposing the fiery red, skinless, muscled body of the Devil. Bolívar's raging red face blazes from under the horned mask of the stereotypical Devil which opens like shutters to the sides. From Bolívar's backside protrudes a mighty dragon's tail, also red, that forms a sort of a slide, on top of which a naked woman sits, preparing to slide down. The tail then shoots up, raising on its tip the lifeless body of another naked woman, with her arms hanging to the sides and legs spread apart. Her posture evokes sexual rapture, rape, and sacrifice, symbolizing the allure and violence of the messianic man. Other naked women around her smile diabolically and make inviting gestures.

El Colorado evokes the cover of the 2012 edition of Rosero's novel, in which Bolívar was depicted as the Prince of Hell from the "Hell" panel of Bosch's triptych *The Garden of Earthly Delights*. The creature from Bosch's painting devours and excretes sinners, while other anguished-looking sinners are pierced by cutting objects. On the center panel of the triptych, which looks very much like today's amusement park, these sinners smile as they partake in torturous-looking entertainments. Bosch's triptych, overflowing with smiling and suffering people, fantastic creatures, and devils, likely inspired the creator of *El Colorado*. In turn, *El Colorado*'s demonic Bolívar replaced Bosch's Prince of Hell on the cover of the 2019 edition of Rosero's novel (figure 6.4). I draw your attention to the mask and the scraps of the general's uniform used as a disguise in the float's representation of Bolívar. Here we see leadership as a performance, and the leader as a histrion hiding devilish ambition, ready to sacrifice everything and everyone to his obsession with the spotlight. Critic David Gil Alzate said about Rosero's novel that the float did not fulfill its promise of carnivalesque renewal because it did not even make it to the streets (Alzate). But the novel ultimately did more than that: it is amazing to see this powerful symbol of the cult of messianic man and its destructive power emerge from its pages and roll into the streets of Pasto, impressing crowds, winning first place, and receiving wide press coverage. We see the demand for non-predatory, non-spectacular leadership reverberate throughout multiple art forms, gain sharper contours, and win the acceptance of large audiences.

Conclusion

"'But he has no clothes on!' said the little child at last." This famous line from Hans Christian Andersen's tale *The Emperor's New Clothes* is exactly what artists, novelists, and filmmakers have recently been saying about The Liberator. In Andersen's tale, everyone admires the Emperor's new imaginary clothes as the pompous Emperor struts around naked. After a small child says the Emperor has no clothes on, everyone acquires the courage to say as much. Portraying Bolívar without pants has happened before: in the 1960s, sculptor Rodrigo Arenas Betancourt imagined him as a naked Greek hero Prometheus, a Titan who stole fire from the gods and brought it to humanity, dooming himself to eternal torment for his crime. In this statue, installed in Pereira, Colombia, the galloping Bolívar is an inspired spirit carrying the fire of liberty in his outstretched hand, and his heroic, muscular nudity signifies the purity of his intentions. The recent portrayals, however, undress Bolívar to bare other, self-interested reasons for holding onto power and glory. Juan Dávila painted Bolívar in pop-art style, as an exhibitionist and a cult celebrity. Bolívar's neat, universally recognizable uniform comes apart in these depictions. When the uniform becomes no more than a costume, the man wearing it is exposed as an actor. The messianic man must have thoroughly tired people's eyes and ears for even The Liberator to be taking jabs on all sides. We can also see the fatigue with the charismatic man in recent book titles—Herbert Morote's *Bolívar: The Liberator and Peru's Number One Enemy* (2007), Isidoro Medina Patiño's *Genocidal Bolívar, a Bipolar Genius* (2009), Pablo Victoria's *The Bolivarian Terror* (2019), and *The Accursed Liberators: the Story of Latin American Underdevelopment* by Augusto Zamora (2020). Bolívar did give the example of holding on to power by any means necessary, while constantly talking about self-sacrifice and democracy. It also did not help that he was claimed as inspiration by opportunistic and authoritarian political actors, Venezuela's Hugo Chávez and the FARC in Colombia. In recent Venezuelan films I have discussed, he remains a selfless demigod. But in Colombian works, he is described as a histrion, with irony, pity, or indignation. A carnival float that materialized in real life, depicting a devilish and pantless Bolívar from novels and art works, was met with acclaim by mass audiences. Are we about done with the messianic man? Are we ready to consider that he may turn out to be a histrion and his dear great Fatherland only a stage?

7

The Profiteer

Political Freedom Becomes Consumer Freedom in Chile

In September 1973, General Augusto Pinochet led a military coup in Chile that overthrew the democratically elected socialist government of President Salvador Allende. The coup marked the beginning of a brutal dictatorship characterized by widespread human rights abuses and repression. Under Pinochet's regime, the government implemented a series of neoliberal economic reforms, designed by economists known as the "Chicago boys." These reforms included privatizing state-owned industries, deregulating the economy, and implementing austerity measures. While these policies initially led to economic stabilization and growth, they also exacerbated social inequalities. This is why in 2019 massive protests shook the country. The protests were sparked by a rise in subway fares of thirty pesos—only four US cents—but they quickly evolved into a broader movement. Chileans protested the high cost of living, low salaries and pensions, and disparities in education and healthcare. One of the slogans, "This is not about 30 pesos, this is about 30 years!" shows the dissatisfaction with the political system and the legacy of the Pinochet dictatorship's neoliberal economic reforms, which had perpetuated and deepened inequality. This chapter shows that recent Chilean films metaphorically represent the democratic politicians who failed to change the country's socioeconomic model inherited from Pinochet by the figure of the father. Unlike the histrionic and imposing fathers examined in the previous chapters, these fathers are avoidant and self-effacing. They have good intentions and convictions but fail to act on them because this means losing their own privileges and they are not prepared to do that. These well-intentioned profiteer fathers appear in the films *Subterra* (2003), *Machuca* (2004), and *No* (2012). The fact that they were missing in the literary inspirations for these films tells us that filmmakers introduce this avoidant father character intentionally, to explain the lack of the political will to change the model inherited from Pinochet. These films adapt stories about important moments in Chile's past that hold the key to the country's present. Filmmakers invite us to reflect on whether the cornerstones of Pinochet's free-market reforms—competition and political marketing, private ownership of businesses, industries, and public services—are conducive to a truly democratic and fair society. Why does Chile's economic growth result in increased socioeconomic inequality? What if this growth is predicated on making employment and life precarious for the very people who produce it? Filmmakers use the opposition of lack and plenty to answer these questions. The fathers in these films belong to the world of plenty and are accomplices, enablers, and beneficiaries of the predatory leadership principles, which materialize covertly, as the impersonal imperatives of the free market. These fathers are so vaporous that it is difficult to know what they really think or want, but they continue to make profit no matter who is in power. They are as self-effacing and pervasive as the neoliberal orthodoxy itself.

Education as Socioeconomic Segregation in *Machuca*

Released in 2003 and directed by Andrés Wood, *Machuca* won the Most Popular International Film Award at the Vancouver International Film Festival and was nominated for the Ariel Award for Best Iberoamerican Film. In *Machuca*, Wood draws on his own experience during Allende's integration program and the coup. Born into a wealthy family, Wood was a student at the elite Colegio Saint George. Wood dedicated the film to the principal, Father Gerardo Whelan, who was jailed for 125 days in the aftermath of the coup. Father Whelan returned to Saint George in 1992 after Pinochet stepped down (Langlois). The film recounts a friendship between a boy from a wealthy family, Gonzalo Infante, and a boy from the shantytown, Pedro Machuca (Matías Quer and Ariel Mateluna). Machuca appears one day at St. George, an elite "English School for Boys" run by an American priest, Father McEnroy. The principal, like the socialist president Salvador Allende, believes that all children should have the right to a good education. Gonzalo comes from a privileged family, as is clear from his last name, Infante, which denotes an heir to the throne. In contrast, Machuca's name comes from *machucar* (to pound, to hit) and denotes physical labor (Park 22). He lives in a poor neighborhood on the other side of the Mapocho River, with his mother, his drunkard father, and a baby sister. The river, which crosses the capital from east to west, serves as the geographical boundary separating the northeastern part of the capital where the upper class lives from the neighborhoods inhabited by the lower classes (Vilches).

The film shows the world of the dominant class as a spiritual void masked by an abundance of luxury commodities and contrasts it with the world of the poor, which is a world of relationships. After meeting Machuca, Gonzalo sees for the first time that ideas and relationships can matter more than things. His mother spends her days shopping for outfits and visiting her lover, an old rich businessman who bribes Gonzalo with imported comic books and "Made in Germany" Adidas sneakers. They do not lack food, even during the economic and political crisis that preceded the coup. Gonzalo's father is an executive with the United Nations Food and Agriculture Organization (FAO), which is devoted to combating world hunger. The only time this family comes together is when they discuss, with dreamy faces, the things that the father can bring them from Rome, where FAO is headquartered. Gonzalo requests an American comic book, his sister a Neil Diamond record, and even the always sour mother lightens up, requesting a pair of Italian shoes and looking at her husband almost lovingly. After Pinochet takes over, the family moves into an even bigger house, with the hated lover sitting in the garden and the mother fretting over the new carpet as movers bring in an abundance of decorative objects and furniture. The family is doing even better than before, but Gonzalo feels even emptier inside, having lost his friends who cared not only about things.

Machuca shows Gonzalo that human connection is not based on commodities. In addition, Machuca teaches him to stand up for what is right. While Gonzalo endures being bullied by an aggressive boy and his sidekicks without much resistance, Machuca has a sense of dignity and is not easily intimidated. When the bullies come after him, Machuca fights back. He is not aggressive—his innate sense of dignity is the foundation of his courage, and he does not care if he gets hurt. When Gonzalo's sister's snobbish, nationalistic boyfriend meets Machuca, he scoffs at his name and threateningly swings nunchucks (karate sticks) in his face. The timorous Gonzalo edges to the side, but Machuca does not budge, remaining still as if studying the man. Gonzalo is surprised that Machuca does not seem to want to learn anything at his elite school and does not appear to take this life-changing opportunity seriously. When Machuca's neighbor Silvana puts him to the test, asking him to translate into English the phrases, "Mi hermana Rosita es bonita" (my sister Rosita is pretty) and, significantly, "Salvador Allende es el presidente de Chile," Machuca responds with imaginary English words. To help Machuca, Gonzalo writes answers on his English test, but he answers some questions incorrectly so they will not get caught. Machuca is upset that he received a lower score on the test than Gonzalo, because he is not versed in the games of conformity that Gonzalo knows so well. Attending the posh school, which affords him the opportunity to enter the world of the Chilean elite, comes at the price of learning to live scared. Machuca is unable to learn that, and he will suffer the consequences.

Machuca's neighbor Silvana (Manuela Martelli), with whom Gonzalo is in love, is another figure who teaches Gonzalo defiance. When they sell cigarettes and flags at the rally of the nationalists, she confronts both Gonzalo's sister's nationalist boyfriend and Gonzalo's mother. The boyfriend takes a cigarette off Silvana's tray without paying as he walks by her. When Silvana rushes to catch up with him, she inadvertently pushes and gets into a brawl with Gonzalo's mother, who came to the rally with her rich female friends. The mother calls Silvana a *rota* (lowlife) and tells her to go back to her slum, and Silvana calls her a *puta* (whore). Gonzalo observes them unnoticed. He looks sad and seems to acquiesce, thinking about his mother's affair with the old businessman, the vacuous immorality of which visibly torments him. Although Silvana quits school to help her father, she understands the political situation in Chile much better than the straight-A student Gonzalo. As the people around them chant "Who doesn't jump is a *momio*" (a fascist, a right-wing conservative), Gonzalo chants and jumps with them and then wonders aloud what a *momio* is, and Silvana is quick to respond, "An ignorant, rich kid like you!" Perhaps more importantly, Silvana stands up to Machuca's father, a defeatist drunkard who comes home only to collect money and drink. Upon seeing Machuca's upper-class friend Gonzalo, Machuca's father lashes out at his son. He tells Machuca that in five years this "friend" will be studying at a university, in ten years he will be working for his father, and in fifteen he will inherit his father's company, while Machuca will be scrubbing toilets the entire time. For the first time we see Machuca unsure of how to respond to aggression, but Silvana is unfazed. She tells Machuca's father that, with his drinking, in two years he will be dead, and she does not flinch when he grabs her by the neck. In the end, Silvana's inability to stand down costs her life. After the coup, when soldiers ransack the shantytown, she tries to protect her father from being beaten by the soldiers. A soldier simply shoots her dead.

Toro, a tall older boy from the shantytown, gives Gonzalo one more example of courage. Toro's defiant behavior, such as turning in his English tests blank and leaving the classroom, is not a pose. He understands that education in this school is a luxury commodity that perpetuates the class system. Gonzalo sees Toro at pro-Allende demonstrations, aware, marching and chanting. When the school bully, a spoiled blond boy, snatches away Machuca's popsicle, which Gonzalo bought for him, and invites him to come suck it to the jeers of the crowd, Toro strikes the bully hard on the head and leaves the scene. None of the boys, not even the bully, denounce Toro, perhaps because they understand that Toro, incapable of conformity and compromise, is not joking. After the military seize the school, the soldiers line the boys up, shave their long hair, and wrap a chain with a huge lock on the school gate. They are protecting the elite boys' space from the encroachment of the poor and, even more importantly, they are making sure that the elite behave as they should. This is when Toro gives the students his final performance of defiance. He sneaks into the courtyard, stands tall, and screams, "Army bastards, go back to the barracks!" (¡Milicos de mierda, vuelvan a sus cuarteles!). All the students rush to the windows and see Toro being led away by the soldiers, likely never to be seen again. The lesson resumes with a student reading from the English textbook, "Jessica is growing up. Soon she will walk, talk, and play with the children of her neighborhood." These lifeless English sentences prepare the boys for a mechanical and meaningless life of conformity. As the new principal Col. Sotomayor puts it, the students must "devote themselves to studying, not anything else" (no otra cosa).

The school principal, Father McEnroy, gives the most impactful example of defiance, and the unstudious Machuca proves to be his best student. A sincere enthusiast of social justice, Father McEnroy (Ernesto Malbrán) inspires both Machuca and Gonzalo to want to become priests, like him. When Silvana teases them that they do not even go to church and are "too horny," Machuca tells her that what matters is "to help people, especially the poor." The optimistic Father believes that growing vegetables and raising pigs will transform his students into caring and understanding citizens who will embrace the shantytown boys like "friends and brothers." After the coup, Father McEnroy (who was replaced by a military man) enters the school worship hall where a new and approved priest is officiating the Mass and praising the military junta. As all look on in fascination, Father McEnroy rapidly consumes all the altar bread, with tears rolling down his cheeks, and announces that this place is no longer holy. No one dares to breathe, let alone to talk, because this act of defiance will surely bring retribution as soon as the military men in the audience catch onto what is happening. As Father McEnroy goes to leave, with military officials on his heels, Machuca instinctively rises and says in English, "Goodbye, Father McEnroy." While Machuca has not cared to learn English or the school discipline before the coup, now he uses the school ritual of greeting and saying goodbye to the principal in English to show solidarity with Father McEnroy and to defy the military officials who are taking him away. Father McEnroy replies, "Goodbye, Machuca," and all students and teachers rise as one, as if on command, intoning in one voice, "Goodbye, Father McEnroy," two times in a row. Even the bully stands up, seeing that everyone else does. To prevent his students from being attacked by the soldiers who begin to understand what is happening, Father McEnroy ends this act of general defiance by saying "Goodbye, boys" and marching out. This scene is a reference to Louis Malle's *Au revoir, les enfants* (*Goodbye, children*), words with which the principal of a boarding school, Father Jean, takes leave of three Jewish children as they are all arrested by the Gestapo and led away, never to be seen again (Sorensen 90). Machuca knows his act of defiance will be punished. Indeed, the new principal, Col. Sotomayor makes a sign to Machuca to come with him, while other students are sent back to their classrooms.

After classes end, Gonzalo goes to look for Machuca in the shantytown, and he sees it ransacked by the military. Machuca must have told the colonel where he lives, so soldiers are everywhere, looking for pro-Allende materials and flags. He watches as the soldiers put the inhabitants to the wall at gunpoint, search them, scream at them, hit them, load them on trucks, and burn papers and flags. Gonzalo sees Machuca subjected to the violence of the soldiers and watches as Silvana is killed. He is terrified but finds salvation in the luxury commodity presented to him by his mother's lover, whom he so despises: the Adidas sneakers, "Made in Germany." When a soldier tells Gonzalo to board the truck with the rest of the slum dwellers, headed to an unknown destination, if any, Gonzalo tells him he is from the other side of the river, and when the soldier does not believe him, he tells him in a commanding tone, "Look at me!" (Mírame). Gonzalo, a child, addresses the adult soldier, who has Indigenous features with a familiar *tú* reserved for servants to make him recognize the future member of the superior class. Seeing the freckles, the red hair, and the imported sneakers, the soldier realizes he has made a mistake and lets him go with light slap (which replaces a hard kick and a shove into the truck). Gonzalo rides out of the burning shantytown on his bike, crying as he pedals away, because he returns to his world of loneliness and conformity with the people whose beliefs and behaviors he despises. He did learn some defiance from his disappeared friends. When the school bully tries to make him write his English test answers again, Gonzalo writes "Asshole" in English across the bully's test, turns in his own test blank, and leaves. He rides to the shantytown but finds that nothing remains but an empty soccer field and ashes (figure 7.1).

The razed shantytown and the empty soccer field serve as a metaphor of the coup and the new "postsocial" reality, as critic Juan Poblete puts it, in which the memory of the predictatorial, "social" past must be evacuated ("Memory of the National" 105). Prior to this scene, Gonzalo's mother's lover is shown reading a newspaper with the headline "FIFA Says That Life in Chile Is Normal" (FIFA dice que la vida en Chile es normal). After the coup, about 40,000 people were brought to the National Stadium, which served as a detention

Figure 7.1. Gonzalo observing the empty soccer field of the razed slum in *Machuca* (2004).

camp for two months. People were detained there and tortured before being transferred to prisons. According to official records, forty-one people were murdered there. Relatives kept watch at the doors to learn of their detained loved ones. The use of the stadium as a detention camp became so notorious that the Soviet Union's team refused to play there arguing that it was "the place of blood." FIFA sent its representatives, who reported they saw no prisoners but rather "detainees whose identity must be established." Some prisoners were kept in locker rooms and underground tunnels. Others were on the bleachers, but the FIFA representatives "seemed to be interested only in the condition of the grass" (Waldstein). They dutifully reported that there was no reason to stop the match from taking place or to move it to a different venue. The Soviet team refused to come, and so, on the day of the match, the Chilean team, wearing uniforms, lined up, greeted the sparse audience, and made at least nine passes before driving the ball into the unprotected goal. The newspapers extolled the athletic valor and the winning spirit of the team. Pinochet's regime's patriotic speeches of victory and order at the time when the opponents were simply killed parallels this imaginary victory. The last scene of *Machuca* (figure 7.1) brings to mind the famous photos of the National Stadium when it was used as a detention center after the coup. In these photos, the field is also empty, except for a few soldiers with machine guns, who set the rules in this game and guard the detainees on the bleachers. In the last scene of the film, Gonzalo occupies the position of the detainees and looks on the field, whose emptiness metaphorically signals the recent presence of the soldiers who took his newfound friends away from him. He now knows what it means to have relationships instead of things and he feels lonelier than ever before. He has understood that his privilege is a disciplinary institution and, whether he likes it or not, he must conform if he wishes to live. His former friends from the land of lack can be killed whether they conform or not, but he has a choice, for which he despises himself because it causes him to betray himself and his friends.

If the courageous Father McEnroy is the model that Gonzalo would like to follow, his own father, Patricio, is a weakling, despite his good intentions. Patricio (Francisco Reyes) thinks that nationalists are stupid and retrograde. He dislikes his daughter's nationalist boyfriend and wonders how she "couldn't get anything better" (no pudo conseguir nada mejor). He is annoyed by his wife's friends, who are only interested in money and talk about how much they earn and what they sell, to which she responds, "At least they are proud of something!" He is annoyed by his wife's superficiality. He dislikes how the conservative parents at the school meeting berate Father McEnroy for his integration efforts, for making their kids study alongside "people that they wouldn't have to ever meet" (gente que no tienen por qué conocer). Gonzalo's father begins to object that "in some sense, it's everyone's fault" but is interrupted by another parent who argues it is paternalistic to give the poor something for free that they did not earn. Instead of responding, the father cringes. He nods enthusiastically when an articulate progressive parent opines that Father McEnroy does something that a lot of parents want: he offers "an education that is more egalitarian and profoundly democratic." When his wife stands up, he cringes in anticipation and tries to prevent her from speaking, and he is right to fear. She sounds like a silly, spoiled child when she asks, "Why put so much effort into mixing apples and pears? I don't mean to say we're better but, geez, we're *so* different!" (pucha que somos distintos). The audience just loves this simple sally and Gonzalo's father's incipient objection that "But this is precisely why this [integration project] is so interesting . . ." is drowned out in the hubbub of approvals. At the same time, even though Gonzalo's father is a well-paid executive with the Food and Agriculture Organization, an international organization dedicated to fighting hunger, he uses his connections with shop owners who hoard merchandise and sell everything on the black market, making fortunes. He acquires food for his family from them and never questions them. In a memorable scene, the father and Gonzalo emerge from the back door of a store, the front of which is covered in signs reading "No meat," "No bread," "No sugar," carrying huge bags filled with these very items. They walk out nonchalantly and defiantly in slow motion to upbeat music, like mafia bosses, Patricio taking a puff on a cigarette, Gonzalo taking bites of a cookie. This scene illustrates that Gonzalo is like his father, not like his new friends or the brave principal. Finally, Patricio proposes they move to Rome, where FAO is headquartered. He'd be paid in dollars and "Socialism is good, but not for us! . . . Not yet." We do not see him again after the coup, but he must be all right because the family moves into an even bigger and more luxurious house. The father's name, Patricio, means "patrician," a member of the Roman ruling class, as opposed to plebeians (who could not participate in government or politics). The father likes the idea of social justice but he also likes his land of plenty. He and his son inherited privileges that they must perpetuate.

The film's source of inspiration is the 2002 novel *Three Years to Be Born* (*Tres años para nacer*), by the writer and poet Amante Eledín Parraguez Lizana. The novel recounts the coup from the perspective of one of the "Machucas," the lower class student integrated into the elite school. This boy, Amador Parra, is very different from the film's carefree, undaunted Machuca. Amador is a diligent student and he is upset that he is so different from the other boys in this new school. He despairs that even his hair lies differently than theirs and that, no matter how often his mother washes and irons his shirt, it looks nothing like theirs. He laments that he cannot even dream of talking to the beautiful, inaccessible, rich female students. He recognizes his classmates' last names from the names of stores, streets, and everyday product brands, even his pencils. He is annoyed by the piles of trash near his shanty and despairs that he, his mother, and his sister "lack the mental clarity to know the right place for things" and cannot organize them neatly. More importantly, unlike in the film, Amador and the other integrated boys keep quiet when the class debates social justice issues, listening instead to the outspoken privileged boys. He is awed by Father Whelan's belief that the school's Christian mission is to make the world more just, true, and fraternal (*Tres años* 114). The priests have students read and discuss news articles, and some students and parents grumble that this is not language teaching but rather communist brainwashing. Amador compares this elite private school to his previous public school, where students cannot fathom careers beyond low-paying physical labor. He concludes that education is a right, that "everyone anywhere on the planet deserves it, regardless of his economic situation" (cualquier persona lo merece en cualquier lugar del planeta, independientemente de su situación económica; 66). After the coup, Amador changes schools, because he is afraid of the new principal Col. Verdugo (which means "executioner" in Spanish and is the surname of the real-life colonel who replaced the principal after the coup). The Colonel warns the students, "This school is out of your league. I don't know how in the world the likes of you got in. This cannot be and, besides, things have changed in this country. We'll get all this in order. We don't want any lazy people here, no delinquents, no armed politicians. We'll conduct a proper cleaning" (este colegio es de otro nivel, no sé cómo llegaron aquí. Esto no puede ser, además las cosas han cambiado en el país, vamos a ordenar todo esto. No queremos gente floja, ni delincuentes, ni políticos armados. Vamos a realizar una limpieza como debe ser; 161). Amador feels threatened and transfers to a different elite school. Although he is disappointed, he is hopeful that there will come a day "when history will dare to include us and make us its protagonists" (la historia se atreverá a incluirnos y hacernos protagonistas de ella; 167). In summary, the novel is about a boy from a poor neighborhood who becomes aware that quality education is a right and is positively transformed by this education. In contrast, the film is about the structural impossibility of change, because the integrated boy is disappeared, and his privileged friend is disciplined.

Both the film and the novel illuminate how elite schools perpetuate the class system in Chile, a situation that did not change under the post-Pinochet governments and has not changed today. Cornejo Chávez shows that democratic governments in Chile consistently apply market-based concepts of efficiency, competition, and privatization to education. As a result, only 30 percent of students go to municipal public schools, as compared to 78 percent in 1981. Fifty-four percent go to semi-private schools subsidized by the Chilean government. Much of government educational spending goes toward these semi-private institutions. The remaining 9 percent of students attend elite private schools. Such socioeconomic segregation, which begins at a young age, brings about a strong sentiment of social injustice. Sixty-seven percent of Chileans reported feeling "very angry that some people have access to a much better education than others" (242). During her first presidential term, Michelle Bachelet, of the Socialist party, vowed to de-market public education. Instead, the 2007 reforms implemented entrepreneurial models, including flexible hiring, individual teacher accountability, pay based on students' performance on standardized tests, and the clientelization of parents and students, which caused many teachers to leave the profession (Gaete Silva et al.). Chávez Cornejo argues that the demands of the 2006 and 2011 mass mobilization of students were co-opted by many advocacy groups that are financed by private companies and banks and promote the privatization of education. In addition, he indicates that advocates of the private ownership of schools, educational centers, and universities are present not only among conservatives but also among center-left politicians (Chávez Cornejo 253). Educational segregation was one of the triggers of the 2019 mass protests in Chile known as Estallido social (Social Outburst). In January 2020, hundreds of students from the far-left union of high school students disrupted the university entrance exam (PSU), the Chilean equivalent of the SAT. They blocked the entrances to the test centers, burned test papers, and clashed with security forces. Only 30 percent of public school students who took the exam in 2018 got a high enough score to apply to college, compared to 43.5 percent of students from semi-private schools and 79 percent of students from fully private schools. A 2016 OECD report on educational inequality found that students' socioeconomic status had a greater impact on their achievement in the sciences in Chile than in any other developed country studied (Nugent). Pinochet deepened educational inequality, and it continues to shape the country.

Machuca metaphorically represents this continued segregation and the triumph of neoliberalism, "which creates a zone without law and rights (where those elements are transformed into parodies of themselves)," as Luis Martín-Cabrera and Daniel Noemi Voionmaa note in their analysis of the film (72). In a recent interview, director Andrés Wood said he did not expect the deep socioeconomic inequality he showed in his film to change before his and older generations die out (Wood, Interview by *Cine Arte*). Wood believes it is symbolic that the leader of the student protest movement, Victor Chaufres, is a grandson of a disappeared detainee, while the secretary of education is the daughter of a Pinochet-era official (the then secretary of education, Marcela Cubillos, daughter of Pinochet's secretary of external relations, Hernán Cubillos). *Machuca* made an impact on society, as we can see in the name of the 2021 law, "Ley Machuca," that requires private schools to enroll 30 percent of their students from underprivileged communities. Interestingly, Parraguez Lizana, the author of the novel on which the film is based, who participated in the integration experiment, compares this measure to a Band-Aid. He says that socioeconomic inequality has increased dramatically since the 1970s. As an educator in underserved communities, he thinks that the market logic of competition transformed education into a luxury item and learning into a race for success. He believes that freedom has little to do with the market concepts of merit, competition, and success. The poor should not have to prove that they deserve a good education. On the contrary, "the powerful should prove they deserve their position to serve the public good" (Son los que tienen el poder los que deben demostrar el mérito que los llevó a ese puesto para trabajar al servicio del bien común; interview by Saldías). These words demonstrate the new attitude to authority, that people in positions of authority are now viewed as public servants, accountable to their constituents. This is the attitude we can see in the 2019 protests.

The father figure introduced in the film, who has noble ideas but chooses to conform instead, reflects the failure of the post-Pinochet governments to respond to these new expectations. Patricio, Gonzalo's father, does not like the caste system or those who do not understand that it is morally wrong. He disapproves of his wife and her friends who believe that their privilege is natural and deserved. But he has no courage to stand up for his principles or even the conviction or the words to formulate them better, as in the scene of the school meeting, and he uses his connections to obtain black-market goods for his family as merchants are making money on creating shortages—even though he works for the international organization ostensibly dedicated to fighting world hunger. He is so avoidant and self-effacing that he is not even shown at the end of the film. But it is obvious that he stayed in Chile and will collaborate with the dictatorship, despite his scorn for the retrograde nationalists who took power. He will live in his new and better house and keep his criticisms to himself now, and so will his son, Gonzalo, until better days. When democracy returns, he will defend equality again, but his words will remain only that—words.

Political Marketing Replaces Politics in *No*

Pablo Larraín, in his Oscar-nominated film *No*, also explains the shallow nature of democracy in modern Chile by portraying the man who made it possible for the democratic coalition to defeat Pinochet as having little knowledge of what democracy means. The protagonist is a professional adman who thrives in Pinochet's Chile. He considers his job well done when he can market a product efficiently, and it does not occur to him that he promotes consumerism through which Pinochet's regime replaced political freedoms. The film then retells a historic event that has been celebrated as the victory of democracy, both in life and literature—the 1988 referendum that Pinochet allowed in order to maintain the semblance of legitimacy—and positions this event as a defeat of democracy rather than its victory.

The neoliberal reforms imposed by Pinochet made Chile a market society, if we use political economist Karl Polanyi's term. These reforms "subordinate[d] the substance of society itself to the laws of the market" (71), instituting individual competition through consumption, atomizing citizens and liquidating political debate. The transition to market society depoliticized Chileans and deactivated civic groups, including political parties, neighborhood organizations, and activist organizations, says Chilean historian Patricio Silva. Even after Pinochet stepped down, politicians who assumed power promoted consensus rather than debate in order to avoid the collapse of democracy in another coup. Both politicians and citizens came to believe that political deactivation meant prosperity while conflict meant crisis. Moreover, in order to succeed in a consumerist and apolitical society, politicians began marketing themselves as political products, relying on commodified political messages, expensive spots, and celebrities. Politics came to be viewed as a media happening (P. Silva 71). Both politicians and citizens embraced the neoliberal orthodoxy that collective efforts are less valuable than individual meritocratic competition, and that "happiness and individual rewards had to be found in the market in a constant attempt to increase the personal levels of consumption of goods" (P. Silva 62). The neoliberal framework turned Chileans into consumers, and democracy into the freedom to consume.

The 2012 film *No* shows how marketing has penetrated all aspects of life in Chile so that restoring democracy in the country becomes the matter of securing better marketing specialists. The adman, René Saavedra (Gael García Bernal), who made possible the victory of the democratic coalition strategically removed all political content from the campaign. He populated his spots instead with generic images of "happiness" (alegría). He insisted that the pro-democracy campaign needed a jingle, as if it were a product. Even the jingle creator, to whom René turns for help, doubts his ability to work on something as serious as politics, but René convinces him and he composes the catchy jingle "Happiness is coming" (La alegría ya viene). René knows that consumers will want a product if they believe it will unlock happiness and success for them, so he markets democracy as just such a product. The adman's ex-wife, frequently beaten and detained at anti-Pinochet rallies, watches with incredulous scorn as he puts together the jingle and the campaign logo (a rainbow), designs the campaign T-shirts, and films incongruous and absurd spots. In one spot, for example, an extremely tall person is walking toward the camera and the sun is rising behind him. René's ex-wife admonishes him sarcastically, "We Chileans are small" (los chilenos somos chicos). Even his colleague Ricardo who directs the spots objects when they film smiling people picnicking in the sunny meadow with baguettes. He tells him, "No one eats baguettes in this country" (nadie come baguettes en este país). René responds that this is what people want to see, that "it looks nice" and "it works" (funciona). Conversely, René runs out of patience with his crew when they film a politician who pompously talks about democracy as a political system because he is afraid his viewers will think it is boring (Patricio Aylwin who succeeded Pinochet as president played himself in this episode, but it is unlikely that the filmmakers made him aware of their intentions). When they finish filming women who dance an imaginary dance with their disappeared husbands, sons, and brothers, René wants to remove this powerful footage (that inspired

Sting's song "They Dance Alone"), concerned that it feels too "weepy" (llorón) and may alienate his target audience.

Most importantly, René freely circulates his advertising ideas between his projects—consumer products, telenovelas, and the pro-democracy campaign—and seems to treat these projects with equal seriousness. The funny mime holding a bottle of the "Free" soft drink from his previous project migrates to the pilot for the No campaign. Afterward, René has no qualms using the news story and interview format he learned while working on the No campaign to publicize an insipid soap opera *Las bellas y audaces*. He invents an entirely uncalled for "news story" that "informs" the audience that "Santa María's tower's heliport welcomed ten women in formal gowns and five men who admired their beauty. Suddenly, the soap opera's leading man Estéban Greve, played by Osvaldo Silva, appeared in a helicopter, with a bouquet of flowers in his hands." René explains to his clients watching the clip that he is using James Bond–style imagery. This telenovela spot, packaged as a news story and significantly, *the film itself,* end with an "interview" with one of the soap opera stars, who shares that she has a hair salon and five children and used to be a dancer in the cabaret Bim Bam Bum. To conclude the film about the campaign which defeated Pinochet with such empty nonsense is to say that this victory is empty, too. Neither the "news story" nor "the interview" have any bearing on the series, they are merely a refreshing packaging for the soap opera—a medium itself designed to sell consumer products. It is not surprising that the adman introduces his concept videos for all three products—the "Free" soft drink, the No campaign, and the soap opera—with the same pompous preamble, "What you're about to see is framed within the current social context. We believe that the country is prepared for a communication of this nature. Today, Chile thinks about its future" (Lo que van a ver a continuación está marcado dentro del actual contexto social. Nosotros creemos que el país está preparado para la comunicación de esta naturaleza. Hoy, Chile piensa en su futuro). While this preamble is appropriate for the pro-democracy campaign, it sounds perfectly grotesque with the soap opera and the soft drink. This means that René makes no distinction between a soap opera and the democracy campaign. He is not equipped to see such distinctions, for reasons we can only guess. He may be ignorant, too cynical, or too practical to take to heart morality, democracy, and other abstract notions that cannot be sold.

René's audience is shown as well—couples lounging in bed, looking on apathetically. They show some interest in the spots but never enough to discuss them with each other. They look at them from a consumer's point of view, as if choosing one of the two products offered to them, YES to Pinochet and NO to

Pinochet. Such shots imply that Pinochet's regime succeeded in extinguishing political convictions. Voters no longer had opinions of their own and did not really care who would win in the end. As Pinochet's minister quips to his own adman, no one will watch this nonsense (the duel between the YES and the No campaigns) because "Everyone will be sleeping. I'm sleeping at that time!" and repeats, "See? Everyone's sleeping" (todo el mundo está durmiendo). The repetition of the word "sleeping" illuminates again the population's lethargic and consumerist attitude toward politics and life. As for the democratic coalition politicians, at first they are outraged after seeing René's concept presentation, calling it "a masquerade," "a campaign to silence what really happened," and "more like a Coca-Cola commercial" than a political message. They want the campaign to show Chileans they are being robbed not only of their political freedom but also of their economic rights: "What needs to be shown is that the dictatorship destroyed the country's economic success because 40 percent of the people are below the poverty line." It is funny to watch René and the politicians expect something else of one another. When the politicians show René their version of the campaign, with images of people being beaten by police, howling in pain, and the grim voiceover explaining torture and abuse, René asks them whether they have anything more (¿No hay nada más?), something "nicer" (más simpático). They ask him the same question after watching his video (¿No hay nada más?). While he means they have too much heavy and scary political content, they mean he has too many empty images that refer to nothing. He convinces them by asking if they think they can win, which is when they relinquish their principles and go with his ideas. The important objection of one politician that "some of us just really want to win, not really change Chile in a profound way," is forgotten.

As in *Machuca*, we see the opposition of emptiness and abundance. The abundance of generic images and objects in advertising hides its lack of meaning and its purpose to make people buy things they do not need. Cultural theorist Jean Baudrillard used the term "simulacrum" to describe consumer society. Images of happiness proliferate and erase the difference not only between the original and the copy but more generally between the true and the untrue, the meaningful and the meaningless. A simulacrum is a copy that goes beyond hiding reality and the fact that this profound reality does not exist. The simulacrum is a copy that "has no relation to any reality whatsoever; it is its own pure simulacrum" (*Simulacra and Simulation* 6). Consumer society, says Baudrillard, is "a gigantic enterprise of production of the artificial and the cosmetic, of pseudo-objects and pseudo-events, which is invading our daily existence" (Baudrillard, *Consumer Society* 126). Everything, including culture and politics, can be made into "a pseudo-object, a simulation, a copy, an imitation, a dearth of a real signification and a superabundance of signs" (110).

This is exactly what René's wife means when she says, "Your campaign is the copy of a copy of a copy of a copy of a copy!" (Tu campaña es una copia de la copia de la copia de la copia). René has no idea what she means and quickly objects "We didn't copy!" (¡Nosotros no copiamos!). He is so clueless that he even repeats this critique to his colleague and rival, the adman who directs the pro-Pinochet campaign and who technically did "copy" his funny skit technique. His colleague (played by Alfredo Castro) looks duly mortified and René triumphant. They both think that copying means to plagiarize, and René is happy his techniques are so good that others steal them (Dzero, "Larraín's Film *No* As a Simulacrum" 125). These two admen are the thoughtless unmoved movers of consumer society, developing and refining persuasion technologies to publicize any content for their clients, no matter how moral or immoral, useful or useless. After the win of the pro-democracy coalition, René carries his son through the rejoicing crowds. He looks with surprise and curiosity at the people in the street, celebrating with such abandon the triumph of the campaign he designed, but he cannot celebrate with them, not knowing exactly what this is about, as his bewildered face shows. Gael García Bernal is famous for playing sympathetic and well-intentioned villains (*Bad Education, The Crime of Father Amaro, Amores perros*), and he is perfect for the role of René, the unwitting champion of democracy who sells it as a product. He seems genuinely unsure of why this is so important to people, and this is also the reason he is able to devise the winning strategy to attract voters who, like him, do not really know what this is all about. We are left to wonder whether his son will know it. They both stand out from the crowd, with their unsmiling faces (figure 7.2). Like Patricio Infante, the father in *Machuca*, he seems to want to serve the cause of democracy, but his actions show he has other priorities.

Interestingly, the father in the literary source that loosely inspired the film is René's opposite. The adman portrayed in the unpublished play *The Referendum* (*El plebiscito*, 2008), Antonio Skármeta, is a true champion of democracy who was punished for his beliefs but did not stand down. As Allende's supporter, he was arrested and tortured after the coup and has been unable to find work since. Compare this character to the successful, apolitical adman of the film, who works at the best marketing firm, has projects to choose from, lives in a fashionable townhouse, owns an expensive sports car, employs a nanny-maid, and pays for his son to attend a private school. The film's adman thrives on consumerism and is unable to see what's wrong with it. In contrast, the play's adman is an intellectual who uses consumerism strategically. He

Figure 7.2. René carries his son through the crowd celebrating the electoral defeat of Pinochet in *No* (2012).

want to explain to Chileans that Pinochet replaced their political freedom with phony consumer choices. "Everyone in Chile stares open-mouthed at televisions in the store windows, where they see things they can only buy if they get into debt. These fools eat up advertising images. They don't see reality . . . They think that if Pinochet stays, someday they'll be able to buy what television makes them covet" (Todo el mundo en Chile con la boca abierta mirando televisión en las vitrinas de las tiendas donde les ofrecen cosas que sólo endeudándose con créditos pueden llegar a comprar. Estos huevones comen imágenes comerciales. No ven la realidad . . . Creen que si sigue Pinochet algún día van a poder comprar todo lo que la televisión les hace apetecible). The adman decides to "make No into a product" because "there is no other way" (lo único que me queda). His loving wife tries to reason with him, "Are you joking? Like a bra, shoes, lipstick, ice-cream, like wine? . . . The 'No to the dictatorship' is not a product . . . It is a profound moral and political decision" (¡No bromees! ¿Como un *brassière*, como un zapato, como un lápiz labial, como un helado, como un vino? . . . El No a la dictadura no es un producto . . . Es una profunda decisión moral y política; Skármeta, *El plebiscito*). But he convinces her. The play was later developed into a novel, *The Days of the Rainbow* (*Los días del arcoíris*), published in 2011. In the novel, the adman is even more strongly invested in defeating Pinochet to save Chile, and even considers suicide in moments of doubt. He laments "the cursed hour" when he agreed to do it, believing it will be his personal "hell," "apocalypse," and "ignominious end of his career" (Skármeta, *Los días* 93, 108). He worries that his strategy is a "mistake" (desatino), "irresponsible fiction," "shame," and "banalization," and he wants to end it all by jumping into the Mapocho River or running until his heart explodes (Skármeta, *Los días* 105, 103, 108). He is beside himself when No wins and interprets it as if, "for the first time, people felt that television spoke to them, not over them" (Skármeta, *Los días* 119). For this adman, winning this campaign is a matter of life and death. Compare this character to the film's adman, who never doubts his success, never uses moral or ethical vocabulary of any kind, and works on marketing a microwave and a soap opera concurrently. In both the play and the novel written by Skármeta, after the heroic father defeats Pinochet, his child recovers from the profound paralysis of thought caused by fear and looks into the future with optimism.

Skármeta, who lived through the dictatorship, praises "the heroic opponents of the dictatorship and the genius admen of the No campaign" (Entrevista digital). He says that "the younger generation that enjoys democracy and freedom do not know what it cost to recover them. They are in a paradise in which they can say what they want, without fearing that their parents will be tortured, killed, or exiled. This is the victory of No" (interview by Soto). In contrast, the director of the film, Pablo Larraín, belongs to the generation that did not experience the dictatorship personally. In addition, he is the son of Hernán Larraín, a right-wing politician who actively supported Pinochet and who served as Secretary of Justice and Human Rights during the conservative politician Sebastián Piñera's first and second presidency until 2022. The director, who describes himself as closer to the left, was criticized for *No*, both by the right, who called it communist propaganda, and by the left, who labeled it superficial and not political enough (Paz Peirano 141). Larraín said the film is about "the piece of the [pro-Pinochet campaign] Yes that won." "Today, Chile is a country that fits in the pockets of eight families. The state became smaller and inequality grew bigger, people are under huge amounts of debt. That logic, which has to do with marketing and with the model imposed on us by Pinochet, is already woven into the campaign and the referendum, because we said no to Pinochet but yes to his system" (Larraín, interview by Palacios). In 2020, Larraín said that "both sides, the right and the left, arrived at the pact of silence." Democracy returned, but "the system, the heart of the system, is still where it was" (interview by Garrido).

Indeed, this is a sharp criticism of the current neoliberal order that the

Figure 7.3. The mime in "Free" soft drink ad and the pro-democracy campaign in *No* (2012).

soft drink "Free," held by a laughing mime, appears in the concept presentation of the No campaign (figure 7.3). It ridicules the neoliberal postulate that free markets and consumer freedom bring about political freedom, promoted in the 1980s by the American academic and intellectual leader of the Chicago School of Economics Milton Friedman. Friedman convinced Pinochet to adopt the reform program designed by the "Chicago boys," a group of Chilean economists who had studied under his mentorship at the University of Chicago. Milton Friedman also served as advisor to Richard Nixon and Margaret Thatcher (Klein 98). In his books *Free to Choose* and *Capitalism and Freedom*, Friedman argues that if the state regulates economic activity, it becomes totalitarian. Free market capitalism, on the other hand, places a check on the government and produces prosperity and political freedom (*Road to Serfdom* 1944; *Constitution of Freedom* 1960). In a 2000 interview, Friedman argued that Chile proved him right on all fronts because, as he had predicted, free markets brought not only economic growth but also Pinochet's defeat and the return of political freedom: "The Chilean economy did very well, but more importantly, in the end the central government, the military junta, was replaced by a democratic society. So the really important thing about Chilean business is that free markets did work their way in bringing about the free society" (Friedman).

Neoliberal orthodoxy has since come under fire, but the idea that free market models are good for democracy because they make politicians listen to voters if they want to win remains very much alive. Political marketing, which is a central topic of *No*, is defended as a way to draw more voters to politics, especially considering that fewer and fewer voters participate in traditional party politics. In *Consumer Democracy: The Marketing of Politics* (2017), entrepreneurship scholar Margaret Scammell argues that eliciting emotions in people makes politics interesting and visceral. To avoid the misinformation and misrepresentation marketers use to defeat opponents, she proposes to develop "widely shared standards of critical evaluation of political marketing that can distinguish the democratically good from bad" (17). In *The Citizen Marketer: Promoting Political Opinion in the Social Media Age* (2021), Joel Penney, another marketing scholar, similarly argues that citizens can use political marketing techniques to "wrest a degree of control over the persuasion process through participatory media actions and interventions" (36). Political scientist Heather Savigny objects that political marketing strategies are exactly the reason that citizens disengage from politics because they "commodify and marketize" it (40). "The culture of consumption influences, even contaminates, politics—and the two spheres affect each other, a consumerist politics and a politicized consumption," writes historian Nicholas O'Shaughnessy (2). Curiously, this is what happens in the last film adaptation I will examine here. The filmmaker chose the commercial genre of melodrama and dissolved the political intention of the literary source. The figure of the father, missing in the book, appears again in this film, as avoidant and insubstantial as the other two fathers in *Machuca* and *No*.

Precarious Jobs in Subterra

In line with neoliberal orthodoxy, the film adaptation *Subterra* argues that free-market capitalism leads to prosperity and freedom of political expression for all members of society, both owners and workers. Its literary inspiration, the classic story collection by the same name by Baldomero Lillo (1904), says the exact opposite. The stories recount how mine workers in the town of Lota in central Chile struggle, and fail, to survive. The precariousness of their situation is the Company's strategy to prevent them from leaving the mine and from organizing to negotiate better conditions. All the stories in the collection are tales of loss. A mother loses her son because in order to save on safety, the company gambles with miners' lives (*Devil's Pit*). A father cannot get his month's pay and is told that he was fined and now owes money to the Company instead (*Payday*). In *The Search*, the Company's overseer confiscates *mate* tea from an old woman, who previously lost her husband and sons to the mine, because she secretly bought the tea in the town instead of the Company store, which is considered theft by the Company, punishable by eviction.

Other stories recount how miners are robbed of solidarity and friendship. The Company strategically pits them against each other, so they make more money for the Company and direct their anger at each other rather than at management. In *The Drill*, the workers of one mine are told by their engineer that the workers of a rival mine are digging to get to the rich undersea coal deposit, and they are ready to "throw [the rivals] inside their mine pit with hoist, machines and everything." The engineer tells them they will have to dig twice as fast as their rivals to get to the deposit first. They work "day and night without stopping for a minute, even a second," so hard that many workers faint, while others "start bleeding from their noses and ears" (reventaban de sangre por las narices y los oídos; 102). The workers make it just a little ahead of the opposing team and throw a bag of garlic and smoldering coals into their tunnel. Acrid smoke spreads through the tunnel so the rival miners cannot enter the tunnel to frame it, and soon it collapses, engulfed by sea waters along with the winners' tunnel. What was the point of working so hard if they did not receive more pay or the coveted coal? But the "winners" do not care about pay: with cries of joy and cheers (gritos y vivas; 105) they celebrate their victory over the poor devils just like themselves, who respond in turn with insults and curses (105). *Firedamp* recounts another destructive result of the failure of solidarity: a young worker rebels against an arbitrary fine and is beaten and humiliated by the Company engineer while his coworkers look on, laughing to please the feared boss. Mocked even by his coworkers, the young man feels like a "cornered beast" (bestia acorralada; 30) and decides to put an end to everything. He furiously hammers a framing beam in place to the sarcastic praise of the engineer who does not know that the tunnel is full of explosive firedamp. Sparks fly and everything explodes. Everyone in the tunnel dies—the victimized worker, his tormentor the engineer, and the complicit coworkers. The Company's tactics to make workers compete against each other rob them of solidarity and make their job and life even more precarious.

The miners are also robbed of the right to be good parents to their children. In *Gate Number 12*, a father brings his ten-year-old son, Pablito, to the mine. The child does not know that he is to begin working as a doorman who opens and closes a door for horse-pulled trains. The foreman accepts the child as replacement for "José's son who was run over yesterday" (el hijo de José aplastado ayer; 15). When Pablito realizes this was not a fun walk and now he will stay all alone in the dark, he weeps and begs his father to take him back home. The father then ties him with a rope by the waist to a bolt in a rock and runs off to his own tunnel, haunted by the child's faint calls for his mother thundering in his ears. In *Payday*, a young widow, who learns that her twelve-year-old son will not get paid because he was fined, invokes divine punishments upon the foreman and, instead of compassion, receives jeers from a crowd of miners. Incensed, she shoves her son, who was dawdling, gaping at a flock of seagulls, and he falls on his face into the mud (44). The Company's cost-cutting policies bring these parents to mistreat their own children as the only thing in their life they can control.

The workers are robbed of solidarity, love, and health, as well as their lives. The Company humiliates workers and forces them to accept deplorable labor conditions, all the while touting their free choice. The story *The Devil's Pit* is about a mine infamous for daily collapses and deaths. The rock is so porous that wooden framing rots very quickly. Since it is too expensive to maintain the framing properly, the Company finds it more economical to pay a little extra to attract workers, despite the risk of losing their lives there. The Company soon cancels the extra pay and tries a new strategy. The foreman tells workers that their current positions are terminated and nothing else is available except spots at the Devil's Pit. When workers complain that this is a trick to make them work there, the foreman rebukes them, "No one is forced here. Just as you are free to refuse the work that you do not like, the Company, for its part, is within its right to take the measures that best suit its interests" (Aquí no se obliga a nadie. Así como Uds. son libres de rechazar el trabajo que no les agrade, la Compañía, por su parte, está en su derecho para tomar las medidas que más convengan a sus intereses; 48). These lives, devoid of rights, relationships, and possessions, are portrayed as free by the very same Company who took everything from these workers. Historian Laura Benedetti described with archival documents how Compañía Explotadora de Lota y Coronel, which belonged to a couple of Chilean Cousiño entrepreneurs, implemented arbitrary fines and pay cuts, arbitrary incarceration and evictions, nine- to twelve-hour shifts, and the token system to discipline their workers. Precarity was the condition of miners' life and the means to control it, writes Benedetti (213).

Nearly a hundred years lie between the publication of the book and the release of the film adaptation, *Subterra* (2003). It was the most expensive film produced in Chile, with over five hundred extras selected from Lota's actual inhabitants. The film fills the lack that defines the miners' life with something (work, school, rights), and makes it look as if they will get access to more in the future (which is the present of the film audience). A whole new set of characters is introduced to bring together the workers and the entrepreneurs-owners. We meet Matías Cousiño and his wife Isidora Goyenecheya, who owned the Lota mine. The noble-minded profiteer father in this adaptation is

Matías Cousiño (Héctor Noguera). He is passionate about scientific progress and inventions. He spends his days devising and tuning tricky mechanisms and corresponding with his "friend Edison" and is excited to see a photographic camera his adopted daughter Virginia brought from Spain. He never visits the mine and leaves everything to Mr. Davis (Ernesto Malbrán, the good American priest from *Machuca*, plays a malevolent foreigner here). He is not opposed to repressive measures but does not want to know the details, advising to proceed with caution. He is not interested in why his workers want to strike or the conditions in which they work. Instead, his ambition is to benefit humanity in general. He designs and builds in Lota the first electricity plant in Chile. Using electric trains to transport ore will make mining more efficient and also provide light to the town of Lota. Things would not have changed with him in charge, but he dies and his wife doña Isidora takes the reins.

The owners' goddaughter, Virginia, is the character who makes them consider that their workers are suffering. At the beginning of the film, Virginia (Paulina Gálvez) returns to Chile from Spain, where she was sent in an attempt to end her relationship with one of the miners, Fernando. As they rekindle their love upon her return, she becomes more and more aware of the workers' plight and communicates it to doña Isidora. The owners, Virginia, and Fernando were not present in the literary source and are vehicles for the rapprochement between the owners and the workers that the film effects. Virginia decides to teach the miners' children, and discovers that they cannot attend school because their parents make them work at the mine. When little Pablito (from the story "Gate Number 12" discussed above) does not return to school because he is left in the mine, Virginia tells her adoptive mother that they are to blame. Doña Isidora (Consuelo Holzapfel) objects that before her husband founded the mine there was nothing, but that plenty of things emerged with it, and that something is better than nothing. Miners are free agents, if they work in the mine or send their children to work instead of school, it is their choice:

> For your information, Virginia, when don Matías Cousiño came here, there was nothing, just a few poor fishermen and farmers. The mine brought people here and gave them a livelihood. We gave them a hospital, a priest, a general store so they don't have to go into town. Brick and ceramic factories where the women can work and the child nutrition center for the neediest children. Tell me, Virginia, if we also offer a school for their children and they would rather send their children to the mine what can we do? They are free.

¿Sabías Virginia que cuando Don Matías Cousiño llegó aquí no había nada? Sólo unos pocos pescadores y campesinos muy pobres. La mina hizo que la gente viniera aquí y que se pudiera ganar la vida con su trabajo. Le hemos dado hospital, tienen un sacerdote. La pulpería para que la gente no tenga que ir al pueblo a comprar sus cosas. Fábricas de ladrillo y cerámica donde las mujeres puedan trabajar . . . y la gota de leche donde podemos atender a los niños más necesitados. Dime Virginia, si además les ofrecemos una escuela y los padres prefieren mandar a sus hijos a la mina ¿qué podemos hacer? Son libres.

The film does show, of course, that Doña Isidora exaggerates the Company's beneficial influence on the community at least up to this point in the film. We see that some miners are not paid their full wages, that the Company store charges the miners much more than the town store, and that children work in the mine because the pay is too low. As opposed to the stories, in the film all these practices are attributed to one individual, the engineer-manager. At first Doña Isidora is angry at Virginia, slapping her for saying that she and her husband are wrong to live in luxury at the expense of their workers. But as the film progresses, Doña Isidora grows more amenable to the idea of social justice. After her husband's death, Doña Isidora fires Mr. Davis, the mine's foreign-born engineer and head manager, as the man responsible for exploiting the workers. She agrees to the workers' demands to prohibit child labor, introduce a minimum wage, and shorten shifts. She unveils the power plant that her husband had built for the mine and the town, sharing the benefits of electricity with the community at large.

The film prophesies unity and harmony between workers and entrepreneurs, showing that working together, they will advance each other's interests and the general progress of Chile. This progress is symbolized by the power plant that the workers themselves would have never been able to build, but which they will now enjoy because the surplus value of their labor was turned into a common good by the owner, that same avoidant father who allowed their repression by the army. Baldomero Lillo, the author of the stories on which the film is based, is made into a character in this film (played by Cristián Chaparro) and works at the Company store while secretly writing his stories. He also helps the miners register their union, making repression more difficult for the Company. In the end, he travels to the capital with his manuscript under his arm, saying that the events described reflect a change in the winds (semillas de nuevos vientos). As Virginia gathers her schoolchildren for a group portrait in the last shot of the film, a voiceover by Baldomero Lillo's character in voiceover says about these children, "Now they were able to face the future with greater dignity" (ahora ellos podían mirar el futuro con mayor dignidad). By the way, if the film implies that schooling will help these children attain dignity, *Machuca* disproves it.

Critic Gastón Lillo argues that the film's reliance on the commercial genre of melodrama converts the class struggle presented in the original stories into motivations of individual characters and embraces the politics of consensus espoused by the democratic governments (148). Indeed, the moral message of the film is far different from Lillo's stories, which show how the workers' precarious existence, lack of rights, and impossibility of friendship and solidarity was structural and integral to the Company's practices. In the film, these practices are the consequence of the cruel and treacherous dispositions of two individual characters, Mr. Davis and his spy, the foreman. They are found out and punished, which implies that these practices will disappear with them. The miners' leader, Fernando, Virginia's lover, pays with his own life to ensure that the evil engineer dies with him, exploding firedamp in the mine tunnel when the fired engineer comes to exact his revenge on the strikers. No one else is hurt in this purposeful and noble death. In contrast, in the original story *Firedamp* the young miner kills not only himself and the engineer but also his coworkers for looking on and laughing at his humiliation. In *Gate Number 12*, the story of the ten-year-old Pablito, whose father left him in the mine, was meant to call attention to child labor as a widespread practice and a consequence of wage theft. In the film, however, it is a unique occurrence and the father in question is the second villain of the story, engineer's spy, the foreman who informs on strike organizers. He, too, is punished: the miners cut off his ear to let everyone know he is a deceitful informer and they exile him from Lota. In the film, his son Pablito returns to school and is seen playing in the sun in the school yard, although it is unclear how his mother and siblings are now to survive at all, without their father and his earnings. If in the original stories' laissez-faire capitalism not only left workers with nothing but took everything from them, in the film it gives workers quite a few things, including some political freedoms. Moreover, the film's promise is that they would eventually get even more.

The film *Subterra* prophesied a better future for workers, but this promised future, which is the present, looks more like that past for a large majority of workers in today's Chile. Pinochet's government gave companies legal tools to exploit workers and took from workers the ability to organize and push back. As a result, wage and income inequality increased between 2000 and 2010, despite the economy growing at a rate of 4.2 percent annually (Gammage et al. 10). In 2017, 1 percent of Chile's population controlled 26.5 percent of the country's wealth, whereas 50 percent of low-income households controlled only 2.1 percent. More than half of Chilean workers do not earn enough to lift an average family of four out of poverty. In order to compensate for low salaries, 70 percent of Chilean households rely on debt. Many Chileans take out new loans to pay for existing loans—a practice known as "bicycling" (bicicleteo). The average annual household debt to income ratio is over 75 percent, which means that Chileans owe more than they earn (Durán and Kremerman 18; "Banco central"). Scholars explain that this impoverishment of vast sectors of the population is the consequence of the expanding labor precarization (Gammage et al. 25; Stecher and Sisto 38).

Labor flexibility, a euphemism for freeing companies from obligations toward their workers, was introduced in 1978 by José Piñera, Pinochet's Secretary of Labor, Social Security, and Mining, one of the Chicago boys and brother of the recent president Sebastián Piñera. The new laws allowed both public and private companies to subcontract workers for essential tasks and made it possible to treat them differently from permanent workers in terms of labor conditions, remuneration, and benefits (Echeverría Tortello 96). Subcontracted workers complete the same tasks as permanent workers but are paid less and have less or no access to benefits, such as health insurance and pension. More importantly, since they formally work for a subcontracting firm, they cannot participate in collective bargaining with their actual employer. If they attempt to organize, they can be easily replaced (Sehnbruch, "A Precarious Labor Market" 77). More than two-thirds of jobs are precarious (poorly paid, unprotected, and insecure), and it is during the rule of the center-left democratic governments that subcontracted and temporary workers began to outnumber permanent workers (Sehnbruch, "How Pinochet's Economic Model Led to the Current Economic Crisis Engulfing Chile"; Gómez Leiva 120). Companies fire permanent workers and hire them back as subcontractors (Fundación Sol). Workers are divided into two classes: those on permanent contract enjoy superior pay, labor conditions, protections, rights, and benefits, and the subcontracted or temporary workers. This division helps save on labor costs and atomizes workers, forcing them to direct their discontent toward each other and away from the management (Standing 17; Manky 582).

In the lucrative mining sector, labor precarization has reached its highest levels. Chile is a leading exporter of copper. The state-owned mining company Codelco makes considerable profits, but over 70 percent of its workers are subcontracted and temporary. Codelco's annual 2018 report states that over 95 percent of its workers are members of unions and benefit from training opportunities, but these numbers include only permanent workers. Therefore, union membership, training, and other benefits only apply to only two out of every seven workers. In fact, the state-owned Codelco subcontracts on an even larger scale than private mining companies. It funnels money to private subcontracting agencies rather than to its workers, demonstrating, again, the "entrepreneurial capture of public resources" (Osorio and Vega). Subcontracted and temporary workers not only lack job security and benefits but also experience inferior pay, insufficient bathroom facilities, inferior cafeteria food, and can only board buses after permanent employees (Hughes 98). The interview with a subcontracted miner quoted below is very telling. He realized the scale of the injustice when he heard politicians on TV say that copper is the engine of progress and economic growth for all Chileans. While he extracted this valuable resource, he felt underpaid and humiliated:

> Yes, I admit: I agreed to the conditions. No unions. I wanted, I needed the pay. But . . . It was the combination of a lot of things: going down to the mine at night, doing the same work as the other guy at my side but knowing he was earning five times as much. I don't know, many things, like feeling that what you're doing is worth little. Or at any rate, much less than what the permanent worker does. But I think the trigger was to find out how much copper cost, at what price Codelco sold it! And we kept on working on miserable salaries . . . I think that's what it was: to see people on TV telling you how great we were doing because of the high international price of copper. And I'd work in the mine and after work, I'd have to wash myself with cold water because we subcontractors didn't have any hot water. And then they tell you that copper belongs to all Chileans.

> Sí, yo lo reconozco: yo acepté las condiciones. Nada de sindicato. Yo quería, necesitaba la paga. Pero . . . Se juntaron muchas cosas. Subir a la mina de noche, hacer la misma tarea que el de al lado pero que cobraba 5 veces más. No sé, muchas cosas, sentir que lo que haces vale poco . . . o por lo menos mucho menos que lo mismo que hace el interno . . . ¡Pero yo creo que el detonante fue saber a cuánto estaba el cobre, a cuánto vendía el cobre CODELCO! Y nosotros seguíamos con salarios miserables . . . Sí, yo creo que fue eso. Ver en la televisión que te digan lo bien que estábamos por el precio internacional del cobre. Y yo trabajaba en la mina y cuando terminaba la faena, me bañaba con agua helada, ¡porque los contratistas no teníamos agua caliente! Y que te digan que el cobre es de todos los chilenos. (Hughes 101)

As the words of this disgruntled man show, listening to politicians who live in the world of plenty angers workers who live in the everyday reality of lack. Democratically elected officials congratulate Chileans on the nation's economic growth but fail to explain that it is predicated on growing job precarity. Sociologist Lorena Pérez-Roa observed how, starting in 2000, a combination of consumerism and low wages led miners to voluntarily relinquish benefits won by their ancestors, such as health and dental insurance. The miners exchanged these benefits for a one-time bonus in order to acquire costly consumer goods and pay debts. Social rights were replaced by individual possessions—not only consumer goods but also credits, which they perceived as assets and a sign of trust on the part of the banks, an appreciation of them as respectable clients (86). Social psychologists Stecher and Sisto say that the growing precarization of work is one of the factors of the 2019 protests. They explain that, in addition to working more and being paid less, workers are increasingly controlled by flexible management models and rendered ever more efficient by means of new information technologies. Workers are pressured to compete with each other to achieve individualized and ever-growing performance goals. This constant pressure to compete is detrimental to workers' mental and physical health and prevents workers from coming together as a collective (Stecher and Sisto 48). The demand to cut costs in order to maximize profits and achieve growth leads to the nationwide precarization of labor. It causes social suffering and brings about a strong sentiment of moral injustice. Baldomero Lillo described the strategies to cut labor costs at the beginning of the last century, yet the 2003 film adaptation presented them as a thing of the past. In a sense, this film whitewashes the neoliberal laissez-faire exploitative model. In the film, the avoidant and irresponsible father builds a power central to share with the community. In addition, his wife agrees to improve working conditions for the workers, and prevents the army from attacking them. In fact, the opposite happened in real life. The workers of doña Isidora's mining company marched to the capital to deliver their petition to her son and received a promise that things will change. Back home, however, the army repressed the leaders. There were evictions and deaths, including deaths of children. This violent repression ended the first wave of strikes (Benedetti 287).

Conclusion

At stake in these three adaptations is the morality of the neoliberal socioeconomic model in modern Chile. Consumerism and the freedom to consume are offered as a substitute for political rights. I used the contrast of plenty and lack to explain the films. In *Machuca*, the slum dwellers lack possessions but have moral principles and the courage to defend them, for which they are eliminated by the military as undesirable and undeserving. The rich live in the land of plenty. They use their privileges and connections to access imported goods and fine foods in the midst of shortages, but they must give up the right to political agency and their moral principles to preserve these privileges. Education remains a tool of socioeconomic segregation and is the reason for the continuing and growing socioeconomic inequality. *No* explains how the plentiful goods that Pinochet offered for consumption obliterated political debate. The adman who enabled the democratic coalition to win the referendum replaced the political content of the campaign with sound bites, jokes, and superficial images of happiness. Political marketing appeals to emotions and distracts voters from the fact that the new socioeconomic model replaced their social rights (health, education, dignity of work) with consumer goods that they can only acquire by taking out loans. Unlike its literary inspiration, *No* portrays the triumph of the democratic coalition as a defeat, because Pinochet's model remained in place. The third adaptation, *Subterra*, attempts to justify that model. Its source, written one hundred years earlier, described the precariousness of the miners' life as the management's strategy to cut labor costs and alienate workers from one another. The film portrays this strategy as the fault of one particular manager, who is fired and killed for his evil doings. It presents the company as providing people with work and a purpose to contribute to the progress of the country, together with creative owners-entrepreneurs. It promises that the miners' children will have a future of dignity. And yet, in this promised future, which is Chile's present, workers also lack job security and dignity. Ironically, during the three decades of post-Pinochet governments, companies began employing these same techniques even more aggressively to increase their profits. Two-tier contracts sow hostility between workers and incapacitate collective action. Chile's economic growth dramatically increased the share of precarious jobs—non-permanent, low-wage, and lacking benefits. All three films introduce the character of a father who means well but lacks the conviction or knowledge and does more harm than good. This character did not exist in the stories that inspired the films. These noble-minded profiteers from the films belong to the land of plenty and represent the lack of will on the part of post-Pinochet democratic governments to share the growing national wealth with the people who produce it.

8

Conclusion

The Clean-Shaven Father, Disfigured, Urinated Upon, Buried Alive, and Blown Up

In this book I have described the trend in post-2000 Latin American cinema to turn harsh and unreliable fathers into a metaphor for predatory leadership. Filmmakers change the source novels and plays to criticize this model of leadership as scolding, name-calling, manipulation, indifference, and neglect. In the original stories, children and wives who fall under the dominion of such men wither away lethargically. Their intellectual and even physical potential for growth is permanently stunted and liberation is impossible, even if their master dies. However, in the films, the children and the wives find the courage to stand up to these terrible fathers, walk away from them, and begin a new life. I want to end this book with films in which a composite version of the predatory leader examined in the previous chapters is destroyed, symbolically or physically: *Pan's Labyrinth* and *Pinocchio* by Guillermo del Toro and *Dance of Reality* and *Endless Poetry* by Alejandro Jodorowsky. Each of these films features an ostentatiously groomed, clean-shaven man, his hair carefully slicked back with copious amounts of gel, his attractive uniform impeccably ironed, and his tall boots meticulously shined. This man is a father and a function in a fascist regime. Flaunting his exaggerated masculinity and self-control, he imitates the leader of the regime, similarly clean-shaven and with his hair slicked back—Joseph Stalin and Chilean dictator Ibáñez del Campo in Jodorowsky's films, and Francisco Franco and Benito Mussolini in del Toro's. By the end of the films, these clean-shaven men end up splattered with paint and have their pictures burned; they have their dictator mustaches and hair shaved off; they are disfigured, stabbed, buried alive, blown up to pieces, urinated upon by a woman, and showered with scatological obscenities.

Commands and Crowd Behavior

These films also present striking visuals of people clicking into a repeating pattern of a crystal lattice. This is achieved with rhythmic and synchronized gestures, such as throwing up a hand in a fascist salute, marching, shouting slogans, and brandishing objects. These audiovisual metaphors are best explained using Elias Canetti's *Crowds and Power*. Canetti examines exercising power and submitting to power as an instinctual, psychosomatic behavior. The mechanism is simple: a command is issued and obeyed, and it remains lodged in the flesh of the obeying person, like an arrow or a sting. Every command obeyed changes the person who obeys it. The sting of the command remains sticking in the flesh, until the person passes the command to someone else. The wound will heal but leave a scar: "Every scar has a story; it is the mark of a particular arrow," as Canetti puts it (309). Children are the natural recipients of commands, and they will pass the commands they receive to their own children.

One way to feel temporarily free of these accumulated stings of command is to become part of a crowd, in which the usual distinctions of rank, class, and status dissolve. As a part of one enormous living organism, one experiences elation in the rhythmic movement of the crowd, becoming just one more stomping foot and one more shouting mouth. When antelopes hear the roar of a lion, which for them is a death verdict and a command to flee, they form a tight group and start galloping, executing one rhythmic movement. To become separated from the herd would mean a sure death, but as long as they are galloping together, executing the same rhythmic movement, the animals do not panic. Canetti writes sarcastically that one may call the common direction of animals fleeing together their "conviction" (310; also see Adorno 123). Using these analogies with herd and pack behavior, as well as religious rituals, Canetti explains the instinctual need for people to join crowds, for the crowds to want to come into existence, and for people to feel thankful to the man who can couch his goals into slogans, simple commands that they can chant together (311). Such commands spread instantly, turn people into a crowd without leaving a sting, and make people forget the stings that lodged in them.

Another way to avoid being marked by the sting of a command is to disobey it. The films I examine here teach precisely that. The film stills included here (figure 8.1, figure 8.2, figure 8.3, and figure 8.4) all depict a scene from the four films by Guillermo del Toro and Alejandro Jodorowsky analyzed in this chapter. In each, a clean-shaven man stares with a surprisingly intense, disproportionate rage at a small child. These men are called upon to be the

Figure 8.1. The fascist leader points at and questions Pinocchio in *Pinocchio* (2022).

impersonal function of command and power, to make individuals click into place in rigid crystal-like structures of fascism, with a repeating pattern of gestures and slogans. Every one of these men carries with him something that leaves a wound, a sting in the flesh of others: a taser baton, a razor, torture instruments, or a gun. The function of these clean-shaven men is to precipitate crowds, to be what Canetti calls "crowd crystals." They remain dormant until a demagogue appears and these men immediately respond, throwing up their hands in salute and making other people do the same. It is natural for people to comply with simple commands, especially children, whose survival is conditional on pleasing the adults on whom they depend. The reason these clean-shaven men always end up with a gun pointed at a small child in these films is *not* because the child is aggressive. These men would understand aggression and would know how to deal with it. However, they cannot understand the friendly child's organic inability to comply with a simple command and click into place in the very clear rigid structure that they precipitate and maintain. Canetti explains that for the crowd, the biggest threat comes from the inside. If one "traitor" cannot click into place, the whole structure will collapse. This explains why the crowd feels persecuted and exhibits hostility toward anyone

Figure 8.2. The fascist Captain Vidal seizes and shakes Ofelia in *Pan's Labyrinth* (2006).

Figure 8.3. The Stalinist father grabs his son by the arm in *Dance of Reality* (2011).

Figure 8.4. The father grabs his son by the neck in *Endless Poetry* (2016).

who for some reason moves out sync with it. This fear of being broken apart explains the crowd's insecurity and hostility, surprising and illogical for such a strong and large unit (Canetti 337). This fear is why the uniformed and clean-shaven men with a gun react hysterically to the child, terrified that no amount of scolding or intimidation can shape this ridiculous piece of human flesh into a crowd unit. The children in these films put a crucial strain on the rigidity of the structure merely by how they look, how they wear their hair, what they say, and even how they hold their hand out for a handshake. Logically, the result of this confrontation is either total destruction or a complete transformation of the clean-shaven man. The one person who does not change at all in the films I will now consider is the unafraid, open, and friendly child. It is a foreign element that breaks apart the crystal lattice of fascism.

Del Toro's *Pan's Labyrinth* (2006) and *Pinocchio* (2022)

The clean-shaven man in del Toro's *Pan's Labyrinth* (*Laberinto del fauno*) is known as captain Vidal, or simply the Captain (played by Sergi López). This name alerts us to the fact that he is not just a man but a function of power. The Captain precipitates and maintains the fascist structure in Spain in 1944. The country is controlled by dictator Francisco Franco, who led a nationalist military rebellion during the Spanish Civil War, established a fascist regime, suppressed political dissent, and promoted nationalist and conservative values. The Captain metaphorically represents Franco in the film, and his mission is to fight the remaining Republican guerrillas hiding in the mountain and control the neighboring localities, importantly, by retaining control over food and distributing it among the locals. The feeding procedure has a rigid physical and audiovisual structure: the locals rhythmically move along in a line to receive their ration while the soldiers carrying out the procedure belch loud rhythmic shouts: "This is our daily bread in Franco's Spain!" and "In a united Spain, there's not a single home without fire or bread!" This rhythmic public feeding of people to make a structure out of them is an important metaphor. Trained animals obtain food from their trainer as a reward for complying with his command. Children obtain food from their parents, and slaves from their master. The master alone has the obligation to feed his dog, and no one else is under any obligation to do it. Canetti gives these examples (305) to explain that feeding is a camouflaged command. Satisfying hunger is a physical necessity and is always conditional on complete compliance with the giver of food, from the very first moments of each human life.

We also observe the Captain precipitate another rigid structure with another feeding. When the town's rich and powerful arrive for a special dinner party at the military outpost, he makes them all click into place in the familiar lattice structure by making the same gesture and exclaiming the same words. At the beginning, the party appears to be a usual gathering of different individuals who came to enjoy each other's company. Some ladies even make an attempt at pleasant chit-chat by asking the Captain's wife (Ariadna Gil) how they met. She puts her hand on the Captain's hand and naively shares that her first husband, a tailor, died in the war, and that he used to make the Captain's uniforms. The Captain pointedly removes his hand from hers and says, "Please, forgive my wife. She hasn't been exposed to the world. She thinks these silly stories are interesting to others." His wife looks miserable, like a child who does not know what she did wrong, but we understand that for the Captain the personal simply does not exist, and that this dinner, a public administration of food, is another camouflaged command that will make those fed click together into a rigid structure. He tells these rich people that from now on, for everyone, and especially for them, there will be only one ration card per family. He pointedly clarifies that the small group of *republicanos* hiding in the woods cannot be fed with the supplies in his control: "We can't allow anyone to send food to the guerrillas in the mountains." This clarification would seem absurd if it were not meant to solidify his image as the sole giver of food in the impressionable minds of his guests. The guests, habituated by their wealth and power to having anything they want, and certainly as much food as they want, timidly try to object that one ration card per family will not be enough for them, but quickly lose heart, acquiesce, and hurry to pile compliments onto the Captain. To appease their new giver of food, they thank him for his selfless service in harsh conditions that he must surely dislike. The Captain coolly replies, "You are wrong about that. I am here because I want to (estoy aquí por gusto). I choose to be here because I want my son to be born in a new, clean Spain." The captain cues his guests, exclaiming, "We're all here because we want to." The guests immediately click into place in the rigid structure that the Captain outlines for them: they throw up their hands holding a drink as in a fascist salute and shout in unison "¡Por gusto!" (Because we want to!).

The child who cannot bring herself to obey the clean-shaven man in this film is Ofelia, the Captain's wife's child from her first marriage. Ofelia had the obligation to attend this dinner, or rather, a disciplinary feeding ritual, as shown above. Her mother made her a shiny green taffeta dress with a mandatory white apron (girls are habituated to occupy a servant's position early on) and shiny shoes. These pieces of clothing shine like Captain's boots and would have made Ofelia look like him. Ofelia (played by Ivana Baquero) fails to attend the dinner because she was given a task by a magical creature: she must extract a golden key from a monstrously sized toad who lives in a burrow. As she executes this mission, giant millipedes the size of her hand are crawling all over her face and body. As the toad explodes, Ofelia is drenched in its slimy remains. When she emerges from the burrow, her shiny shoes are a sorry sight, and the shiny new dress that she so prudently hung on a branch before going in lies in the mud. Film scholar Dolores Tierney notes that Ofelia's preference for filth and the abject signifies her protest and a refusal to take her place in the symbolic order signified by her stepfather (117). We recall that Kafka's frightening father often called him "vermin," and that the meek hero of the short story "Metamorphosis" turns into vermin, "Ungeziefer," and dies after the father wounds him with an apple. We also recall that the Nazis called the Jews "Ungeziefer" (Despiniadis 69), and that in German the word also means "an unclean animal unsuitable for sacrifice," similar to Agamben's *homo sacer*, a person who can be killed without committing a crime but who cannot be sacrificed, a bare life form whose life is not worth living. The child in this film is an anomaly: she prefers being covered with bugs, dirt, and slime to sitting at dinner in a pretty dress with the clean-shaven personification of command who she cannot bring herself to call "father," to her mother's dismay.

Ofelia's second task is to attend yet another dinner, with another monstrous host—a pale zombie-like monster whose eyes are in his palms. He sits at a long table laden with the most tempting foods. The monster, another giver of food, actually feeds on little children lured in by the feast. A mound of little shoes towers nearby, immediately bringing to mind similar piles in photos from the Nazi death camps. Here the command is shown in its primitive state, as the lion's roar announcing imminent death (Canetti 306). In another frame, the monstrous giver of food bites off the head of a fairy who led Ofelia to this chamber, looking identical to Goya's painting *Saturn Devouring His Son*. In this legend, Saturn, afraid of being overthrown by one of his children, devoured them all, until Jupiter, hidden by his mother, liberated all the children Saturn had swallowed and they overthrew him together. Ofelia was told not to touch any of the monster's treats, but as she cannot obey commands, she takes a grape and puts it in her mouth. This is when the host wakes up, and Ofelia barely escapes with her life. The Pale Man and the Captain, two monstrous givers of food, make obvious that their food is a command and a death verdict. Throughout the film, Ofelia quietly resists the simple and natural wisdom about "the hand that feeds you." Her inability to comply with simple commands, anomalous in such a small child, in the end drives the clean-shaven man to shoot her dead. This is excessive—he already took his newborn son from her hands, and all she does is say no and shake her head. It would be enough to just ignore her, walk away from her, or at most push or kick her. But the Captain can no longer deal with Ofelia's barely audible "no"s and thus ends her life.

In del Toro's stop-motion animated film *Pinocchio* (2022), we meet another clean-shaven man and another aberrant child who lacks the natural instinct to comply with commands. The man (voiced by Ron Perlman) is known as "Podestá," which, like "Captain," is not a name but a function of command, an appointment as local authority in Mussolini's Italy. He is raising his son in his image, showing him off as a perfect genetic specimen of Italian Fascist youth, pulling up his eyelids and baring his teeth for others to admire. Podestá is appalled by Pinocchio (voiced by Gregory Mann), whom Geppetto crudely nailed together in a state of angry drunkenness, with nails sticking out of his neck in the back. But no matter the looks, Podestá needs a perfect soldier, and since Pinocchio cannot be killed and is made of "fine Italian pinewood," the clean-shaven man becomes more excited about him than his own son. Pinocchio's father, Geppetto (David Bradley), is also looking for perfection. His first son died because of a perfect pinecone, without missing scales, which Geppetto told him to find. Del Toro's Pinocchio never learns to listen to his elders and is never rewarded with becoming "a real boy." He is the opposite of his counterpart from the original book by Carlo Collodi, *Adventures of Pinocchio* (1881). Collodi's Pinocchio journey is about learning the importance of work, discipline, and obeying the elders. This is why Umberto Eco called *Pinocchio* a bildungsroman rather than a fairy tale (2).

It is remarkable that del Toro's Pinocchio does not learn a single lesson; instead, everyone learns from him. Like the other children I discuss here, he knows the most important and unintuitive thing—to not obey when he is issued a simple command. After meeting Pinocchio, Podestá's son musters the courage to say no to his father for the first time in his life: "I can say no to you. I am not afraid." Geppetto, Pinocchio's maker, also learns from him. When he first sees Pinocchio come to life, he denies him, horrified: "You are not my son! Get away from me!" Watching Pinocchio explore the objects in the house and exclaim, "Love it! Love it!" Geppetto shouts, "Don't touch it!" and "Don't!" and locks him up in the storage closet. Pinocchio refuses to stay locked up and follows him to church, where he experiences the hostility of the crowd and its horror at confronting something that it will not be able to integrate, something that can explode it from within. They shout "Demon!" "Monster!" "An abomination!" "Unholy thing!" "Burn him!" and "Chop him up!" They curse Geppetto. When the clean-shaven man comes up to ask, "Who controls you?" Geppetto hurries to say, "I control him, of course," and holds his hand over the boy's mouth to stop him from talking, but Pinocchio angrily snaps back, "Who controls you?" "No one talks to Podestá like that," Geppetto tells him. On several occasions Geppetto compares him to his dead son Carlo, who never behaved like that and who was a perfect boy. The lesson of this tale is for Geppetto: *he* learns to accept and love Pinocchio as he is, not the other way around, as in the original Italian tale.

The crowd is right to fear Pinocchio: any attempt to insert him into a crowd brings it to collapse. In one example, Podestá brings Pinocchio to a fascist youth camp, determined to turn him into a perfect soldier. In Mussolini's Italy, children in these camps were equipped with uniforms and wooden rifles and were organized in military hierarchies. They practiced parade ground exercises and military rituals, such as raising the flag and pledging the oath of allegiance. The stay at the camp fostered an emotional attachment to the fascist regime and particularly to Mussolini himself. Even the architecture of these camps was meant to inspire nationalist fervor in the boys (Winkelmann). When del Toro was told that the letter M on the camp gate in the film was too grotesquely huge, he replied that it came from an actual photograph (interview with Holub). In the camp, Pinocchio participates in a real-time tactics game in which the boys, divided into two camps, shoot at each other with guns loaded with paint. As with other disciplinary rituals, he makes a mockery of it, a game of friendship, and the enraged clean-shaven man gives his son a real gun and tells him to shoot Pinocchio. Pinocchio's placement in the fascist youth camp dismantles its rigid structure of order-compliance, and the son of the clean-shaven man refuses to obey him for the first time in his life. As the enraged father prepares to mete out terrible punishments, he is blown up by a missile. The second time Pinocchio is inserted into a fascist crowd, he again explodes it from within. His task was to publicize fascism in a performance: accoutered with boots, helmet, and a machine gun, he rides a tank and an eagle, singing an ode to the fatherland and Mussolini: "Il Duce, il Duce / we sing and we pray / Like an eagle soaring / magnificent and free." Like Ofelia, Pinocchio cannot put the outfit he is given to its intended use of fitting into a crowd directed by the clean-shaven man. When the Duce himself arrives to see the show, Pinocchio turns the act into total anarchy. Flying around over the audience in his eagle prop, he showers the Duce with words denoting excreta: "Il Duce, il Duce / go smell your farts and pray / Eat your boogers, your slime / you can also have mine / like a bag of poop / magnificent and free." The delighted crowd chants the abject words after Pinocchio. The Duce commands his lieutenants to burn the theater and, of course, shoot Pinocchio.

In these films, the figure of the clean-shaven man is viciously maltreated and showered with abject insults. Captain Vidal from *Pan's Labyrinth* is stabbed in the chest and back and also shot, but, before that, he is disfigured: the right corner of his mouth is cut to his ear (figure 8.5). The gaping wound makes the captain look like the Joker, with his ear-to-ear smile. When he stitches it up with a sewing needle and coarse thread, without flinching, he resembles both Terminator and Frankenstein. The Duce is showered with obscenities. And both lose their name. The Captain tells the doctor to save the baby over his wife in case of complications during delivery, because his son will bear his name and his father's name. When he is about to be shot by the rebels at the end of the film, he asks them to give his watch to his son when he grows up and begins a pompous farewell with "Tell him . . . ," but they cut him short: "He won't even know your name." The same loss strikes the Duce, whose title of "His Excellency" on the show's celebratory poster is scratched out and corrected by Pinocchio to "His Excremency" (Sua Escremenza), and his name changed from Mussolini to Puzzo (the Stinker in Italian, as the Duce was known in the dialect spoken in Rome, Er Puzzone, figure 8.6).

That the bad father and leader is stripped of his name becomes particularly interesting if we recall that Lacan conceptualized the paternal figure as "The Name of the Father"—the linguistic and symbolic order. The Name of the Father represents the opposite of the abject universe of the mother (specifi-

Figure 8.5. Captain Vidal stiches up the cut on his mouth in *Pan's Labyrinth* (2006).

cally associated with abject bodily fluids), which the child must leave behind. Playing with the fact that in French, the Name of the Father sounds the same as the No of the Father, Lacan described the paternal function as the order of law, prohibition, and guilt. It ensnares people in language and symbols and marks them with "hieroglyphics of hysteria, blazons of phobia, labyrinths of the Zwangsneurose [obsessional neuroses], charms of impotence, enigmas of inhibition, oracles of anxiety, . . . seals of self-punishment, disguises of perversion" (52). Philosopher Slavoj Žižek stresses the coercion implied in the paternal metaphor: the Name (and the No) of the Father is experienced subjectively as "perverse fantasies about what the person who is the bearer of this No 'really wants.'" The No of the Father is not a clear law, such as "You shall not kill" but "the truncated injunction 'You shall not!'—do what? . . . you yourself should know or guess what you should not do, so that you are always and a priori put in an impossible position of always and a priori being under suspicion of violating some (unknown) prohibition" (lxvi).

Thus, to watch a film that extirpates the name of the father figure is to witness the abolition of the entire symbolic order of the masculine male: the discipline, the punishment, the guilt—in short, the very source of command. No wonder that the destruction of the father in the films is excessive, anarchical, and exhilarating.

Figure 8.6. Pinocchio makes fun of Mussolini in *Pinocchio* (2022).

Figure 8.7. The wife urinates on her husband in *Dance of Reality* (2011).

Conclusion: The Clean-Shaven Father, Disfigured, Urinated Upon, Buried Alive, and Blown Up · 213

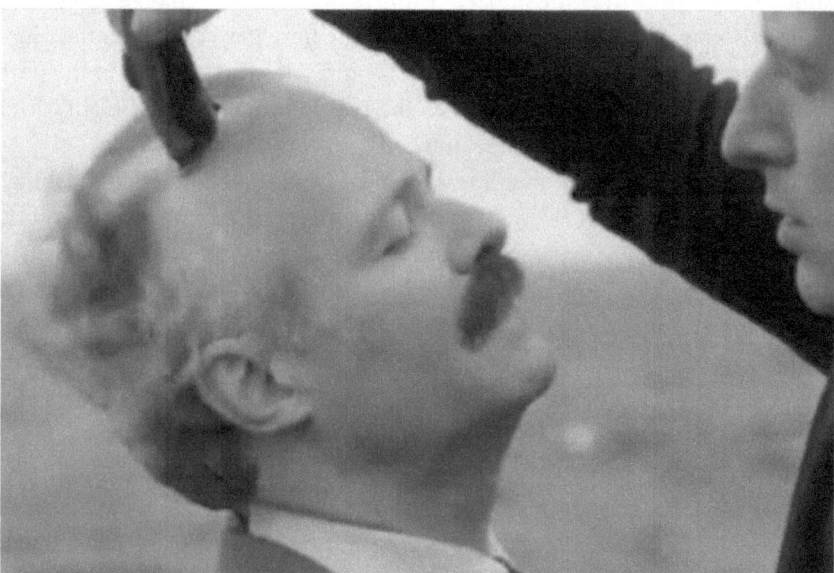

Figure 8.8. The son shaves his father's head and his Stalinist mustache in *Endless Poetry* (2016).

Jodorowsky's *Dance of Reality* (2011) and *Endless Poetry* (2016)

Alejandro Jodorowsky, the avant-garde filmmaker who was born in Chile and lives in France, also drowns the clean-shaven man, his own father and a Stalinist, in the abject in the adaptation of his autobiography, *Dance of Reality* (*Danza de la realidad*). The father is lengthily urinated upon by a woman (figure 8.7), and his slicked-back hair and Stalinist mustache are shaved off (figure 8.8); he is also tortured and buried alive, among other things, and stripped of his name. In the film, the Chilean leader of the fascist regime figures as a prototype and inspiration for the clean-shaven father, just like Franco and Mussolini in del Toro's films, and he is also abjectified: he is so suspiciously attached to his special white horse Bucephalus that he is shown having an orgasm while riding it. Again, the clean-shaven man's antagonist is a child who is unable to understand simple commands, that is to say, little Jodorowsky himself. The boy's otherness is made obvious by his long, wavy blond hair, clearly a woman's wig (Jodorowsky likes to use theatrical props to materially manifest intangible concepts). The father decides to save the boy from growing up "a fag" (maricón). An ardent Stalinist, he shapes the boy into a little copy of himself, cutting his long hair, dressing him in a military uniform like his own, and taking him along for manly pursuits. It is painful to watch this child take pleasure in being noticed by the father, trying to change and please him, as is natural for children. The child in the film, played by Jeremías Herskovits, is the young Alejandro Jodorowsky himself, who grew up in the port town of Tocopilla in northern Chile. The real Jodorowsky, aged eighty-five, appears in the film as well, embracing and consoling the lonely boy.

The father's training in manliness includes pulling, shoving, and pushing, as well as urinating on religious symbols in which the boy found comfort, saying, "God does not exist, we die and we rot;" tickling his son with a feather and forbidding him to laugh; slapping his son in the face while the boy must say "Harder!"; and pulling out his tooth without anesthesia. Influenced by Surrealism and Artaud's theater of cruelty, Jodorowsky conjures powerful sensory images to explore "madness, hallucination, and fear" (Fleming 113), as well as "manipulation, obsession, jealousy, perversity, and other dark sides of human psyche" (Cho).

Of course, the boy, despite his strong and honest desire to please, always disappoints the father, especially when he must click into place in a crowd. For example, the father, who is the leader of the town's volunteer firefighters, decides that the boy should be the company's mascot. He gives him a beautiful uniform, scarlet with gold accents. The occasion is a midnight funeral procession to bury a member of the company who died in a fire the day before. The impressionable boy, forced by the father to look at the carbonized corpse when it was found, is imagining himself sharing a grave, full of white maggots, with the corpse that says in a sepulchral voice the father's words: "We die and we rot!" As in *Pan's Labyrinth*, the child receives a clean, beautiful piece of clothing as a camouflaged command to separate himself from the abject world of the mother and enter the ordered world of the father, the symbolic order. And again, the child, dressed in this beautiful piece of clothing, wallows in the mud, covered in vermin. As in *Pan's Labyrinth*, the child chooses the abject over the clean and brings the ordered structure to collapse. The imaginative boy faints from terror, disrupting the rhythmic marching and torch-brandishing, and the father, embarrassed and angry, takes him home. When the boy recovers, having slept for two days straight, and tries to win back the father's favor, the father has been waiting for him. With an angry and depressed face, he tells him: "You acted like a coward. Now they are laughing at me. If the son is a coward, the father must be too" (the father's paranoid fear materializes immediately in front of them as two firefighters sitting in the gazebo and laughing at him, saying, "A Jew is always a Jew!"). The father throws the boy's beautiful uniform into a tin bowl, pours gasoline on it, and sets it aflame. He grabs the dismayed boy by the neck as if he were a kitten that had peed on the floor and says "Look!" This terrible father seems to come from the pages of Kafka's *Letter to My Father*, which inspired so many novelists and filmmakers (as discussed in chapter 5).

In his interviews about this film, Jodorowsky said he wanted to heal his soul by sending his father on a journey of redemption in the second half of the film. By the time he began working on the film, his father had long been dead. In fact, the filmmaker never returned to Chile after leaving for Paris at twenty-two and throwing his address book into the waves, as we read in his 2001 autobiography of the same title (*Danza de la realidad* 173). The director made his father into a hero and his mother into a loving and powerful woman. In reality, as we learn from the autobiography, Jodorowsky's mother was cold with her son even when he was young, telling him that she had her tubes tied after she got pregnant with him because she wanted no other children with his "brute" of a father. She was obese from stifling her fear of her husband and from boredom due to sitting all day behind the counter of the family store. She dreamed of becoming an opera singer, but the father beat these dreams out of her with a stick (Jodorowsky's interview with Naranjo).

In the film, Jodorowsky's mother, played by opera singer Pamela Flores, regains her dignity. She is a luxuriously curvy, beautiful, strong woman who sings all her lines in soprano. It is the mother who begins the fascist father's transformation by standing over him and urinating on him lengthily, with her vulva in close-up the whole time. The symbols of female sexual anatomy dominate in all films I examine here: they overpower the phallic symbols of the father's power. Fallopian tubes also visually dominate *Pan's Labyrinth*, in the shape of the faun's horns and the tree under which Ofelia's beautiful dress becomes irremediably dirty (Tierney 118), both of which figure in the film's promotional poster. In *Pinocchio*, the shape of the Blue Fairy with giant wings also brings to mind fallopian tubes, as well as Pinocchio's constant throwing his hands up in the air, in surprise and excitement, and these images also figure in the film's posters. In Jodorowsky's film, the mother urinates on her husband, purportedly to cure him of the plague that he contracted, while the city officials are banging on the door threatening to burn the house to prevent the spread of the disease. As she is urinating on him, she stands over him as he lies supine under her on the ground. This scene impacted and puzzled many viewers and critics, but of course, a woman dousing a violent male in an abject body fluid is another powerful way to deactivate his potential for violence, as we have seen in del Toro's films. This scene (figure 8.7) is not only abject, but also anarchical and carnivalesque in Bakhtin's sense. It visually reverses the entire pyramid of the authoritarian worldview, in which the man is positioned on top, over women and children, described by cognitive linguist George Lakoff (81).

After having been urinated upon, Jaime recovers not only from the plague, but also from the impulse to inflict purposeless violence on his son and wife. He sets out to assassinate the Chilean strongman Carlos Ibáñez del Campo, who came to power in 1927. Ibáñez ruled by decree, suspended elections, named his allies to the Senate and the Chamber of Deputies, and arrested and exiled his political opponents. Ibáñez was popular because he borrowed copiously from American banks to finance public spending, until the Great Depression stopped the flow of money. Jaime fails to rid his country of the dictator because he is unaware of the fact that his idol, Stalin, is just like Ibáñez. He fails because this same compulsion to violate other people by giving them absurd commands lives in him too, and his journey is about extirpating this compulsion from himself. Following him on this journey, we see this compulsion represented in surprising, surreal, and powerful metaphors. One of them is a bizarre dog show in which dogs of all shapes and sizes are accoutered in bizarre costumes and made to sit still. This eerie happening is decorated with many Chilean flags, is hosted by a priest, and is accompanied by a string quartet of nuns. Ibáñez himself arrives, either to attend or adjudicate, and the nuns play the national anthem. The sight of all that sickens Jaime, and he says with tears in his eyes, "I don't want to live in the world of dressed-up dogs! It makes me sick!" This surreal scene is not merely a "funny and Jodorowskian" auteurial signature (as critic Peter Bradshaw put it). On the symbolic level, it represents the totalitarian fantasy that the state can organize people into one "living organism" and obliterate all individual and group identities. The idea of *Volkskörper*, the people's body, extends an invitation to every individual to become a part of one strong living organism of the nation and dissolve in it. It was precisely the great spiritual rebirth that German, Italian, Spanish, and Chilean Nazis promised to the cheering masses (Mussolf, Etchepare, and Stewart; Gruegel). Hannah Arendt's insight into totalitarianism helps us understand the deep meaning of the dressed-up dogs scene. Totalitarian societies only pretend to be pyramidal, like its authoritarian predecessors, in which every little leader of each level and group bears a little bit of the authority of the man at the top and can play at imitating this man—der Führer (Germany), il Duce (Italy), el Caudillo (Spain), or el Jefe (Chile). In reality, the pyramidal structure of authority and well-defined functions are only an "ostensible, spurious imitation" (Arendt, *The Origins of Totalitarianism* 405). These multiple groups are purposefully assigned identical and confusing functions, so that any of these groups together with its leader can be removed at any moment without anyone noticing. The dressed-up dogs standing still in bizarre costumes represent what people must be in a totalitarian structure—replaceable functions that only look like individuals.

Not surprisingly, Jaime discovers an affinity with Ibáñez and is seduced by his charisma. To get closer to the strongman he wants to kill, Jaime obtains the position of caretaker for his beautiful white horse Bucephalus. Soon, like the strongman himself, Jaime shown to have an erotic, orgasmic experience with the horse. This is another powerful metaphor of the totalitarian man's solitude and longing for love. With people, the strongman tries to realize this longing in a perverted way, by making them obey, but complying makes people resent him, so he must look for love elsewhere, not among people. Jaime confesses to the horse the solitude and repression which made him into what he is: "I never knew affection because I grew up in the street among cruel people who locked me in a fortress where I remain to this day." These lines reveal the hostile loneliness of the strongman, in which he is stuck. As Ángel Rama puts it, the desire for power is "a voracious and devastating passion that leaves no space in the soul for anything else. It takes up the person's entire spiritual life and must be paid for by a terminal solitude" (53). Soon Jaime catches himself thinking that the crimes of the strongman he is planning to kill come "not from a wicked soul but from an overwhelming generosity," and must force himself to hate the man, shouting, "No! *He is not a good father!* He is a disgusting pig!" (my italics). The strongman is a bad father of the people, just like Jaime is a bad father of the family. Establishing a link between them again illustrates Lakoff's metaphor of the family as a nation. Indeed, all cleanshaven men in the films analyzed here explicitly model themselves on the fascist leader. This is why Jaime fails to kill the strongman. He is captured and tortured by the Chilean Nazis. He becomes amnesiac, *forgets his name*, and lives in a slum with a dwarf woman who calls him "Cuco." These experiences of abjection make Jaime a different, loving, and repentant man. He returns home looking like Jesus, wearing a white tunic and long hair, and falls to his knees before his wife and child. The wife lifts him up in her arms and then gently lowers him down, cradling him like the Virgin cradles Jesus in Michelangelo's *Pietà*. The last act of this transformation is shooting the picture of himself in his old authoritarian hypostasis between the eyes. After this, the picture, alongside the pictures of Stalin and Ibáñez, goes up in flames. His wife sums it up: "You found in Ibáñez all you admired in Stalin. You are the same as they are! You have lived in the guise of a tyrant."

Unfortunately, after all this hard work, the father comes back as cleanshaven, uniformed, and fearsome as before in the film's sequel, *Endless Poetry* (*Poesía sin fin*, 2015). In this film, Alejandro is a young man. The return of the fearsome father coincides with the return of Ibáñez del Campo to the presidency in 1952, as a candidate of the Agrario Laborista Party. This party was created by the *nacistas* (as the Chilean Nazis were known) from the earlier party, Movimiento Nacional Socialista, which desintegrated after the fall of Nazi Germany. Ideologically, though, the organization did not change, and it continued to position the state as "above all a living organism, efficient, constructive" (Etchepare and Stewart 592). In this second film, which narrates Alejandro's adolescence, Jaime moves the family and his Casa Ucrania store to the capital and we see him grabbing the son by the neck again, as when he burned his firefighter's uniform in the first film and told him "Look!" In this scene (figure 8.4), Jaime grabs Alejandro by the neck to command him to spot thieves in the store. Alejandro acquiesces and makes a sign to him when he sees a young girl putting something under her shirt. Jaime jumps out from behind his counter and drives the girl outside, slapping her in the face, where he undresses her in front of the crowd that quickly gathers to look. Not one of the assembled people says a word, mesmerized by the spectacle of male dominance. Meanwhile, Alejandro is in the bathroom vomiting nonstop, purging his body of "so much shame and forbidden tears," failing once again to follow his father's instructions, this time to give a few kicks to the victim himself. Vomit is also an abject body fluid, signifying that Alejandro is physically unable to be clean and masculine like his father. He soon puts on a public spectacle of his own to separate himself forever from his family. At a gathering at the grandparents' house, he hacks down the lime tree growing in the backyard, to everyone's horror at the sacrilege, and is told to never come back.

After this symbolic separation from the father, Alejandro organizes a puppet theater, performs in a circus, and forms friendships with artists and poets. The female symbol of fallopian tubes, so prominent in the films discussed above, dominates this film as well, in the figure of Alejandro, dressed as a clown and spreading out to the sides giant angel wings, which also appears in the film posters. In another scene, Alejandro attaches his mother's corset to a balloon, and it rises and drifts away. However, Alejandro cannot help seeing another rhythmic crowd taking shape around him. We see another visual of the crystal-like rigid structure, a crowd marching after Ibáñez del Campo mounted on his white horse. Alejandro places himself in front of the crowd and raises his hands to stop them, but the strongman simply urges his horse to go around him and the crowd marches on, without breaking up. All people in the crowd are wearing identical white plastic masks, symbolizing their transformation into units of a totalitarian structure. They brandish red flags with a black swastika on them and brooms. Ibáñez's electoral motto was "Ibáñez to power, broom to sweep" (Ibáñez al poder, escoba a barrer). The broom represents the fascist leader's promise to rid the organic body of the state of corrupt, unclean elements. Alejandro, trying to break up the marching crowd, tears the broom out of the hands of one masked person and hits that person on the head with its soft bristles. But the crowd marches on, like zombies, after their leader.

The film ends with another transformation of the clean-shaven father. He will be shaven to a sarcastic exaggeration, including his eyebrows, his fearsome mustache, and his slicked-back hair, the trademark attributes of authoritarians which the clean-shaven men in these films represent: Stalin, Hitler, Mussolini, Franco, and Ibáñez del Campo. In this highly symbolic scene, Alejandro prepares to board the boat bound for Europe. There is no boat in sight and Alejandro will depart by going down a staircase leading nowhere, into the water. There are no other people, because the only departure that matters is his departure from his father. The father runs after him to stop him from leaving, pulling him by the sleeve, and saying that he needs a helper at the store. Alejandro replies that he has always been a prisoner, not a helper. The enraged Jaime slaps his son in the face, but Alejandro slaps him back. (This is a performative cure Jodorowsky recommended to a woman traumatized by her abusive mother. The mother reacted by saying, "You slapped me once, but you should have slapped me a hundred times!" as we read in *Danza de la realidad*, 342.) Then the father suddenly closes his eyes and goes limp in his son's hands, like an inanimate puppet. Alejandro recites a poem to him and shaves his hair and mustache (figure 8.8). The poem, which Jodorowsky also published on his site and social media accounts with the title *Letter to My Father*, is a rewrite of the famous letter that Kafka wrote to his father and that was returned to him, unopened, by his mother. In his letter, Kafka laments that he spent his life locked up like a prisoner in his father's absurd rules, mockery, and insults. Jodorowsky, in his poem-letter recited in the film by the actor who plays him as a young man, thanks his father for being cruel because it made him actively search for spirituality, poetry, and art. The actor playing Jaime opens his eyes, now shining with love, and his entire body language is different—from neurotic, repressed, and violent it becomes relaxed and gentle. The father smiles and says, "Goodbye, my son, I bless you," they kiss on the lips, and the young man departs. The old filmmaker appeared in the scene too, like a puppeteer, holding the two actors by the waist, and gave his young self a hair clipper (Dzero, "Under the Skin Cinema").

Both actors in this scene are Jodorowsky's sons: his oldest, Brontis, plays Jaime, and his youngest, Adán plays, Jaime's younger self. Making the film impacted the brothers strongly. Adán was actually unable to do the shaving in the film, so Jodorowsky had to do that himself. After the filming, Adán traveled to the Chilean desert and shaved his own head (Melnyk 117). Brontis confessed that he had no point of reference to play his terrible grandfather Jaime because he had only met him once, for a coffee. Instead, Brontis played none other than his father, Alejandro Jodorowsky himself, such as he was when he first met him for the first time, at the age of seven, to star in his film *The Mole* (*El Topo*, 1973). In this cult classic, Alejandro played little Brontis's father—a pitiless gunslinger, who compels his son to bury a picture of his mother and his one toy in order to become a man, and later abandons him and kicks him in the mouth as a goodbye. Brontis is Alejandro's first child, and Adán—his last. "One is a different father with a fifth son," mused Brontis (Brontis Jodorowsky).

His father readily acknowledges: "I failed [Brontis] in the film, and I failed him in real life" (*El Topo* 168). "I was a cold, strict, and competitive father," he readily revealed, "I behaved with him exactly like my father acted with me" (*Danza de la realidad* 341). Jodorowsky went a long way to become a different father. Even at the age of forty he was yet unable to answer personal questions, however superficial, about his traumatic childhood years without closing his eyes, as he says in an interview, "It's embarrassing for me to answer realistic questions. That's why I close my eyes" (*El Topo* 136). With time, he came up with a technique to heal old traumas with short surreal acts which he invents for himself and for the people who turn to him for help. He calls his symbolic cures "psychomagic" (psicomagia), and slapping the parent who was abusive in childhood was one of such cures Jodorowsky recommended and included in the film, as I discussed above. On his quest to become a good father, Jodorowsky realized that he avoided physical contact with his first two sons, just like his father Jaime, who, in his homophobia, never touched him to express affection but only to punch, shove, pull, and drag. The filmmaker thought of a way to change that. He meditated and called forth a vision in which he met his father and, in spite of his initial resistance, embraced and rocked him in his arms (*Danza de la realidad* 232). He asked his second son Cristóbal to do the same to him. With his youngest son Adán, affectionate touch has become for him a natural aspect of parenthood. He was both a father and a mother to Adán, who recalls how "you [Jodorowsky] always smelled my hair and my skin, telling me that I smelled wonderfully nice. You always told me that I was going to be tall, that I was talented, that I was beautiful, that I was a prince," and how every morning he ran to his dad's room to cuddle with him, "listening to your breathing and your heart beating" (Carta al padre). This physical, prelinguistic contact connotes the abject universe of the mother, "a kind of fusion between mother and nature," as opposed to the father's linguistic universe, "where embarrassment, shame, guilt, desire, etc. come into play" (as Julia Kristeva, who pioneered the study of the abject, puts it; 74). Adán wrote these lines in an open letter to his father, which he entitled *Letter to My Father* (*Carta al padre*) to signal that this is another rewrite of Kafka's letter. Kafka recounts the continual emotional abuse he suffered from his father and can recall *only one* kind gesture on his father's part, a ridiculously insignificant one—when he was sick in bed with a fever, his father stopped in the doorway and waved at him. The memory of this singular gesture brings Kafka to tears as he is writing the letter: "At such times one could lie down and cry for one's good fortune—as I am crying now as I write" (Kafka 24). In contrast, Adán tears up because he realizes how good his father was to him: "I am crying now because I never took the time to tell you all that. You are a wonderful father. My tears flow, these are the tears of love" (Adán Jodorowsky). Acting in the film, he learned how bad fathers can be.

The Crying Man versus the Clean-Shaven Man

The boy in Jodorowsky's films is not afraid of shedding tears, for which the father calls him a "faggot," "coward," and even, somewhat puzzlingly, a "whore." Pinocchio, too, is unafraid of showing his feelings, for which Podestá calls him "an abnormal boy." The crying man is the opposite of the clean-shaven man, who is trained to repress his emotions. Psychologists Shields, Kuhl, and Westwood found that military personnel repress emotions because they are afraid of sliding into the abject identity of failed masculinity, recalling the taunts of "faggot," "pussy," and "wimp" widely used during military training (216). C. J. Pascoe in her book *Dude, You're a Fag!* shows that adolescent boys are socialized to call each other "fag" in a kind of discursive contest, to establish dominance and to stave off the fear of being seen as unmasculine. The abject identity of "the fag" represents penetrated masculinity, and "to be penetrated is to abdicate power" (11), become womanized, and, therefore, subjugated, like women are supposed to be in this construct. This is why males engage in these repeated rituals of "compulsory masculinity." Suppressing emotions, on the one hand, and aggressive assigning of "the fag" identity to each other is a "socialization process in which all youth—boys and girls, straight and gay, feminine and masculine—suffer." Compulsory masculinity is a normative and policing mechanism (Pascoe 24). The incongruous "whore" insult that the father applies to his little son in *Dance of Reality* betrays a paranoid horror of penetrated masculinity and loss of power on the part of the clean-shaven man.

Del Toro's and Jodorowsky's films undo compulsory masculinity by putting a defenseless, kind child at the disposal of a cruel father figure. This setup provokes strong emotions in people and makes them cry. Viewers who saw *Pinocchio* called it "mesmerizing" and "haunting," and described how it made them cry: "shedding tears," "I'm not ashamed to have cried," "I am a teary mess at the end," "break your heart," "hits hard, bringing me to tears," "I DON'T CRY and I cried through the whole movie. I find crying a weakness, but this really truly moved me" (IMDb *Pinocchio* Movie Reviews). People who saw *Dance of Reality* also shared that they were moved to tears—"I don't know why but I was teary during some scenes even though they had no resemblance to my life"—and described it as "utterly overwhelming," "a devastating, gobsmacking punch in the face." One person cried and laughed and was moved to buy a flower for a long-lost friend: "I left the cinema feeling very happy and filled with a joy for life. In fact, I met an old friend that I hadn't seen for a very long time and the film inspired me to buy him a rose from a street vendor and say thank you for his friendship" (IMDb *Dance of Reality* Movie Reviews).

Prompted by his interviewer's outburst of emotion ("I am actually struggling to kind of hold on to myself"), Del Toro shared that he too wept while working on *Pinocchio* and felt the urge to talk to his family: "Every time I see the movie, every time we went through the screenplay, every time we saw the dailies, I would tear up. And I wanted to call my mother or my father or call my kids." He also said that he has been thinking about *Pinocchio* for a good part of his life, since 2000 (he could not find a studio that would give him full control of the film until recently, with Netflix). This is why the film sums up his experiences as a father and a son: "I am 58. I've been a kid. I've been a parent. I have failed or been failed to" (del Toro, interview with Martin). For del Toro, working on this film was a way to become aware of the scripts he inherited from his own father and found himself reproducing, willy-nilly, with his own children:

> One of the things that happened to me as an adult is that I tried to avoid the things that I thought my father did wrong by doing the exact opposite and the results were exactly the same. Meaning one morning I realized I was acting like my dad. That was a big reckoning. I lost my dad five years ago and I was able to make a lot of peace with the idea of the father figure. But I also see how fathers tend to not listen or not see their kids for what they are, just what they want them to be. (interview with Holub)

In making *Pinocchio*, del Toro identified himself for the first time with the father figure—not the clean-shaven one, of course, but with Pinocchio's maker Geppetto, who at the end of the film embraces Pinocchio and tells him, "Be who you are, exactly as you are. I love you." In the same breath, the director explains the connection between the clean-shaven man as a father and a fascist ruler. The strongman is "the darkest sort of father figure you can think of" (interview with Ryan). Fascism and the man who can attractively present it to the masses exercise an attraction on "the stray souls," by "the glamor," "the pageantry," "the rigidity and sort of paternal structure" (interview with Martin).

Del Toro explained that working on *Pinocchio* "changed and healed a lot of things that I had in me as a father and a son" and proved to be "a catharsis" (interview with Ryan). Jodorowsky also spoke about his autobiographical films as "a healing of my soul": "I needed to heal my interior child. I suffered in that town. I wanted to go back and conquer that town. And I wanted to bring that child back, and to change my past" (interview with Ebiri). Like del Toro, Jodorowsky makes an explicit connection between a bad father and a fascist ruler. The experience of growing up with a bad father draws people to strongmen, Jodorowsky believes. "Chile is a country of the absent father," because it is normal for men to abandon their families, and "this is why we had Ibáñez, this is why we had Pinochet" (interview with Naranjo). Jodorowsky believes that attraction to strongmen arises in unfree minds, because growing up with a bad father perverts the idea not only of family but of leadership in general, again evoking Lakoff's conceptualization of the leader of the nation as the father of the family. As Jodorowsky puts it, "the dictator came because people wanted, the limited mind wanted" (interview with Whalen). Canetti explains the attraction of fascism in much the same way: "If one is nothing oneself, there is a peculiar kind of servile gratification to be got from ending in the belly of power" (295). Arendt also has harsh words for closed minds who cannot tolerate the unpredictability of reality and must escape into the "rigid, fantastically fictitious consistency of an ideology" (352).

In addition to making viewers cry and loathe the compulsively masculine man, the films also quite literally do away with him. His clean-shaven, pulchritudinous physique in del Toro's films signals that it is a kind of masquerade, that soon he will have a kind of "wardrobe malfunction," reveal his monstrosity, and come undone. In *The Shape of Water*, the man loses two fingers; he has them reattached, but they rot and he tears them off. In *Pinocchio*, such a man is sprayed with paint and exploded. In *Pan's Labyrinth* he is disfigured, stabbed, and shot dead. In *Devil's Backbone*, he is disfigured and killed by sharp sticks. In Jodorowsky's *Dance of Reality* the father is subjected to torture. Feminist theorist Laura Mulvey said that being beautiful and desirable, an erotic object to be looked at, is a function in cinema traditionally reserved for women (815). Film scholar Barbara Creed has written of males turned into abject, masochistic, and feminized bodies in horror films (130). Critic Ann Davies applies these insights to del Toro's beautiful male. He is feminized because he is positioned in the film as an object to be looked at and, at the end of the film, when he is disfigured and stabbed, he is penetrated—hurt and made to secrete blood, like a woman (146). Abjectifying these clean-shaven men makes them repugnant rather than awe-inspiring and neutralizes the fear they use to control people.

We cannot help but note that all these films turn the original story on its head. *Pinocchio* is the opposite of the original character in Collodi's book. *Pan's Labyrinth* grants the victory to the rebels, whereas we know that it would be historically accurate to grant that victory to the Captain (Francisco Franco, whom the Captain symbolically represents, crushed the *republicanos* and ruled until 1975, dying peacefully in his bed). In *Dance of Reality* and *Endless Poetry*, Jodorowsky adapts his own biography, in which the fearsome and authoritarian father has always remained such, until his death at the age of 100. Yet in his films, Jodorowsky made him undergo humiliating trials and change into a loving father. These are part of a larger trend in post-2000 Latin American cinema to adapt older literary sources for the screen to emphasize the harm that a predatory father and leader does to the family and the country. But del Toro and Jodorowsky go farther than any other filmmaker discussed in this book. The artistic impulse is no longer about changing the source in order to criticize the predatory father more harshly, walk away from him with less damage, or bring him down faster. It is about extirpating that father, taking away his name and the symbolic order of prohibitions, guilt, and discipline for which he stands. It is also about transforming the father completely, in order to shape a different idea of a leader in the viewers' minds, a leader who does not want to make his children and citizens into impersonal functions of command but talks to them and depends on their feedback.

Although, of course, this would be wishful thinking. We know that people who live to dominate others do not open letters, do not wish to hear a word of contradiction, and do not participate in debates. They panic at the thought that someone might tell them they did something wrong. They must preserve their inner rigidity, too fragile to endure the strain of even one "no." In Jodorowsky's second film, the transformed father returns, just as clean-shaven and angry as he has always been, in the first film and in real life. "Shut up!" he keeps screaming at the boy all along, "You look like a whore, not like a man!" "Silence," the clean-shaven man in del Toro's *The Shape of Water* orders his wife as she is making passionate little noises to please him during sex. "Shoot the puppet," says Podestá, referring to Pinocchio. "Shoot the puppet," says the Duce, referring to Pinocchio. "I am the master, you are the slave! And you will do as I command," the circus director says to Pinocchio. No, the true purpose of these films is to show friendly children who are unresponsive to coercion and women who are sick of commands. The wife urinates on the clean-shaven man in *Dance of Reality*. His son slaps him back in *Endless* Poetry. The mute woman in *The Shape of Water* looks into his eyes defiantly and spells out in sign language "F-U-C-K Y-O-U." Pinocchio screams gleefully to the Duce, "Go smell your farts and pray." Ofelia refuses to give the man his son and his servant Mercedes tells him that his son won't even know his name. These new words and images rescript behavior. Authoritarian people will continue to expulse commands and wait for commands to comply with, until their last day. As for the rest of us, we can see that it is not written that we should live like soldiers, in constant expectation of command (as Canetti puts it; 312). These films show how to break free from the compulsion to keep looking for new masters and new subordinates. To repeat Jodorowsky's words, "Art can begin to take limits off the mind" (interview with Whalen).

WORKS CITED

Films

A Wonderful World [*Un mundo maravilloso*]. Directed by Luis Estrada. Bandidos Films, 2006.
Behind the Sun Abril [*Abril despedaçado*]. Directed by Walter Salles. Videofilmes, 2001.
Bolívar soy yo. Directed by Jorge Alí Triana. CMO Producciones. 2002.
Bolívar, el hombre de las dificultades. Directed by Luis Lamata. Alter Producciones Audiovisuales, 2012.
Bolívar: una lucha admirable. Created by Juana Uribe. Caracol Televisión, 2019.
Brainstorm [*Bicho de sete cabeças*]. Directed by Laís Bodanzki. Buriti Filmes, 2000.
The City of God [*Cidade de Deus*]. Directed by Fernando Meirelles, 02 Filmes, 2002.
City of Men. Directed by Paolo Morelli. 02 Filmes, 2017.
Dance of Reality. Directed by Alejandro Jodorowsky. Le Soleil Films, 2013.
El Chivo. Created by Humberto Olivieri. RTI Colombia and Televisa, 2014.
El clan. Directed by Pablo Trapero. K&S Films, 2015.
El Comandante. Created by Moisés Naím, directed by Felipe Cano and Henry Rivero. RCN Televisión, 2017.
Elite Squad. Directed by José Padilha. Zazen Produções, 2007.
Endless Poetry. Directed by Alejandro Jodorowsky. Le Soleil Films, 2016.
Feast of the Goat [*La fiesta del Chivo*]. Directed by Luis Llosa. Future Films, 2005.
Hell [*El infierno*]. Directed by Luis Estrada. Bandidos Films, 2010.
Herod's Law [*La ley de Herodes*]. Directed by Luis Estrada. Bandidos Films, 1999.
History of a Clan [*La historia de un clan*]. Directed by Luis Ortega. Telefe, 2015.
To the Left of the Father [*Lavoura arcaica*]. Directed by Luiz Fernando Carvalho. Video Filmes, 2001.
Machuca. Directed by Andrés Wood. Tornasol Films, 2004.
Madeinusa. Directed by Claudia Llosa. Oberón Cinematográfica, 2006.
Magallanes. Directed by Salvador Del Solar. Péndulo Films, 2015.
No. Directed by Pablo Larraín. Fabula Productions, 2012.
Pan's Labyrinth [*Laberinto del fauno*]. Directed by Guillermo Del Toro. Tequila Gang, Estudios Picasso, 2006.
Pinocchio. Directed by Guillermo Del Toro. Netflix, 2022.
Subterra. Directed by Marcelo Ferrari. Infinity Films, 2003.
Tear This Life Out [*Arráncame la vida*]. Directed by Roberto Sneider. Altavista Films, 2008.
The Blue Hour [*La hora azul*]. Directed by Evelyne Pégot-Ogier. Panda Films, 2014.

The Crime of Father Amaro [*El crimen del padre Amaro*]. Directed by Carlos Carrera. Alameda Films, 2002.
The Diary of Bucaramanga [*Diario de Bucaramanga*]. Directed by Carlos Fung. SPM Producciones, 2013.
The Liberator [*Libertador*]. Directed by Alberto Arvelo. San Mateo Films, 2013.
The Mechanism [O mecanismo]. Directed by José Padilha. Zazen Produções and Netflix, 2018–2019.
The Milk of Sorrow [*Teta asustada*]. Directed by Claudia Llosa. Oberón Cinematográfica, 2009.
The Perfect Dictatorship [*Dictadura perfecta*]. Directed by Luis Estrada. Bandidos Films, 2014.
The Shape of Water. Directed by Guillermo Del Toro. Double Dare You, Searchlight Pictures, 2017.
The Time of the Hero [*La ciudad y los perros*]. Directed by Francisco Lombardi. Inca Films, 1980.

Literary Sources

Carrano Bueno, Austregésilo. *Canto dos malditos*. Rio de Janeiro: Editora Rocco, 2004.
Collodi, Carlo. *The Adventures of Pinocchio*. Knopf, 1988.
Cueto, Alonso. *La hora azul*. Anagrama, 2005.
Cueto, Alonso. *La pasajera*. Seix Barral, 2015.
Jodorowsky, Alejandro. *La danza de la realidad*. Madrid: Ediciones Siruela, 2001.
Kadare, Ismail. *Broken April*. Vintage, 2003.
Kafka, Franz. "Home-Coming." *The Complete Stories*. Schocken Books, 1971, pp. 492–93.
Kafka, Franz. "Judgment." *The Sons: The Judgment, The Stoker, The Metamorphosis, and Letter to His Father*. Schocken, 1989, 1–16.
Kafka, Franz. "Metamorphosis." *The Complete Stories*. Schocken Books, 1971, pp. 114–65.
Kafka, Franz. *Letter to my Father*. Translated by Howard Colyer, Lulu Press, 2008.
León, Luis Alberto. *La cautiva*. Lima, 2014. Theatrical script.
Lins, Paulo. *Cidade de Deus*. [*City of God*] Translated by Alison Entrekin, Black Cat, 2006.
Lillo, Baldomero. *Sub terra: Cuadros mineros*. Nascimiento, [1904] 1970.
Lizana Parraguez, Amante Eledín. *Tres años para nacer*. Editorial Académica Española, 2018.
Márquez, Gabriel García. *The General in His Labyrinth*. Translated by Edith Grossman, Knopf, 1989.
Mastretta, Ángeles. *Arráncame la vida*. Mexico, D.F.: Cal y Arena, 1994.
Nassar, Raduan. *Ancient Tillage*. Translated by Karen Sotelino, Penguin, 2017.
Palacios, Rodolfo. *El clan Puccio*. Buenos Aires: Planeta, 2015.
Pavlovsky, Eduardo. *Paso de dos*. Buenos Aires: Ediciones Búsqueda de Ayllu, 1990.
Quierós, Eça de. *The Sin of Padre Amaro*. Translated by Nan Flanagan, M. Reinhardt, 1962.
Rosero, Evelio. *Feast of the Innocent*. Translated by Ann McLean and Anna Milsom, London: MacLehose, 2015.
Skármeta, Antonio. *El plebiscito*. Unpublished play, 2008.

Skármeta, Antonio. *Los días del arcoíris*. Alfaguara, 2011.
Vargas Llosa, Mario. *Captain Pantoja and the Special Service*. Translated by Gregory Kolovakis, Harper and Row, 1973.
Vargas Llosa, Mario. *Death in the Andes*. Translated by Edith Grossman, Penguin, 1996.
Vargas Llosa, Mario. *Feast of the Goat*. Translated by Edith Grossman, Alfaguara, 2001.
Vargas Llosa, Mario. *Fish in the Water*. Translated by Helen Lane, Penguin, 1994.
Vargas Llosa, Mario. *Time of the Hero*. Translated by Lysander Kemp, Grove Press, 1966.

Secondary Sources

Abreu, Luis Gerónimo. "Así lo dijo Luis Gerónimo Abreu." *Maduradas*, 20 Aug. 2019, maduradas.com/asi-lo-dijo-luis-geronimo-abreu-simon-bolivar-seguramente-habria-armado-una-trifulca-tiempos.
Acosta, Luis Jaime. "Nuevo distanciamiento Colombia y Venezuela por guerrilla." *Reuters*, 11 Jan. 2008.
Adios a Macondo: Informe Latinobarómetro 2021. Latinobarómetro, 7 Oct. 2021.
Adorno, Theodor, Else Frenkel-Brunswik, Daniel J. Levinson, and Nevitt Sanford. *The Authoritarian Personality*. New York: Harper and Row, 1950.
Adorno, Theodor. "Freudian Theory and the Pattern of Fascist Propaganda." *The Essential Frankfurt School Reader*. Continuum, 1988, pp. 118–37.
Agamben, Giorgio. *Sovereign Power and Bare Life*. Stanford University Press, 1998.
"Albano Harguindeguy a Robert Cox: 'No soy Jesucristo.'" *Perfil*, 27 Mar. 2016, www.perfil.com/noticias/politica/albano-harguindeguy-a-robert-cox-no-soy-jesucristo-no-puedo-decirle-a-lazaro-levantate-y-anda-20160327-0080.phtml.
Altozano, Manuel. "Adolfo Scilingo, el recluso modelo que no se arrepiente de sus crímenes." *El País*, 29 Mar. 2015.
Alvarado, Abel. "Tens of Thousands Protest as Milei's Austerity Measures Hit Argentina's Public Universities." *CNN*, 24 Mar. 2024.
Alzate, David Gil. "*La carroza de Bolívar*. Simetría de dos revoluciones fracasadas en Colombia." *Estudios de literatura colombiana*, vol. 38, 2016, pp. 145–62.
Andermann, Jens. "December's Other Scene: New Argentine Cinema and the Politics of 2001." *New Argentine and Brazilian Cinema: Reality Effects*, edited by Jens Andermann and Álvaro Fernández Bravo, Palgrave, 2013, pp. 223–237.
Andrade, Gabriel, and Jairo Lugo-Ocando. "The Angostura Address 200 Years Later: A Critical Reading." *Iberoamericana*, vol. 47, no. 1, 2018, pp. 74–82.
Anguita, Eduardo, and Daniel Cecchini. "Borges y la dictadura: del almuerzo con Videla a la reunión con las Madres y la condena a los militares en tiempos de sangre y plomo." *Infobae*, 13 July 2019.
Arana, Marie. *Bolívar: The American Liberator*. Simon and Schuster, 2013.
Arendt, Hannah. *Eichmann in Jerusalem*. Viking Press, 1963.
Arendt, Hannah. *The Origins of Totalitarianism*. Harcourt, 1985.
Aríco, José M. *Marx and Latin America*. Brill, 2014.
Armada, Alfonso. "El Chivo rumia su lujuria en Manhattan." *ABC España*, 1 Mar. 2003, www.abc.es/cultura/teatros/abci-chivo-rumia-lujuria-manhattan-200303010300-165171_noticia.html.

ArtForum. "Alejandro Jodorowsky Speaks Out After El Museo del Barrio Calls off Retrospective." *Artforum*, 31 Jan. 2019, www.artforum.com/news/alejandro-jodorowsky-speaks-out-after-el-museo-del-barrio-calls-off-retrospective-242092.

Astiz, Alfredo. "Palabras finales." *Así se publicó*, Oct. 2011, asisepublico.blogspot.com/2011/10/palabras-finales-del-capitan-alfredo.html.

Astiz, Alfredo. Interview with Gabriela Cerruti. *Nuestras voces*, 29 Aug. 2017, www.nuestrasvoces.com.ar/entendiendo-las-noticias/alfredo-astiz-no-me-arrepiento-nada.

Atanacio, Vanessa Laura. "Ni pasivas ni descorporizadas: las películas *Madeinusa* y *La teta asustada* de Claudia Llosa." *Trayectorias de los estudios de género*, edited by Fanni Muñoz, Cecilia Esparza, and Martín Jaime Ballero, Pontificia Universidad Católica del Peru, 2019.

Auyero, Javier. "'From the Client's Point(s) of View': How Poor People Perceive and Evaluate Political Clientelism." *Theory and Society*, vol. 28, no. 2, 1999, pp. 297–334.

Ayuero, Javier, and Claudio Benzecry. "The Practical Logic of Political Domination: Conceptualizing the Clientelist Habitus." *Sociological Theory*, vol. 35, no. 3, 2017, pp. 179–99.

Aznárez, Juan Jesús. "*El crimen del padre Amaro* se convierte en la película más taquillera de México." *El País*, 16 Sept. 2002, elpais.com/diario/2002/09/16/espectaculos/1032127201_850215.html.

Bailey, John, and Pablo Parás. "Perception and Attitudes About Corruption and Democracy in Mexico." *Mexican Studies*, vol. 22, no. 1, 2006, pp. 57–81.

Bailey, Kay E. "El uso de los silencios en *Arráncame la vida* por Ángeles Mastretta." *Confluencia*, vol. 7, no. 1, 1991, pp. 135–42.

Balardini, Lorena. "Argentina: Regional Protagonist of Transitional Justice." *Transitional Justice in Latin America*, edited by Elin Skaar, Jemima García-Godos and Cath Collins, Routledge, 2017, pp. 50–66.

Balasco, Lauren M. "The Double Transition of Transitional Justice in Peru: Confronting the Appeal of Iron-fist Policies." *The International Journal of Human Rights*, vol. 20, no. 8, 2016, pp. 1177–98.

"Banco Central: deuda total de los hogares chilenos alcanzó el 75,4% de sus ingresos disponibles." *CNN Chile*, 6 July 2020, www.cnnchile.com/economia/banco-central-deuda-hogares-754-ingresos-disponibles_20200706.

Bandura, Albert. *Moral Disengagement: How People Can Do Harm and Live with Themselves*. Worth Publishers, 2016.

Bañuelos, Claudio. "*Bendice* el obispo Ramón Godínez las limosnas dadas por narcotraficantes." *La Jornada*, 20 Sept. 2005, www.jornada.com.mx/2005/09/20/index.php?section=politica&article=022n1pol.

Barragán, Almudena, and María Julia Castañeda. "Las mujeres gritan 'Basta!'" *El País*, 25 Nov. 2021.

Barreto, José Ramón. "Me llevó la tenacidad y la fortaleza de Simón Bolívar." *El Universo*, 14 July 2019.

Bataille, Georges. "Sacrifice, the Festival and the Principles of the Sacred World." *The Bataille Reader*. Blackwell, 1997, 200–10.

Bataille, Georges. *Literature and Evil*. Marion Boyars Publishers, 2001.

Battle, Diego. 2015. "El clan, un récord para el cine nacional." *La Nación*, 18 Aug. 2015, www.lanacion.com.ar/espectaculos/el-clan-un-record-para-el-cine-nacional-nid1819947.
Baudrillard, Jean. *Simulacra and Simulation*. University of Michigan Press, 1981.
Baudrillard, Jean. *The Consumer Society*. Sage, 1998.
Benedetti, Laura. *La cuestión social en Concepción y los centros mineros de Coronel y Lota (1885–1910)*. Concepción: Ediciones del Archivo Histórico de Concepción, 2019.
Bentes, Ivana. "Global Periphery: Aesthetic and Cultural Margins in Brazilian Audiovisual Forms." *New Argentine and Brazilian Cinema: Reality Effects*, edited by Jens Andermann and Álvaro Fernández Bravo, Palgrave, 2013, pp. 103–18.
Binder, Christina. "The Prohibition of Amnesties by the Inter-American Court of Human Rights." *German Law Journal*, vol. 12, no. 5, 2011, pp. 1204–30.
Binggeli, Nelson, Stuart N. Hart, and Marla R. Brassard. *Psychological Maltreatment of Children*. Sage, 2001.
Block, Elena. *Political Communication and Leadership: Mimetisation, Hugo Chávez and the Construction of Power and Identity*. Routledge, 2017.
Bodevin, Leon. "Naturaleza y cultura: una lectura elemental de *Arráncame la vida* de Ángeles Mastretta." *Revista de crítica literaria latinoamericana*, vol. 29, no. 57, 2003, pp. 159–69.
Boesten, Jelke. "Anger at Violence against Women in Peru Spills over into Protest." *The Conversation*, 10 Aug. 2016, theconversation.com/anger-at-violence-against-women-in-peru-spills-over-into-protest-63087.
Boesten, Jelke. "The State and Violence Against Women in Peru: Intersecting Inequalities and Patriarchal Rule." *Social Politics*, vol. 19, no. 3, 2012, 361–82.
Bolívar, Simón. "Proclama del dictador presidente." *Biblioteca virtual Miguel de Cervantes*, www.cervantesvirtual.com/obra-visor/colombia-otros-documentos-3/html/0260de94-
82b2-11df-acc7-002185ce6064_1.html.
Bolívar, Simón. *Textos. Una antología general*. Mexico: UNAM, 1982.
Bolognesi, Luiz. *Bicho de sete cabeças*. São Paolo: Editora 34, 2002.
Bonaparte, Napoleon. "Proclamation to the French People on His Second Abdication, June 22, 1815." *Napoleon's Addresses*, edited by Ida M. Tarbell, 1897. *Wikisource*, en.m.wikisource.org/wiki/Napoleon%27s_Addresses.
Bonaparte, Napoleon. "To the Legislative Body Before the Battle of Jena, October, 1806." *Napoleon's Addresses*, edited by Ida M. Tarbell, 1897. *Wikisource*, en.m.wikisource.org/wiki/Napoleon%27s_Addresses.
Bradshaw, Peter. Review of *The Dance of Reality*. *The Guardian*, 20 Aug. 2015, www.theguardian.com/film/2015/aug/20/the-dance-of-reality-review-my-father-the-hero.
Brannigan, Augustine. *Beyond the Banality of Evil: Criminology and Genocide*. Oxford University Press, 2013.
Braun, Ilja. "Raduan Nassar's '*Lavoura arcaica*: Rebellion Against the Patriarchal Taboo.'" *Quantara*, 1 Jan. 2005, en.qantara.de/content/raduan-nassars-lavoura-arcaica-rebellion-against-the-patriarchal-taboo.
Brennan, David. "Police Are Killing More and More People in Brazil's Favelas." *Newsweek*, 31 Oct 2019.

Burt, Jo-Marie. "A Deal with the Devil: The Fujimori Pardon." *NACLA*, 5 Jan. 2018, nacla.org/news/2018/02/23/deal-devil-fujimori-pardon.

"Bussi, el militar de hierro que terminó a las lágrimas." *Perfil*, 28 Aug. 2008, www.perfil.com/noticias/politica/bussi-el-militar-de-hierro-que-termino-a-las-lagrimas-20080828-0036.phtml.

Caballero, Jorge. "*Arráncame* . . . muestra cómo nos volvimos hijos del fraude, dice Daniel Giménez Cacho." *La Jornada*, 2 Sept. 2008, www.jornada.unam.mx.

Cabral, Francisco. "Auteur of the Reactionary." *Jacobin Magazine*, 22 Mar. 2018.

Campanella, Juan José. Interview with Sara Cano. *Castellón Plaza*, 8 July 2019, https://castellonplaza.com/juan-jose-campanella-.

Campi, Eric, and Paulo Henrique Pompermaier. "*Lavoura arcaica* é a utopia por um mundo melhor." *Revista Cult*, 28 Oct. 2016, revistacult.uol.com.br/home/lavoura-arcaica-e-a-utopia-por-um-mundo-melhor.

Canetti, Elias. *Crowds and Power*. New York: Farrar, Straus, and Giroux, 1984.

Canqui, Elisa. "El trabajo forzoso y los pueblos indígenas." Permanent Forum on Indigenous Issues, New York, 16–27 May 2011.

Capriles, Colette. "La política por otros medios: espectáculo y cesarismo del siglo XXI." *Cuadernos unimetanos*, vol. 30, 2012, pp. 54–62.

Carrasco Freitas, Marlos. "Poder Judicial declara 'ilegal' partido A.N.T.A.U.R.O." *Infobae*, 31 Oct. 2024.

Carrera, Carlos. "El conflicto de la iglesia en *El crimen del padre Amaro*." *El Proceso*, 27 June 2002, www.proceso.com.mx/cultura/2002/6/27/el-conflicto-de-la-iglesia-en-el-crimen-del-padre-amaro-67377.html.

Carrera, Carlos. Interview by José Antonio Fernández. *Revista Pantalla*, 8 Oct. 2002, www.revistapantalla.com/telemundo/entrevistas/?id_nota=2800.

Carrera, Carlos. Interview with Renata Marrufo. *Diario Yucatán*, 25 Nov. 2019, www.yucatan.com.mx/espectaculos/2019/11/25/carlos-carrera-con-la-animacion-moviendo-su-vida.html.

Carroll, Rory. *Comandante*: Hugo Chávez's Venezuela. New York: Penguin, 2013.

"Carroza ganadora 2018 El Colorado." *YouTube*, uploaded by GVILive, 6 Jan. 2018, www.youtube.com/watch?v=jUYnCrN6IFY.

Castro Rocha, João Cezar de. "Dialética da marginalidade." *Folha de São Paolo*, 29 Feb. 2004.

Castro, Pedro. "El caudillismo en América Latina, ayer y hoy." *Política y Cultura*, vol. 27, 2007, pp. 9–29.

Castro, Vanessa Maria de. "Why Did Bolsonaro's Supporters Vote for Him?" *In Spite of You: Bolsonaro and the New Brazilian Resistance*, edited by Conor Foley, OR Books, 2019, pp. 71–85.

Catunda, Júlia. "Querem calar, custe o que custar . . . Austregésilo Carrano." IATDI, 25 May 2010, www.iatdi.com.br/si/site/jornal_materia?codigo=324.

Chernick, Marc. "The FARC at the Negotiating Table." *Colombia: Building Peace in a Time of War*, edited by Victoria Bouvier. United State Institute of Peace, 2009, pp. 65–94.

Cho, Seongyong. Review of *Santa Sangre*. Rogerebert.com, 9 Mar. 2011.

Cobb, Ben. *Anarchy and Alchemy: The Films of Alejandro Jodorowsky*. Creation, 2007.

Codelco. 2018 Annual report. www.codelco.com/memoria2018/site/docs/20190408/20190408190123/codelco_annual_report_2018.pdf.

Collins, Cath, and Boris Hau. "Chile: Incremental Truth, Late Justice." *Transitional Justice in Latin America*, edited by Elin Skaar, Jemima García-Godos, and Cath Collins, Routledge, 2017.

Collyns, Dan. "Peru's former presidential candidate sentenced for journalist's murder," *The Guardian*, 13 Apr. 2023.

"Condenaron a Miguel Etchecolatz." *Infobae*, 26 Oct. 2018, www.infobae.com/politica/2018/10/26/condenaron-a-miguel-etchecolatz-a-prision-perpetua-por-crimenes-de-lesa-humanidad.

Cornejo Chávez, Rodrigo. "Políticas y reformas escolares: el experimento educativo chileno y su evolución." *Privatización de lo público en el sistema escolar. Chile y la agenda global de educación*, edited by Carlos Schneider Ruiz, Leonora Reyes Jedlicki, and Francisco Herrera Jeldres, LOM Editores, 2018.

Correa, Raquel, and Elizabeth Subercaseaux. *Ego sum Pinochet*. Interviews with Augusto Pinochet. Santiago de Chile: Zig-Zag, 1989.

Corrales, Javier. "Latin America's Neocaudillismo: Ex-Presidents and Newcomers Running for President . . . and Winning." *Latin American Politics and Society*, vol. 50, no. 3, pp. 1–35.

Costa, Sérgio. "Entangled Inequalities." *The Social Life of Economic Inequalities in Contemporary Latin America*, edited by Margit Ystanes and Iselin Åsedotter Strønen, Palgrave, 2018, pp. 59–80.

Creed, Barbara. "Dark Desires: Male Masochism in the Horror Film." *Screening the Male: Exploring Masculinities in Hollywood Cinema*, edited by Steve Cohan and Ina Rae Hark, Routledge, 1993, pp. 118–33.

"*The Crime of Padre Amaro*: User Reviews." *IMDb*, m.imdb.com/title/tt0313196/reviews?ref_=tt_urv.

Cruikshank, Stephen A. "Bandits and Biopolitics: Power, Control, and Exploitation in *Cidade dos Homens* (2007)." *Word Hoard*, vol. 5, 2016, pp. 7–19.

Cuarón, Alonso. Interview with Marcela Valdés. *The New York Times*, 13 Dec. 2018.

Cueto, Alonso. "El aniversario de un peruano." *El Comercio*, 26 Mar. 2021.

Cueto, Alonso. *La piel de un escritor*. Lima: Fondo de Cultura Económica, 2015.

Cueva, Álvaro. "La dictadura perfecta." *Milenio*, 19 Oct. 2014, www.milenio.com/opinion/alvaro-cueva/ojo-por-ojo/la-dictadura-perfecta.

Cuevas, Pamela. "El nivel de endeudamiento de hogares chilenos sigue sin aflojar." *Diario financiero*, 6 Dec. 2020.

Cunha, Mariana and Antônio Márcio da Silva. *Human Rights, Social Movements and Activism in Contemporary Latin American Cinema*. Palgrave, 2018.

Da Silva, Luiz Inácio "Lula." 2003 Discurso de posse. *Biblioteca presidência da República*, 2003.

Da Silva, Luiz Inácio "Lula." 2007 Discurso de posse. *Biblioteca presidência da República*, 2007.

Dassin, Joan. Introduction. *Torture in Brazil: A Shocking Report on the Pervasive Use of Torture*. Brazil Archdiocese of São Paulo. University of Texas Press, 1998.

Davies, Ann. "The Beautiful and the Monstrous Masculine: The Male Body and Horror in *El espinazo del diablo*." *Studies in Hispanic Cinemas*, vol. 3, no. 3, 2006, pp. 135–47.

Dávila, Juan. Interview with Paco Barragán. *Art Pulse*, n.d., artpulsemagazine.com/interview-with-juan-davila.

Debord, Guy. *The Society of the Spectacle*. Zone Books 1994.

Del Solar, Salvador. Interview. *Nodal Cultura*, 4 Mar. 2016, www.nodalcultura.am/2016/02/entrevista-exclusiva-a-salvador-del-solar-en-el-peru-llevamos-anos-sin-poder-dialogar-sobre-lo-ocurrido-en-los-tiempos-violentos.

Del Toro, Guillermo. Interview with Christian Holub. *Entertainment Weekly*, 19 Dec. 2022, ew.com/movies/guillermo-del-toro-explains-why-he-wanted-to-add-fascism-to-pinocchio.

Del Toro, Guillermo. Interview with Lucía Lizárraga, *Brunoticias*, 10 Mar. 2018, brunoticias.com/guillermo-del-toro-pide-a-jovenes-hacer-cine-fe-estilos-huevos.

Del Toro, Guillermo. Interview with Mario Amaya, *Revista Boca*, 18 Feb. 2018, www.eltiempo.com/bocas/entrevista-con-guillermo-del-toro-director-de-la-forma-del-agua-182794.

Del Toro, Guillermo. Interview with Michel Martin. *Texas Public Radio*, 10 Dec. 2022, www.northcountrypublicradio.org/news/npr/1142099390/guillermo-del-toro-says-making-his-pinocchio-was-healing.

Del Toro, Guillermo. Interview with Patrick Ryan. *USA Today*, 8 Dec. 2022, www.usatoday.com/story/entertainment/movies/2022/12/08/pinocchio-guillermo-del-toro-interview/10791402002.

Del Toro, Guillermo. Interview with Roxy Simons. *Newsweek*, 9 Dec. 2022, www.newsweek.com/why-guillermo-del-toro-wants-netflix-pinocchio-celebrate-disobedience-facism-1765642.

Del Toro, Guillermo. Interview with Ryan Gilbey. *The Guardian*, 15 Jan. 2022, www.theguardian.com/film/2022/jan/15/guillermo-del-toro-i-saw-real-corpses-when-i-was-growing-up-in-mexico.

Despiniadis, Costas. *The Anatomist of Power: Kafka and the Critique of Authority*. Black Rose Books, 2019.

Dickson, Kent. "Trauma and Trauma Discourse: Peruvian Fiction After the CVR." *Chasqui*, vol. 42, no. 1, 2013, pp. 64–76.

Dieleke, Edgardo. "*O sertão nao virou mar*: Images of Violence and the Position of the Spectator in Contemporary Brazilian Cinema." *Visual Synergies in Fiction and Documentary Film from Latin America*, edited by Miriam Haddu and Joanna Page, Palgrave, 2009, pp. 67–86.

Dore, Elizabeth. *Myths of Modernity: Peonage and Patriarchy in Nicaragua*. Duke University Press, 2006.

Doris, John, and Dominic Murphy. "From My Lai to Abu Ghraib: The Moral Psychology of Atrocity." *Midwest Studies in Philosophy*, vol. 31, 2007, pp. 25–55.

Ducoudray Holstein, Henry La Fayette Villaume. *Memoirs of Simón Bolívar*. Boston: S.G. Goodrich, 1829.

Duncan, Cynthia. "Reading Ángeles Mastretta's *Arráncame la vida* through the Lens of Mexico's Golden Age of Cinema." *Rocky Mountain Review*, vol. 63, no. 2, 2009, pp. 171–93.

Durán, Gonzalo, and Marco Kremerman. "Los verdaderos sueldos de Chile." *Estudios de la Fundación Sol,* Sept. 2021, www.fundacionsol.cl/blog/estudios-2/post/los-verdaderos-sueldos-de-chile-2021-6796.
Dzero, Irina. "*La fiesta del Chivo*, Novel and Film, on the Transition to Democracy in Latin America." *Latin American Research Review,* vol. 51, no. 3, 2016, pp. 85–100.
Dzero, Irina. "Larraín's Film *No* and Its Inspiration, *El plebiscito:* Chile's Transition to Democracy as a Simulacrum." *Confluencia,* vol. 31, no. 1, 2015, pp. 120–31.
Dzero, Irina. "Under the Skin Cinema: Alejandro Jodorowsky Tells Abject Secrets in *Dance of Reality* and *Endless Poetry.*" *Film International,* vol. 105, 2024, pp. 38–51.
Echeverri, Marcela. *Indian and Slave Royalists in the Age of Revolution.* Cambridge University Press, 2016.
Echeverría Tortello, Margarita. "La historia de la regulación de la subcontratación." *La historia inconclusa de la subcontratación.* Chile: Dirección del Trabajo, 2010, pp. 91–139.
Eco, Umberto. Introduction. *Pinocchio.* New York Review of Books, 2008.
El Colorado. YouTube, uploaded by GVI Live, 18 Mar. 2018, www.youtube.com/watch?v=jUYnCrN6IFY.
"El día en que las Madres encararon a Harguindeguy por los desaparecidos." *Clarín,* 11 July 2007, www.clarin.com/ediciones-anteriores/dia-madres-encararon-harguindeguydesaparecidos_0_SJTWp8e1RKl.html.
"El gobierno incluyo al represor Alfredo Asiz en el listado de presos en condiciones de salir de la cárcel." Infobae, 20 Mar. 2018, www.infobae.com/politica/2018/03/20.
"Estela de Carlotto repudió el pedido del genocida Etchecolatz," *Infocielo,* 27 Aug. 2018, infocielo.com/nota/95201/estela_de_carlotto_repudio_el_pedido_del_genocida_etchecolatz_para_volver_a_la_policia_bonaerense.
Estrada, Luis. Interview by Joshua Partlow. *Washington Post,* 30 Dec. 2014, washingtonpost.com/news/worldviews/wp/2014/12/30/is-luis-estrada-the-conscience-of-mexico.
"Estrenan en Zulia el largometraje Diario de Bucaramanga." Gobierno de Venezuela, 5 Apr. 2019, www.minci.gob.ve/estrenan-en-zulia-el-largometraje-diario-de-bucaramanga-en-homenaje-a-hugo-chavez.
Etchecolatz, Miguel. *La otra campaña de Nunca Más.* Argentina (no publisher), 1988.
Etchepare, Jaime Antonio, and Hamish J. Stewart. "Nazism in Chile. A Particular Type of Fascism in South America." *Journal of Contemporary History,* vol. 30, no. 4, 1995, pp. 577–608.
Feitlowitz, Marguerite. *A Lexicon of Terror: Argentina and the Legacies of Torture.* Oxford University Press, 2011.
Fichter, Manfred M. "The Anorexia Nervosa of Franz Kafka." *International Journal of Eating Disorders,* vol. 6, no. 3, 1987, pp. 367–77.
Finchelstein, Federico. *The Ideological Origins of the Dirty War: Fascism, Populism, and Dictatorship in Twentieth Century Argentina.* Oxford University Press, 2014.
Finol, Mary Cruz. "Miniserie sobre Simón Bolívar se transmitirá por Netflix en junio." *Papagayo News,* 7 June 2019.
Fleming, David. *Unbecoming Cinema.* Intellect Books, 2017.
Frayssinet, Fabiana. "Child Slavery Lingers in Latin America." *Real Change,* 30 May 2018, www.realchangenews.org/news/2018/05/30/child-slavery-lingers-latin-america.

Freud, Sigmund. "Notes upon a Case of Obsessional Neurosis." *Freud Reader*, edited by Peter Gay, Norton and Company, 1989, pp. 309–50.

Freud, Sigmund. *Totem and Taboo*. Routledge, 2001.

Friedman, Milton. Interview. *PBS*, 1 Oct. 2000, pbs.org/wgbh/commandingheights/shared/minitext/int_miltonfriedman.html.

Fujimori, Alberto. "Mensaje a la nación, el 5 de abril de 1992." Congreso de la República, 1992, www.congreso.gob.pe/Docs/participacion/museo/congreso/files/mensajes/1981-2000/files/mensaje-1992-1-af.pdf.

Fundación Sol. "Precariedad laboral y modelo productivo en Chile." Dec. 2011, fundacionsol.cl/cl_luzit_herramientas/static/wp-content/uploads/2011/12/Ideas-1-Tendencias-del-Trabaj02.pdf.

Gaete Silva, Alfredo, María Castro Navarrete, Felipe Pino Conejeros, and Mansilla Devia. "Abandono de la profesión docente en Chile." *Estudios pedagógicos*, vol. 43, no. 1, 2017, pp. 123–38.

Galarraga Cortázar, Naiara. "Un video revela una explosiva reunión." *El País*, 23 May 2020.

Galarza, Delfina. "Massera: 'Me siento responsable, pero no culpable.'" *Diario Publicable*, 30 Oct. 2015, www.diariopublicable.com/especiales/4363-alegato-de-massera.html.

Gammage, Sarah, Thomás Alburquerque, and Gonzálo Durán. "Poverty, Inequality and Employment in Chile." International Labour Office, Conditions of Work and Employment Branch, 2014.

García Orso, Luis. "El crimen del Padre Amaro." *Xipe Totek*, vol. 12, no. 1, 2003, pp. 97–105.

García, Santiago. "Cine durante la dictadura." *Leer Cine*, 18 Mar. 2018, www.leercine.com.ar/cine-durante-la-dictadura.

Garrastazu Médici, Emilio. *A justificada confiança*. Biblioteca presidência da República, 1973.

Garrastazu Médici, Emilio. *O nascimento do governo*. Biblioteca presidência da República, 1974.

Gay, Robert. "Clientelism, Democracy, and Violence in Rio de Janeiro." *Clientelism in Everyday Latin American Politics*, edited by Tina Hilgers, Palgrave, pp. 89–99.

Gedan, Benjamin. "Much of Argentina Wants Its Populists Back." *NPR News*, 10 Aug. 2019.

Gentile, Emilio. "Sacralization of Politics." *Totalitarian Movements and Political Religions*, vol. 1, no. 1, 2000, pp. 18–55.

Ginzberg, Victoria. "Torturador, represor, asesino, dictador y fusilador," *Pagina 12*, 25 Nov. 2011, www.pagina12.com.ar/diario/elpais/1-182038-2011-11-25.html.

Gómez Leiva, Sandra. "La subcontratación en la minería en Chile." *Polis*, vol. 8, no. 24, 2009, pp. 111–31.

González Iñárritu, Alejandro. Interview with Fernanda Solórzano. *Letras Libres*, 1 Sept. 2020, letraslibres.com/revista/entrevista-con-alejandro-gonzalez-inarritu-yo-queria-que-amores-perros-fuera-una-pelicula-sensorial.

González, Beatriz. Interview with Luisa Espino. *El Español*, 16 Mar. 2018, www.elespanol.com/el-cultural/arte/20180316/beatriz-gonzalez-cosas-historia-no-puede-contar/292472484_0.html.

Gordillo Aldana, Claudia Solanlle. *Seguridad mediatica la propaganda militarista en la Colombia contemporánea*. Bogota: Uniminuto, 2014.

Gottschall, Jonathan. *Storytelling Animal: How Stories Make Us Human.* Harcourt, 2012.
Green, Melanie, and Timothy Brock. "In the Mind's Eye: Transportation-Imagery Model of Narrative Persuasion." *Narrative Impact: Social and Cognitive Foundations,* edited by Melanie Green, Jeffrey J. Strange, and Timothy C. Brock, Lawrence Erlbaum, 2002, pp. 315–42.
Gruegel, Jean. "Nationalist Movements and Fascist Ideology in Chile." *Bulletin of Latin American Research,* vol. 4, no. 2, 1985, pp. 109–22.
Gullino, Pablo. "Día común, doble vida. Sobre *Historia de un clan.*" *Imagofagia,* vol. 13, 2016, pp. 1–7.
Hagene, Turid. "Political Clientelism in Mexico: Bridging the Gap Between Citizens and the State." *Latin American Politics and Society,* vol. 57, no. 1, 2014, pp. 139–62.
Hay, Colin. *Why We Hate Politics.* Cambridge University Press, 2007.
Hegarty, Paul. *Georges Bataille, Core Cultural Theorist.* Sage, 2000.
Hernández, María Camila. "Colombia: el sonido de la cacerola en una protesta social inedita." *France 24,* 27 Nov. 2019.
Herrera, Carlos. Entrevista con Adolfo Scilingo. *Memoria viva,* May 2008 [1997], memoriaviva5.blogspot.com/2008/06/entrevista-con-adolfo-scilingo-ex.html.
Holzner, Claudio. "The End of Clientelism? Strong and Weak Networks in a Mexican Squatter Movement." *Mobilization,* vol. 9, no. 3, 2004, pp. 223–40.
Horowitz, Irving Louis. "Castro and the 'Caudillo.'" *The National Interest,* vol. 91, 2007, pp. 66–71.
"How People Decide What News to Trust on Digital Platforms and Social Media." *American Press Institute,* 17 Apr. 2016, www.americanpressinstitute.org/publications/reports/survey-research/trust-news.
Hughes, María Fernanda. "Precariedad laboral en Chile. Prácticas de resistencia en los sindicatos de trabajadores tercerizados de la Gran Minería chilena." *Revista de Estudios Marítimos y Sociales,* vol. 9, no. 10, 2016, pp. 84–111.
"Hugo Chávez: su ultimo mensaje." *YouTube,* uploaded by Cubadebate, 8 Mar. 2013, www.youtube.com/watch?v=4WcwJI9hzLI.
"Iñárritu on Film Metaphysics." *YouTube,* uploaded by American Film Institute, 26 May 2020, m.youtube.com/watch?v=ISLPZwLyK_o.
"Iván Márquez enseña la espada de combate de Bolívar recuperada por las FARC." *Rebelión,* 27 Feb. 2010, www.rebelion.org/noticia.php?id=101273.
Janson, Gregory, Jolynn V. Carney, Richard J. Hazier, and Insoo Oh. "Bystanders' Reactions to Witnessing Repetitive Abuse Experiences." *Journal of Counseling and Development,* vol. 87, no. 3, 2009, pp. 319–26.
Jodorowsky, Adán. "Carta a mi padre." *Plano sin fin,* 18 Feb. 2015, planosinfin.com/carta-a-mi-padre-carta-de-adanowsky-a-alejandro-jodorowsky.
Jodorowsky, Alejandro. "No Attachment to Dust." Interview with *Bluefat Magazine. Bluefat,* n.d., www.bluefat.com/1108/Alejandro_Jodorowsky2.htm.
Jodorowsky, Alejandro. *El Topo.* Producciones Pánicas, 1970.
Jodorowsky, Alejandro. Interview with Andrew Whalen. *Player One,* 23 July 2017.
Jodorowsky, Alejandro. Interview with Bilge Ebiri. *Roberebert.com,* 22 May 2014, www.rogerebert.com/interviews/interview-alejandro-jodorowsky-on-the-dance-of-reality-and-the-healing-power-of-art.

Jodorowsky, Alejandro. Interview with Budd Wilkins. *Slant Magazine*, 8 Aug. 2020, www.slantmagazine.com/film/interview-alejandro-jodorowsky-on-psychomagic-the-theater-of-cruelty-and-more.

Jodorowsky, Alejandro. Interview with Eric Benson. "This is Not a Film. This is the Healing of My Soul." *The New York Times Magazine*, 14 Mar. 2014.

Jodorowsky, Alejandro. Interview with Eric Benson. *The New York* Times, 14 Mar. 2014, www.nytimes.com/2014/03/16/magazine/the-psychomagical-realism-of-alejandro-jodorowsky.html.

Jodorowsky, Alejandro. Interview with René Naranjo. *BioBioChile*, 19 May 2013, www.biobiochile.cl/noticias/2013/05/19/alejandro-jodorowsky-por-la-danza-de-la-realidad-este-filme-es-una-curacion-para-mi.shtml.

Jodorowsky, Brontis. Interview with Clarence Tsui. *Hollywood Reporter*, 25 July 2015, www.hollywoodreporter.com/news/general-news/brontis-jodorowsky-playing-his-grandfather-593417.

Johnson, Tim. "Mexico's 'Maquiladora' Labor System Keeps Workers in Poverty." *McClatchy Newspapers*, 17 June 2012, www.mcclatchydc.com/news/nation-world/world/article24730981.html.

"Jorge Videla, el dictador que nunca cuestionó su accionar." *La Nación*, 18 May 2013, www.nacion.com/el-mundo/perfil-jorge-videla-el-dictador-que-nunca-cuestiono-su-accionar.

Kadare, Ismail. "Living with Ghosts." Interview with Julian Evans. *The Guardian*, 16 Sept. 2005, www.theguardian.com/books/2005/sep/17/featuresreviews.guardianreview8.

Kalizsky, Adrián. "Habla el represor Scilingo: 'Estar preso es muy llevadero.'" *El Salto*, 21 Oct. 2018, www.elsaltodiario.com/argentina/exclusiva-habla-el-exrepresor-scilingo-estar-preso-es-muy-llevadero.

Kauffmann, Stanley. Review of *The Crime of Padre Amaro*. New Republic, 25 Nov. 2002, pp. 24–25.

Kay, Jeremy. "Everybody Has 20 Offers on the Table." *ScreenDaily.com*, 25 Mar. 2022, www.screendaily.com/features/everybody-has-20-offers-on-the-table-latin-american-producers-on-premium-tv-drama-boom/5169000.article.

King, John. *Magical Reels: A History of Cinema in Latin America*. Verso, 2000.

Klein, Naomi. *The Shock Doctrine: The Rise of Disaster Capitalism*. Metropolitan Books, 2007.

Krause, Enrique. "Against the Populist Passions." Interview with Jay Nordlinger. *The National Review*, 10 Feb. 2020.

Kristeva, Julia. *Powers of Horror: An Essay on Abjection*. Columbia University Press, 1982.

Lacan, Jacques. *Ecrits: A Selection*. Routledge, 1980.

LaCapra, Dominick. "Lanzmann's *Shoah*: 'Here There Is No Why.'" *Critical Inquiry*, vol. 23, no. 2, 1997, pp. 231–69.

LaCapra, Dominick. Interview with Amos Goldberg. *Yad Vashem: The World's Holocaust Remembrance Center*, 9 June 1998, www.yadvashem.org/articles/interviews/dominick-lacapra.html.

Lacroix, Louis Peru de. *Diario de Bucaramanga: vida pública y privada del Libertador Simón Bolívar*. Madrid: Editorial América, 1924.

Lakhani, Nina. "Mexico: World's Deadliest Country for Journalists." *The Guardian*, 22 Dec. 2020.
Lakoff, George. *Moral Politics: How Liberals and Conservatives Think*. Chicago University Press, 2016.
Langlois, Ed. "Priest-Educator an Inspiration for Film." *Catholic Sentinel*, 10 Feb. 2005.
Larraín, Pablo. Interview by José Miguel Palacios. *The Brooklyn Rail*, Nov. 2012, brooklynrail.org/2012/11/film/the-problems-of-fictionpablo-larran-with-jos-miguel-palacios.
Larraín, Pablo. Interview by Mónica Garrido. *La Tercera*, 2 Sept. 2020, latercera.com/culto/2020/09/02/pablo-larrain-dijeron-que-estaba-vendiendo-historia-chilena-y-obteniendo-ganancias-de-su-doloroso-pasado.
Larraín, Pablo. Interview with Gregorio Belinchón, *El País*, 19 Jan. 2020.
"Las pruebas que comprometen a Humala." Human Rights Watch, 2017, www.hrw.org/sites/default/files/report_pdf/peru0917sp_web_4.pdf.
Lattanzio, Ryan. "Alejandro G. Iñárritu Compares Modern Cinema to a 'Whore That Charges Money.'" *Indiewire*, 19 Aug. 2019.
Laukkanen, Tatu-Ilari. "A Prophecy of Bolsonaro: Masculinity and Populism in *Elite Squad* Films." *The Culture and Politics of Populist Masculinities*, edited by Ouili Hakola, Lexington Books, 2021, pp. 167–86.
Lavery, Jane E. *Angeles Mastretta: Textual Multiplicity*. Tamesis, 2015.
Lazar, Sian. "Personalist Politics, Clientelism and Citizenship: Local Elections in El Alto, Bolivia." *Bulletin of Latin American Research*, vol. 23, no. 2, 2004, pp. 228–43.
Leal, Henrique Pedro. "Bolsonaro and the Far Right." *Open Democracy*, 24 Apr. 2017, www.opendemocracy.net/en/democraciaabierta/bolsonaro-and-brazilian-far-right.
Leñero, Vicente. Interview with Silvia Cherem. "A medio juego." *Revista de la Universidad de México*, 2006, pp. 7–18.
Leñero, Vicente. Interview with Stuart A. Day. *Chasqui*, vol. 33, no. 2, 2004, pp. 17–26.
Liberato, Ana. *Joaquín Balaguer, Memory, and Diaspora: The Lasting Political Legacies of an American Protégé*. Lexington Books, 2013.
Lillo, Gastón. "Notas para una lectura política de la película chilena *Subterra* de Marcelo Ferrari (2003)." *Cinémas d'Amérique Latine*, vol. 21, 2013, pp. 139–49.
Lizana Parraguez, Amante Eledín. Interview by Washington Saldías. *Pichelemu News*, 15 Aug. 2020, www.pichelemunews.cl/index.php/all-categories-list/reportajes/amante-eledin-parraguez-machuca-sus-raices-pichileminas-y-la-educacion.
Llosa, Claudia. "Ha habido un cambio de paradigma que ha democratizado el cine." *Escuela Universitaria de Artes de Madrid*, n.d., taiarts.com/alumni/claudia-llosa.
Llosa, Claudia. Interview with Edward M. Chauka, Rafael Ramirez, and Carolina Sitinsky-Cole. *Mester*, vol. 39, 2010, pp. 45–55.
Llosa, Claudia. Interview with Ricardo Bedoya-Wilson and José Carlos Cabrejo-Cobián, *Ventana indiscreta*, no. 2, 2009, pp. 52–54.
Londoño, Ernesto, Letícia Casado, and Manuela Andreoni. "Turmoil in Brazil." *The New York Times*, 24 Apr. 2020.
Lopez Rosell, Patricia López. "Mapocho River Keeps Rich and Poor Apart in Chile's Capital." *EFE*, 27 Mar. 2019, efe.com/efe/english/life/mapocho-river-keeps-rich-and-poor-apart-in-chile-s-capital/50000263-3936930.

López, Oscar. "Mexico Exonerates Ex-Defense Chief Who Was Freed by the U.S." *The New York Times,* 14 Jan. 2021.

Loret de Mola, Carlos. "Los casos impunes de Felipa, Pío, Bartlett, Sandoval y Robledo muestran la corrupción en México." *Washington Post,* 13 Dec. 2020.

"Lula defende nova relação entre polícia e moradores das favelas do RJ." *O Tempo,* 28 Abr. 2013.

Lum, Kathryn. "The Effects of Bolsonaro's Hate Speech on Brazil." *Monitor Racisim,* Jan. 2019, monitoracism.eu.

Lynch, John. *Caudillos in Spanish America, 1800–1850.* Clarendon Press, 1992.

M-19. "Bolívar, tu espada vuelve a la lucha." *Cedema,* 17 Jan. 1974, www.cedema.org/ver.php?id=3718.

"Maduro se retracta y alaba la serie *Bolívar,*" uploaded by Luigino Bracci Roa, *YouTube,* 31 July 2019, www.youtube.com/watch?v=ndOPJ0M-3mU.

Malca, Camila Gianella. "Peru: Changing Contexts for Transitional Justice." *After Violence: Transitional Justice, Peace, and Democracy,* edited by Elin Skaar, Jemima García-Godos, and Cath Collins, Routledge, 2015, pp. 94–124.

Manky, Omar. "Resource Mobilization and Precarious Workers' Organizations: An Analysis of the Chilean Subcontracted Mineworkers' Unions." *Work, Employment and Society,* vol. 32, no. 3, 2018, pp. 581–98.

Mannarino, Juan M. "Mariana, la hija de Etchecolatz." *Revista Anfibia,* 2018, revistaanfibia.com/cronica/marche-contra-mi-padre-genocida.

"'Mano dura,' el plan de gobierno de Keiko Fujimori para Perú." *Chicago Tribune,* 25 Jan. 2021, www.chicagotribune.com/espanol/sns-es-keiko-fujimori-propone-mano-dura-para-gobernar-peru-20210125-epwtnai77je47bdf20lkrnop3m-story.html.

Marks, Laura. *The Skin of Film.* Duke University Press, 2000.

Marquez Travae, Marques. "Are you breeding cockroaches in that hair?" *Black Brazil Today,* 12 June 2021.

Márquez, Gabriel García. "El enigma de los dos Chávez." *Voltairenet,* 1999, www.voltairenet.org/article120084.html.

Márquez, Gabriel García. Interview with Maria Sampler. *Semana,* 4 Oct. 1989.

Martín-Cabrera, Luis, and Daniel Noemi Voionmaa. "Class Conflict, State of Exception and Radical Justice in *Machuca* by Andrés Wood." *Journal of Latin American Cultural Studies,* vol. 7, 2007, pp. 63–80.

Martínez-Fernández, Andrés. "Money Laundering and Corruption in Mexico." *American Enterprise Institute,* 23 Feb. 2021, www.aei.org/research-products/report/money-laundering-and-corruption-in-mexico-confronting-threats-to-prosperity-security-and-the-us-mexico-relationship.

Marínez, Ibsen. "*Bolívar soy yo.*" *El País,* 13 Sept. 2016.

Martínez, José David. "El Bolívar desnudo de Pereira." Jodamaro https://jodamar0701blog.wordpress.com/bolivar-desnudo-de-pereira/

Marx, Karl, and Friedrich Engels. Letter to Friedrich Engels from February 14, 1858. *Briefwechsel.* Dietz Verlag, 1949, p. 357.

Marx, Karl. "Bolivar y Ponte." *The New American Cyclopaedia,* vol. 3. Appleton and Co., 1863, pp. 440–46.

Massera, Emilio. *El camino a la democracia.* Orestes, 1979.

Mastretta, Ángeles. "Entre la aventura y el litigio." Interview with Gabriella de Beer. *Nexos*, 1 Apr. 1993.

Mastretta, Ángeles. "La escritura como juego erótico y multiplicidad textual." Interview with Jane Livery. *Anales de Literatura Hispanoamericana*, vol. 30, 2001, pp. 313–40.

Mastretta, Ángeles. "Mi novela es una historia, no un ensayo feminista." Interview with Braulio Peralta. *La Jornada*, 11 June 1985, p. 25.

Mastretta, Ángeles. "Women of Will in Love and War." Interview with Barbara Mujica. *Americas*, vol. 49, no. 4, 1997, pp. 36–43.

Mayer, Frederick. *Narrative Politics: Stories and Collective Action*. Oxford University Press, 2014.

Mbembe, Achille. "Necropolitics." *Public Culture*, vol. 15, no. 1, pp. 11–40.

Meirelles, Fernando. Interview with Demetrios Matheou. *The Faber Book of New South American Cinema*, edited by Demetrios Matheou, Faber, 2010, pp. 122–35.

Mello, William. "Poverty and Politics: Bolsonaro, Neoliberalism's Authoritarian Alternative." *Nonsite*, vol. 34, 12 Mar. 2021, nonsite.org/poverty-and-politics-bolsonaro-neoliberalisms-authoritarian-alternative-and-the-ongoing-assault-on-democracy-in-brazil.

Melnyk, George. *Transformative Cinema of Alejandro Jodorowsky*. Bloomsbury Academic, 2023.

Meretoja, Hannah. *The Ethics of Storytelling*. Oxford University Press, 2017.

"Mexican Prosecution Opens Corruption Investigation Against Ex-President Peña Nieto and Ex-Minister Luis Videgaray." *Mercopress*, 14 Aug. 2020.

"Mexico Files U.S. Lawsuit Against Ex-security Chief Linked to Sinaloa Cartel." *Reuters*, 21 Sept. 2021.

"Mexico President Backs Dropping of Drug Case Against Ex-defense Minister." *Reuters*, 15 Jan. 2021.

Miguel, Marlon. "Psychiatric Power: Exclusion and Segregation in the Brazilian Mental Health System." *Democracy and Brazil: Collapse and Regression*, edited by Bernardo Bianchi Jorge Chaloub, Patrícia Rangel, and Frieder O. Wolf, Routledge, 2020, pp. 250–67.

Ministerio de la Mujer y Poblaciones Vulnerables. *Casos atendidos a personas afectadas por hechos de violencia. Enero-diciembre, 2019*. Lima: MMPV, 2019, www.mimp.gob.pe/contigo/contenidos/pncontigo-articulos.php?codigo=33.

Morello, Gustavo. *The Catholic Church and Argentina's Dirty War*. Oxford University Press, 2015.

Mulvey, Laura. "Visual Pleasure and Narrative Cinema." *Film: Psychology, Society, and Ideology*, edited by Leo Braudy and Marshall Cohen, New York: Oxford, 1999, pp. 803–15.

Mussolf, Andreas. *Metaphor, Nation and the Holocaust: The Concept of Body Politics*. London: Routledge, 2014.

Nagib, Lúcia. *Realist Cinema as World Cinema*. Amsterdam University Press, 2020.

Navarro, Mireya. "Political Theater: At the Intersection of Ruler and Ruled." *The New York Times*, 23 Feb. 2003.

Neruda, Pablo. "Canto a Bolívar." *Residence on Earth*. Translated by Donald D. Walsh, New Directions Publishing Corporation, 1973, pp. 334–36.

Neruda, Pablo. *Confieso que he vivido. Memorias*. Seix Barral, 2011.

Nery, Erick Matheus. "José Padilha quebra a cara com Sérgio Moro." *Noticias da TV*, 27 May 2022, noticiasdatv.uol.com.br/noticia/celebridades/jose-padilha-quebra-cara-com-sergio-moro-e-critica-bolsonaro-fui-idiota-81896.

"Nicolás Maduro Moros—New Target." US Department of State, 26 Mar. 2020, www.state.gov/nicolas-maduro-moros-new-target.

Nikas, Jack. "Bolsonaro's New Ally in Questioning Brazil's Elections: The Military." *The New York Times*, 12 June 2022.

Noriega, Carlos. "Un represor fue el congresista más votado en Perú." *Página 12*, 28 Jan. 2020, www.pagina12.com.ar/244214-un-represor-fue-el-congresista-mas-votado-en-peru.

Nugent, Clara. "Why Chile's SATs Have Become the New Frontline of Inequality Protests." *Time*, 23 Jan. 2020, time.com/5770308/chile-student-protests.

"Odebrecht Case: Politicians Worldwide Suspected in Bribery Scandal." *BBC*, 17 Apr. 2019.

O'Leary, Daniel Florence. *Bolívar and the War of Independence*. University of Chicago Press, 1975.

Oliveira Rocha, Renato. "O vínculo de *Cidade de Deus* com a realidade." *REVELL Revista de Estudos Literários da UEMS*, vol. 2, no. 7, 2013, pp. 19–32.

Ortega, Luis. Interview with Hernán Guerschuny. *Centro de extensión profesional, Directores argentinos cinematográficos*, n.d., cepdac.org/entrevista-a-luis-ortega.

Ortega, Luis. Interview with Nando Varela Pagliaro. *Medium*, 30 Aug. 2015, medium.com/@varelapagliaro/entrevista-a-luis-ortega-el-crimen-te-da-una-identidad-66a67dcaee7e.

O'Shaughnessy, Nicolas. *Marketing the Third Reich*. Routledge, 2018.

Osorio, Sebastián, and Francia Vega. "Salario y estrategias de ganancia empresarial en la minería privada y estatal del cobre." *El Mostrador*, 18 Aug. 2013, m.elmostrador.cl/noticias/opinion/2013/08/18/salario-y-estrategias-de-ganancia-empresarial-en-la-mineria-privada-y-estatal-del-cobre.

Ostry, Jonathan, Prakash Loungani, and Davide Furceri. "Neoliberalism: Oversold." *Finance and Development*, June 2016, pp. 43–42.

Oubiña, David. "Footprints: Risks and Challenges of Contemporary Argentine Cinema." *New Argentine and Brazilian Cinema: Reality Effects*, edited by Jens Andermann and Álvaro Fernández Bravo, Palgrave, 2013, pp. 31–41.

Padilha, José. Interview with Demetrios Matheou. *The Faber Book of New South American Cinema*, edited by Demetrios Matheou, Faber, 2010, pp. 173–85.

Pagán-Teitelbaum, Iliana. "Glamour in the Andes: Indigenous Women in Peruvian Cinema." *Latin American and Caribbean Ethnic Studies*, vol. 71, 2012, pp. 71–93.

Page, Joanna. "Beyond Reflexivity: Acting and Experience in Contemporary Argentine and Brazilian Cinema." *New Argentine and Brazilian Cinema: Reality Effects*, edited by Jens Andermann and Álvaro Fernández Bravo, Palgrave, 2013, pp. 73–87.

Page, Joanna. *Crisis and Capitalism in Contemporary Argentine Cinema*. Duke University Press, 2009.

Palacios, Rodolfo. *El clan Puccio*. Planeta, 2015.

Palaversich, Diana. "Cultural Dyslexia and the Politics of Cross-Cultural Excursion in Claudia Llosa's *Madeinusa*." *Bulletin of Hispanic Studies*, vol. 90, no. 4, 2013, pp. 489–501.

"The Pandemic Strikes: Responding to Colombia's Mass Protests," *Crisis Group*, report 90, 2 July 2021.
Park, Moisés. "Machuca (2004): Melodrama y horror." *Polifonía*, vol. 9, 2019, 20–33.
Parra, Andrés. "Chávez era un monstruo de la comunicación." *Semana*, 11 Dec. 2016, www.semana.com/cultura/articulo/entrevista-a-andres-parra-sobre-su-personaje-hugo-chavez/508724.
Pascoe, C.J. *Dude, You're a Fag: Masculinity and Sexuality in High School.* University of California Press, 2012.
Payan, Tony. Introduction. *A War That Can't Be Won.* Arizona University Press, 2011.
Paz Peirano, María. "A Tale of Neoliberalism." *Contemporary Latin American Cinema: Resisting Neoliberalism?* edited by Claudia Sandberg and Carolina Rocha, Palgrave, 2018, pp. 135–52.
Paz, Octavio. "Crítica de la pirámide." *El laberinto de la soledad. Postdata. Vuelta a el laberinto de la soledad.* Mexico City: Fondo de Cultura Económica, 1999, pp. 287–318.
Pégot-Ogier, Evelyne. Interview by Luis Ramos. *Cinencuentro*, 9 Mar. 2016, cinencuentro.com/2016/03/09/entrevista-la-hora-azul-evelyne-pegot-ogier-pelicula-la-novela-alonso-cueto.
Penney, Joel. *The Citizen Marketer: Promoting Political Opinion in the Social Media Age.* Palgrave, 2021.
Pereira, Tiago. "Redes reagem a Bolsonaro." *Rede Brazil atual*, 30 May 2022.
Pérez-Roa, Lorena. "Consumo, endeudamiento y economía doméstica: una historia en tres tiempos para entender el estallido social." *Hilos tensados: para leer el octubre chileno*, edited by Kathya Araujo, Santiago: Universidad de Chile, 2019, pp. 83–106.
"The Perfect Dictatorship: User Reviews." *IMDb*, m.imdb.com/title/tt3970854/reviews?ref_=tt_urv.
Phillips, Dom. "How Brazil's Militias Wield Terror to Seize Power from Drug Gangs." *The Irish Times*, 14 July 2018.
Plantinga, Carl. *Screen Stories: Emotion and the Ethics of Engagement.* Oxford University Press, 2018.
Poblete, Juan. "National Cinema." *The Routledge Companion to Latin American Cinema*, edited by Marvin D'Lugo, Ana M. López, and Laura Podalsky, Routledge, 2018.
Poblete, Juan. "The Memory of the National and the National as Memory." *Latin American Perspectives*, 2015, vol. 42, no. 3, pp. 92–106.
Podalsky, Laura. "The Affect Turn." *New Approaches to Latin American Cultural Studies: Culture and Power*, edited by Juan Poblete, Routledge, 2018, pp. 237–54.
Podalsky, Laura. *The Politics of Affect and Emotion in Contemporary Latin American Cinema.* Palgrave, 2011.
Polanyi, Karl. *The Great Transformation.* Rinehart, 1957.
Premici, Sebastián. "Explotación laboral en el sector rural." *Página 12*, 26 Mar. 2019, www.pagina12.com.ar/183322-explotacion-laboral-en-el-sector-rural.
Preston, Julia, and Samuel Dillon. *Opening Mexico: The Making of a Democracy.* New York: Farrar, Straus and Giroux, 2004.
"Propaganda en la dictadura argentina." Uploaded by Guillermo Martínez Vásquez. Youtube, 29 June 2016, www.youtube.com/watch?v=LX1GkDhWNj4.

"Provocación ante el aniversario del golpe." *Página 12*, 21 Mar. 2018, www.pagina12.com.ar/102797-provocacion-ante-el-aniversario-del-golpe.

Quintero, Inés. "Sobre la serie 'Bolívar' de Netflix." *Prodavinci*, 17 July 2019, prodavinci.com/sobre-la-serie-bolivar-de-netflix-es-cuento-no-es-historia.

Quijano, Aníbal. "Coloniality of Power, Eurocentrism, and Latin America." Nepantla: Views from the South, vol. 1, no. 3, 2000, pp. 533–80.

Quiroz, Karem Barbosa. "Daniel Urresti: su abogada renunció." *El peruano*, 3 Feb. 2021, elcomercio.pe/politica/daniel-urresti-su-abogada-renuncio-en-plena-audiencia-del-juicio-por-el-caso-hugo-bustios-noticia.

Quispe, Oscar M. "Caso Madre Mía se reactiva y no descartan citación de Ollanta Humala." *Perú21*, 24 Sept. 2020, peru21.pe/politica/caso-madre-mia-se-reactiva-y-no-descartan-citacion-de-ollanta-humala-noticia/?tmp_ad=30seg.

Rama, Ángel. *Los dictadores latinoamericanos*. Mexico: Fondo de Cultura Economica, 1976.

Rama, Borja. "La Fiscalía de México implica al expresidente Peña Nieto en un soborno de seis millones." *ABC*, 2 Sept. 2021.

"Ranks of Mexican Poor Swell to Reach Nearly Half of the Population." *Reuters*, 5 Aug. 2021.

Reato, Ceferino. *Disposición final: la confesión de Videla sobre los desaparecidos*. Buenos Aires: Sudamericana, 2012.

Reid, Michael. *The Forgotten Continent*. Yale University Press, 2007.

"Reportaje del periodista Manuel Ruiz. El Colorado, Pasto 2018." Uploaded by Grupos, música y cultura nariñense, *YouTube*, 9 Jan. 2018, www.youtube.com/watch?v=Qdw4PSJ0YeU.

Reséndez, Andrés. "North American Peonage." *Journal of the Civil War Era*, vol. 7, no. 4, 2017, pp. 597–619.

Reséndez, Andrés. *The Other Slavery: The Uncovered Story of Indian Enslavement in America*. Harcourt, 2016.

Rey, Carlos. "Ideario bolivariano y la democracia en la Venezuela del siglo XXI." *Revista Venezolana de ciencia política*, vol. 28, 2005, pp. 167–91.

Reyes, Ana María. "Beatriz González's Case for Critical History Painting." *Simón Bolívar: Travels and Transformations of a Cultural Icon*, edited by Mareen G. Shanahan and Ana María Reyes, University Press of Florida, 2016, pp. 148–68.

Ribke, Nahuel. "Netflix and Over the Top Politics? *The Mechanism* TV Series and the Dynamics of Entertainment Intervention." *Critical Studies in Television*, vol. 16, no. 1, 2021, pp. 47–61.

Rivas Molina, Federico. "El Latinobarómetro registra en 2018 el 'annus horribilis' de las democracias de América Latina." *El País*, 9 Nov. 2018, elpais.com/internacional/2018/11/09/america/1541766116_145827.html.

Rocha, Camila, Esther Solano, and Jonas Medeiros. *The Bolsonaro Paradox*. Springer, 2021.

Rodríguez-Bravo, Eglee Teresa, *Reimaginando a Bolívar en la cultura latinoamericana*. 2016. Wayne State University, Doctoral dissertation.

Rodríguez, Rene. "Sins of the Flesh, Relevancy of the Story Make *El crimen del Padre Amaro* Timely." *Hispanic*, vol. 15, no. 11, 2002, p. 62.

Roett, Riordan. *The New Brazil*. Washington, DC: The Brookings Institution, 2010.

Rohter, Larry. "Distressing Portrayal by Garcia Marquez: Bolivar's Feet of Clay." *The New York Times*, 6 June 1989.
Roncagliolo, Santiago. "El abuelo Vargas Llosa les da la bienvenida." *El Comercio*, 16 Nov. 2018, elcomercio.pe/opinion/columnistas/abuelo-vargas-llosa-les-da-bienvenida-santiago-roncagliolo-noticia-578017-noticia.
Roniger, Luis. "Favors, 'Merit Ribbons,' and Services: Analyzing the Fragile Resilience of Clientelism." *Clientelism in Everyday Latin American Politics*, edited by Tina Hilgers, New York: Palgrave, 2012, pp. 25–40.
Rosero, Evelio. "Lo único más importante que la escritura es la lectura." Interview with Alonso Rabí. *Ojo público*, 15 Dec. 2015, ojo-publico.com/136/evelio-rosero-lo-unico-mas-importante-que-la-escritura-es-la-lectura.
Rosero, Evelio. Interview with Enrique Patiño. *El País*, 1 Feb. 2012, elpais.com/cultura/2012/02/01/actualidad/1328115600_1328124376.html.
Rousseff, Dilma. Pronunciamento à nação. *Biblioteca presidência da República*, 2011. www.biblioteca.presidencia.gov.br.
Sabet, Daniel M. "Corruption or Insecurity? Understanding Dissatisfaction with Mexico's Police." *Latin American Politics and Society*, vol. 55, no. 1, 2013, pp. 22–45.
Sáez-Pardo, Melchior. "Las dos caras de Adolfo Scilingo." *Equipo Nizkor*, 19 Jan. 2005, www.derechos.org/nizkor/espana/juicioral/doc/melchor5.html.
Salles, Walter. Interview. *Revista continente*, 2003. www.revistacontinente.com.br/sumario/182/1002-a-contenente/revista/cinema/18431-walter-salles-entrevista.html.
Salles, Walter. Interview with Matheou Demetrios. *The Faber Book of New Latin American Cinema*. Faber & Faber, 2010, pp. 31–112.
Sánchez Prado, Ignacio. *Screening Neoliberalism: Transforming Mexican Cinema, 1988–2012*. Vanderbilt University Press, 2014.
Sañudo, José Rafael. *Estudios sobre la vida de Bolívar*. Pasto: Editorial de Díaz Castillo, 1925.
Savigny, Heather. *The Problem of Political Marketing*. Continuum, 2011.
Scammell, Margaret. *Consumer Democracy: The Marketing of Politics*. Cambridge University Press, 2017.
Scherer, María, and Nacho Lozano. *El priísta que todos llevamos dentro*. Penguin Random House, 2016.
Schröter, Barbara. "Clientelismo político: ¿existe el fantasma y cómo se viste?" *Revista Mexicana de Sociología*, vol. 72, no. 1, 2010, pp. 141–75.
Scilingo, Adolfo. *¡Por siempre nunca más!* Buenos Aires: Editorial del Plata, 1996.
Schroeder Rodríguez, Paul A. *Latin American Cinema*. University of California Press, 2016.
Seffer, Kristin. "Clientelism a Stumbling Block to Democratization? Lessons from Mexico." *Latin American Perspectives*, vol. 42, no. 5, 2015, pp. 198–215.
"Según el 'Tigre' Acosta, en la ESMA 'se privilegiaba la vida.'" *Diario registrado*, 19 June 2015, www.diarioregistrado.com/over-gear_uplighter_sapidity.
Sehnbruch, Kirsten. "A Precarious Labor Market." *Democratic Chile: The Politics and Policies of a Historic Coalition, 1990–2021*, edited by Kirsten Sehnbruch and Peter M. Siavelis, Lynne Reinner, 2014, pp. 263–80.

Sehnbruch, Kristen. "How Pinochet's Economic Model Led to the Current Economic Crisis Engulfing Chile." *The Guardian*, 30 Oct. 2019.

Seoane, María, and Vicente Muleiro. *El dictador: la historia secreta y pública de Jorge Rafael Videla*. Buenos Aires: Sudamericana, 2016.

Sheridan, Mary. "Former Aide Ties Mexican Ex-president Peña Nieto to Millions in Bribes." *Washington Post*, 11 Aug. 2020.

Shields, Duncan M., David Kuhl, and Marvin J. Westwood. "Abject Masculinity and the Military: Articulating a Fulcrum of Struggle and Change." *Psychology of Men and Masculinity*, vol. 18, no. 3, 2017, pp. 215–25.

Silió, Elisa. "Jorge Alí Triana ironiza sobre Bolívar." *El País*, 10 Apr. 2003.

Silva, Patricio. "Doing Politics in a Depoliticised Society: Social Change and Political Deactivation in Chile." *Bulletin of Latin American Research*, vol. 23, no. 1, 2004, pp. 63–78.

Silva, Sebastián. Interview with Nick Dawson. *Filmmaker Magazine*, 16 Oct. 2009, filmmakermagazine.com/1390-sebastian-silva-the-maid.

Singer, Matthew. "Buying Voters with Dirty Money: The Relationship between Corruption and Clientelism." Annual Meeting of American Political Society Association, 3–6 Sept. 2009, Toronto. Conference Presentation.

Skármeta, Antonio. Entrevista digital. *El País*, 27 May 2011, elpais.com/cultura/2011/05/27/actualidad/1306508400_1306516519.html.

Skármeta, Antonio. Interview by Marcelo Soto. "Antonio Skármeta y la chispa del *No*." *Revista Capital*, 28 Jan. 2013. www.capital.cl/antonio-skarmeta-y-la-chispa-del-no.

Smith, Nigel. "Magaly Solier." *Indiewire*, 27 Aug. 2010, www.indiewire.com/2010/08/futures-magaly-solier-star-of-altiplano-and-the-milk-of-sorrow-245051.

Sneider, Roberto. Interview with Ada Aparicio Ortuñes. *Casa de America*, 2008, www.casamerica.es.

Soares, Luiz Eduardo, André Batista, and Rodrigo Pimentel. *Elite da tropa*. Objectiva, 2006.

Sørbøe, Celina Myrann. "Urban Development in Rio de Janeiro During the 'Pink Tide.'" *The Social Life of Economic Inequalities in Contemporary Latin America*, edited by Margit Ystanes and Iselin Åsedotter Strønen, Palgrave, 2018, pp. 107–28.

Sorensen, Kristen. *Media, Memory, and Human Rights in Chile*. Palgrave, 2009.

Spigariol, André, and Jack Nicas. "Brazil's Polls Were Wrong," *The New York Times*, 22 Oct. 2022.

Standing, Guy. *The Precariat: The New Dangerous Class*. Bloomsbury Academic, 2011.

Stecher, Antonio, and Vincente Sisto. "Trabajo y precarización laboral en el Chile neoliberal." *Hilos tensados: para leer el octubre chileno*, edited by Kathya Araujo, Universidad de Chile, 2019, pp. 37–94.

"Tear This Heart Out: User Reviews." *IMDb*, m.imdb.com/title/tt1130981/reviews?ref_=tt_urv.

Teixera, Pablo. "Brazil to Issue 'Dirty List' of Employers Using Slave Labor." *Reuters*, 2 June 2019.

Thiher, Allen. *Understanding Franz Kafka*. University of South Carolina Press, 2018.

Tierney, Dolores. *New Transnationalisms in Contemporary Latin American Cinemas*. Edinburgh University Press, 2018.

Tosoni, Magdalena. "Notas sobre el clientelismo político en la ciudad de México." *Perfiles latinoamericanos*, vol. 29, 2007, pp. 47–69.

Trapero, Pablo. Interview with Danny Leigh. *The Guardian*, 14 Sept. 2016, www.theguardian.com/film/2016/sep/14/pablo-trappero-argentina-hit-film-the-clan-puccio-family-interview.

Trapero, Pablo. Interview with Emanuel Bremermann. *El Observador*, 16 Oct. 2018, www.elobservador.com.uy/nota/pablo-trapero-entre-el-clan-puccio-el-buenos-aires-rural-y-el-negocio-de-la-cocaina-20181015192735.

Trapero, Pablo. Interview with John Hopewell. *Variety*, 30 Nov. 2012, variety.com/2012/film/news/trapero-preps-clan-puccio-thriller-1118062895.

Trevino-Rangel, Javier. *Policing the Mexican Past*. Palgrave, 2022.

Triana, Jorge Alí. Interview with Oswaldo Osorio. *Cinefagos*, 2003, www.cinefagos.net/index.php/cine-colombiano/entrevistas/57-entrevista-con-jorge-alriana.

Triana, Jorge Alí. Interview with Oswaldo Osorio. *Cinéfagos*, n.d., www.cinefagos.net/index.php/cine-colombiano/articulos-y-ensayos/56-420-festival-de-cine-de-cartagena?r=47369ku41kbepksc0-q.

Tuckman, Jo. "Mexican Media Scandal: Secretive Televisa Unit Promoted PRI Candidate." *The Guardian*, 26 June 2012.

Tuckman, Jo. *Mexico: Democracy Interrupted*. Yale University Press, 2012.

"Urresti: Fiscalía decidirá si hay apología en 'La Cautiva.'" *El Comercio*, 1 Dec. 2015.

"User Reviews: *Dance of Reality*." *IMDb*, m.imdb.com/title/tt2301592/reviews/?ref_=tt_ov_rt.

"User Reviews: *Pinocchio*." *IMDb*, www.imdb.com/title/tt1488589/reviews?ref_=tt_urv.

Uzcategui, Rafael. *Revulution as a Spectacle*. See Sharp Press, 2011.

Valencia, Sayak. *Gore Capitalism*. Semiotext(e), 2018.

Valero, Roque. "Bolívar, el hombre de las dificultades es un legado histórico de Chávez." *Noticias24*, 18 Dec. 2013.

Vargas Llosa, Mario, Abraham Guzmán Figueroa, and Mario Castro Arenas. Informe de la Comisión Investigadora de los sucesos de Uchuraccay. Lima: Editora Perú, 1983.

Vargas Llosa, Mario. "Bataille or the Redemption of the Evil." *Making* Waves. Farrar, Strauss, and Giroux, 1996, pp. 117–26.

Vargas Llosa, Mario. "Eso no debe repetirse jamás." *Rumbo*, vol. 327, 2000, pp. 46–59, issuu.com/diariolibre/docs/revista_rumbo_327.

Vargas Llosa, Mario. "Nuevas inquisiciones." *El País*, 17 Mar. 2018, elpais.com/elpais/2018/03/16/opinion/1521215265_029385.html.

Vargas Llosa, Mario. Interview. *The Cambridge Companion to Mario Vargas Llosa*, edited by Efraín Kristal and John King, Cambridge University Press, 2012, pp. 212–20.

Verbitsky, Horacio. *El vuelo*. Buenos Aires: Sudamericana, 2006.

Videla, Jorge Rafael. *Mensajes presidenciales*, vol. 1. Argentina: Presidencia de la República, 1976.

Vieira, Evaldo. *A ditadura militar: 1964–1985*. São Paulo: Cortez, 2014.

Vilches, Patricia. "Andrés Wood's *Machuca* and *Violeta Went to Heaven:* The Geographical Spaces of Conflict in Chile." *Latin American Perspectives*, vol. 43, no. 5, 2016, pp. 45–61.

Waldstein, David. "In Chile's National Stadium Dark Past Shadows Copa América Matches." *The New York Times*, 17 June 2015, www.nytimes.com/2015/06/19/sports/soccer/in-chiles-national-stadium-dark-past-shadows-copa-america-matches.html.

Wallis, Daniel. "Venezuela's Chávez Unveils 3D Image of Hero Bolivar." *Reuters*, 24 July 2012.
Walsh, Rodolfo. "Open Letter to the Military Junta." Translated by Arturo Desimone, *The Inverse Journal*, 20 Jan. 2022, www.inversejournal.com/2022/01/20/rodolfo-walshs-1977-open-letter-to-the-military-junta-in-argentina-introduced-and-translated-by-arturo-desimone.
Warf, Barney, and Sheridan Stewart. "Latin American Corruption in Geographic Perspective." *Journal of Latin American Geography*, vol. 15, no. 1, 2016, pp. 133–55.
"'We Won't Be Trampled On': Striking Mexican Workers Vow to Fight the Fight." *The Guardian*, 19 Feb. 2019.
Winkelmann, Arne. "The Colonie as a Political Instrument." *Le Colonie: The Children's Holiday Camps of Fascist Italy*, www.lecolonie.com/texts.htm.
Weber, Max. *Economy and Society*. University of California Press, 1978.
Wood, Andrés. Interview by Jorge de Elizade. *Imaginación atrapada*, 7 Oct. 2005, www.imaginacionatrapada.com.ar/Cine/entandreswood.htm.
Wood, Andrés. Interview. *Cine-Arte Magazine*, 25 Jan. 2020, www.cineartemagazine.com/2020/01/entrevista-andres-wood.html.
Zarazaga, Rodrigo. "Brokers beyond Clientelism: A New Perspective through the Argentine Case." *Latin American Politics and Society*, vol. 56, no. 3, 2014, pp. 23–45.
Zavala Kahn, Sebastián. "*La Hora azul*, de Evelyne Pegot-Ogier." *En Lima*, 18 Oct. 2016, enlima.pe/blog/cine/critica/la-hora-azul-de-evelyne-pegot-ogier.
Zevallos-Aguilar, Juan. "*Madeinusa* y el cargamontón neoliberal." *Wayra*, vol. 2, no. 4, 2006, pp. 71–81.
Zimbardo, Philip. *The Lucifer Effect*. Random House, 2008.
Zimmerman, Seth. "Elite Colleges and Upward Mobility to Top Jobs and Top Incomes." *American Economic Review*, vol. 109, no. 1, 2019, pp. 1–47.
Žižek, Slavoj. *For They Know Not What They Do: Enjoyment as a Political Factor*. Verso, 1991.

INDEX

Abjectification, 207, 210, 221
Adorno, Theodor, 139, 143–46, 159
Agamben, Giorgio, 114, 127, 143, 207
Andermann, Jens, 15
Andrés Wood, 182
Arendt, Hannah, 72, 74–76, 216, 223
Aylwin, Patricio, 184

Bakhtin, Mikhail, 215
Balaguer, Joaquín, 32, 33, 41
Banality of evil, 23, 75, 81
Bandura, Albert, 70
Bare life (Agamben), 127
Bataille, Georges, 29–30
Baudrillard, Jean, 186
Benjamin, Walter, 143
Bernal, Gael García, 102, 104, 184, 187
Biopolitics, 127
Blue Hour, The (*La hora azul*, Evelyne Pégot-Ogier), 43–44
Blue Hour, The (*La hora azul*, Alonso Cueto), 43
Boesten, Jelke, 51–53
Bolívar, Simón: appropriation by the FARC, 163; carnival and parody as responses to Bolívar cult, 169; deification and appropriation by Hugo Chávez, 158; Pablo Neruda's praise of, 154; in pop art: 146–50
Bolívar, una lucha admirable (Caracol Televisión), 162
Bolívar I Am (*Bolívar soy yo*, Jorge Alí Triana), 165–66
Bolsa Família, 136–39
Bourdieu, Pierre, 88
Broken April (Ismail Kadare), 121–22

Canetti, Elias, 143, 205, 206, 223, 225
Carnival symbolism, 42, 76, 168–70
Captive, The (*Cautiva*, Alberto León), 46–47

Carrera, Carlos, 102, 104, 108
Caudillismo, 6, 10, 41, 151
Chávez, Hugo: appropriation and deification of Bolívar's image, 158; portrayal as modern caudillo and charismatic leader, 159; subject of critique and satire in Colombian and Venezuelan media, 159–61
City of God (*Cidade de Deus*, Fernando Meirelles and Kátia Lund), 129–30
City of Men (*Cidade dos Homens*, Paulo Morelli), 130–31
Clan, The (*El clan*, Pablo Trapero), 58–60
Clan Puccio, The (*El clan Puccio*, Rodolfo Palacios), 64–69
Clennen, Sofia A., 13
Clientelism, 88–90
Compadrazgo, 87, 103
Compulsory masculinity, 221
Corruption, 5, 13, 28
Creed, Barbara, 223
Crime of Padre Amaro, The (*El crimen del padre Amaro*, Carlos Carrera), 101–7
Crime of Father Amaro, The (*O crime do padre Amaro*, José Maria Eça de Queirós), 103
Cueto, Alonso, 28, 43–45, 60

Dance of Reality, The (*La danza de la realidad*, Alejandro Jodorowsky), 213–19
Dávila, Juan, 146–50
Debt peonage, 7, 90–91
del Solar, Salvador, 22, 28, 44–47
del Toro, Guillermo, 205–13, 221–23
Dirty War (Argentina, 1976–1983): clandestine detention, 61; secrecy, 73; Triple A (Argentine Anticommunist Alliance), 59
Dore, Elizabeth, 7, 8, 10, 90, 91
Duque, Iván, 4

Elite Squad (*Tropa de elite*, José Padilha), 128, 132–36
Endless Poetry (*Poesía sin fin*, Alejandro Jodorowsky), 219

FARC (Revolutionary Armed Forces of Colombia), 163, 166
Feast of the Goat, The (*La fiesta del Chivo*, Luis Llosa), 28, 30, 41
Feast of the Innocent, The (*Carroza de Bolívar*, Evelio Rosero), 24, 166–68
Freud, Sigmund, 17, 18, 29, 33, 159
Fujimori, Alberto, 11, 28, 40–42, 52
Fujimori, Keiko, 53

García Bernal, Gael, 102, 104, 184, 187
García Márquez, Gabriel, 2, 146, 159, 164, 165
General in His Labyrinth, The (*El general en su laberinto*, Gabriel García Márquez), 146, 164–65
González, Beatriz, 150

Herod's Law (*La ley de Herodes*, Luis Estrada), 6, 92, 100, 106, 109
History of a Clan, The (*Historia de un clan*, Luis Ortega), 92, 97, 100, 106
Human sacrifice: in Bataille, 30; in Vargas Llosa, 28–30

Impunity: Full Stop Law (Ley de Punto Final, Argentina), 77; Mexico, 5; Peru 51–53
Iñárritu, Alejandro, 17, 104

Jodorowsky, Alejandro, 15, 16, 213–21

Lacan, Jacques, 18, 26, 210, 211
LaCapra, Dominick, 42, 76
Lakoff, George, 1, 17, 131, 138, 215, 217, 223
Larraín, Pablo, 183, 189
León, Alberto, 27, 48
Liberator, The (*El Libertador*, Alberto Arvelo), 156–57
Llosa, Claudia, 15, 27, 28, 48, 49, 50
Llosa, Luis, 28, 30, 41

Madeinusa (Claudia Llosa), 22, 27, 48–51
Magallanes (Salvador del Solar), 44–46
Magnificence of evil, 76

Marx, Karl, 154, 167, 168
Mastretta, Ángeles, 111, 112
Mbembe, Achille, 114, 133
Meirelles, Fernando, 16, 129, 130
Menem, Carlos, 11, 77, 78, 79
Milk of Sorrow (*Teta asustada*, Claudia Llosa), 9, 48–50
M-19 (Movimiento 19 de Abril), 163
Moral disengagement, 75
Montesinos, Vladimiro, 42
Mulvey, Laura, 223

Nagib, Lúcia, 16
Nassar, Raduan, 117, 118, 120
National Reorganization Process (Proceso de Reorganización Nacional, Argentina), 57
Necropolitics, 133
Neoliberalism, 4, 11, 13, 14, 15, 25, 40, 96, 98, 172–73, 182, 183, 184, 190, 191, 199
Neruda, Pablo, 154, 155, 158
No (*No*, Pablo Larraín), 183–88

Ortega, Luis, 56, 63, 64, 68, 70, 80

Padilha, José, 16, 132, 135, 136
Palacios, Rodolfo, 64, 71–73
Pan's Labyrinth (*El laberinto del fauno*, Guillermo del Toro), 205–8, 230
Parraguez Lizana, Amante Eledín, 180, 182
Pascoe, C. J., 221
Passenger, The (*La pasajera*, Alonso Cueto), 44–45
Patriarchy, 6, 50, 52
Patronage, 87, 90
Peru, internal conflict in, 1980–2000: Shining Path (Sendero Luminoso, Peru), 22, 42, 48, 50–52, 54; Truth and Reconciliation Commission (Peru), 28, 44, 53, 54; Uchuraccay (massacre site), 29
Pavlovsky, Eduardo, 79
Pégot-Ogier, Evelyne, 43, 44
Perfect Dictatorship, The (*La dictadura perfecta*, Luis Estrada), 95–98
Piñera, José, 197
Piñera, Sebastián, 189
Plantinga, Carl, 17
Podalsky, Laura, 15
Poblete, Juan, 14, 177

Political Caesarism, 151, 156, 159
PRI (Partido Revolucionario Institucional), 87

Quijano, Aníbal, 12, 13, 150

Rama, Ángel, 217
Reséndez, Andrés, 6, 7, 90, 91
Roncagliolo, Santiago, 28
Rosero, Evelio, 24, 146, 166–68

Salinas, Carlos, 11, 91
Salles, Walter, 15, 122–26
Scilingo, Adolfo, 71–73, 82–84
Sehnbruch, Kirsten, 4, 197
Shape of Water, The (Guillermo del Toro), 225
Stalin, Joseph, 155, 201, 204, 213–19
Subterra (*Subterra*, Marcelo Ferrari), 193–97

Tear This Heart Out (*Arráncame la vida*, Ángeles Mastretta), 107–10
Tear This Heart Out (*Arráncame la vida*, Roberto Sneider), 110–12
Three Years to Be Born (*Tres años para nacer*, Parraguez Lizana), 180–81
Tierney, Dolores, 14, 50, 129, 207, 215
Time of the Hero, The (*La ciudad y los perros*, Francisco Lombardi), 37

To the Left of the Father (*Lavoura arcaica*, Luiz Fernando Carvalho), 117–20
Toledo, Alejandro, 3, 42, 53, 54
Tony Manero (*Tony Manero*, Pablo Larraín), 14, 20, 21, 145
Tosoni, María Magdalena, 9, 88
Transgression: in Bataille, 30; in Freud, 29; in Vargas Llosa, 30
Trapero, Pablo, 56, 58–60, 68, 70, 101
Triana, Jorge Alí, 33, 146, 165, 166,
Trujillo, Rafael Leónidas, 32–35, 39, 41, 51, 145

Uribe, Álvaro, 163
Urresti, Daniel, 48, 54

Valencia, Sayak, 99
Vargas Llosa, Mario: *Captain Pantoja and the Special Service* (*Pantaleón y las visitadoras*), 28; *Death in the Andes* (*Lituma en los Andes*), 28–29; *Feast of the Goat, The* (*La fiesta del Chivo*), 30–32; *Pez en el agua* (*Fish in the Water*), 37–41; *Time of the Hero, The* (*La ciudad y los perros*); Uchuraccay, 29
Videla, Jorge Rafael, 10–12, 21, 23, 57, 68, 69, 73, 77, 80–82

Žižek, Slavoj, 18, 211

Irina Dzero is associate professor of Spanish at Kent State University. Dzero publishes on authoritarianism in Latin America and Russia.

www.ingramcontent.com/pod-product-compliance
Lightning Source LLC
Chambersburg PA
CBHW030824230426
43667CB00008B/1358